High Finance in the €uro-Zone

Competing in the
New European Capital Market

"Most analysts have underestimated the fundamental institutional revolution unfolding in Europe. Professors Ingo Walter and Roy Smith are the exceptions ... they masterfully grasp the complex dynamics of Europe's launch of an integrated market."

Alfred Steinherr, Chief Economist, European Investment Bank, Luxembourg

"The euro is a stimulus to overhaul the structure of financial markets in Europe. Walter and Smith provide an excellent assessment of the implications for investment banking in Europe, covering the process of financial market integration in Europe and the implications both for markets and for individual players. The Walter/Smith book is likely to become a required reading for those dealing with financial market issues, and their lessons for future developments are highly relevant for policymakers, practitioners, and researchers alike."

Professor Dr Horst Siebert, President, Institute for World Economics, Germany

High Finance in the €uro-Zone

Competing in the New European Capital Market

Ingo Walter *and* Roy C. Smith

Withdrawn

FINANCIAL TIMES
Prentice Hall

An imprint of **Pearson Education**

London · New York · San Francisco · Toronto · Sydney · Tokyo · Singapore
Hong Kong · Cape Town · Madrid · Paris · Milan · Munich · Amsterdam

PEARSON EDUCATION LIMITED

Head Office
Edinburgh Gate
Harlow CM20 2JE
Tel: +44 (0)1279 623623
Fax: +44 (0)1279 431059

London Office:
128 Long Acre
London WC2E 9AN
Tel: +44 (0)20 7447 2000
Fax: +44 (0)20 7240 5771
Website:www.financialminds.com

First published in Great Britain in 2000

© Pearson Education Limited 2000

The right of Ingo Walter and Roy C. Smith to be identified as
authors of this work has been asserted by them in accordance
with the Copyright, Designs and Patents Act 1988.

ISBN 0 273 63737 1

British Library Cataloguing in Publication Data
A CIP catalogue record for this book can be obtained from the British Library.

This publication is designed to provide accurate and authoritative
information in regard to the subject matter covered. It is sold with the
understanding that neither the authors nor the publisher is engaged in
rendering legal, investing, or any other professional service. If legal advice
of other expert assistance is required, the service of a competent professional
person should be sought.

The publisher and contributors make no representation, express or implied, with
regard to the accuracy of the information contained in this book and cannot accept
any responsibility or liability for any errors or omissions that it may contain.

10 9 8 7 6 5 4 3

Typeset by Northern Phototypesetting Co. Ltd, Bolton
Printed and bound in Great Britain by Biddles Ltd, Guildford & King's Lynn

The Publishers' policy is to use paper manufactured from sustainable forests.

About the authors

Ingo Walter is the Charles Simon Professor of Applied Financial Economics at the Stern School of Business, New York University, and also serves as Director of the New York University Salomon Center, an independent academic research institute founded in 1972 to focus on financial institutions, instruments and markets.

Professor Walter received his AB and MS degrees from Lehigh University and his PhD degree in 1966 from New York University. He taught at the University of Missouri – St Louis from 1965 to 1970 and has been on the faculty at New York University since 1970. From 1971 to 1979 he was Associate Dean for Academic Affairs and subsequently served a number of terms as Chairman of International Business and Chairman of Finance. Since 1985 he has also been affiliated with INSEAD in Fontainebleau, France, as Professor of International Management.

Professor Walter's principal areas of academic and consulting activity include international trade policy, international banking, environmental economics, and economics of multinational corporate operations. He has published numerous papers in professional journals in these fields and is the author or editor of 25 books, the most recent of which are *Global Banking* (New York: Oxford University Press, 1997), *Street Smarts: linking leadership, professional conduct and shareholder value in the securities industry* (Boston: Harvard Business School Press, 1997), and *The Politics of European Financial Integration: the battle of the systems* (Cambridge: MIT Press, 1997).

At present, his research and consulting interests focus on competitive structure, conduct and performance in the international banking and financial services industry, as well as international trade and investment issues.

He has served as adviser to various government agencies, international institutions, banks and corporations, and has held a number of board memberships.

Roy C. Smith has been on the faculty of the Stern School of Business at New York University since September 1987 as a professor of finance and international business. Prior to assuming this appointment he was a General Partner of Goldman Sachs & Co., specializing in international investment banking and corporate finance. Upon his retirement from the firm to join the faculty, he was the senior international partner. During his career at Goldman Sachs, he set up and supervised the firm's business in Japan and the Far East, headed business development activities in Europe and the Middle East and served as President of Goldman Sachs International Corporation while resident in the firm's London office from 1980 to 1984.

Mr Smith received his BS degree from the US Naval Academy in 1960, and his MBA degree from Harvard University in 1966 after which he joined Goldman Sachs. He was an Adjunct Professor of Finance at New York University in 1979–80, and was a founding member of the Board of Advisors of the Center for US–Japan Business and Economic Studies at New York University. He is a frequent guest lecturer at other business schools in the US and in Europe.

Mr Smith's principal areas of research include international banking and finance, global capital market activity, mergers and acquisitions, leveraged transactions, foreign investments, the problems of third world debt, and privatization of Eastern European businesses.

In addition to various articles in professional journals and op-ed pieces, he is the author of *The Global Bankers*, EP Dutton, 1989, *The Money Wars*, EP Dutton, 1990 and *Comeback: the restoration of American banking power in the new world economy*, Harvard Business School Press, 1993. He is also co-author with Ingo Walter of *Investment Banking in Europe: restructuring in the 1990s*, Basil Blackwell, 1989, *Global Financial Services*, Harper and Row, 1990, *Global Banking*, New York: Oxford University Press, 1997, and *Street Smarts: linking leadership, professional conduct and shareholder value in the securities industry*, Boston: Harvard Business School Press, 1997.

Mr Smith is currently a Limited Partner of Goldman Sachs, a Director of Harsco Corporation, a former Director of Tootal plc, a UK Corporation, and a founding partner of Large, Smith & Walter, a European financial services consulting company.

Contents

PART III

LOOKING AHEAD

Preface

....

Early in 1999, when the dew was still fresh on the dawn of the euro and the economic and monetary union in Europe (EMU), an event took place in Milan that in many ways symbolized what the new era was to be all about. The event was the announcement by Olivetti on 20 February that it would soon launch a hostile takeover bid for Italy's largest company, the recently privatized Telecom Italia. The bid valued Telecom Italia at $58 billion. It was by far the largest takeover bid ever proposed in Europe. A furore soon followed in the media. How could this be? Olivetti was one-fifth the size of Telecom Italia. Although privatized, Telecom Italia was still a semi-government institution, and the Italian government was capable of controlling its future. How could Olivetti manage a hostile takeover of a company like that? Besides, hostile takeovers were an Anglo-American thing, rarely attempted in Europe and mostly unsuccessful when they were. Olivetti announced that its deal would be for a mixture of cash, floating-rate bonds and stock, but the bond portion would be for a huge amount, perhaps as much as $10 billion, at a time the corporate bond market in Europe was very small indeed, and when there really was no market for low-rated issues at all.

This deal, however was just the beginning of a cascade of gigantic European mergers and acquisitions that occurred during 1999, the last year of the century. Indeed, there were 26 deals involving 21 target companies with market values over $10 billion each announced in 1999. These totalled about $685 billion. And ten of the deals were hostile attempts to take over one European company by another. Indeed, the year got off to such a fast start that Olivetti's remarkable bid for Telecom Italia was in fact the fourth $10 billion European deal of the year!

Soon after Olivetti stepped up, Banque National de Paris (BNP) announced the launch of simultaneous hostile takeovers for two of its rivals, Société Générale and Banque Paribas. Other very large banks similarly became targets later in the year. Banca Commerciale Italiana (BCI) was targeted by Unicredito in March and by Banca Intesa in May. In the autumn National Westminster Bank in Britain became the target of two separate hostile bids by Bank of Scotland and Royal Bank of Scotland. The NatWest bids apparently were prompted by its unpopular move in September to take over Legal & General Insurance in the UK for $17 billion which the market considered greatly overpriced. And in December 1999 Internationale Neder-landen Groep (ING) announced and then tactically withdrew a bit for Crédit Commercial de France (CCF). In all, 15 of the takeover attempts exceeding $10 billion involved banks or insurance company targets.

The industrial sector in Europe was equally active. For several years, European industry had been undergoing restructuring and consolidation in a number of sectors, with an emphasis on improving shareholder value. In May 1999, Hoechst and Rhône-Poulenc announced their $27 billion friendly cross-border merger. In July, the French oil companies Total-Fina and Elf-Acquitaine began battling to see which one would take over the other for $450 billion plus. In October Mannesmann's friendly offer for the UK wireless phone company Orange plc was announced. This soon triggered the world's biggest takeover attempt ever, the effort by Vodaphone (which had acquired Air Touch in the US earlier in the year for $60 billion) to take over Mannesmann for nearly $130 billion. The year ended with investors in doubt as to how this one would turn out. There was some sympathy in the market for Mannesmann's defensive view that it would eventually be worth more to shareholders if left alone, but the arbitrageurs and the institutional shareholders of both companies saw a lot of value in the merger premium being offered by Vodaphone. Mannesmann's chairman said repeatedly that the decision as to which way things went should be left to shareholders, and that the company would not resort to a 'barbed wire' defence by employing available 'show-stopping' German anti-takeover measures. No major German company had ever said that before, but the sentiment was immediately applauded by the chairman of Germany's largest institutional investor, the insurance giant Allianz AG. The principle of share-holder rights and maximization of shareholder value had never been more widely appreciated in Europe.

These deals could not have been imagined in Europe only a few years before. Nor could they have been executed, since the vast resources of finance in debt and equity markets needed to support them did not then exist. But in 1999, over $1,400 billion of new euro and international bond issues were launched, a 65 per cent increase over 1998. And of the 1999 issues, nearly 60 per cent were denominated in the new European currency, the euro. There was also a torrent of Euro-MTN (medium-term note) issues – $600 billion, a record year. Euro-commercial paper outstandings at year-end were $170 billion, a new record and up 28 per cent on the previous year. Internationally syndicated bank loans also reached record levels in 1999, as financing packages for mergers and restructuring packages were arranged. Non-investment-grade and securitized bond markets also sprang to life in 1999, exceeding all previous levels of activity in Europe as bridge loans for takeovers and buyouts were funded in the market and as new ideas about bond collateral were tried. In November 1999, for example, the government of Italy raised $4.8 billion by selling bonds backed by the collateral of unpaid social security payments and set up a collection network to bring the delinquents to book. These levels of activity, in combination, clearly relocated the world's largest and most active corporate debt financing centre to Europe, not New York. So, as far as the debt markets were concerned, the launch of the euro was a resounding success.

Equity markets in Europe also flourished in 1999, especially for new issues and initial public offerings (IPOs). All equity issues by European corporations totalled $181 billion, more than double the amount of 1998 and about 15 times the volume of such issues a decade earlier. In one week during November 1999, *The Wall Street Journal Europe* reported 134 European initial public offerings in preparation, 83 of which were by companies in Germany. New forms of venture capital, private equity and leveraged buyout financing were also appearing rapidly, and at least four 'small company' stock exchanges had been set up to encourage wider public ownership.

These developments certainly represent great changes in the European financial landscape. Much of that which we were about to forecast in this book, had already come to pass even before the book had made it into print. But all of this activity has not been just the result of bull market conditions and a generally favourable economic climate. They reflect far more fundamental, deep-rooted changes. A totally new economic order has been brought to Europe, one of different values, and certainly different capabilities and methods. Europe at the *fin de siècle*, was vastly different from what it had been 20 years before, and was well on its way to becoming something else again over the next couple of decades. Europe, the ancient bastion of national chauvinism, economic protectionism, fragmented markets, government ownership of business assets, politicized institutions, corporate rigidity and elitism, and traditional internecine relationships was changing fast into a powerful, streamlined, semi-Americanized, market-valued version of itself. As such, the new unified Europe actually seemed capable of becoming the world's largest marketplace for goods and services, a goal outlined at the time of the Single Market Act 15 years earlier, but not much believed at the time.

If Europe does become the world's largest unified marketplace, it would certainly challenge its efficient US competitor as the 21st century's global economic centre of gravity. Such an event would be one of great importance to both Europeans and Americans and for the rest of the world. If this happens, it will be because two decades of economic and financial overhaul and reform have been surprisingly effective, and the cynical and suspicious

European (and US) public has accepted them, on balance, as being both for the best and here to stay.

The overhaul and reforms were underway long before the euro came on the scene. Indeed, EMU was frequently seen all along as only a distant beacon to encourage reformers and market operatives onward to a better time. Now it has arrived, and we begin to overlook and forget the many difficulties that had to be overcome to get there. Chief among these was persuading European governments to give up a great deal of the sovereignty they cherished in governing their national economic affairs. That power would be transferred first to the private sector, and second into an unknown and dubious political vessel, the EU, requiring continuous co-operation between 15 and eventually even more different countries. Surely this would have been impossible had the countries involved not realized that they had to do it. Their economic future as serious players in an increasingly globalized economic universe was otherwise doubtful. They had to adapt to the world's new economic realities or be marginalized.

The long road travelled

European progression, from whence it came to where it is now, has been a long but exceptionally speedy journey. From the euro-sclerosis of the seventies to the present, many significant milestones have been passed without which the journey could not have been the same. Much credit is due to Margaret Thatcher, whose first efforts at financial and economic reforms were so successful as to attract admiration and emulation from various parts of Europe. She abolished foreign exchange controls, lowered taxes, fought union power and intransigence, ushered-in Big Bang, which reformed Britain's antiquated financial markets, and sold-off hordes of businesses that had come to be owned by the government. She did a lot in her first few years and much of it succeeded as Europe watched in quiet disbelief. Britain post-Empire had been a reliable butt of jokes among the continentals. Now, nobody was laughing.

By the mid-eighties, enough of Thatcher's magic had worked to cause the other countries of the EU to take a fresh look at the 1958 Treaty of Rome, which had fallen well short of creating the unified and transparent market for European goods and services that had once been envisioned. A study was commissioned, supported by many important business and academic leaders – the so-called Checcini Report. The task force decided that national restrictions on the free flow of commerce and investment were killing European growth and dissipating the principal advantages of membership in the EU.

They resolved to create the unified market, which would establish in a Europe of 325 million people and combined GDP equal to that of the US, 'an area without internal frontiers in which the free movement of goods, services, persons and capital is ensured'. This marvellous Single Market Act was approved by European heads of state in 1985 and by national legislatures in 1986, and went into effect in 1992.

But before it did, many other reforms were gathering steam. Following Britain's lead, privatization programmes were undertaken by virtually all European countries, and a great many outside Europe as well. Several hundred billions of dollars of shares of public corporations were sold by governments during the eighties, and many more were set up to be sold later. These actions raised funds for the various governments, enabled improvements in operating results, and spread ownership of the shares among the investing public, helping to build-up national capital markets.

As a result, much improvement has been achieved in the economic condition of Europe since the Checcini Report was submitted in 1985. A vast amount of deregulation has occurred, which has brought the powerful forces of the free-market into every corner of Europe. The result has been major improvements in the governance of corporations and institutions, in the scale and efficiency of financial markets and in the confidence that European firms such as Olivetti, BNP and Vodaphone now show in themselves. And there is much more to come. Especially as companies ready themselves for open competition in a single-currency market with all its opportunities and dangers, and for the need to define their successes in terms of returns on investment and increased market value. These are the ultimate code-words for creating wealth, improving standards of living and the quality of life. Although it sometimes does not seem like it – and there are periodic reminders that there are still those who disagree – Europe has in fact bought into the programme.

Europe today

As a result of the long march to reform, much progress has been made in placing European capital markets, investment and financial restructuring activity in the centre of the global arena. As of the end of 1998, for example, the market capitalization of all outstanding European Union debt and equity securities was $17,300 billion ($17.3 *trillion*), or 30 per cent of a vastly expanded world total of (an incredible) $58,800 billion. Of this amount, $12,600 billion, or 21 per cent, was accounted for by the euro-zone countries. The US was still the world's largest financial market, with $27,500 billion of securities outstanding (47 per cent of the total world market value), but the European share was both competitive and increasing (*see* Fig. 1).

In Europe, capital markets continue to accept new privatization activities and affect new issues of securities necessary to finance mergers and acquisitions and other forms of corporate restructuring. The debt markets are likewise in constant use in the redistribution of funding sources for governments and agencies of the euro-zone countries, and the increased activity in those markets is in turn attracting substantial numbers of corporate issuers that have not used them before – €32.7 billion in the first four months of 1999, compared to €7.4 billion a year earlier. At the same time, the euro has provided a more stable and capitalized base for the offshore eurobond market, already the largest non-governmental, investment-grade debt securities market in the world. In the early months of eurobond market activity following the January 1999 launch of the new currency, the euro was in fact the preferred currency of issuance, at least temporarily supplanting the dollar despite its deadline relative to the dollar of some 13 per cent by the end of the year.

Fig 1 Capitalization of major securities markets – nominal value outstanding, 1998 (US$bn)

Country of issuance	Bond market				Equity market	Total market capitalization
	Government	Corporations	Euro and foreign bonds	Total bonds		
US	$7,550	$5,795	$738	$14,083	$13,451	$27,534
EU11	4,812	2,319	1,320	8,451	4,160	12,611
EU4	809	692	512	2,013	2,751	4,764
Total EU	5,621	3,011	1,832	10,464	6,911	17,375
Japan	3,118	1,212	293	4,623	2,496	7,119
Rest of the world	190	764	1,224	2,178	4,604	6,782
World total	**$16,479**	**$10,782**	**$4,087**	**$31,348**	**$27,462**	**$58,810**

Source: BIS, IFC

Europe's share of the world's money management business was also approximately 30 per cent in 1998. At that time, ten of the world's leading asset managers – those with $100 billion or more in assets-under-management – were European, and the share of all assets managed by them was 37 per cent. There were 24 asset managers from the US on this list, representing 50 per cent of total AUM. The European market position, however, was developed well in advance of the kinds of reforms in funding pension systems that took place in the US in the seventies and eighties. These reforms are now underway, and will inevitably result in far more assets being set aside for management by European market professionals in the not too distant future. Thus Europe can be expected to continue growing as a centre for investment management activity (*see* Fig. 2).

Fig 2 Top global money managers (assets under management exceeding $100m) as of April 1998

Asset managers	Total assets under management (US$bn)	Number of managers
US	$5,112	24
Switzerland	1,760	3
Japan	1,323	3
UK	862	3
France	500	1
Germany	450	2
Netherlands	140	1
Total	**$10,147**	**37**
Total European	$3,712	10
European % of total	**37%**	**27%**

Calculated from data reported in *Euromoney*, August 1999 (non-US asset managers) based on InterSec Research Corp. data, and *Institutional Investor*, July 1999 (US asset managers)

Finally, the European share of the global corporate restructuring market – the market for mergers and acquisitions – was 51 per cent in 1999 after the completion of nearly $900 billion of transactions (*see* Fig. 3). This transactions volume reflected efforts of European corporations to alter business strategies in response to higher standards of market discipline and performance that were demanded by their increasingly sophisticated and vocal institutional shareholders, and by the new economic and financial realities of Europe. Free market-access throughout Europe by both traditional and new competitors forms the centre of the new regime. To succeed in this environment (or to avoid failing) companies seem to agree that they must 'restructure', or make their operations more economically efficient. For every European company that has been involved in an actual merger or acquisition, several others have introduced significant internal reforms. This is especially evident among Europe's largest companies, such as Mannesmann, Siemens, Philips, Veba and Hoechst, which aggressively have sold businesses no longer fitting into their new configurations, reduced headcount, and made new strategic investments and alliances. When industry leaders engage in such activities, their competitors must follow.

Fig 3 European mergers and acquisitions (completed transactions only)

	1999		1989	
	Value (US$bn)	%	Value (US$bn)	%
Intra-European transactions	$575.5	34.1	$130.1	23.1
European cross-border transactions	292.0	17.2	74.3	13.2
Total European	**867.5**	**51.3**	**204.4**	**36.3**
Intra-US transactions	588.7	34.8	250.1	44.4
US cross-border transactions	303.4	18.0	85.6	15.2
Total US	**892.1**	**52.8**	**335.7**	**59.6**
(Double counted transactions)	219.1	13.0	46.3	8.2
Total global transactions	**1,689.6**	**100**	**563.5**	**100**

Source: Thomson Financial Securities Data Company

The convergence of these activities, and the forces behind them, is gradually making a huge difference to Europe's economic future, even if it sometimes seems marked by political rhetoric recalling the 'good old days' and the traditions of business-government-labour consensus, and the continuing heavy hand of regulation, taxation and bureaucracy. The standards for the investment of capital in Europe have been raised to market levels. If the standards are too low to accommodate the risks involved and the returns expected by the market, then capital will avoid Europe, strangling investment and economic growth. But market levels of performance are difficult to meet without changing the template from one shaped by the requirements of the old, mixed economy to one shaped mainly by the private-sector and market actions.

Certainly the momentum that has developed in support of the new template will last for several more years, at least. The need to raise standards of market competitiveness in exchange for better economic outcomes for all citizens will continue to be the main driver in the marketplace for banking and financial services well into the early years of the new century. We do not suggest that these changes will last for ever, or that future experimentation with different templates may not be tried. But we do say that the force behind the trends of the last few years must necessarily continue, and that Europe will be a different place because of it. We will see a place more like the US, but also a place emerging as a much more focused and coherent commercial and financial centre in the world, possibly even larger and more important than the US itself.

What this book is about

This volume is a sequel to a book we wrote on the same general subject a decade earlier, *Investment Banking in Europe – Restructuring for the 1990s* (Oxford: Basil Blackwell, 1990). It is about the changes that have occurred since that time and that are still occurring in various key areas of European finance – mainly investment banking and other wholesale financial services – at the start of the 21st century.

We begin with two chapters to help define the economic and regulatory territory. Both of these are continuing to evolve as the new Europe does, and we spend some time discussing the background and frameworks within which further changes can be expected.

Next we address changes and developments in the principal financial marketplaces of investment banking – debt, equities and mergers and acquisitions. Then comes the extraordinary phenomenon of privatization, in which economic power and the rights of control are shifted from the public sector to the private sector, and how it has helped shape other events and will continue to be a force in the European marketplace for some time to come. The shifting sands of corporate governance in general, and in an increasingly free market environment, then attracts our attention as do parallel and closely related developments in the rapidly growing field of asset management.

Finally, we try to take all of this in and consider what effects it has on how individual firms in wholesale banking must run their own businesses. There are many kinds of firms and many ways for courses to be charted. But at the end of the day, similar goals and objectives must be met. Rising to these challenges is the task that managers of today's investment banks must face.

Acknowledgements

We are grateful to Gayle De Long, Yonghong Mao, Ann Rusolo and Robyn Vanterpool for their outstanding help in assembling data and preparation of the manuscript for publication.

Many thanks.

Professor Ingo Walter
Professor Roy C. Smith

PART I

Legacies and forces of change

CHAPTER 1

The euro and financial sector reconfiguration

Introduction of the euro represents a sea change in the environment of modern global finance. In the three decades since the end of the Bretton Woods system in 1971, and against great odds, Europe has forged a platform that could ultimately emerge as a viable challenger to the US as the world's premier financial market. It was a difficult birth, but if ever the saying 'no pain, no gain' applies in the context of macro-financial reform, this is it.[1]

Financial institutions are extraordinarily sensitive to even small changes in their environment. Increases in interest rate or exchange rate volatility can create wholly new markets for risk management products. Equally, these businesses, often built up at huge expense, can be wiped out overnight if volatility drops. Regulatory concerns about counterparty or liquidity risk in over-the-counter markets can drive transactions on to organized exchanges and their standardized contracts, and eliminate much of the innovation that is most easily undertaken in over-the-counter markets. Similar effects could be caused by changes in tax codes, transaction costs, information technologies, and an array of variables that form the environmental overlay for business strategy in the financial services industry. These are parameters that management has to think about carefully, build a consensus on, before placing strategic bets. When mistakes are made in devising core strategies in the financial services industry, they are usually big ones.

The advent of the euro is probably the most important recent development in the environment of the world's financial institutions, and therefore has to be carefully related to the strategies of financial firms. Other contemporary issues, such as emerging market financial crises, regulation of hedge funds, and Japan's continued economic doldrums, pale by comparison. The euro will redefine a large part of the global financial landscape of the 21st century. Strategies of European financial services firms in their home markets have already been profoundly affected by competitive conditions that have yet to be fully delineated. Meanwhile, outsiders, notably US firms long used to competing in a massive single currency market, have big strategic plans for the euro-zone. In some cases they have already made incursions into European financial services markets that would have been undreamed of a few years ago. As financial reconfiguration in the euro-zone proceeds alongside continued technological advance in both the wholesale and retail domains, as regulatory and tax policy alignment continues to change the rules of the game, and as clients become increasingly performance-oriented and promiscuous, core strategies of financial firms – many of which continue to think in terms of institutional boundaries instead of financial processes – will come under additional stress.

In some ways, reconfiguration of the euro-zone financial structure is merely the latest in a series of forces that have propelled the transformation of the global financial services sector. Some of these are regulatory initiatives designed to make national financial systems more efficient and competitive – notably US deregulation in 1974, British deregulation in 1986, and less dramatic regulatory liberalization in various continental European countries in the eighties and nineties, with Japan bringing up the rear in the late nineties.

It is not surprising that the pacing of regulatory change has been related to the competitive performance of the financial firms at the centre of this process. In the regulatory domain as well are broad-based agreements on capital adequacy standards and consolidated supervision, carried out at a global level under the auspices of the Bank for International Settlements and at the regional level by the European Union, as well as market access issues anchored multilaterally both in the WTO General Agreement on Trade in Services and various EU financial services directives.

Developments in the global macro-environment were equally important, including the convergence of exchange rates and interest rates in the euro-zone. Politically, the ascendancy of free market thinking beginning in the early eighties was a global phenomenon that gradually penetrated the euro-zone and affected everything from bank regulation to corporate governance. Not least, rapid technological change inexorably drove down information and transaction costs, promoting massive changes in the financial intermediation process.

All of these were broad-gauge, global developments whose ever more powerful impact was felt in the financial services industry – most dramatically at the wholesale end – over several decades and whose benefits were progressively harvested by end users of the financial system along the way. The advent of the euro, with all its dramatic aspects, can be regarded as another phase in this progression, one that complements rather than substitutes a broader set of revolutionary developments affecting the financial industry.

Suppositions

A strategic exercise aimed at creating a high-performance financial services franchise in the evolving euro-zone has to start by taking a view on the basic drivers of the financial markets and their impact on the prospective size and structure of the sub-markets for wholesale and retail financial services.

As we expect this book to have some use as a guide to those conducting such strategic exercises, we have set out some of the main suppositions and expectations upon which we base our view of the financial and economic environment in Europe over the next few years. This is an environment that has already been affected by the introduction of the euro, and also by a variety of powerful forces released by reforms and acts of deregulation by the EU and several member countries.

Economics

- The euro-zone will hold together and gradually be expanded to encompass the remaining EU countries, with the European Central Bank earning the required broad-based political support, complemented by fiscal convergence in accordance with the Maastricht targets and the Stability Pact and including some degree of convergence in tax regimes.

- The euro will rapidly consolidate the reduction in foreign exchange and hedging costs facing corporations, households and investors, estimated in 1999 to be approximately $58 billion per annum.

- The massive euro-zone home market will allow realization for the first time of economies of scale equivalent to the home market advantage of US producers of goods and services, potentially leading to lower costs and prices and improved profitability.

- Transparency in euro-zone product and labour markets will dramatically increase comparability of prices, costs, taxes and profitability, all of which will intensify competitive pressures in markets for goods and services, labour and capital.

- Improvements in pricing transparency and competition will at the same time help increase real incomes at the household level and, through lower costs, the global competitiveness of European industry.

- Increased consolidation will occur in both the manufacturing and services sectors, notably banking, through M&A transactions and corporate restructurings. Much of this is already under way, but the euro will accelerate the pace.

- Disproportionate growth will become evident in the euro-zone service industries, particularly if currency unification accelerates economic growth. Services will gradually grow towards the economic significance they hold in the US.

- There will be a winding down of government subsidies in the euro-zone under pressure from the EU competition authorities and budgetary constraints – an important factor in market-based economic restructuring.

- Rigidity in labour, occupational and geographic mobility, compensation levels and social charges are likely to persist, triggering progressive relocation to low-cost production environments within the euro-zone, to the Eastern European periphery and to emerging economies. However, there will be progressive improvement in European labour mobility, particularly at the high-skill end of the spectrum, facilitated by gradual government standardization of pensions and job requirements. Roughly 20 per cent of the EU workforce is likely to be affected by M&A and structural adjustments, with perhaps 5 per cent job losses extended over many years and cushioned by the growth of small firms and an underground economy estimated to employ 28 million people (20 per cent of the workforce).

- Euro-zone governments have begun a process of adjustment in social support structures, including measures to hold down healthcare costs, reforms of social security systems, large-scale privatization of state-owned enterprises, and other market-based reforms. These have, however, varied in speed and intensity among the participating countries, being perhaps most advanced in the Netherlands and Ireland, and least advanced in France.

- Strong improvements in innovation and entrepreneurial performance are likely, based on a world-class scientific and technical infrastructure and building on already powerful global positions in industries such as biotechnology, wireless communications and business software.

The government bond market

● Eleven euro-zone government bond markets, estimated at $2 trillion in 1999, are roughly comparable in size to the US. There will be growing standardization of government bonds in the euro-zone, including auction calendars and interest calculations, as well as new instruments such as inflation-indexed bonds denominated in euros.

● The changed fiscal environment will constrain the issuance of national government bonds and the rate of growth of the market, and push financing on to municipalities and other public finance entities, sometimes with state guarantees.

● Trading in euro-zone government bonds, driven historically by interest rate and exchange rate factors among the participating countries, is likely to be driven mainly by credit spreads in the future. The 23 basis point and 20 basis point spread between Germany and Portugal and Belgium respectively, in early 1999 is far smaller than those between the states in the US. Without sovereign bailouts, these may be too narrow. Euro-zone government bonds will be subject to conventional rating criteria and corporate spreads will no longer be capped by home country government spreads.

The corporate bond market

● The euro-zone corporate bond market was estimated at $180 billion in 1999, one-sixth the size of the US, with limited liquidity. Outstandings may rise to $800 billion over ten years as capital market financing replaces bank financing, as a high-capacity, liquid euro-zone market replaces fragmented national markets, and as national investment restrictions are scrapped.

● Incremental demand for assets denominated in euros can be expected to lower average interest rates and the cost of capital facing euro-zone corporations even in the presence of growing demand for financing in euros. Increased trading volume and market liquidity will reduce transaction costs for investors and issuers.

● The market for non-investment grade debt in Europe has grown rapidly as investors search for yield and as the financing requirements of small, high-growth companies increase, a development that is likely to continue.

● The market for asset-backed securities in the euro-zone, very small in comparison to that in the US, will grow rapidly as various tax and regulatory impediments are removed, and as banks rethink how much capital they should have tied up in their lending books. Already some of the pioneering securitization of commercial loans has taken place in Europe, with significant mutual gains for borrowers, investors and intermediaries.

The market for equities

● Euro-zone equity market capitalization was estimated to be $3 trillion in mid-1999, compared to about $10 trillion in the US, with various forecasts pointing to a tripling over a decade or so. The euro-zone's 32 stock exchanges in 1998 (compared to eight in the US) and 23 derivatives exchanges (compared to seven in the US) will consolidate rapidly even as trading, clearance and settlement systems become more efficient.

● Secondary markets for equities in the euro-zone will increasingly be characterized by block trading, as large institutional investors grow in importance, and with that the need for risk management, capital and institutional distribution capability. There will be growing use of innovative, equity-linked financial instruments and structured transactions for which the national European markets were previously too small, too fragmented and illiquid, too tightly regulated or too uncompetitive to make them attractive.

● The creation of euro equity benchmarks such as the Dow Jones Euro Stoxx 50 and the FTSE Eurotop 100 will strengthen performance orientation of asset managers as well as corporations, promoting the shift from national to sectoral asset allocation.

● Accelerated development of initial public offerings (IPOs) and the small-cap equity market can be foreseen, promoted by the success of markets such as the Nouveau Marché in France and the Neuer Markt in Germany, as well as growth in the volume of management buyouts (MBOs), leveraged buyouts (LBOs), venture capital and private equity.

Retail financial services

● Retail financial services markets in the euro-zone will change only gradually, due to wide differences in preferences and the historical dominance of certain types of institutions such as savings banks, mortgage banks, co-operative banks and postal savings banks, as well as equally significant differences in the insurance industry.

- New products and retail distribution channels will gradually encroach on legacy structures, as they have already done in the case of bancassurance, which will gradually make the retail financial services market more open to competition, both cross-border and between domestic strategic groups.

- As demographics strain the already heavy reliance in most euro-zone countries on unfunded (pay-as-you-go) or underfunded pension schemes, governments are being forced to introduce pre-funded pension systems. New schemes will focus on defined contribution formulas that shift management responsibility to beneficiaries, suggesting a growing role for mass distribution and branding of pension products. This will eventually form massive, performance-driven managed pools of fixed-income securities and equities. As involuntary 'noise' traders, these will make a disproportionate contribution to euro-zone financial market liquidity and efficiency.[2]

- The euro-zone mutual fund industry will be contested by banks, insurance companies, independent fund management companies, and financial conglomerates. However, retail financial services in the euro-zone will be subject to strong consumer protection measures at the national level, which may delay penetration of non-traditional and innovative products and distribution channels.

If these suppositions are broadly borne out by the facts, the euro-zone market for financial services is likely to be a very dynamic one indeed, both in terms of its overall prospects within the broader context of the global financial system and in terms of its structure. This runs across the entire spectrum of wholesale and retail financial activities. There is plenty of growth potential in wholesale capital market activities as the new government bond market envelops the constituent national markets and as the corporate and asset-backed bond markets accelerate the replacement of bank debt, as in the US. Equity markets should develop rapidly as well, propelled by rising volumes of new issues and an expanding need for equities in pre-funded pension plans as some of the euro-zone countries come to grips with the demographic reality of ageing populations. Economic sectors, individual corporate prospects, and credit quality will replace currencies in asset allocation strategies. At the retail level, clients will face an increasing array of financial services from a wide variety of vendors using traditional and non-traditional approaches to distribution, with local and regional financial services oligopolies confronting unprecedented challenge.

Reconfiguration of euro-zone financial services

The potential for change brought about by the euro is set against a state of substantial overcapacity and inefficiency in broad segments of the euro-zone's financial services industry. There is too much capital and there are too many people employed in the production and distribution of financial services – as there have been in the US. Both will be removed in a process of restructuring and consolidation that has only just begun. It will take a long time, most particularly in the retail sector in view of the importance of government-related and co-operative institutions in Europe that are not subject to the shareholder value discipline. The ruthlessness of the US restructuring process will be somewhat less prominent, and this is likely to slow down the movement to a new equilibrium in terms of financial structure. And of course nobody wants to be shaken out, so tenacious rearguard actions will be mounted by vulnerable players even as new entrants – including the ubiquitous Americans hardened by their own structural revolution – crowd into the European marketplace.

Figure 1.1 shows some of the differences between European and US financial sector restructuring via mergers and acquisitions, with US intra-sector M&A volume during the period 1985–99 almost three times the European volume in banking, three times as large in securities, and twice as large in insurance. This despite the fact that the EU plus Switzerland comprises a larger economic region than the US. Inter-sector M&A volume was higher in Europe for banks buying insurance companies, presumably due to the popularity of bancassurance and the absence of legal barriers.

Fig 1.1 Volume of in-market mergers and acquisitions in the US and Europe, 1985–98 (US$bn)

Acquiring institution	US target institution			Europe target institution		
	Banks	Securities	Insurance	Banks	Securities	Insurance
Commercial banks	480 (53.4%)	25 (2.8%)	0.3 (0.0%)	265 (40.9%)	22 (3.4%)	22 (3.4%)
Securities firms	5 (0.6%)	112 (12.5%)	31 (3.5%)	35 (5.4%)	57 (8.8%)	35 (5.4%)
Insurance companies	73 (8.1%)	16 (1.8%)	156 (17.4%)	47 (7.3%)	12 (1.9%)	153 (23.6%)

Source: DeLong, Smith and Walter (1999)

Fig 1.2 Volume of cross-market mergers and acquisitions in the US and Europe, 1985–98

Acquiring institution	US-non-US target institution			Intra-Europe target institution			Europe-non-Europe target institution		
	Banks	Securities	Insurance	Banks	Securities	Insurance	Banks	Securities	Insurance
Commercial banks	32.1 (22.3%)	7.4 (5.1%)	0.2 (0.1%)	37.6 (21.7%)	6.7 (3.9%)	0.4 (0.2%)	39.0 (22.8%)	6.8 (4.6%)	1.0 (0.4%)
Securities firms	5.7 (4.0%)	25.2 (17.5%)	6.0 (4.2%)	8.8 (5.1%)	17.0 (9.8%)	1.9 (1.1%)	19.6 (11.5%)	19.6 (11.2%)	22.2 (3.4%)
Insurance companies	0.6 (0.4%)	4.1 (2.8%)	20.2 (14.0%)	20.2 (11.6%)	1.5 (0.9%)	79.4 (45.8%)	1.1 (9.3%)	3.8 (2.5%)	57.9 (48.4%)

Source: DeLong, Smith and Walter (1999) and Thomson Financial Securities Data Company. The first figure is the dollar value (in billions) of M&A activity and the second number in parentheses is the percentage of the total (these sum to 100 for each 3×3 matrix). Figures reported are the sum of the equity values of the target institutions

Figure 1.2 shows the cross-border aspects of financial services M&A activity during 1985–99. Most important among US acquisitions abroad are investment firms buying other investment firms (notably British merchant banks and asset managers) and insurance companies buying foreign insurance companies. Intra-European cross-border transactions are mainly intra-sectoral, with almost half occurring in the insurance industry. When European firms acquire non-European ones (mainly in the US and Japan), this is again largely on an intra-sector basis.

Competitive challenges

Developing and implementing strategies in firms hoping to secure a permanent and profitable place in the euro-zone financial services config-uration thus presents a challenge that will test the mettle of even the most far-sighted and determined managers. The challenge centres around seven basic questions:

● *Strategic positioning.* Given the foregoing environmental suppositions governing the euro-zone, what are the target markets – in terms of clients, products and geographic spread – that promise the most attractive oppor-tunities for growth over time?

● *Prospective market structure.* How are these targeted markets likely to evolve in terms of competitive structure? There is not much sense in going through the effort and expense of gearing up for what looks like a poten-tially profitable market if, at the end of the day, competitors are doing the same thing and market structure ends up approximating perfect compe-tition, incapable of supporting attractive, sustained returns on the capital employed. Herd-like behaviour is well known among financial services managers and strategists, especially in the face of major parameter shocks such as the creation of the euro-zone, and it may be advisable to stay out of the way of the stampede.

● *Core competencies.* What is the firm really good at, in terms of its baseline market position and franchise, creativity and innovation, flexibility, ability to manage complexity, and command of financial and human resources? What competitive resources can be rolled out geographically or focused on defensible market segments in response to euro-zone developments?

● *Operating economies.* To what extent are there economies of scale, cost economies of scope and production efficiencies that can be exploited in order to reinforce the firm's competitive position?

- *Revenue synergies and earnings diversification.* Are there revenue economies of scope that can be exploited by linking products and clients, and are these cross-selling gains likely to prevail across the euro-zone for target retail and/or wholesale client segments? Are there significant earnings stability gains to be had by diversifying across clients, financial services activities and geographies within the euro-zone?

- *Institutional configuration.* What types of institutional configurations do the strategic positioning considerations suggest are the ones most likely to maximize the value of the enterprise, running across the institutional spectrum from massive euro-zone universals or multifunctional financial services conglomerates to specialists that are highly focused on best-in-class delivery of specific types of financial services?

- *Ability to execute.* Based on the firm's existing situation and an objective assessment of competitive strengths and weaknesses – a 'reality check' – is it reasonable to envision its transformation into what will be required in the light of the environmental suppositions, given resource and managerial constraints, with some but not excessive urgency?

Financial intermediation in the countries comprising the euro-zone has traditionally been heavily dominated by commercial banks, insurance companies and savings institutions, together capturing about 85 per cent of all financial assets in the system in 1998, compared with about 40 per cent in the US. If the same economics of disintermediation apply in both regions, one would expect the role of classic euro-zone intermediaries to decline dramatically over time. In order to 'go with the flow' banks will have to develop viable strategies to compete in mutual fund management, pension fund management, capital market access, asset securitization, custody and securities transaction processing, etc. So will insurance companies and savings institutions. And there will be plenty of room for specialists. In short, the financial services industry has begun a profound shake-up which will ultimately settle into some sort of institutional equilibrium, although nobody is yet quite sure how that will look. If the US is any sort of guide, it will be a highly varied and dynamic field of players.

Searching for operating economies and revenue synergies

As in many other industries, a major purported benefit associated with the advent of the euro is the realization for the first time of significant economies of scale and economies of scope. For the first time as well, an unprecedented degree of competitive pressure will bear on long-sheltered European financial firms, and force them to manage better. Regardless of scale or scope benefits, this will create a leaner, more cost-effective set of competitors, to the benefit of both their shareholders and the European financial system. Individually or in combination, economies of scale and scope in euro-zone financial firms will lead to increased profit margins or will be passed along to clients in the form of lower prices, resulting in a gain of market share. Diseconomies of scale will have the opposite effects. The potential impact of the euro on operating economics (production functions) of financial firms is so important – and so often used to justify mergers, acquisitions and other strategic initiatives – that available empirical evidence is central to the whole argument.[3]

Economies of scale

Whether economies of scale exist in financial services has been at the heart of strategic and regulatory discussions about optimum firm size in the financial services sector. Can an increase in the average size of firms by itself create a more efficient financial sector and can it increase shareholder value?

For example, large organizations may be more capable of the massive and 'lumpy' capital outlays required to install and maintain the most efficient information technology and transactions processing infrastructures. If extremely high technology spend levels result in higher efficiency, large financial services firms will tend to benefit in competition with smaller ones. However, smaller organizations ought to be able to pool their resources or outsource scale-sensitive activities in order to capture such gains.

In an information- and distribution-intensive industry with high fixed costs such as financial services, there should be ample potential for scale economies – as well as potential for diseconomies of scale attributable to disproportionate increases in administrative overheads, management of complexity, agency problems and other cost factors once very large firm size is reached. If economies of scale prevail, increased size will help create systemic financial efficiency and shareholder value. If diseconomies prevail, both will be destroyed.

Examples of financial sector mega-mergers in 1998 alone included Deutsche Bank and Bankers Trust as the first intercontinental mega-deal, creating the world's largest bank with combined assets of $849 billion in November 1998; Swiss Bank Corporation and Union Bank of Switzerland to form UBS AG ($749 billion); and Citicorp and Travelers Group to form Citigroup ($702 billion). In January 1999, Banco Santander and Banco Central Hispanoamericano formed BSCH ($300 billion). There were other deals between First Chicago NBD and BancOne, and BankAmerica and NationsBank, the 1999 takeover of Paribas by Banque Nationale de Paris and the 2000 takeover of National Westminster Bank by Royal Bank of Scotland. Bankers regularly argue that bigger is better from both systemic and share-holder value perspectives, and usually point to economies of scale as a major reason for this. What is the evidence?

Many studies of economies of scale have been undertaken in the banking, insurance and securities industries.[4] Virtually all of them have found that economies of scale are achieved with increases in size among small banks (below $100 million in asset size), although some have shown that the scale economies may also exist in banks falling into the $100 million to $5 billion range. There is very little evidence so far of scale economies in the case of banks larger than $5 billion and no evidence whatsoever of scale economies among very large banks. Figures 1.3 and 1.4 show the 20 largest European and US banks, all of which are much larger than the size of banks for which any empirical evidence of scale economies has been found. The data also show the top 20 European banks to be much larger than the top 20 US banks. The inability to find major economies of scale among large commercial and universal banks is also true of insurance companies and broker-dealers.[5] Furthermore, the consensus among empirical studies of the matter seems to be that scale economies and diseconomies generally do not result in more than about a 5 per cent difference in unit costs of financial services firms.[6]

So, for most banks and non-bank financial firms in the euro-zone, except the very smallest, scale economies seem likely to have relatively little bearing on competitive performance. This is particularly true since many of the smaller European institutions are linked together in co-operatives or other structures that allow any economies of scale to be maximized centrally, or are specialists not particularly sensitive to the kinds of cost differences usually associated with economies of scale in the financial services industry. Big deals such as those cited above, and most of the mega-mergers that may appear in the euro-zone in the coming years, are unlikely, whatever their other merits, to contribute very much in terms of scale economies unless the fabled

Fig 1.3 Top 20 European bank performance data, November 1998

	Bank	Total assets ($bn)	Market cap ($bn)	Market cap as % of assets	Tier 1 equity	ROAE (post-tax)	Net int margin	Ln growth 8 years	P/E	P/B
1	UBS	749	69.2	9.24%	7.5	21.6	1.0	n.a.	15.50	2.94
2	Deutsche Bank	693	33.4	4.82%	5.1	15.0	1.3	11.9	11.70	1.76
3	ABN-Amro	501	31.8	6.35%	7.2	18.3	1.7	28.1	16.00	2.12
4	Hypovereinsbank	492	31.3	6.36%	5.0	17.7	1.3	n.a.	n.a.	n.a.
5	HBSC	487	55.5	11.40%	9.8	17.7	2.8	n.a.	12.00	2.02
6	Credit Suisse	477	46.4	6.56%	10.3	2.2	0.9	13.1	18.60	3.2
7	Dresdner	462	24.7	5.35%	5.7	15.0	1.3	8.5	19.70	2.04
8	ING Groep	456	55.2	12.11%	7.0	13.5	2.3	17.0	15.60	1.47
9	Société Générale	418	18.2	4.35%	6.2	10.4	1.2	9.5	13.50	1.65
10	Barclays	406	35.6	8.77%	7.3	22.9	3.4	-0.5	12.20	2.70
11	Banque Nationale de Paris	346	14.6	4.22%	5.5	10.1	1.1	4.6	12.40	1.39
12	Commerzbank	343	13.8	4.02%	6.0	10.4	1.3	14.6	13.90	1.37
13	National Westminster	311	30.2	9.71%	8.1	18.6	3.3	1.2	12.80	2.37
14	Lloyds TSB	234	64.8	27.69%	9.1	27.7	3.6	10.0	18.10	5.49
15	San Paolo-IMI	200	12.0	6.00%	11.0	5.2	1.8	11.8	20.80	2.25
16	Santander	186	21.9	11.77%	8.3	22.2	2.6	30.2	19.90	3.33
17	BBV	147	26.9	18.30%	9.0	19.4	2.9	10.6	25.00	4.88
18	Bank Austria	126	6.9	5.48%	5.9	8.5	1.5	n.a.	6.40	1.07
19	Banco di Roma	119	10.3	8.66%	6.9	n.a.	2.4	n.a.	16.80	1.80
20	BCI	117	12.0	10.26%	7.8	5.1	2.9	12.2	23.40	2.32
	Total **UK and continental average**	**7,270**	**614.7**	**8.46%**	**7.4**	**14.6**	**1.7**	**10.9**	**14.5**	**2.06**

Source: Goldman Sachs

Fig 1.4 Top 20 US bank performance data, November 1998

Bank	Total assets ($bn)	Market cap ($bn)	Market cap as % of assets	Tier 1 equity	ROAE (post tax)	Net int margin	P/E	P/B
1 Citigroup	702	107.0	15.2%	8.3	6.5	5.1	n.a.	n.a.
2 Chase Manhattan	357	48.7	13.6%	8.3	14.9	3.1	13.2	2.20
3 JP Morgan	299	16.6	5.6%	7.4	5.3	0.7	17.3	1.68
4 BankAmerica	264	99.9	37.8%	7.4	7.7	3.6	14.6	2.12
5 First Union	235	57.4	24.4%	7.1	23.5	3.8	15.5	3.31
6 Norwest/Wells Fargo	196	50.0	25.5%	n.a.	n.a.	n.a.	n.a.	n.a.
7 Bankers Trust	156	6.0	3.8%	7.0	n.a.	1.0	8.7	1.44
8 BancOne	120	57.3	47.8%	9.2	21.8	5.3	14.4	2.81
9 Fleet Financial	100	22.7	22.7%	6.9	18.6	4.6	15.5	2.68
10 National City	83	21.2	25.5%	8.8	19.0	4.1	16.2	2.94
11 Key Corp	78	13.3	17.1%	6.7	18.1	4.2	13.7	2.38
12 PNC Bank	76	15.1	19.9%	7.4	20.5	3.8	15.4	2.75
13 BankBoston	74	10.8	14.6%	7.0	16.3	4.0	12.5	2.30
14 Wachovia	66	18.7	28.3%	8.1	18.2	6.2	20.4	3.52
15 Bank of NY	64	23.6	36.9%	7.5	24.2	3.2	20.6	4.76
16 Sun Trust Bank	61	14.6	23.9%	7.2	13.3	3.9	19.6	2.79
17 State Street	51	10.1	19.8%	14.3	20.0	1.8	23.4	4.51
18 Mellon Bank	48	15.7	32.7%	6.8	20.3	4.0	18.5	3.60
19 SouthTrust	36	6.0	16.7%	6.8	14.4	3.7	14.3	2.27
20 Comerica	34	10.0	6.5%	7.2	23.0	4.6	17.2	3.73
Total	**3,100.0**	**624.7**	**20.2%**	**7.6**	**15.7**	**3.6**	**14.3**	**2.4**
Average top 20 / **US banks average**	**155.0**	**40.5**	**21.0%**	**8.6**	**16.2**	**3.7**	**15**	**2.85**

Source: Goldman Sachs

'economies of superscale' turn out to exist – these, like the abominable snowman, have unfortunately never been observed in nature.

The basic fallacy seems to be management's emphasis on firm-wide scale economies when the really important scale issues are encountered at the level of individual financial services. There is ample evidence, for example, that economies of scale are both significant and important for operating economies and competitive performance in areas such as global custody, processing of mass-market credit card transactions, and institutional asset management, but are far less important in other areas such as private banking and M&A advisory services. Unfortunately, empirical data on cost functions that would permit identification of economies of scale at the product level are generally proprietary and therefore unavailable. Still, it seems reasonable that a scale-driven, pan-European strategy may make a great deal of sense in specific areas of financial activity even in the absence of evidence that there is very much to be gained at the firm-wide level.

Economies of scope

There should also be potential for economies of scope in the euro-zone financial services sector – competitive benefits to be gained by selling a broader rather than a narrower range of products – which may arise either through supply- or demand-side link-ups. Indeed, managements of universal banks and financial conglomerates often argue that broader product and client coverage, and the increased throughput volume and/or margins this makes possible, leads to shareholder value enhancement.

On the supply side, scope economies involve cost savings achieved through sharing of overheads and improving technology via joint production of generically similar services. Cost diseconomies of scope may arise from such factors as inertia and lack of responsiveness and creativity that may come with increased firm size and bureaucratization, 'turf' and profit attribution conflicts that increase costs or erode product quality in meeting client needs, or serious cultural differences across the organization that inhibit seamless delivery of a broad range of financial services.

Most empirical studies have failed to find cost economies of scope in the banking, insurance or securities industries, and most of them have concluded that some diseconomies of scope are encountered when firms in the financial services sector add new product ranges to their portfolios.[7] However, many of these studies involved institutions that were shifting away from a pure focus on banking or insurance, and may thus have incurred considerable costs in expanding the range of their activities. If this diversification effort involved significant front-end costs – which were included on the accounting statements during the period under study – undertaken to achieve expansion of market share or increases in fee-based areas of activity, then we might expect to see any strong statistical evidence of cost diseconomies of scope (for example, between lending and non-lending activities of banks) reversed in future periods. If investment in staff, training and infrastructure in fact in the future bears returns commensurate with this expenditure, then neutral or positive cost economies of scope may well exist. Still, the evidence so far remains inconclusive.

On the revenue side, economies of scope attributable to cross-selling arise when the all-in cost to the buyer of multiple financial services from a single supplier – including the cost of the service, plus information, search, monitoring, contracting and other transaction costs – is less than the cost of purchasing them from separate suppliers. Revenue diseconomies of scope could arise, for example, through agency costs that may develop when the multi-product financial firm acts against the interests of the client in the sale of one service in order to facilitate the sale of another, or through problems encountered in attempting to manage highly complex organizations, or as a result of internal information transfer considered inimical to the client's interests.

Despite an almost total lack of hard empirical evidence, it is nonetheless reasonable to suggest that revenue economies of scope may indeed exist, but that these are likely to be very specific to the types of services provided and the types of clients served.[8] Strong cross-selling potential may exist for retail and private clients between banking, insurance and asset management products (one-stop shopping), for example. Yet such potential may be absent between trade-finance and mergers and acquisitions advisory services for major corporate clients. So demand-related scope economies in the euro-zone are clearly linked to a firm's specific strategic positioning across clients, products and geographic areas of operation.[9] Indeed, a principal objective of strategic positioning in the 'new' model of European financial services is to link market segments in a coherent pattern – what might be termed 'strategic integrity' – that permits maximum exploitation of cross-selling opportunities, and the design of incentives and organizational structures to ensure that such exploitation actually occurs. These are, however, extraordinarily difficult to achieve and must work against multi-product vendor behaviour on the part of corporate and institutional clients as well as a new generation of retail clients comfortable with non-traditional approaches to distribution such as the Internet.[10]

Production efficiency

Besides economies of scale and cost economies of scope, financial firms of roughly the same size and providing roughly the same range of services can have very different cost levels per unit of output. There is ample evidence of such performance differences, for example, in comparative cost-to-income ratios among banks or insurance companies or investment firms both within and between national financial services markets. The reasons involve differences in production functions, efficiency and effectiveness in the use of labour and capital, sourcing and application of available technology, and acquisition of inputs, organizational design, compensation and incentive systems – i.e. simply in better management.

Various studies have found large disparities in cost structures among banks of similar size, suggesting that the way banks are run is more important than their size or the selection of businesses they pursue.[11] The consensus based on US experience seems to be that average unit costs in the banking industry lie some 20 per cent above 'best practice' firms producing the same range and volume of services, with most of the difference attributable to operating economies rather than differences in the cost of funds.[12] This suggests that any shareholder value gains in many of the financial services mergers of the nineties were more highly associated with increases in production efficiency than with reductions in competition. If very large institutions are systematically better managed than smaller ones (which may be difficult to document in the real world of financial services), there may be a link between firm size and operating efficiency. In any case, both from a systemic and shareholder value perspective, management is (or should be) under constant pressure through their boards of directors to do better, to maximize operating efficiency in their organizations, and to transmit that pressure throughout the enterprise. If the euro-zone intensifies that pressure, this may in the end be one of the most significant sources of financial sector performance gains.

Taken together, the empirical evidence suggests very limited prospects for firm-wide cost economies of scale and scope among major financial services firms, and operating efficiency seems to be the principal determinant of observed differences in cost levels among banks and non-bank financial institutions. Demand-side economies of scope through cross-selling may well exist, but are likely to apply very differently to specific client segments and can be vulnerable to client promiscuity in response to sharper competition and new distribution technologies. Based on these considerations alone, therefore, there appears to be room in the euro-zone for viable financial services firms that range from large to small and from universal to specialist in a rich mosaic of institutions, as against a competitive monoculture dominated by financial mastodons.

Market structures in euro-zone financial services

In addition to the strategic search for operating economies and revenue synergies in the euro-zone financial services industry of the future, firms will also seek to dominate markets in order to extract economic rents. Europe has a long history of imperfect market structures and sometimes cartel formation in various industries, and the financial services market has been no different.

Concentration and market power

The role of concentration and market power in the financial services industry is an issue that empirical studies have not yet examined in great depth, although in many national markets for financial services suppliers have shown a tendency towards oligopoly. Supporters have argued that high levels of national market concentration are necessary in order to provide a platform for a viable pan-European or global competitive position. Opponents argue that monopolistic market structures without convincing evidence of scale economies or other size-related gains serve mainly to extract economic rents from consumers or users of financial services and redistribute them to shareholders, cross-subsidize other areas of activity, or reduce pressures for cost-containment. They therefore advocate vigorous antitrust action to prevent exploitation of monopoly positions.[13]

One way to measure market concentration is the Herfindahl-Hirshman index.[14] This index is low when market structure approaches perfect competition (e.g. commodity markets) and rises as market structure becomes more concentrated through monopolistic competition, oligopoly and price leadership, and ultimately monopoly. As Fig. 1.5 suggests, across a broad range of industries the index appears to be related to profitability in terms of margins and returns on equity. A key strategic issue is therefore the likely future competitive structure of financial services in the euro-zone. Financial services market structures differ widely among nations, with high levels of concentration in countries such as the Netherlands, Finland and Denmark, and low levels in relatively fragmented financial systems such as the US and Germany. The market concentration issue is perhaps best considered separately for wholesale and retail financial services.

Fig 1.5 Returns on capital and global concentration

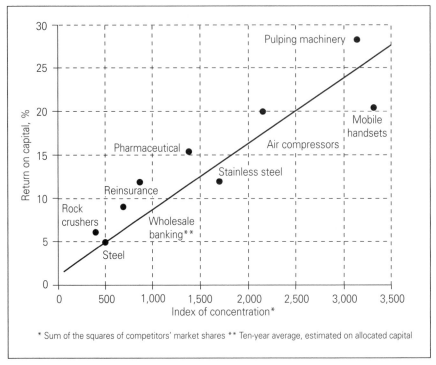

* Sum of the squares of competitors' market shares ** Ten-year average, estimated on allocated capital

Source: J.P. Morgan and author estimates

Wholesale financial services

The competitive structure that prevails in the euro-zone for wholesale financial services is likely to be similar to that prevailing in the global market. National markets for wholesale financial services in the euro-zone countries are already increasingly contested, with corporate and institutional clients under pressure to find the best and most competitively priced products regardless of vendor. As discussed in Chapter 8, US and European firms have made impressive incursions on traditional domestic client relationships. This is likely to be reinforced by the euro. The pan-European wholesale banking market should be highly fluid, as has long been the case in the US. This is good news for the euro-zone financial system as a whole, but not such good news for shareholders expecting sustained high profitability from wholesale banking activities. Nor is there much evidence so far that size as conventionally measured (e.g. by assets or capital) makes much difference in determining wholesale banking market share.

Retail financial services

The situation is likely to be very different with respect to market structure in retail financial services. Here the geography of local and regional market concentration is clearly more important, and what will no doubt be a very low euro-zone Herfindahl-Hirshman index for retail banking, insurance and investment services as a whole can mask high levels of regional or local concentration that are capable of supporting monopolistic pricing. The key question here is whether the advent of the euro will trigger the kind of geographic cross-penetration observed in the US after the relaxation of inter-state banking restrictions in the nineties.[15] US retail financial services markets have become increasingly contestable, with large national and super-regional banking networks such as Bank of America, Key Corp., Fleet Financial and First Union battling it out for regional market share with smaller, local institutions surprisingly adept at survival.

Figure 1.6 shows that, among all types of financial services firms doing business with the general public, only banks and savings institutions have shown significant increases in concentration (eight-firm ratio) during the period 1988–97 – from 22.3 per cent to 35.5 per cent – while concentration has decreased substantially in the life insurance industry. Even in the case of banks, the Herfindahl-Hirshman index has *decreased* from 2,020 in 1988 to 1,949 in 1997 in urban areas, and from 4,316 to 4,114 in non-urban areas – this during a period of dramatic industry consolidation in the US. These conclusions are not much different for the top European banks, especially in view of stiff competition from co-operatives and state-owned banks and savings institutions.

Research shows that retail banking clients remain strongly dependent on financial services firms with a local presence, and where there is a high level of concentration this is reflected in both interest rates and deposit rates.[16] However, the most profitable firms in the industry were not clearly identified with highly concentrated markets, suggesting that other competitive factors seem to be more important. On the other hand, bank mergers that increased local concentration sufficiently to trigger Department of Justice antitrust guidelines (a Herfindahl-Hirshman index exceeding 1,800 and a 200-point increase in the index as a result of the merger) were associated with reduced deposit rates. The US has implemented a legislative constraint against excessive market concentration in the form of the Riegle-Neal Act, which limits the share of retail deposits captured by mergers to 30 per cent in a given state and 10 per cent nationally, although these limits do not apply in the case of organic growth.[17] Despite continued consolidation and capacity reduction

Fig 1.6 Concentration trends in the US financial services industry

	Number of US bank charters	Number of banking organizations	Eight-firm concentration ratio	Life insurance		Property-liability insurance		Securities firms		Savings institutions		Credit unions	
				Number of firms	Asset share of eight largest firms	Number of firms	Asset share of eight largest firms	Number of firms	Capital share of ten largest firms	Number of firms	Asset share of eight largest firms	Number of firms	Asset share of eight largest firms
1988	13,130	9,881	22.3%	1,367	41.7%	940	32.5%	6,432	57.5%	3,175	13.5%	13,875	6.3%
1989	12,727	9,620	22.6%	1,288	40.4%	1,193	32.4%	6,141	61.8%	3,100	15.0%	13,371	6.5%
1990	12,370	9,391	22.3%	1,223	39.0%	1,272	32.4%	5,827	63.6%	2,725	18.2%	12,860	6.7%
1991	11,949	9,168	25.7%	1,221	38.1%	1,267	32.2%	5,386	62.1%	2,386	19.9%	12,960	6.8%
1992	11,496	8,873	26.4%	1,177	37.2%	1,232	32.2%	5,260	62.2%	2,086	19.3%	12,594	7.4%
1993	11,001	8,446	28.1%	1,187	36.4%	1,197	31.5%	5,292	63.4%	1,726	17.7%	12,317	7.7%
1994	10,491	8,018	29.7%	1,082	35.3%	1,187	31.3%	5,426	60.9%	1,532	19.2%	11,991	7.9%
1995	9,984	7,686	30.4%	1,054	34.9%	1,179	33.7%	5,451	59.3%	1,420	21.7%	11,687	7.9%
1996	9,575	7,421	34.3%	1,001	34.7%	1,138	36.1%	5,553	58.5%	1,322	21.3%	11,392	7.8%
1997	9,216	7,234	35.5%	n.a.	n.a.	n.a.	n.a.	5,597	55.5%	1,201	30.6%	11,238	8.0%

Source: Allen N. Berger, Rebecca S. Demsetz and Philip E. Strahan (1998) The Consolidation of the Financial Services Industry: Causes, Consequences, and Implications for the Future. New York: Federal Reserve Bank of New York.

in the industry, in 1998 almost 300 new US commercial bank charters were issued. There remains stiff competition from mutual fund companies, broker-dealers and insurance companies – i.e. intense competition both within and between strategic groups.

It seems likely that the kind of contestable retail financial services market that exists in the US will be slower in coming to the euro-zone. Pan-European mass-market branding is not easy to achieve. Local and national consumer preferences remain strong, with no particular reason to change unless there are demonstrable gains in terms of pricing or service quality provided by foreign firms. Nationally entrenched retail financial firms have generally improved their performance to the point that foreign players have a difficult time doing much better, and penetrating local markets by acquisition can be prohibitively expensive. So far, successful cross-border retail businesses are largely in niches such as private banking or consumer finance, with broader-based incursions such as Deutsche Bank in Italy or ING in Belgium confined to special situations.

Still, change will come, especially with a new generation of consumers less tied to local vendors and with new ways of delivering financial services. Markets that are already highly concentrated and characterized by high margins will be increasingly challenged. This suggests that the euro will eventually undermine existing monopolistic market structures, with little prospect of high levels of retail market concentration in the euro-zone as a whole in the foreseeable future.

Asset management

The asset management industry – where the top firms comprise a mixture of European, US and Japanese firms and at the same time a mixture of banks, broker-dealers, independent fund management companies and insurance companies, as discussed in Chapter 8 – is perhaps the most contestable in the financial services industry. Any number can play, as long as they have strong distribution, performance and client service capabilities. With a Herfindahl-Hirshman index of 540 for the top 40 firms in the industry (*see* Fig. 8.14) and very little sign of increasing concentration in recent years, this sector of the euro-zone's financial system is likewise likely to remain highly competitive. Despite this, the quality of earnings in asset management is relatively high, and provides an anchor for financial firms that are also engaged in much more volatile parts of the business.

State-owned financial firms

The role of the state at the national, regional and municipal levels will also have a major impact on competitive structure and performance in the euro-zone, and remains rather unclear. As noted, in the euro-zone the state is far more heavily involved than in the US, ranging from the European Investment Bank through the German Landesbanken to municipal savings banks. Public guarantees and other forms of support, as well as performance pressures, are very different from those facing investor-owned financial firms. When public- and private-sector firms meet in the market, competitive outcomes will clearly be affected. Consequently, the value extracted from a given market structure may be substantially smaller than expected in the presence of explicit or implicit subsidies imbedded in the activities of state-linked firms in the market. Similar points could be made with respect to co-operatives and mutuals, which play a major role across much of the euro-zone.

One can conclude that the euro is unlikely to have much of an impact on market concentration in wholesale financial services, which is basically a globalized industry, or in asset management. At the same time, it may gradually reduce regional and local market concentration by introducing new competitors. If this is correct, a good proportion of the gains associated with restructuring and competitive development in the euro-zone financial services sector will flow to end users rather than shareholders. This will place an even greater premium on astute strategic positioning and execution on the part of financial firms.

Universal banks and financial conglomerates

Proponents of universal banking as the dominant current and future form of strategic organization of financial services argue that the aforementioned operating economies and synergies, as well as non-destructive competition, can best be assured if the core of the evolving financial system in the euro-zone comprises bank-based, multifunctional financial organizations.[18] It has also been argued, for example, that shares of European-type universal banks incorporate substantial 'franchise value' due to their conglomerate nature and importance in national economies, which could well serve to inhibit extra-ordinary risk-taking.[19] This conclusion is, however, at variance with the observed, massive losses incurred in recent years by European universal banks in lending to highly leveraged firms, real estate lending and emerging market transactions.

There is also the argument that greater diversification of income from multiple products, client groups and geographies creates more stable, safer, and ultimately more valuable institutions. Indeed, there is some evidence that this is the case.[20] The main risk-reduction gains appear to arise from combining commercial banking with insurance activities, rather than with securities activities. Such arguments may, however, exaggerate the risk-reduction benefits of universal banking because they tend to ignore many of the operational costs involved in setting up and managing these activities.[21]

It is certainly the case that a number of large financial institutions will play a major role in the future financial configuration of the euro-zone. Failure of one of these institutions is likely to have unacceptable systemic consequences, and the institution is virtually certain to be bailed out by taxpayers, as happened with comparatively much smaller institutions in the US, Switzerland, Norway, Sweden, Finland and Japan during the eighties and early nineties.[22] Consequently, too-big-to-fail (TBTF) guarantees create a potentially important public subsidy for universal banking organizations.

Of course, 'free lunches' usually don't last too long, and sooner or later such guarantees invariably come with strings attached. Possible regulatory responses include tighter limits on credit and market risk exposures, stronger supervision and surveillance intended to achieve 'early closure' in advance of capital depletion, and structural barriers to force activities into business units that can be effectively supervised in accordance with their functions, even at the cost of lower levels of production efficiency and scope economies.

Conflicts of interest

The potential for conflicts of interest is endemic in the kinds of multifunctional financial services firms that characterize the euro-zone, and runs across the various types of activities in which they are engaged.[23]

First, when firms have the power to sell affiliates' products, managers may no longer dispense 'dispassionate' advice to clients and may have a salesman's stake in pushing 'house' products, possibly to the disadvantage of the customer. Second, a financial firm that is acting as an underwriter and is unable to place the securities in a public offering may seek to ameliorate this loss by 'stuffing' unwanted securities into accounts over which it has discretionary authority. Third, a bank with a loan outstanding to a client whose bankruptcy risk has increased, to the private knowledge of the banker, may have an incentive to induce the corporation to issue bonds or equities to the general public, with the proceeds used to pay down the bank loan.[24] Fourth, in order to ensure that an underwriting goes well, a bank may make below-market loans to third-party investors on condition that the proceeds are used to purchase securities underwritten by its securities unit. Fifth, a bank may use its lending power activities to coerce a client to also use its securities or securities services. Finally, by acting as a lender, a bank may become privy to certain inside information about a customer or its rivals that can be used in setting prices, advising potential buyers in a contested acquisition or helping in the distribution of securities offerings underwritten by its securities unit.

Mechanisms to control conflicts of interest can be market-based, regulation-based, or some combination of the two.

In most of the euro-zone countries few impenetrable walls exist between banking and securities departments within universal banks, and few external firewalls exist between a universal bank and its non-bank subsidiaries (e.g. insurance).[25] Internally, there appears to be a reliance on the loyalty and professional conduct of employees, both with respect to the institution's long-term survival and the best interests of its customers. Externally, reliance appears to be placed on market reputation and competition as disciplinary mechanisms. The concern of a bank for its reputation and fear of competitors are viewed as enforcing a degree of control over the potential for conflict exploitation. The US, on the other hand, has had a tendency since the thirties to rely on regulation, and in particular on 'walls' between types of activities. Either way, preventing conflicts of interest is an expensive business. Compliance systems are costly to maintain, and various types of walls between business units can have high opportunity costs because of inefficient use of information within the organization.[26]

The conflict of interest issue may seriously limit effective strategic options. For example, inside information accessible to a bank as lender to a target firm would almost certainly prevent it from acting as an adviser to a potential acquirer. Entrepreneurs are unlikely to want their private banking affairs dominated by a bank that also controls their business financing. A mutual fund investor is unlikely to have easy access to the full menu of equity funds available through a universal bank offering competing in-house products. These issues may be manageable if most of the competition is coming from other universal banks. But if the playing field is also populated by aggressive insurance companies, broker-dealers, fund managers and other specialists, these issues will prove to be a continuing strategic challenge to management.

Is there a conglomerate discount embedded in universal banks?

It is often argued that the shares of multi-product firms and business conglomerates tend (all else being equal) to trade at prices lower than shares of more narrowly focused firms. There are two reasons why this 'conglomerate discount' is alleged to exist.

First, it is argued that, on the whole, conglomerates tend to use capital inefficiently. A number of studies in the non-financial sector have assessed the potential benefits of diversification (greater operating efficiency, less incentive to forego positive net present value projects, greater debt capacity, lower taxes) against the potential costs (higher management discretion to engage in value-reducing projects, cross-subsidization of marginal or loss-making projects that drain resources from healthy businesses, misalignments in incentives between central and divisional managers).[27] The evidence seems to show an average value loss in multi-product firms to the order of 13–15 per cent, as compared to the stand-alone values of the constituent businesses for a sample of US corporations during the period 1986–91. This value loss was smaller in cases where the multi-product firms were active in closely allied activities, and the bulk of value erosion in conglomerates is attributed to overinvestment in marginally profitable activities and cross-subsidization.[28]

Such findings may well apply to diversified activities carried out by financial firms as well. If retail banking and wholesale banking are evolving into highly specialized, performance-driven businesses, one may ask whether the kinds of conglomerate discounts found in industrial firms may not also apply to universal banking structures and other types of financial conglomerates, especially as centralized decision making becomes increasingly irrelevant to the requirements of the specific businesses.

A second possible source of a conglomerate discount is that investors in shares of conglomerates find it difficult to 'take a view' and add pure sectoral exposures to their portfolios. Investors may avoid such stocks in their efforts to construct efficient asset-allocation profiles. This is especially true of highly performance-driven managers of institutional equity portfolios who are under pressure to outperform cohorts or equity indexes. So the portfolio logic of a conglomerate discount may indeed apply in the case of a multi-functional financial firm that is active in retail banking, wholesale commercial banking, middle-market banking, private banking, corporate finance, trading, investment banking, asset management and perhaps other businesses. In effect, a financial conglomerate's shares are a closed-end mutual fund of a broad range of assets.

Both the portfolio selection and capital misallocation effects (perhaps mitigated by the franchise and TBTF effects mentioned earlier) may thus weaken investor demand for financial conglomerate shares, and lower their equity prices. In the context of the euro-zone, management of universal banks and other types of financial conglomerates will have to come up with a compelling set of counter-arguments, particularly when investors have the choice of placing their bets on more narrowly focused financial specialists.

Linkages between financial and non-financial firms

In most of the euro-zone countries, including France and Germany, banks and insurance companies have traditionally held large-scale shareholdings in non-financial corporations or have been part of multi-industry holdings of financial groups. There are various historical reasons for this, such as politically driven interests of the state to intervene directly in the control of industry and past economic crises that forced banks to capitalize debt in the face of threatened client bankruptcies. There are also portfolio reasons, such as insurance companies' need to invest massive reserves in the absence of

Fig 1.7 Sustainable returns and capital allocation of German banks by business line

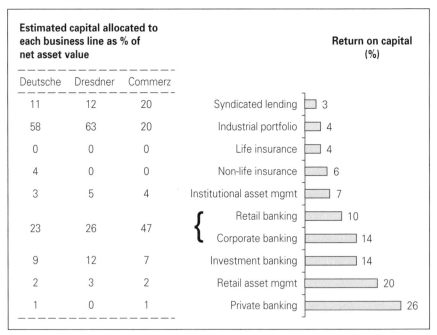

Source: Schroders estimates (March 1999)

sufficiently broad and deep local capital markets – inevitably leading to major equity positions in non-financial corporations as well as banks. And there are relationship reasons, with banks viewing shareholdings in client firms as an important part of 'Hausbank' ties that would attract most of the client's financial services business, even as clients themselves value the presence of a reliable lender who looks beyond a purely arm's length credit relationship. These issues are discussed in greater detail in Chapter 7.[29]

Certainly the earnings structures of European-style financial conglomerates are complex and difficult. Figure 1.7 shows an estimate of 'sustainable' earnings patterns for the major German universal banks, which demonstrate not only very different levels in terms of lines of business but also the imbedded complexity of the linkages between them – and creating the incentive to begin serious restructuring of long-term shareholdings.

Strategic options

The introductory discussion presented here is centred around a common sense approach to strategic positioning and execution after the launch of the euro. Put simply, it's all a matter of doing the right thing, and then doing it right. This invariably requires an astute assessment of the prospective competitive battlefield, both in terms of market prospects and competitive structures, which has to be based on a number of suppositions reflecting a well argued consensus among those creating the strategy. If important suppositions turn out to be wrong, key parts of the strategy will be wrong too.

Once a judgement has been reached as to key client groups, geographies and product portfolios that promise to generate acceptable risk-adjusted returns to shareholders, a strategic configuration has to be devised for the institution that can extract significant economies of scale and scope and that can be managed effectively to achieve strong operating economies. Such an optimum configuration may be termed 'strategic integrity'. It forms what the Germans call a 'soll-Zustand' (what *ought to be*). This compares with the 'ist-Zustand' (what *is*), i.e. how the institution stacks up against competitors, traditional and non-traditional, in the cold light of day, and what will be required to compete effectively in the future in terms of capital, human and managerial resources and organizational change.

Comparing reality to strategic objectives in the presence of a critical time element usually produces a number of show-stoppers. Rejecting losers among strategic options is just as important as selecting winners, and is often much more difficult, especially when opportunistic moves beckon and time is short. Failure to reject losers can result in a disproportionate number of strategic errors in the financial services sector – often at great expense to shareholders.

Finally comes strategic implementation: marshalling resources, controlling costs, getting the troops on board, building a high-performance 'super-culture' over what inevitably will be a number of often very different 'sub-cultures', getting the right people, and then providing effective leadership. The devil is always in the detail.

If a strategic direction taken by the management of a financial firm in the euro-zone does not exploit every source of potential value for shareholders, what is the purpose? Avoiding an acquisition attempt from a better managed suitor who will pay a premium price does not seem nearly as unacceptable today as it may have been in the past. In a world of more open and efficient markets for shares in financial institutions, shareholders increasingly tend to have the final say about the future of their enterprises.

NOTES

[1] See, for example, Story and Walter (1997) *Political Economy of Financial Integration in Europe*, Manchester: Manchester University Press, and Cambridge: MIT Press.

[2] See Walter (1999) 'The asset management industry in Europe: competitive structure and performance under EMU', in Dermine, Jean and Hillion, Pierre (eds) *European Capital Markets With a Single Currency*, Oxford: Oxford University Press.

[3] These effects should be directly observable in financial services suppliers' cost functions and in overall performance measures. Unfortunately, studies of scale and scope economies in financial services are unusually problematic. The nature of the empirical tests used, the form of the cost functions, the existence of unique optimum output levels, and the optimizing behaviour of financial firms all present difficulties. Limited availability and conformity of data present serious empirical problems. And the conclusions of any study that has detected (or failed to detect) economies of scale and/or scope in a sample selection of financial institutions does not necessarily have general applicability. For a survey, *see* Berger, Demsetz and Strahan (1998).

[4] See Saunders (1996) *Financial Institutions Management*, 2nd edn. Burr Ridge, Ill: Irwin, for a useful survey.

[5] See Cummins and Zi (1998) for insurance companies ('Comparisons of frontier efficiency levels', *Journal of Productivity Analysis*, June) and Goldberg, Hanweck, Keenan and Young (1991) for broker-dealers ('Economies of scale and scope in the securities industry', *Journal of Banking and Finance*, 15).

[6] An examination of the world's 200 largest banks (Saunders and Walter, 1994) found evidence that the very largest banks grew more slowly than the smaller among the large banks during the eighties, but that limited economies of scale did appear among the banks included in the study. More recently, there is some scattered evidence of scale-related cost gains of up to 20 per cent for banks up to $25 billion in size (Berger and Mester, 1997). Among German universal banks, Lang and Wetzel (1998) found diseconomies of scale in both banking and securities services.

[7] Saunders and Walter (1994), for example, found negative supply-side economies of scope among the world's 200 largest banks – as the product range widens, unit costs seem to go up. Scope economies in most other studies of the financial services industry are either trivial or negative. For a survey, *see* Saunders (1996).

[8] *See*, for example, Walter (1988) *Global Competition in Financial Services*, Cambridge, Mass: Ballinger – Harper & Row.

[9] Op. cit.

[10] Recent consumer surveys in the US show that client reactions to multi-product vendor relationships are viewed very positively in principle, but in fact US retail clients have, throughout the nineties significantly increased the average number of financial services firms they deal with.

[11] Berger, Hancock and Humphrey (1993) 'Bank efficiency derived from the profit function', *Journal of Banking and Finance*, April; Berger, Hunter and Timme (1993) 'The efficiency of financial institutions: a review of research past, present and future', *Journal of Banking and Finance*, April.

[12] Akhavein, Berger and Humphrey (1996) 'The effects of megamergers on efficiency and prices: evidence from a bank profit function.' Paper presented at the *Conference on Mergers of Financial Institutions*, New York University Salomon Center, October 11. In addition, Siems (1996) finds that the greater the overlap in branch-office networks, the higher the abnormal equity returns in US bank mergers, while no such abnormal returns are associated with increasing concentration levels in the regions where the bank mergers occurred.

[13] In Canada, two mega-mergers that would have reduced the number of major financial firms from five to three were disallowed by the authorities in late 1998 despite arguments by management that major US financial services firms would provide the necessary competitive pressure to prevent exploitation of monopoly power.

[14] The Herfindahl-Hirshman index is the sum of the squared market shares ($H=\Sigma s^2$), where $0<H<10,000$ and market shares are measured, for example, by deposits, by assets, or by capital. H rises as the number of competitors declines and as market-share concentration rises among a given number of competitors.

[15] Insurance and investor services were never subject to such restrictions, although there continues to be prudential regulation at the state level.

[16] *See*, for example, Kwast, Starr-McCluer and Wolken (1997) 'Market definition and the analysis of antitrust in banking', *Antitrust Bulletin*, 42, 973–95, Berger and Hannan (1987) 'The price-concentration relationship in banking', *Review of Economics and Statistics*, 71; and Prager and Hannan (1999) 'Do substantial horizontal mergers generate significant price effects?', *Journal of Industrial Economics*.

[17] The merger of BankAmerica and NationsBank in 1998 created a national market share of 8 per cent for the new Bank of America, which is very close to the limit but can be circumvented by moving assets off the balance sheet or non-deposit funding.

[18] This argument is made in Van den Brink (1998) 'Universal banking: an answer to the challenges facing the financial sector', ABN AMRO (*mimeo*).

[19] Demsetz, Saidenberg and Strahan (1996) find some evidence that the higher a bank's franchise value, the more prudent management tends to be, so that large universal banks with high franchise values should serve shareholder interests as well as stability of the financial system – and the concerns of its regulators – with a strong focus on risk management, as opposed to banks with little to lose.

[20] Saunders and Walter (1994) carried out a series of simulated mergers between US banks, securities firms and insurance companies in order to test the stability of earnings of the 'merged' as opposed to separate institutions. The opportunity set of potential mergers between existing firms and the risk characteristics of each possible combination were examined. The findings

suggest that there are indeed potential risk-reduction gains from diversification in multi-activity financial services organizations, and that these gains increase with the number of activities undertaken.

[21] For example, only the financial firms in existence for the full 1984–8 period are considered in Saunders and Walter (1994) *Universal Banking in the United States*, New York: Oxford University Press.

[22] The speed with which the central banks and regulatory authorities reacted to the 1996 Sumitomo copper trading scandal signalled the possibility of safety-net support of the global copper market, in view of major banks' massive exposures in highly complex structured credits.

[23] For a detailed discussion, *see* Saunders and Walter (1994), Chapter 6.

[24] An example was the 1995 underwriting of a secondary equity issue of the Hafnia Insurance Group by Den Danske Bank, distributed heavily to retail investors, with proceeds allegedly used to pay down bank loans even as Hafnia slid into bankruptcy. This case went before the courts. *See* Smith and Walter (1997) *Street Smarts: Linking Professional Conduct and Shareholder Value in the Securities Industry*, Boston: Harvard Business School Press.

[25] For a comprehensive catalogue of potential conflicts of interest, *see* Gnehm and Thalmann (1989) 'Conflicts of interest in financial operations: problems of regulation in the national and international context'. Working Paper, Swiss Bank Corporation, Basel.

[26] A detailed discussion is contained in Smith and Walter (1997) *Global Banking*, New York: Oxford University Press, Chapter 8.

[27] *See*, for example, Berger and Ofek (1995) 'Diversification's effect on firm value', *Journal of Financial Economics*, 37.

[28] *See* Berger and Ofek (1995). In empirical work using event study methodology, John and Ofek (1994) show that asset sales by corporations result in significantly improved shareholder returns on the remaining capital employed, both as a result of greater focus in the enterprise and value gains through high prices paid by asset buyers.

[29] *See also* Walter (1993) *High-Performance Financial Systems*. Singapore: Institute for Southeast Asian Studies, and Story and Walter (1997) *Political Economy of Financial Integration in Europe*, Manchester: Manchester University Press, and Cambridge: MIT Press.

CHAPTER 2

Towards a single financial market in Europe

With the euro successfully introduced by the 11 EMU countries, and barring any unforeseen setbacks, the outlines of the single financial market are beginning to take shape. It is a market that will rival in size that of the US, which (except for the civil war period) has had a single currency for more than 200 years. Creation of the market has three more or less distinct elements:

- macro-economic convergence and the crafting of monetary union
- free trade in financial services and a common chartering process for financial institutions
- regulatory convergence and an agreed framework for prudential super-vision and market practices.

These three elements define the platform on which the battle for supremacy in wholesale financial services will be fought. In this chapter we consider each of these core elements of the euro marketplace, and how it is likely to affect the competitive structure of the wholesale banking industry.

Financial firms based in the euro-zone – mainly universal banks – fully expect to capture a major share of the deal flow in this massive market. But outside firms – notably those based in the US, the UK and Switzerland – have big plans for their role in the new market as well, and are zeroing in on expanding their already impressive share of the euro deal flow – some have estimated the US firms' share of European investment banking earnings to have approached 70 per cent. At the same time, a battle is being waged among financial centres where the value-added is actually carried out. At stake are jobs and incomes in the financial services industry, which in turn are linked to many other sectors of the economy. Few countries in the euro-zone are prepared to let their share of financial services value-added wither, yet industry dynamics suggest that this is exactly what will happen to many of them.

The regulatory setting

The securities industry worldwide has been, and will continue to be, subject to significant public authority regulation and supervision due to the fiduciary nature of the business, the potential for financial fraud, and the possibility of serious social costs associated with financial failure. Indeed, small changes in financial regulation can bring about massive changes in financial markets activity.

Fundamental to the European regulatory environment was the elimination of all capital controls among the EU member countries in 1990, resulting in a unified financial market for cross-border monetary transfers. Beyond this is the constellation of regulations bearing on the establishment and operation of credit institutions, securities firms and insurance companies, as well as the markets themselves. To the extent that information flows among counterparties in financial markets are imperfect, regulation can improve the operation of financial systems. The greater the information asymmetries, the greater the value of regulation. Bodies such as the Securities and Exchange Commission (SEC) in the US that force firms to produce timely accounting statements, the US Financial Accounting Standards Board (FASB) that lays down accounting rules and standards, and bank supervisors who both monitor and produce information about financial institutions, play an extremely important role in engendering investor confidence in financial markets and institutions.

Panic and instability is likely to occur in financial systems for two reasons. First, the nature of bank deposits is such that depositor place in line (queuing) matters when banks become distressed (unlike mutual fund contracts where investors share any remaining assets on a pro rata basis. Second, the true value of bank assets is usually uncertain because of the general use of 'book' rather than market value accounting rules and infrequent asset trading, hence the limited availability of current price information on the value of many loans in a bank's asset portfolio.

For both reasons, bad news regarding a specific bank or even banks in general creates incentives for depositors (and other investors) to withdraw funds. Bank runs can, in turn, have contagion effects on other (sound) financial institutions and the financial system as a whole, so that a case can be made for the public provision of deposit insurance schemes and a lender-of-last-resort (LOLR) facility – so-called 'safety nets'. These must be carefully designed to avoid moral hazard and adverse selection problems that could amplify the potential burden on the taxpayer, who in turn has the right to demand vigorous regulation to contain such potential problems. Unfortunately, greater regulation in the form of capital adequacy requirements, reserve requirements, gap limits, lending limits, geographic and line-of-business limits, and similar constraints may themselves serve to erode financial market efficiency and competitiveness.

In going about their business, regulators continuously face the possibility that inadequate regulation will result in costly failures, as against the possibility that overregulation will create opportunity costs in the form of financial efficiencies not achieved, or in the relocation of firms to other, more friendly regulatory regimes. Since any improvements in financial stability can be measured only in terms of damage that did not occur and costs that were successfully avoided, the argument surrounding financial regulation is invariably based on 'what if' hypotheticals. In effect, regulators are constantly compelled to rethink the balance between financial efficiency and creativity on the one hand, and safety and stability of the financial system on the other. They face the daunting task of designing an 'optimum' regulatory and supervisory structure that provides the desired degree of stability at minimum cost to efficiency, innovation and competitiveness – and doing so in a way that effectively aligns such policies among regulatory authorities internationally and avoids 'fault lines' across regulatory regimes. There are no definitive answers with respect to optimum financial regulatory structures and policies. There are only 'better' and 'worse' solutions as perceived by those to whom the regulators are ultimately responsible.

Achieving optimum regulatory structures in an integrated financial market such as the euro-zone, characterized by intense competition among regulatory jurisdictions, may well be impossible without a significant degree of co-ordination and possibly even of regulatory centralization. It is for this reason that future EU regulatory outcomes are so important for the structure and performance of the single European financial market.

Regulatory trade-offs

Figure 2.1 outlines the regulatory issues surrounding the securities industry, and the financial services sector more generally. The right-hand side of the diagram identifies the policy trade-offs that invariably confront those charged with designing and implementing a properly structured financial system. On the one hand, they must strive to achieve maximum static and dynamic efficiency with respect to the financial system as a whole, as well as the competitive viability of financial institutions that are subject to regulation. On the other hand, they must safeguard the stability of institutions and the financial system, in addition to helping to assure what is considered 'acceptable' market conduct, including the politically sensitive implied social contract between financial institutions and small, unsophisticated customers. The problem of safety net design is beset with difficulties such as moral hazard and adverse selection, and becomes especially problematic when products and activities shade into one another, when on- and off-balance sheet activities are involved, and when domestic and offshore business is conducted simultaneously.

Fig 2.1 Regulatory trade-offs, techniques and control in the securities industry

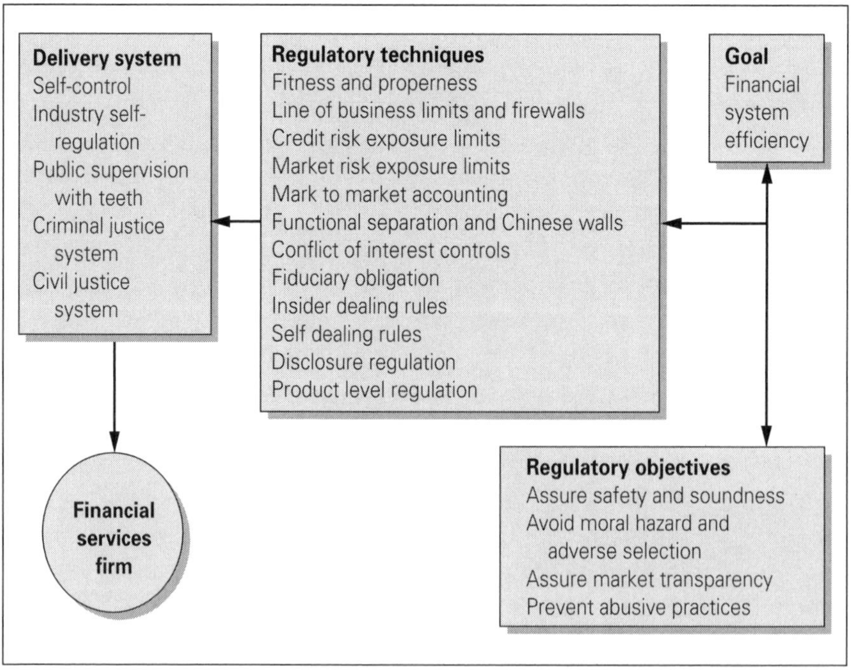

The principal options regulators have at their disposal, identified in Fig. 2.1, range from 'fitness and properness' criteria under which a financial institution may be established, continue to operate or be shut down – including jurisdiction issues, line of business regulation (what types of business financial institutions may engage in), adequacy of capital and liquidity, limits on various types of exposures – to policies governing marking-to-market of assets and liabilities. Regulatory initiatives, however, can have a distortive impact on financial markets, and regulation becomes especially difficult when financial markets evolve rapidly and the regulator can easily get one or two steps behind.

A third element identified in Fig. 2.1 involves the regulatory vehicles that may be used, ranging from reliance on self-control on the part of boards and senior managements of financial firms concerned with protecting the value of their franchises, to industry self-regulation and public regulators with teeth (including criminal prosecution).

Just as there are trade-offs implicit in Fig. 2.1 between financial system performance and stability, there are also trade-offs between regulation and supervision, with some regulatory options (e.g. capital adequacy rules) fairly easy to supervise but full of distortive potential due to their broad-gauge nature, and others (e.g. fitness and properness criteria) possibly highly cost-effective but devilishly difficulty to supervise. Finally, there are trade-offs between supervision and performance, with some supervisory techniques far more costly to comply with than others. Regulators must try to optimize across this three-dimensional set of trade-offs under conditions of rapid market and industry change, blurred institutional and activity demarcations, and international regulatory fault lines.

Global deregulation

As markets became more performance-oriented and regulators became more sophisticated, sequential and sometimes competitive, liberalization of national financial markets took hold from the mid-seventies. Beginning with the New York Stock Exchange's introduction of negotiated securities commission rates on 1 May 1975, the US followed up by liberalizing the rules governing public securities issues and private placements, easing restrictions on commercial banks' investment banking activities, and introducing tax changes designed to make its financial market more attractive to foreign issuers and investors – leading to 25 years of 'mini-bangs'.

Britain's 'Big Bang' followed, with the liberalization of restrictive pricing, trading practices and market access rules, announced in 1983 and implemented in 1986. Britain had repealed exchange controls in 1979, and later vigorously opposed EU tax initiatives that would have diminished the competitive attractiveness of London's financial markets. The country made far-reaching regulatory reforms in banking, securities and insurance in 1998 by creating a super-regulator, the Financial Services Authority (FSA), and relieving the newly independent Bank of England of supervisory responsibility.

Japan did not begin financial deregulation until 20 years after the US, with its own 'Big Bang' near the end of the century, having lost some of its early promise as Asia's pre-eminent financial hub. Struggling against massive credit and corruption problems affecting virtually every part of the financial services sector, and even its regulators, Japan seemed committed for the first time to serious liberalization that included opening the door for foreign financial institutions and asset managers to participate in its high-savings economy.

France, meanwhile, took pride in what it had achieved during the late eighties in developing efficient and innovative markets for derivatives and local securities, and worked in the nineties to remedy its remaining regulatory and transparency shortcomings. Germany, the world's largest importer of financial services, intent on overcoming its longstanding reputation as an 'industrial giant but a financial dwarf', announced in the mid-nineties important institutional and regulatory changes intended to make Frankfurt the pre-eminent financial centre of continental Europe by the year 2000. The Netherlands styled Amsterdam as the 'financial gateway to Europe' but seemed destined to be mainly a niche player along with Luxembourg and Dublin, as well as being the home base for a few powerful financial institutions. Along the way, there were many other 'mini-bangs' in Canada, Australia, Switzerland and a number of emerging financial markets such as Chile, Mexico and Brazil – often under far-reaching national programmes of market-oriented economic reforms – and in Asia which endured the threat of financial collapse in the late nineties.

In short, governments in one country after another sought a better balance between the efficiency of the financial markets and the stability of the financial system, with almost all of the regulatory change favouring more efficient capital markets.

The euro-zone framework

The regulatory overlay across the euro-zone is anchored in EU directives covering the right of banks and securities firms to engage in business throughout the region, the adequacy of capital, and the conduct of business in the constituent financial markets, as well as the establishment and marketing of collective investment vehicles.

The single passport

The regulatory framework covering EU banking activities can be traced to the 1977 First Banking Directive, which allowed banks based anywhere in the EC to establish branches or subsidiaries in any other member country (freedom of establishment) on the condition that banking regulations in the host country were fully observed. It also required member states to establish a licensing system for credit institutions, including minimum 'fit and proper' criteria for authorization to do business.

Under the 1988 Second Banking Directive, a single EU banking licence allows credit institutions authorized to do business in any member state to have full access to other EU national markets for all credit services without separate authorization. This includes deposit taking, wholesale and retail lending, leasing, portfolio advice and management, and trading in securities. Prudential control over all banks authorized to do business in the EU, including subsidiaries (which come under a separate 1983 EU directive on consolidated supervision), is exercised by home countries.

Non-banking securities firms are covered by the Investment Services Directive (ISD). Again, home country agencies – public authorities or professional self-regulatory organizations (SROs) appointed by public authorities – have the power to license, supervise and regulate investment firms. Institutions duly registered and supervised by EU home countries are essentially free to establish a commercial presence and to supply securities services in any member country without separate authorization. Investment firms holding membership in stock exchanges in their home countries are likewise free to apply for full trading privileges on all EU stock, options and futures exchanges. Close collaboration is envisaged between the European Commission, the authorities responsible for securities markets and institutions, and banking and insurance authorities.

Foreign-based financial institutions are treated in accordance with the principle of 'reciprocal national treatment' and, once certified by a member country, notionally fall under the same 'single passport' rules as EU financial institutions as long as their home countries are not found to discriminate against EU-based institutions. The benefit of the single passport is available only to EU subsidiaries of foreign financial institutions. Branches are not eligible and cannot be 'certified'. This is a major point because of the capital cost of running significant financial market activities through subsidiaries. The same issue comes up in US banking law, with foreign and domestic commercial banks able to deal in the securities market (other than government bonds) only through separately capitalized subsidiaries of bank holding companies.

Capital adequacy

The capital-to-assets ratio required of banks and securities firms has a direct impact on their funding costs, as well as their ability to execute transactions, and hence their ability to offer competitive financing to clients. The move towards international agreement on regulatory capital achieved momentum with an Anglo-American initiative announced in January 1987 to strengthen the international banking community and create a level playing field among competing banks globally. As agreed in the 1988 Basle Accord, banks became subject to a minimum 8 per cent ratio of capital (composed of not less than 4 per cent 'core' capital) to risk-weighted assets (defined to include off-balance sheet exposures) by the beginning of 1993. Besides contributing to banking stability, the Basle Accord was intended to promote a level playing field for credit institutions regardless of their home base. In the EU context, the Basle Accord made further harmonization of capital standards for credit institutions largely superfluous.

The comparable EU initiative for the securities industry is the Capital Adequacy Directive (CAD), covering both securities firms and the securities activities of banks. Its provisions range from matching capital against position (market) risks, to minimum levels of firm capital covering all eventualities and EU-wide enforcement of maximum exposure limits.

Conduct-of-business rules

Whereas under the EU 'single passport' banks and securities firms are under the control of home country authorities, conduct-of-business rules regarding EU financial markets are the exclusive responsibility of host country authorities. Financial institutions doing business in the EU must deal with 15 different sets of rules (including the ecrobond market), although these have gradually converged towards a consensus on minimum acceptable conduct-of-business standards in the single market which seek to optimize the balance between market efficiency and regulatory soundness.

Areas of particular interest with respect to conduct-of-business rules include insider trading and information disclosure. For example, the view that insider trading is a crime, rather than a professional indiscretion, is relatively new in most of Europe – few people have been jailed for insider trading, and in several EU countries it is not a criminal offence. With regard to information disclosure in securities new issues, there has been only limited standardization of the content and distribution of prospectuses covering equity, bond and eurobond issues for sale to individuals and institutions in the member countries.

Rules governing trading conduct continue to evolve in the euro-zone countries. For example, omission of investment advice and secondary market trading (including short trading and margin rules) from the ISD was controversial, as were the complaints procedures specified in the directive in the event of infractions of host country rules.

Finally, rules governing the creation and distribution of mutual funds, as well as harmonization of capital income taxation, are critical for the functioning of a single financial market under the euro. These are considered in Chapter 8.

Regulation and the securities industry

In recent years the importance of the securities industry has increased considerably worldwide. More financial transactions now occur in these markets than take place in banks. These transactions and financial flows, including the activities of mutual funds, pension funds and other institutional investors, dominate global financial behaviour. Market developments have generally overtaken regulatory developments, which often have not been adapted sufficiently to compensate for the changed realities of the marketplace. Banking and securities regulation, for example, remain quite dissimilar.

On balance, the banks carry a regulatory burden that, in terms of the requirements and costs of compliance, is vastly greater than that which applies to the securities industry. In part, this is because of the difference in regulatory inheritance of the two industries. In the US, for example, when Congress passed the Securities Act of 1933, it focused on 'truth in new issues', requiring prospectuses and creating underwriting liabilities to be shared by companies and their investment bankers. It then passed the Securities Act of 1934, which set up the Securities and Exchange Commission and focused on the conduct of secondary markets. Later on, in the sixties, it passed the Securities Investor Protection Act, which provided for a $600 million fund (paid in by the securities industry and supported by a line of credit from the US Treasury) to protect investors who maintain brokerage accounts from losses associated with the failure of the securities firms involved.

None of these measures, however, provided for the government to guarantee deposits with securities dealers, nor did they in any way guarantee investment results. So there was less need to get 'inside' the securities firms – the taxpayer was not at risk.

Although the SEC developed into a forthright regulator, willing to use its powers to protect individual investors and ensure the integrity of the markets, most of the discipline to which US securities firms have been subject since

1934 has been provided by the market itself. Prices have risen and fallen. Many investors have lost money. Many securities firms have failed or have been taken over by competitors. Others have entered the industry with a modest capital investment and succeeded. Firms are in fact 'regulated' by the requirements of their customers, their creditors and their owners – requirements demanding marked-to-market accounting, adequate capitalization and disclosure of all liabilities, as well as supervisory and legal proceedings. Customers, presumably, require good service and honest dealings or they will change brokers. These market-driven requirements have proven to be as effective as regulators as any body established by the government.

Things have been very different in the euro-zone. There has been no tradition of separation of commercial and investment banking of the type that existed in the US from 1933 to 1999 and only in later years was considerably softened. Instead, the 'universal banking' model has predominated in virtually all the euro countries, stretching from Finland to Portugal. Banks have been able to engage in all types of financial services – retail and wholesale, commercial banking, investment banking, asset management, as well as insurance underwriting and distribution. In some euro-zone countries they have also held major long-term stakes in insurance companies (and vice versa) as well as industrial companies, sometimes as part of major banking-industry conglomerates (*see* Chapter 7). Savings banks, co-operative banks, state-owned banks, private banks and in some cases more or less independent investment banks (notably in France, Italy and the Netherlands) have also been important elements in some of the national markets.

In general, the euro-zone financial environment has been far more bank-dominated than that of the US, with correspondingly less highly developed capital markets. The regulatory environment has clearly reflected this. In general, bank supervision has been in the domain of the national central banks or lodged with independent supervisory agencies working in co-operation with the central banks and responsible for all aspects of universal bank regulation, with the exception of insurance and in some cases specialized activities, such as mortgage banking, which are often placed under separate regulatory domains. Consequently independent securities firms, domestic or foreign-based, have had to be chartered as 'banks' in most euro-zone countries in order to be encompassed in the national regulatory system.

Bank failure

Given their multiple areas of activity centred around core commercial banking functions (taking deposits from the general public and making commercial loans), the major European players in the investment banking business can be considered 'too big to fail' in the context of their national regulatory domains. This means that, unlike in the US or Japan, significant losses incurred in the securities business (such as credit losses) could bring down the bank. Given the possible systemic impact of failure, the bank is therefore likely to be bailed out by taxpayers through a government takeover, recapitalization, forced merger with a government capital injection, or a number of other techniques. This means that European financial regulators find it as necessary to safeguard the securities business as the banking business. Failure to provide this kind of symmetry in regulation could end in disaster.

No bank failure in the euro-zone has been triggered by securities losses. But, as in the case of Barings in the UK, it can easily happen. It was the firm's disastrous trading activities in Singapore and Japan which ultimately brought it down. However, it was the responsibility of the Bank of England, as home country regulator, to supervise its global activities. The case demonstrated how difficult this is to do. Predictably, it has resulted in closer scrutiny by the regulators.

There is also the question of whether an investment bank that is part of a TBTF universal banking group carries inherent advantages or disadvantages in competition against independent securities firms. Proponents of the latter argue that they are forced to pay greater attention to managing risks, managing costs and ensuring profitability in a mark-to-market environment in part because there is no lender of last resort for the individual securities firm. Even in the case of massive failures (e.g. Barings or Drexel Burnham Lambert in the US) central banks allowed the failure to run its course, taking care only to provide sufficient liquidity to the market during the crisis period.

Regulatory controls

As financial market activities have become increasingly integrated across national and offshore markets, regulatory regimes have also had to become more international. New regulations were imposed in the eighties to provide for minimum capital adequacy and for the conduct of banks within the European Union. The capital adequacy rules were implemented under the auspices of the Bank for International Settlements (BIS), and subsequently were adopted by all EU members, Switzerland, the US and Japan. The Second Banking Directive of the EU permits banks with a licence to operate in one EU country to operate in all, subject to home country regulatory supervision. Banks may participate as they wish in unregulated markets, such as foreign exchange, commodities and the eurocurrency and eurobond markets, but their activities as institutions remain subject to overall control of the home country banking regulators.

In the securities industry, international regulatory controls are more complex. There is no requirement for home country regulation of the global activities of US or Japanese non-bank firms. Regulation is thus a case of compliance with all the local regulations of each of the countries in which a firm may operate, usually through a local entity such as a subsidiary that the local regulators can get their teeth into if they have to. National regulatory requirements are often very different from one another. This creates the massive task of monitoring regulatory compliance for each of the firms, and a certain amount of inefficient duplication of regulatory capital. Still, the essence of the regulatory differences between securities firms and the banks is that the banks are subject to more explicit limitations on their businesses – especially through the requirement to maintain minimum amounts of capital – than are the securities firms. The latter, however, are subject to the costs of maintaining expensive global and local compliance systems, and since they are dependent on banks for much of their funding, they have to meet acceptable credit standards.

There has been lively debate about the effectiveness of firm self-regulation in the securities industry, since firms continue to suffer from incidents of misconduct despite the often devastating effects on their franchises. Control through industry self-regulation is likewise subject to substantial controversy, especially in the UK, which relies heavily on this approach and where, for example, the Investment Management Regulatory Organization (IMRO), the self-regulatory body governing pension funds, failed to catch the disappearance of the Maxwell pension money, and the Personal Investment Authority (PIA) for years failed to act against deceptive insurance sales practices at the retail level.[1]

There are, of course, always political charges of the fox watching the henhouse. For example, the City of London has come in for a good deal of criticism for the 'easygoing ways' that have done so much to contribute to its competitive success in the global marketplace.[2] But reliance on public oversight for financial regulation has its own problems, since virtually any regulatory initiative is likely to run up against powerful vested interests that would like nothing better than to bend the rules in their favour.[3] Even the judicial process that is supposed to arbitrate or adjudicate matters of regulatory policy may not always be entirely free of political influence or popular opinion.

The net regulatory burden

It is useful to think of financial regulation and supervision as imposing a set of 'taxes' and 'subsidies' on the operations of financial firms exposed to them. On the one hand, the imposition of reserve requirements, capital adequacy rules, interest/usury ceilings and certain forms of financial disclosure requirements can be viewed as imposing implicit 'taxes' on a financial firm's activities in the sense that they increase costs. On the other hand, regulator-supplied deposit insurance, lender-of-last-resort facilities and institutional bailouts serve to stabilize financial markets and reduce the risk of systemic failure, thereby lowering the costs of financial intermediation. They can therefore be viewed as implicit 'subsidies' provided by taxpayers.

The difference between these tax and subsidy elements of regulation can be viewed as the net regulatory burden (NRB) faced by financial firms in any given jurisdiction. Financial firms tend to migrate towards those financial environments where NRB is lowest (assuming all other economic factors are the same). NRB differences can induce firms to relocate where transactions are done as long as the savings realized exceed the transaction, communication, information and other economic costs of doing so. Since one can argue that, in today's global financial marketplace, transaction and other economic costs of relocating are likely to be small, one can expect financial market participants to be extremely sensitive to changes in current and perceived NRBs among competing regulatory environments. To some extent, the regulators responsible for particular jurisdictions appear to recognize this sensitivity and – in their competition for employment and value-added creation, taxes and other revenues – have engaged in a form of competition over NRB levels, a kind of 'regulatory arbitrage'.[4]

Competition will spark a dynamic interplay between those demanding and those supplying financial services, as banks and securities firms seek to reduce their NRB and increase their profitability. If they can do so at low cost, they will actively seek product innovations and new avenues that avoid cumbersome and costly regulations. This may be easier when there are multiple and overlapping domestic regulatory bodies, as well as in the global case of multiple and often competing national regulatory authorities.

A domestic financial system such as that in the US may have multiple regulatory authorities, complemented by a host of other regulators at the state and local levels. For example, at the federal level, financial activities could fall into the regulatory domain of the Federal Reserve Board, the Comptroller on the Currency, the SEC and the Commodity Futures Trading

Commission, to name just the major regulatory agencies. Each of the 50 states also has its own regulatory body to deal with banking, securities and insurance. Every city and municipality has an agency responsible for local income taxes, real estate taxes, transfer taxes, stamp duties and so on, all of which affect the NRB bearing on financial firms. The situation is further complicated by ambiguity regarding the definition of a bank, a security, an exchange and so forth – blurring the lines of demarcation between both products and firms, and raising questions about which regulatory agency holds jurisdiction.[5]

Offshore markets

NRB associated with regulations in onshore financial markets creates opportunities to develop a parallel, offshore market for the delivery of similar services. Barriers such as political risk, minimum transaction size, firm size and credit quality help temper the migration of financial activity abroad, although offshore markets can be used to replicate a variety of financial instruments such as forward contracts, short-term commercial paper, long-term bonds, eurocurrency interest rate futures, and the like, many of which are exposed to significant NRB by national financial authorities. These pose a general competitive threat to onshore securities or banking activities, although entry and exit costs, currency conversion costs and distance-related delivery costs, plus uncertainties surrounding these costs and problems of management control, act as effective barriers to complete NRB equalization across countries.

The rise of regulatory competition and the existence of offshore markets thus underscores the fact that financial services firms often face a range of alternatives for executing transactions in any of several financial centres. The development of offshore currency and bond markets in the sixties was a case where borrowers and lenders alike found they could carry out the requisite market transactions more efficiently and with sufficient safety by operating offshore, in what amounted to a parallel market. Domestic regulators, however, usually want the transactions to be conducted within their financial centres – driven by their desire to maintain an adequate level of prudential regulation, sustain revenues from the taxation of financial services, support employment and output in the financial services industry and linked economic activities, or simply maximize their regulatory domain. Thus the market for financial regulation is 'contestable' in the sense that other national regulatory bodies or offshore opportunities offer (or threaten to offer) rules that may be more favourable than those of the domestic regulator.

As any factor of production or economic activity gains mobility, it becomes increasingly difficult to subject it to regulation. Communication costs are low and capital mobility is high, so it is becoming less and less feasible for a state or a nation to impose an NRB that stands too far apart from world norms. Still, it is likely that a long-run equilibrium can be sustained with a positive overall NRB. Financial firms ought to value location in the midst of an important and orderly market, their access to financing by lenders of last resort, and the opportunity to be headquartered in a stable and secure political climate. Indeed, we observe that those markets which are almost totally unregulated, such as the eurocurrency market (with NRB approaching zero), have not in fact completely dominated financial transactions subject to location shifting. If financial institutions find it in their interest to pay some regulatory tax, the economic question then centres around the sustainable magnitude of this net regulatory burden.

This dynamic is unlikely to be very different in the euro-zone. National regulatory regimes will continue to compete within the framework of global and EU capital adequacy and investment services directives, and it seems probable that the progressive convergence in regulation of banks, securities firms and other types of financial firms will continue. Players based in the more heavily regulated countries will successfully lobby for liberalization, and there will be an emergence among regulators of a broad-gauge consensus on minimum acceptable standards that will eventually be accepted by those countries with substandard regulatory regimes. The objective is to optimize the balance between market efficiency and regulatory soundness, so that market forces are free to become the main determinants of what transactions are carried out, where, and by whom.

The battle of financial centres

Banks and securities firms, as well as the end users of financial services, have a broad choice of locations for carrying out their activities. Back-office operations (e.g. payments functions, clearing and settlement of financial transactions) can be physically separated from marketing functions and client interface with no loss of service quality and significant potential for cost improvement. In theory, only certain activities in today's technological environment still need to be carried out in direct physical proximity to the client; most others tend to gravitate towards the most cost-effective siting. This is certainly true at the wholesale end of the industry, and it is becoming more true of retail financial services too, as remote delivery (e.g. via the Internet) captures a greater market share.

The financial services sector has thus become a much more mobile industry, one that is particularly sensitive to operating differences in costs and regulatory burdens. Indeed, the industry can be considered to cover a spectrum of activities, ranging from potentially high-mobility functions such as data processing, investment management, institutional sales and trading, and remote servicing of mass markets, to low-mobility functions that require direct and personal contact with clients such as corporate borrowers, local governments, investors and private individuals.

The economics of high-mobility activities can be described as centrifugal, or supply oriented. Modern information and transaction technologies make it increasingly possible to conduct such activities in remote locations in order to take advantage of lower taxes, labour or real estate costs and other production considerations that can differ widely both interregionally and internationally, as well as potential economies of scale and scope. Transactions processing is probably the best example of an activity that can be physically separated from other parts of the financial value chain. Why undertake data entry for insurance claims in Munich when Ireland or Portugal offer a plentiful supply of lower-cost, skilled and motivated labour, lower rents, and significant tax breaks in the same currency zone. Why not pool or outsource some processing-intensive activities to a vendor such as IBM, Andersen Consulting or Electronic Data Systems, which may be able to do it cheaper and better with increased scale economies in low-cost locations, providing significant operating economies and at the same time liberating a large amount of capital – even to the extent of selling back-office facilities to such firms and buying back transactions processing services. Issues related to quality control, speed, security, reliability, confidentiality and the value of information based on transaction flows may, of course, limit such rationalization of production.

The economics of low-mobility financial activities can be described as centripetal, i.e. agglomeration or demand oriented. They are driven by proximity to clients, trading counterparties or organized securities markets, personal contacts, social relationships and other qualitative factors. There is no way to develop a private banking relationship, or to structure a complex corporate finance transaction involving investment bankers and lawyers, without close personal interaction. Although technically feasible, it is not clear that a portfolio manager or securities trader can do his or her job as well in a remote location away from colleagues and competitors, and away from the excitement and 'smell' of the market. Still, modern technology can often be used to convert front-office to back-office activities, and thereby loosen ties to client-linked and agglomeration-oriented locations.

Technology is the major factor affecting the balance of centrifugal and centripetal forces acting on the location of financial activities, and therefore on the underlying economics of financial centres in Europe (as it has in the US) and globally. Traditionally, the centripetal forces have dominated in the financial services industry, and have assured the dominance of the major financial centres. This now seems to be changing, permitting 'unbundling' of financial activities and allowing the centrifugal forces to start making themselves felt.

One can envisage the mobility of functions within a sphere (*see* Fig. 2.2) that extends from those activities requiring direct and personal contact with clients such as corporate borrowers and issuers, government entities, institutional investors, fund consultants and private individuals, all the way out to back-office functions, investment management and remote servicing of routine retail client transactions. One can also imagine a threshold, radiating out from the centre of the sphere in Fig. 2.2, where the supply-related centrifugal forces may begin to outweigh the demand side or agglomerative centripetal forces for specific segments in the financial services value chain with a given state of technology. This threshold has traditionally been biased

Fig 2.2 Centrifugal and centripetal locational mapping of financial services

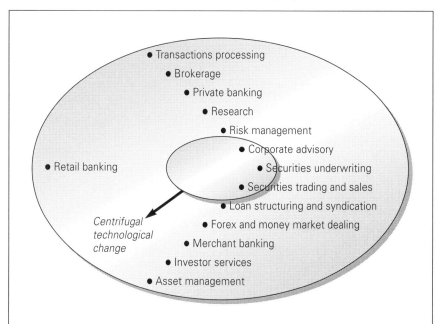

towards centripetal forces, with the requirement for all functions to be carried out in-house and on-site in major financial centres. The need to be near to clients, as well as to legal and accounting services and other firms competing in the market, has tended to bias location towards these centres.

Technological change, and the ability to unbundle the various financial functions, appears to have moved that threshold significantly towards the periphery in Fig. 2.2, with back-office activities, investment management and remote client servicing easily done from sites well removed from the centre of the firm and away from the traditional financial agglomerations. The key question for the traditional financial centres is how much further that threshold can move to the periphery, and how sensitive that movement is to factors such as labour cost and quality, tax and regulatory differences, and the available economic infrastructure.

For example, relocation of back-office and data processing (DP) operations is perhaps the most mobile part of a complex process of rationalizing information and transactions processing in financial firms. Back-office capacity must be on-line to handle existing and expected business volume, transactions security and a variety of contingencies ranging from power failures to software problems. Relocation of these functions to major DP 'factories' serving multiple functions and clients from remote sites is often feasible. On the other hand, measures that would achieve maximum cost economies may compromise proprietary information and complete control. For this reason, outsourcing and pooling of back-office functions has limits. It is certainly feasible for some functions, but probably not for others. Most initiatives towards back-office outsourcing and pooling in the investment banking industry have not borne fruit, unlike similar efforts in mass retail transactions processing or securities custody.

Competition among financial centres is thus in part a contest for market share in centripetal value-added activities, and in part a battle to retain as much as possible of centrifugal value-added activities.

How do financial centres compete?

Two more or less distinct types of financial centres can be identified. One is the functional centre, where transactions are actually undertaken and value is created in the design and delivery of financial services. Examples of traditional functional centres include New York, London and Hong Kong across a wide range of financial activities from syndicated lending to M&A advisory services, and Boston, Chicago, Frankfurt, Paris and Tokyo with a more specialized range of activities. The other is the booking centre for transactions whose underlying value is mainly created elsewhere. Examples in this category include the Bahamas, Cayman Islands, Channel Islands, Liechtenstein and Vanuatu. In order to attract financial booking business, one prerequisite is a favourable tax climate for non-residents, a benign regulatory and supervisory environment as well as (sometimes) strict financial secrecy or blocking statutes. Centres such as Bermuda, Luxembourg, Singapore and Zurich, as well as several newer ones such as Dublin, might be considered among the established dual-capacity financial centres, combining both functional and booking dimensions.

What kinds of factors seem to determine competitiveness among functional centres? A number of studies suggest that the following 'environmental' considerations seem to be of importance:[6]

● the rate of economic growth
● the country's established industrial base
● its international trade and investment intensity relative to GDP
● its political and macro-economic stability
● the cost of operations
● the quality of the labour force[7]
● the quality of the infrastructure, including time zone overlaps.

There are also several other key elements that seem to determine the success of financial centres:

● *Agglomeration economies and liquidity.* The larger the number of financial firms already in place and the greater the volume of financial activity (market depth) – as well as the larger the percentage of the skilled workforce active in the financial services industry – the more likely a financial centre is to attract still more participants. A high degree of liquidity, notably for block trades and good after-hours trading capabilities, is critical for financial centres to attract significant wholesale business. It also includes a strong equity component – ranging from actively traded shares of large-cap global companies to IPOs and private equity – with significant turnover and deep institutional investor participation.

● *Product range and propensity to innovate.* A broad range of banking services, securities and derivatives, and strong innovative capabilities, can be critical for successful financial centres. Those which have developed into major wholesale players tend to be governed by relatively permissive regulators whose default response to a new product or a new financial structure is 'yes, unless there are compelling reasons to prohibit', as opposed to 'no, unless there are compelling reasons to permit'.

● *Transparency.* The issue here is whether transactions in a financial centre are undertaken in a fair and open marketplace, and whether an adequate infrastructure exists for financial end users and intermediaries. This includes the appropriate regulatory and enforcement infrastructure, mediation or arbitration, or recourse to the courts in civil or criminal actions. Transparency applies both to dealing in financial instruments and to the financial instruments themselves, including making issuers as well as underwriters liable for incomplete or false information in the case of securities sold to the public. It also includes a uniform accounting and legal infrastructure that meets global standards.

● *Immediacy and transactional cost-effectiveness.* The role of time is critical in the operation of financial centres – the time it takes to make a trade, affirmation and confirmation of the trade, as well as clearance and settlement of the trade. Basic standards that have been set by the international financial community, such as immobilization and dematerialization of securities, delivery versus payment, clearance and settlement time, must be met or exceeded by a financial centre that hopes to attract significant transactions volume. Low transactions costs, notably in the form of commissions and spreads, clearance and settlement services, back-office operations, custody services, telecommunications and other financial infrastructure services, are critical for the success of wholesale financial centres.

● *Contestability.* The issue here is whether new players find it possible to develop the access to clients and markets and the organizational forms necessary to compete effectively in a particular financial market. The presence of cartels and exclusionary market practices such as limitations on exchange membership or discrimination by regulators can do much to impede the development of a financial centre.

● *Taxation.* Taxes enter into the competitive performance of financial centres in two ways. The first involves the taxation of capital income, and there is a long tradition of specialist financial centres that have done very well by capitalizing on tax avoidance and evasion on the part of depositors and investors under the protection of national sovereignty, financial secrecy and blocking statutes. Examples include the Channel Islands, Luxembourg, Switzerland and various Caribbean and Pacific islands. The second involves taxation of financial transactions and earnings of the financial intermediaries, where Ireland or Bermuda are good examples.

Most tax-driven financial centres comprise niche players as against the major global wholesale centres where taxation tends to play a relatively minor role.[8]

● *Net regulatory burden.* As discussed above, the difference between 'charge' and 'subsidy' elements of regulation can be viewed as the net regulatory burden faced by financial firms in any given jurisdiction. Financial firms tend to migrate towards those financial environments where NRB is lowest – assuming all other economic factors are the same.[9]

Factors that do not appear to be important in determining the competitive position of financial centres, according to empirical studies, include the position of a particular city as a political capital, its age, or the role of the country in the shifting geopolitical environment.[10] The competitive significance of a financial centre's simultaneous role as central bank headquarters remains debatable.

The market for markets

Vigorous competition among financial services firms is today joined by equally vigorous competition among financial centres. This competition can be framed in terms of static and dynamic efficiency properties, with comparative weaknesses in efficiency, liquidity or creativity driving financial transaction streams and the associated value-added to high-performance centres where they can form the basis of a major source of employment and economic growth. London, New York and Tokyo have battled for years for advantage as financial 'hubs' on the world stage. London (outside the euro-zone, at least at the start) has competed vigorously for European dominance against Frankfurt, Amsterdam, Luxembourg, Paris and Zurich on the increasingly level regional playing field. In order to capture market share, regulatory initiatives have been the key policy factors in the battle for value-added in financial intermediation. They have affected all the major financial centres, and have intensified competition among them.

The development of offshore currency and bond markets in the sixties was an early example of how borrowers and lenders alike could carry out the requisite market transactions more efficiently and with sufficient safety and professionalism by operating outside national financial markets, in what amounted to a parallel market.[11] The US interest equalization tax (IET), imposed in order to deal with the balance of payments problems at the time, was intended to force international companies to finance their expansion outside the US in order to reduce capital outflows. This was accompanied by limits imposed on foreign equity investments by the Office of Foreign Direct Investment (OFDI). Together with tax and regulatory advantages (including the use of bearer securities and the absence of new-issue disclosure rules), the IET represented a policy shift that made new debt issues in the US relatively unattractive for many borrowers, and eurobond issuance developed rapidly in London after 1963.

Initially considered a temporary and insignificant departure from the US corporate bond market, growth of the eurobond market over the next two decades was spectacular, especially as more and more financial firms became involved and the market's infrastructure and depth matured. Eurobond issuers came to include most of the major corporate and institutional borrowers around the world, and in 1986 dollar-denominated eurobond volume for the first time surpassed US domestic corporate bond market new-issue volume. Despite US repeal of the IET and the OFDI rules in 1974, intro-duction of Rule 415 (shelf) registration procedures in 1982 to streamline and enhance competition in the securities issuing process, elimination of the withholding tax on interest due to foreign investors in 1984, and adoption of Rule 144A in 1990 to liberalize trading in non-public offerings, eurobond market activity never returned to New York to any significant extent. This suggests a ratchet effect at work. Once financial activity migrates and a demonstrably successful market develops elsewhere, it is virtually impossible to reverse its course.

Similar developments occurred in the eighties and nineties in Europe, as local trading in various German and French financial instruments faced challenges from London, which captured significant market share by virtue of greater efficiency, transparency, regulatory advantages and ultimately market depth, with efforts to re-attract the deal flow back to the countries of the issuers only partly successful at the start but progressively more successful – at least for Frankfurt – more recently. An important objective of regulatory reform in virtually every country has been to support the competitive prospects of its financial centres, or at least to delay the migration of activities to financial centres abroad.[12]

Picking the winners

Financial centres in Europe are caught in a vigorous struggle for market share and value creation in primary and secondary-market financial intermediation and transactions processing. Each of the world's financial centres embodies powerful entrenched interests that will help identify winners and losers. It seems clear that this is well recognized by the authorities, and is reflected in policy debates. For example, during the regulatory debates on the 1986 UK Financial Services Act, the global competitive performance of financial institutions and markets in London was considered of paramount importance. US regulators at the federal and local levels have increasingly taken global competitive aspects into account in assessing proposals for financial reform. In countries such as Canada, Australia, Germany, France, Japan, the Netherlands and Switzerland, discussions of conditions affecting the financial services industry are invariably set against the need to maintain competitive position against London and New York. None of these financial centres is prepared to see its significance on the global stage decline, and all are acutely aware of the benefits of achieving a greater share of financial activity.

In 1998, the EU still supported a highly fragmented system of 32 stock exchanges and 23 futures and options exchanges, among which only one market, London, came close to meeting the rapidly evolving needs of the large capital markets participants. London itself risked becoming marginalized by financial centres inside the euro-zone, despite the fact that its equity market capitalization exceeded twice that of Frankfurt, even as continued fragmentation within continental Europe was perpetuated by differences in legal, tax and corporate governance considerations. However, especially under the pressure of a single currency and in the presence of electronic links and low-cost transactions services available to market participants – for example, the EU Investment Services Directive permitted national exchanges to place trading screens in other financial centres – this traditional European market fragmentation was doomed.

In anticipation, Easdaq in London worked to create a pan-European, over-the-counter exchange modelled on Nasdaq (the National Association of Securities Dealers Automated Quotation System) in the US to attract new, high-growth companies. National markets in Frankfurt, Paris, Brussels and Amsterdam tried to do the same thing and link up in the form of EuroNM to compete with both Nasdaq and Easdaq. Comparable initiatives were launched among the Nordic countries. Frankfurt, Paris and Zurich derivatives exchanges banded together to compete with London's Liffe, which in turn linked up with US derivatives exchanges. Meanwhile, rival initiatives encompassed derivatives markets, equity indexes and an interest rate benchmark for the euro. A rapid shake-out of the various competing market initiatives, based on how they met efficiency and liquidity criteria, was well under way by the late nineties. The indications were for a single, order-driven electronic market in Europe dominating trading in shares of the major international companies and the regional exchanges accounting for the bulk of European trading activity in mid-cap and small-cap shares, with the bond markets dominated by over-the-counter (OTC) trading and similarly consolidated interest rate derivatives markets.

In July 1998, the London Stock Exchange and Deutsche Börse announced a co-operative venture that could lead to a pan-European market for equities after the introduction of the euro. The Deutsche Börse was already linked to Nasdaq, which itself was merging with the American Stock Exchange and the Philadelphia Stock Exchange to form a more effective competitor to the New York Stock Exchange. The Amsterdam and Brussels exchanges indicated an interest in joining the Frankfurt-London link-up as well, complementing existing links between Frankfurt and Vienna and a merger of the Frankfurt (DTB) and Zurich (Soffex) derivatives exchanges to form Eurex. Shortly thereafter the Paris Bourse, which had been left out of the initiative and in all likelihood could join only as a junior partner with a 20 per cent stake, announced a rival alliance combining most of the remaining European exchanges, including a link to the New York Stock Exchange. The argument was that Europe, like the US, could afford two competing exchanges, although many suspected that the French initiative was mainly a ploy to improve its bargaining position in negotiations for participation in the London-Frankfurt market platform – which itself has run into significant implementational difficulties. Like all organized exchanges, those in Europe face growing challenges from electronic communications networks (ECNs) and other market utilities whose ultimate configuration – technical as well as competitive – remains hard to discern.

It is indeed useful to note that the large, integrated US capital market supports only one major stock exchange and one major OTC trading system, alongside a number of specialist exchanges and continued challenge from electronic order-driven exchanges. This may well be an appropriate indicator for the constellation of financial centres in a future integrated European financial market capable of effectively supporting the rapidly growing needs of global financial intermediaries and end users. With respect to financial centres, the US supports a single wholesale market for transactions execution (New York) that is not the seat of monetary policy and financial regulation (Washington), with a reasonable argument to be made that a bit of geographic distance between the markets and their regulators can actually be helpful. The US also supports widely dispersed asset management centres (Boston, Chicago, Philadelphia, Stamford, San Francisco), and sometimes no distinctive centres at all where the necessary information, interpretation and transactions services can all be delivered electronically and in real time. It also has specialist centres focusing on particular financial instruments (Chicago) or industries (Palo Alto) that have their roots in history or ongoing economic developments.

As in any industry, comparative advantage and the interplay of free markets will ultimately determine who wins and who loses in the battle for supremacy among financial centres in an age of enhanced mobility of financial value-added. The name of the game is creating value in a fast-moving, innovative and fiercely competitive contest on an ever-changing playing field. Those institutions judged to be world-class players in the years ahead will have mastered this skill. So will the successful financial centres, in the process capturing for their nations some very substantial real economic gains even as the more mobile parts of the financial value chain migrate to cost-effective sites outside the main centres.

The way forward

The regulatory environment is central to the evolution of the investment banking industry and the locations where investment banking activities are conducted. Optimizing in the context of a trade-off between financial efficiency and stability of the financial system, together with appropriate market conduct, is never easy. Overregulation leads to opportunity costs in the form of inefficient allocation of capital, as well as migration of financial activities to less highly regulated jurisdictions. Underregulation may promote financial collapse and all the costs associated with systemic crises. Even a finely balanced degree of regulation carries with it the risks associated with moral hazard and adverse selection if there are significant perceived asymmetries between those standing to gain from financial activities and those having to bear the costs of financial crises.

If a sound regulatory balance is difficult to strike within a single sovereign state, it is more difficult to achieve in a regional or global environment where differences in regulation and its implementation can lead to migration of financial activities in line with relative net regulatory burdens. A federal state such as the US constrains NRB differences that emerge – although there are some. A confederation such as the countries belonging to the euro-zone has much greater scope for NRB differences, despite the harmonization embedded in the EU's Second Banking Directive, the Investment Services Directive and the Capital Adequacy Directive. Each of these represents an appropriate response to the regulatory issues involved, but it still leaves open the prospect of significant regulatory differences among the participating countries and hence the persistence of fault lines across national regulatory systems – particularly as countries strive for a share of financial value-added and the associated real economic gains. Financial markets regulation imposes both benefits and costs on participants, and it is optimum rather than minimum regulation that will attract transactions flows to particular markets.

In the euro-zone, the indigenous investment banking industry is largely embedded in big universal banks which are too big to fail. These in turn have to compete on a global playing field with investment banks that are independent or structured as separately capitalized affiliates of bank holding companies. This suggests an impact on competitive dynamics, with the former benefiting from an implied taxpayer guarantee but at the same time deprived of the need to be quite as sharp in managing their risks, their costs and their business opportunities.

Assuming no regulatory and protectionist backsliding, the European financial market environment is likely to be of a kind that will allow a variety of players to compete in each other's markets geographically, cross-client, and cross-product, including insurance, real estate and various areas of commerce. The European regulatory setting should thus continue to evolve along the lines of the universal banking model, without significant geographic constraints, and provide a relatively level playing field for all kinds of financial institutions to compete for business across the entire financial inter-mediation spectrum. This could provide a platform for some European institutions to mount a serious challenge in North American and Asian financial markets. Symmetry of regulation and creation of a level playing field, especially between banks and non-bank financial institutions and investment vehicles, will be an important determinant of the composition of market participants and the structure of transactions flows. Europe seems well on its way to creating such a playing field, one that will be highly competitive and fully capable of competing with markets elsewhere in the world.

NOTES

[1] 'Heat turned on self-regulation', *Financial Times*, 28 July 1995. *See also* Securities and Investments Board (1995) *Regulation of the United Kingdom Equity Markets*, London: SIB.

[2] 'Top business court under fire', *New York Times*, 23 May 1995.

[3] *See* Kane, Edward J. (1987) 'Competitive financial reregulation: an international perspective', in Portes, R. and Swoboda, A. (eds) *Threats to International Financial Stability*, London: Cambridge University Press.

[4] *See* Levich, Richard and Walter, Ingo (1990) 'Tax-driven regulatory drag: European financial centers in the 1990s' in Siebert, Horst (ed.) *Reforming Capital Income Taxation*, Tübingen: J.C.B. Mohr/Paul Siebeck.

[5] Edward Kane (op. cit.) has argued that regulation itself may be thought of in a market context, with regulatory bodies established along geographic, product or functional lines competing to extend their regulatory domains. Financial firms understand this regulatory competition and try to exploit it to enhance their market share or profitability, even as domestic regulators try to respond with reregulation in an effort to recover part of their regulatory domain.

[6] *See*, for example, Goldberg, Lawrence and Hanweck, G. (1990) 'The development and growth of banking centers and the integration of local banking markets', *The Review of Research in Banking and Finance*, Spring; Helseley, R.W. and Levi, M.D. (1988) 'The location of international financial centers', *Annals of Regional Science*, May; Helseley, R.W. and Levi, M.D. (1989) 'The location of international financial center activity', *Regional Studies*, January; Choi, S.P., Tschoegl A. and Yu, C.M. (1986) 'Banks and the world's major financial centers, 1970–80', *Weltwirtschaftliches Archiv*, March.

On penetration of foreign banking organizations in domestic markets, *see* Goldberg, Lawrence and Saunders, Anthony (1981) 'The determinants of foreign banking activity in the United States', *Journal of Banking and Finance*, March; Hultman, Charles and McGee, L.R. (1989) 'Factors affecting the foreign banking presence in the US', *Journal of Banking and Finance*, November; and Grosse, Robert and Goldberg, Lawrence (1991) 'Foreign bank activity in the United States: an analysis by country of origin', *Journal of Banking and Finance*, December.

On comparative growth of banks, *see* Dohner, R. and Terrell, H.S. (1988) *The Determinants of the Growth of Multinational Banking Organizations 1972–86*, Board of Governors of the Federal Reserve System, IFDP No. 326, June; and Goldberg, Lawrence and Hanweck, G. (1991) 'The growth of the world's 300 largest banking organizations by country', *Journal of Banking and Finance*, June.

[7] Quality, motivation and availability especially of skilled labour critical in the supply of financial services is a determining factor in the success of financial centres. Openness to highly skilled and motivated labour and management from abroad, including attractive and hospitable living and working conditions, is an important related variable.

[8] Levich, Richard and Walter, Ingo (1990) 'Tax-driven regulatory drag: European financial centers in the 1990s' in Siebert, Horst (ed.) *Reforming Capital Income Taxation*, Tübingen: J.C.B. Mohr/Paul Siebeck.

[9] As noted, Kane has argued that regulation itself may be thought of in a market context. *See* note 5.

[10] *See*, for example, Goldberg, Lawrence and Hanweck, G. op. cit.

[11] For a discussion, *see* Smith, Roy C. and Walter, Ingo (1997) *Global Banking*, New York: Oxford University Press.

[12] For an early study, *see* Kane, Edward (1987) 'Competitive financial reregulation: an international perspective' in Portes, R. and Swoboda, A. (eds) *Threats to International Financial Stability*, Cambridge: Cambridge University Press.

Development of the new euro marketplace

CHAPTER 3

The market for fixed income securities

Fixed income securities have been traded in Europe for centuries. Mainly, these were obligations of governments, but issues by cities, and specially chartered corporations and railroads also occurred from time to time. Often, people living outside the country in which they were issued bought these securities. From the beginning, they were traded on exchanges throughout Europe. By 1900 the markets were robust and varied, and they remained that way until World War I, after which there followed a period of almost 50 years in which the markets were shallow and inactive. The bond markets in Europe really did not recover their prior levels of activity until the late sixties.

The rebirth of European financial markets

At the end of World War II, the European capital markets were virtually non-existent. In 1944, the Bretton Woods agreement among the Allies restored a gold-based, fixed exchange rate standard, and by 1947 the Marshall Plan had begun to transfer significant financial resources into Europe. But there was still little demand for securities. What demand there was (from Swiss banks or other investors) was satisfied by purchasing dollar-denominated bond issues in New York. There were, however, some stirrings in the banking market as local corporations, European subsidiaries of non-European companies, central banks and other financial institutions discovered they could deposit dollars which they had accumulated outside the US with certain banks in London that would retain them as dollars and pay dollar interest rates.

Eurodollars first

Thus was born the 'eurodollar', which was simply a dollar-denominated deposit in a bank or branch located outside the US. Such deposits were beyond the US regulatory umbrella, so that liquidity reserves did not have to be held against them. Original depositors included the financial arm of the Soviet Union and other East-bloc states wanting to avoid placing their holdings in the US. Eurodollar interest rates were related to US deposit rates, but only loosely at first when rate differentials of 100 basis points or more were not uncommon, encouraging US banks to arbitrage the market. Despite the lower deposit rates, depositors were happy to utilize these accounts to avoid the costs of transferring the money back and forth across the Atlantic, and also to avoid disclosing information about themselves and their financial affairs to US authorities. In time, a small group of eurodollar banks set deposit and lending rates for the market and established the convention of a daily posting of a London Inter-Bank Offering Rate (LIBOR). This was the rate at which banks would lend eurodollars to each other. Its companion was the London Inter-bank Bid Rate (LIBID) at which banks could borrow from each other. Non-banks paid a premium to borrow, and received lower deposit rates.

The eurodollar deposits became transferable in the sixties, when the euro-CD (certificate of deposit) was introduced by Citibank, and soon a market was functioning in these instruments that usually carried initial maturities of 30, 60 and 90 days. During the fifties and early sixties, the US balance of payments deficit with Europe was rising steadily, so that increasing quantities of dollars began to accumulate in London and other major European cities. Some of the surplus was retained as reserves by the central banks, some of it was lent back to banks in the US, but an increasing quantity was invested in eurodollar CDs and bank deposits.

The US discourages foreign bonds

Also during the early sixties, non-US governments and municipalities began to borrow money in the US through the issuance of 'foreign bonds'. In foreign bond issues, a borrower such as the City of Oslo would file a registration statement with the US SEC for an issue of US dollar bonds to be offered for sale to US investors. These bonds were tailored to appeal to US bond buyers (mostly insurance companies) and were generally fixed-rate for 15 or 20 years. They carried an interest rate that reflected a significant 'foreign premium' – an interest rate differential above the rate at which a comparably rated US bond for the same maturity would be priced. Although this foreign premium could be 100 basis points or more, and the issuer was obliged to pay interest and principal in US dollars, most issuers had few other viable sources of finance so they came to the US market readily.

While the rates paid by these issuers were pitched to attract US buyers, bond sales were often difficult nevertheless. Insurance companies were restricted as to the total quantity of non-US investments they could hold, and most portfolio managers had lost their ability to appreciate or understand European credit ratings in the long interval since the last wave of foreign borrowing in the US during the twenties. To bolster sales and complete the transactions, the underwriters of the bonds looked to sophisticated investors in Europe who were familiar with the credits and had confidence in them. For such investors, the interest rates being offered were very attractive, and as a result a high percentage of the customers for the bonds – often as much as 70 per cent – were European. Indeed, what was really happening in the foreign bond market was that European issuers, in the absence of a local bond market, were forced to go to the US domestic market. But once the bonds were issued, the US sold them back to investors in Europe. Such a condition begged for a European market to be developed, but as long as the US firms could manage the issues and find the investors across Europe (something few European banks were capable of doing since their distribution was entirely local), there was no need.

However, the success of the foreign bond business (now called 'Yankee bonds' in the US) began to alarm US authorities which were under pressure to reduce a capital account weakness that in turn contributed to the US balance of payment deficit. Under the Bretton Woods system, the dollar had to be maintained at a value of $35 per ounce of gold. If the growing number of overseas dollar-holders was unwilling to continue to hold them, they could sell the dollars to their central bank, which would either hold them as dollar reserves or return them to the US for gold. Perhaps these dollar-holders had accumulated all they wanted because an increasing outflow of US gold resulted, which alarmed the US public.

To halt the 'haemorrhaging' of capital flowing out of the country – although the flows in fact were quite modest, and the US had plenty of gold – the US administration initiated the 'interest equalization tax'. This required foreign borrowers to restore to the US Treasury any interest rate benefits they obtained from issuing securities in the US. The tax, of course, killed the foreign bond market. The administration also signalled to European central banks that it would regard their gold purchases unfavourably, and so those central banks not wishing to offend the US further increased their reserve holdings of dollars. Others, however, particularly the Banque de France under the de Gaulle administration, continued to request gold for virtually all its incoming supply of dollars.

The US government also tried other measures to reduce the increasing surplus of dollars abroad, and the deficits that caused it. A variety of relatively small measures were introduced to help, the most significant of which was the establishment of the Office of Foreign Direct Investment Control, which prevented US corporations from borrowing in the US for long-term investment programmes outside the country. If a company wanted to build a plant somewhere in Europe, for example, it had to finance it outside the US – it could not export US capital for the purpose. This rule irritated many US businesspeople, who believed the policy significantly increased the cost of investing abroad. Suddenly, US borrowers had to find long-term financing in Europe.

A new market emerges

It soon became apparent that all the elements of supply and demand for a bond market in Europe were in place. Ready-to-go borrowers existed from among those European governments and US corporations that had been turned away from the US bond market by the government's actions. Investors in Europe were already accustomed to buying these bonds, and in addition, central banks might like to switch out of holding an increasing supply of low-yielding US treasury securities or eurodollar deposits in their reserves to higher paying dollar bonds of other countries.

So the first eurobond was invented in 1963 by quick-witted bankers at S.G. Warburg & Co. in London. They investigated different devices, finally settling on an odd creature that had a number of contradictory features. A eurobond was, in effect, nominally a 'private placement' in all countries in Europe in order to be exempt from local registration as a public security, but it was also a 'publicly traded instrument' by virtue of its listing on the London and/or Luxembourg stock exchanges to satisfy institutional customers. Though offered in Europe, the security was denominated in dollars to target the enormous supply of eurodollars and to discourage European securities regulators from thinking that the issue had anything to do with them. The US Securities and Exchange Commission, however, did not buy into this concept, and insisted that eurobonds were in fact public offerings and had to be registered with the SEC if any were to be sold in the US. This led to elaborate steps being taken to prevent eurobonds from appearing in US markets, or sales being made to US citizens or residents.

To satisfy the Swiss banks, which were expected to take considerable quantities of the bonds, several other conditions were added. The bonds had to be in bearer form, i.e. payable only to the bearer presenting the bonds for payment, so that no investor identification would be required. They also had to carry annual coupons (instead of semi-annual, as was the US practice) as a concession to practices in the European sovereign bond market and to simplify coupon clipping and account administration by the banks on behalf of their customers. The Swiss also insisted that their investors would not purchase bonds unless the interest rates were guaranteed by the issuers against any future withholding taxes. Maturities could not be greater than 15 years, and the issuers would have to agree to pay full commission rates to the Swiss banks for acting as the investors' agents.

To tempt a first issuer, Sir Siegmund Warburg called his old friend Guido Carli, governor of the Banca d'Italia, and a guinea pig was found. The Italian state highway commission, Autostrade, would issue $15 million of 15-year bonds paying 5½ per cent interest, guaranteed by the Republic of Italy. Warburg was to syndicate the issue broadly within Europe and invited leading banks from Germany, Holland and Belgium to co-manage it – by regulation, Swiss banks at the time were not able to underwrite international bonds. The issue was successful, and paved the way for more. Before long, the eurobond market was launched.[1] In 1963 the market managed $148 million of new issues, in 1968 more than $3 billion. By 1985, the volume of new eurobond issues was well in excess of $100 billion.[2]

Initially, the leading managers of eurobond issues were British merchant banks, such as Warburg, which knew the securities business and also the whereabouts of large European investors. Many of them also managed a considerable volume of British investment funds for their clients. When the US corporations came into the market to finance their foreign direct investment requirements, however, the large US investment banks began to get involved in order to protect their clients' relationships.

Euromarket characteristics

The euromarket, technically, is a market for offshore funds. The market does not officially exist in institutional terms, nor does any country regulate it. Yet it has operated effectively for nearly four decades, allowing money to flow untaxed between countries. In September 1998, approximately $4,100 billion eurobonds were outstanding, about 30 per cent of all bonds outstanding in Europe. The eurobond market has become very good at adapting to developments in the foreign exchange market, and for many years eurobonds have been available in most major currencies – eurodollars, euroyen, euroDM, etc. and even euro-euros. In 1998, dollar issues represented about 46 per cent of all outstanding eurobonds, EMU currencies about 26 per cent, yen 11 per cent, and other currencies 17 per cent.

The eurobond market is operated by reputable and competent banking institutions and is very attractive to investor clients seeking financial safety, good returns and anonymity. The typical investor has been described by euromarket operatives as a 'Belgian dentist', meaning a middle-class European with a relatively high income, who transacts through a bank in modest quantities and welcomes an opportunity to keep some of his income and assets invisible to tax authorities. More realistically, however, the market serves significantly wealthy families and individuals, both shady and distinguished, who want safe investments while avoiding taxes. These investors come from all over the world.[3]

The world's only unregulated market

The market has been tolerated by European governments because it does not involve the public sale of securities to individuals (or retail investors) inside particular countries, and therefore is outside the jurisdiction of each. Sales may be made, however, to wholesale investors (i.e. professional, institutional investors) and these investors may place the securities in accounts which they manage for individuals. As a result, securities issued in the euromarket may not be sold to retail investors except through the agency of a bank or other qualified representative.

The retail market for corporate securities in Europe (especially debt securities) has never been very significant. Until recently, the market was dominated by non-US institutional investors – from central banks and government agencies, commercial banks (acting for their own accounts and for customers), unit trusts and investment funds, insurance companies, retirement funds and similar fiduciaries, hedge funds, corporations and international speculators to a mixed bag of criminals and shady characters. Investors come from all parts of Europe, Asia, the Middle East, Latin America and many Third World countries. The eurobond market is the principal trading arena for such investors.

These global investors are understood to be able to look after themselves and conduct adequate investigation into the investment merits of the securities they purchase on behalf of their clients. They are acting under the principle of *caveat emptor*, and the regulators are happy not to interfere. Accordingly, there are no information disclosure requirements, no fair trading rules, few courts willing to accept jurisdiction over trading practices, and recovering losses or damages through the legal system is very difficult. In effect, the market has become a self-regulated entity, using industry associations and the leading asset managers to establish standards which others are expected to adopt or be rejected from syndicates, credit arrangements or secondary market trading. Some governments, such as the UK, have begun to regulate certain activities of securities firms operating within its jurisdiction that may relate to eurobond trading. On the whole, however, the market has been allowed to develop into a large *laissez faire* enterprise in which more or less anything goes.

There are no restrictions as to who can participate in the market. Underwriting abilities are prized, but so are innovation and the ability to copy a competitor's idea in record time. All commissions and service fees are negotiable, and competition for new issue mandates is intense and sometimes rough. Frequent issuers shop around for the lowest rates, banks will often deliberately take losses on deals in order to show their importance as an underwriter in published 'league' tables, or stuff poorly priced deals into passive customer accounts to get rid of them. As long as the client has other concerns, such as staying ahead of the taxman, complaints about a little underperformance are likely to be few.

Multinational market users

The issuers, too, come from all over the world to utilize the 'international bond markets', a term which combines issues in the eurobond market with those (far smaller) amounts that continue to be issued as 'foreign bonds' in national markets. The issuers comprise supra-nationals (such as the World Bank), European Union agencies (such as the European Investment Bank), national governments and their agencies, banks, corporations and special financing vehicles. Issuers from Europe, the US and Japan have been the most numerous, but there are also issuers from emerging markets in Asia, Latin America and Eastern Europe. In December 1998, there were more than $4,600 billion of international bonds outstanding, $1,874 billion of which (40 per cent) were issued by EU-15 countries (72 per cent of those issued by EMU countries had already been converted to euros). Issuers from the US constituted only 17 per cent, and issuers from Japan, international institutions and emerging markets represented less than 10 per cent each. Figure 3.1 shows the diverse nature of international debt security issuers.

Fig 3.1 International debt securities by nationality of issuer (US$bn)

Countries	Amounts outstanding			Net new issues[1]	
	1996	*1997*	*1998*	*1997*	*1998*
All countries	$3,144.6	$3,512.0	$4,233.6	$574.5	$592.4
Developed countries	2,548.7	2,830.1	3,425.4	450.0	486.6
US	388.3	553.7	797.2	177.6	234.0
EU 15	1,459.1	1,568.4	1,873.9	225	232.8
EU 11	1,027.1	1,111.4	1,360.7	178.9	188.7
Japan	341.9	318.1	315.3	–0.7	–24.0
Other	359.4	389.9	439.0	48.1	43.8
Developing countries	231.4	302.2	329.3	78.8	21.3
International institutions	310.3	303.4	376.1	20.7	60.2
Total market[2]	**3,454.9**	**3,815.4**	**4,609.7**	**595.2**	**652.6**

[1] Net new issue = net of redemption of bonds
[2] Total market = all countries plus international institutions

Source: Bank for International Settlements

Reminiscent of the early days of the US foreign bond market, much of the Japanese new issue volume is placed with investors in Japan. The issuers prefer the unregulated features of the eurobond market to strict limitations imposed on them at home, and the investors often have no other way to buy bonds issued by the major Japanese corporations. US corporations, initially but no longer restricted to issuing bonds through overseas subsidiaries guaranteed by the parent company, have been active borrowers and enjoy tight pricing against rate levels in New York. In 1990, the SEC authorized its Rule 144A, which enabled sales of eurobonds in the US to be handled as unregistered private placements. Since the rapid growth of the interest rate and currency swap markets during the eighties, pricing for bond issues of all types has been extremely competitive with US domestic market alternatives. With the abolition over the past 20 years of capital controls limiting investment flows between countries, continuing deregulation of market access, and improved telecommunications and information technology, the eurobond market has become fully integrated with domestic markets for fixed-income securities.

Sophistication and innovation

Euromarket participants are very sophisticated. They understand investment opportunities around the world, foreign exchange effects, and derivative instruments such as warrants and options to purchase or sell securities. With approximately 500 international banks and investment banks involved in the market, it is highly competitive.

Many firms compete on the basis of innovation and bold initiative. As a result, the euromarket saw the first significant use of the floating-rate note, the dual currency bond, the zero coupon bond, the warrant bond, the swapped foreign currency bond, the first ECU and euro-denominated securities, and a variety of other new ideas. It also saw the first use of the 'bought deal', an issue fully underwritten by one bank, the 'tap' issue (sold on demand, not all at once), and the 'note-issuance facility' for distributing 'euro-commercial paper'. More recently, the eurobond market has begun to accept some of the more complex and controversial products of the US bond market, such as asset-backed issues and non-investment grade or 'junk bonds'.

Secondary market trading

The bond market is facilitated by the volume of trading in the foreign exchange markets, which during 1998 averaged about $1,500 billion a day.[4] Trading is encouraged by arbitrage and proprietary programmes undertaken by investors and large market-makers and financial intermediaries all over the world. The availability of currency swaps and other forms of derivative instruments, all of which have increased steadily since their introduction to the market in the mid-eighties, is helpful to traders. With swaps, traders can manufacture 'synthetic' securities by combining a bond and a swap contract, for example to create a bond with a different financial exposure. Such synthetic securities permit arbitrage or hedging against authentic positions. As long as profit-making opportunities exist, market operatives will take positions to benefit from them.

Trading in financial derivative instruments has grown substantially in Europe, in the over-the-counter markets (mainly for swaps) but also on futures exchanges in London, Paris, Frankfurt and Zurich. Swaps are by far the largest component of the financial derivatives market, with nearly $38,000 billion notional amount outstanding at the end of 1998. Exchange-traded derivatives, by comparison, totalled $16,500 billion notional amount (see Fig. 3.2). The availability of such extensive trading in derivatives also assisted market makers in taking positions in ECU-denominated bonds, for which markets have existed since the early eighties. The ECU was a unit of denomination representing a blend of EU country currencies that preceded the euro, and was effective as a means for eliminating intra-European currency risk. The ECU market operated as a valuable forerunner of the market in bonds denominated in euros.

Fig 3.2 Markets for selected financial derivative instruments (US$bn)

Instruments	Notional amounts outstanding at end-year				
	1998	*1997[1]*	*1996*	*1995*	*1994*
Exchange-traded instruments	**$16,461.7**	**$12,207.3**	**$9,879.6**	**$9,188.6**	**$8,862.9**
Interest rate futures	9,453.7	7,489.2	5,931.2	5,863.4	5,777.6
Interest rate options[2]	5,433.8	3,639.9	3,277.8	2,741.8	2,623.6
Currency futures	59.5	51.9	50.3	38.3	40.1
Currency options[2]	30.4	33.2	46.5	43.5	55.6
Stock market index futures	415.0	216.6	195.9	172.4	127.7
Stock market index options[2]	1,069.3	776.5	378.0	329.3	238.4
OTC instruments[3]	**46,512.3**	**28,733.4**	**25,453.1**	**17,712.6**	**11,303.2**
Interest rate swaps	36,262.0	22,115.5	19,170.9	12,810.7	8,815.6
Currency swaps[4]	2,253.1	1,584.8	1,559.6	1,197.4	914.8
Interest rate options[5]	7,997.2	5,033.1	4,722.6	3,704.5	1,572.8

Data: Futures Industry Association, various futures and options exchanges, ISDA and BIS calculations
[1] For OTC instruments, end-June 1997
[2] Calls and puts
[3] Data collected by ISDA only; the two sides of contracts between ISDA members are reported once only
[4] Adjusted for reporting of both currencies; including cross-currency interest rate swaps
[5] Caps, collars, floors and swaptions

Source: BIS 68th Annual Report (Table VIII.5), 1999

Euromarket trading opportunities, however – as in other markets in fixed-income securities – often depend heavily on market volatility. Before the introduction of the euro, that volatility was affected not only by changing national market conditions, but also by global market linkages and changing foreign exchange and interest rates in different parts of Europe and the rest of the world. Many (but not all) observers believe that increasing trading volume in cash markets and derivatives contributes to a dampening of volatility. Indeed, the volatility of long-term US government bonds and the dollar-DM rate (an important link between US and European markets) declined significantly from the mid-eighties until the introduction of the euro in January 1999. Particularly in the run-up period to the euro, when countries were seeking to align their economic and monetary policies, volatility decreased, but trading volume was still high as investors made bets on which currencies would be selected to enter EMU. The euro, of course, has eliminated all volatility between the 11 participating countries, and should contribute to the overall reduction of euromarket volatility.

Trading volume also increases when markets are used more extensively by borrowers and investors of all types. The greater the volume, the more liquid and efficient the markets, and the tighter the pricing. In such markets, the easy arbitrage trades (in which the same securities are quoted at different prices in different locations) disappear entirely. Many market participants have discovered that trading profitably in increasingly efficient markets is not an easy business. Indeed, much money was lost in Europe (and in the US) during 1994, a bear market year for bonds, due to dramatic increases in interest rates by traders who had open positions instead of fully hedged ones. The traders had discovered that the cost of hedging consumed all their expected profits, so they decided instead to bet on their feel for how the market would develop. Getting the feel wrong was certainly an expensive exercise for many trading firms, and indeed probably cost S.G. Warburg & Co., the eurobond pioneer, its independence.

The world's largest corporate bond market

As a result of increased use by all market participants, the eurobond market has grown into Europe's largest general-purpose, fixed-income securities market serving private sector issuers from all over the world. The volume of eurobonds outstanding increased by 35 per cent from 1996 to 1998. They vastly exceed the amount of all corporate bonds issued in national markets in Europe – more than $4,200 billion of eurobonds were outstanding at the end of 1998, as compared to $3,000 billion of corporate bonds outstanding in all European national markets combined.

For the market to be accessed, however, issuers have to be substantial borrowers, preferably with investment-grade bond ratings from at least one of the major rating agencies. Despite the fact that the market has actively handled issues for European government entities, banks and other financial institutions, and large industrial corporations, the latter has been the most conservative in employing the services of the market.

In 1999, new issues of international bonds totalled $1,394 billion, compared with $1,196 billion of new issues of investment-grade bonds in the US market. This was the sixth time in eight years that the volume of international bond new issues had exceeded the volume of new issues of investment-grade bonds in the US. Thus, by such a standard, the eurobond market has become the world's largest market for corporate bonds, even though the European corporate sector is still underrepresented. As this condition changes, the global importance of the eurobond market will increase (*see* Fig. 3.3).

Fig 3.3 Volume of new issue activity 1992–9 (US$bn)

	1999	1998	1997	1996	1995	1994	1993	1992
US corporate bonds								
Medium-term notes	397.9	308.6	284.7	255.3	404.9	282.8	260.3	169.4
Investment-grade debt	1,195.8	504.2	726.1	518.9	417.3	342.5	389.2	281.1
Collateralized securities	559.0	560.9	378.0	252.3	154.1	252.5	478.9	428.2
Below investment grade	108.7	149.9	125.3	121.4	30.2	36.4	69.5	53.7
Municipal debt	219.3	279.7	214.8	181.7	154.9	161.3	287.8	231.7
Total	**$2,480.7**	**$1,803.3**	**$1,728.9**	**$1,329.6**	**$1,161.4**	**$1,075.5**	**$1,485.7**	**$1,164.1**
International debt issues								
Euro medium-term notes	607.8	598.0	420.0	392.6	251.6	257.2	149.8	96.9
Euro and foreign bonds	1,393.8	846.9	635.2	537.4	385.1	485.2	482.7	335.9
Total	**$2,001.6**	**$1,444.9**	**$1,042.4**	**$930.0**	**$636.7**	**$742.4**	**$632.5**	**$432.8**

Source: Thomson Financial Securities Data Company

National bond markets in Europe

National bond markets in EU countries as of September 1998 totalled $10,464 billion of outstanding issues, of which government or public sector issuers comprised more than 56 per cent. Government bonds of the Euro-11 countries, however, accounted for almost all (86 per cent) EU government bonds (*see* Fig. 3.4).

Fig 3.4 European bond market – amounts outstanding at September 1998 (US$bn)

Country	Total bonds outstanding	National public sector bonds	National private sector bonds	International bonds
EU 11	**$8,451**	**$4,812**	**$2,319**	**$1,320**
Germany	2,480	856	1,127	497
Italy	1,698	1,231	362	105
France	1,479	743	483	253
All others	2,794	1,982	347	465
EU 15	**10,464**	**5,621**	**3,011**	**1,832**

Source: Bank for International Settlements

Governments dominate ...

Within the EU, government bodies in the largest countries – Germany, Italy and France – account for about half of all outstanding government sector debt. Germany was the largest EU issuer of bonds, amounting to $2,480 billion of outstanding debt in 1998. Only 35 per cent of this debt was sovereign, issued by government borrowers. Total German debt has more than doubled since 1989, the year the Berlin Wall came down and programmes commenced designed to integrate the new *Länder* into the Federal Republic, federal, state, municipal and other public sector entities.

Before 1990, the preferred method for distributing German government debt was through the sale to savings institutions of privately placed promissory notes with limited marketability, so-called *Schuldscheine,* with only about 27 per cent of German government debt sold in public offerings in 1980 – a share that increased to 43 per cent in 1989. But after unification, the government found other ways to sell paper, and introduced securitized bonds that were offered to the public. These were mainly mortgage-backed bonds, called *Pfandbriefe,* issued by state-controlled savings banks and mortgage institutions and counted in the bond market statistics as part of the corporate bond sector. By 1996, publicly placed *Pfandbriefe* had reached an all-time high of 63 per cent of all German public sector instruments, and in 1998 the total amount of *Pfandbriefe* outstanding (more than $900 billion) exceeded the total amount of sovereign debt outstanding of Italy, German and France combined.

Foreign investors were attracted early to the increasing supply of long-term German government bonds (*Bunds*) and commenced active trading in them. In the run-up to EMU the Bundesbank attempted to modernize the government bond markets further by offering different instruments (e.g. six-month zero-coupon *Bubills*, and two-year *Schaetzes*) which complemented the maturity structure of existing government securities. Also, in July 1997, the long-term bunds became strippable.[5]

In Italy, with $1,700 billion outstanding in 1998, government bonds represented about 72 per cent of the total domestic bond market, and in France, with $1,479 billion outstanding, 50 per cent was accounted for by the government sector. Both countries had endeavoured to reduce their fiscal deficits to enter EMU, and accordingly neither market was growing.

... And converge

In anticipation of EMU and the requirements to meet the Maastricht Treaty criteria for admission, fiscal and monetary policies in Europe were aligned, with the result that interest rates of the major government issues converged. This paved the way for more trading in the varying government instruments, and increased confidence in the government sector paper of many of the EU countries, including – in addition to Germany, Italy and France – Holland, Belgium and Spain. In early 1998 a rally began in the European 30-year sector, and the markets absorbed several new 30-year issues from these countries.

Figure 3.5 shows the largest and most liquid bonds in the 20–30-year sector from the major issuers among the euro-zone governments. Together, these 16 bonds had the equivalent of $130 billion in market capitalization at April 1997. They ranged in duration from 11.5 to 15 years. The figure also shows the bond yields forward to 1 January 1999 (when they were re-denominated into euros) versus their durations. It shows that for a 24-year bund with a 13-year duration, and a 26-year Italian BTP issue with a similar duration, there was no more than a 20 basis point differential in forward yields more than 18 months before unification.[6]

Fig 3.5 European forward yields

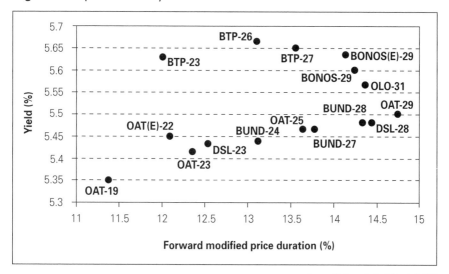

Source: Goldman Sachs & Co., April 1998

Corporates are different

Corporate and other bonds issued by all EU countries in 1998 (i.e. companies, banks and savings institutions) amounted to more than $2,300 billion sold in domestic markets, and $1,000 billion of international bonds, including eurobonds. These bonds were sold within the country of issuance and to other investors inside and outside the EU, but were predominantly bought by institutional investors, both from the EU and other countries. Germany's corporate bond market was the largest after the US, followed by Japan, Italy, France, Sweden and Belgium, all of which had outstanding issues exceeding $100 billion in market value at the end of 1998.

These figures, however, belie reality to some degree, since the corporate sector is actually primarily banks and savings institutions that finance their requirements in the market to on-lend to customers. For example, in Germany the 'corporate sector' represented 37 per cent of the bond market in 1996. Of this amount, however, 'financial' sector issuers represented 99.8 per cent. Only 0.2 per cent (or less than $2 billion) was accounted for by 'non-financial' or industrial borrowers. In Italy and France, the corporate sector in each country accounted for 14.5 per cent of the total bond market in 1996, and there was a breakdown between financial and non-financial borrowers similar to that in Germany. On the other hand, the larger industrial issuers from these countries are becoming accustomed to using the eurobond market for their funding requirements. In 1996, German companies (including some banks) carried out $335 billion of new eurobond issues; French companies did $167 billion; and Italian companies $94 billion. The overlapping of the national corporate markets by the contiguous eurobond market is to be expected in a broad continental marketplace in which the larger, more internationally known issuers can approach a larger, more global investor base with beneficial results in interest costs.

The underutilization of the bond markets by non-financial corporations in Europe, however, is a long-standing condition of European finance. It is rooted in traditional relationships with specific banks (e.g. the German *Hausbanken*), a lack of market awareness by corporate financial officers, and a lack of need to improve old practices. However, aggressive US and other investment banks have been soliciting larger European companies for years and these companies, under pressure to improve their returns to stockholders, have adopted a more modern financial outlook and are familiar with, and frequently utilize, financing opportunities away from the *Hausbank*. As distinct national currencies are replaced by the euro, bankers and borrowers alike are bound to look further afield for their financing opportunities, and those *Hausbanken* that do not respond to the new competitive environment or equip themselves to offer the best priced financing to their clients will be the ones left behind.

Growth rates in bonds

Though larger in 1998 than at any other time, the world and European bond markets experienced a decline in the rate at which they had been growing since the early eighties, according to a Merrill Lynch study. The world bond market reached its peak growth rate, of 18.3 per cent, in 1985–6. After that, the rate of growth declined (with deficit reduction efforts by governments and substantially reduced world inflation and interest rates), to 7 per cent in 1993. In 1996, the world bond market grew at 8 per cent. The European bond market growth rates followed this pattern closely.[7]

The markets after the euro

When the euro went into effect in January 1999 for the participating countries (EMU-11), excluding Britain, Denmark, Greece and Sweden (EMU-4), the EMU-11 constituent bond markets were similar, collectively, in size, liquidity and efficiency to those of the US. With the euro, however, the

European bond markets will be subjected to a number of additional changes and developments that will affect the structure of the market and its supply and demand characteristics.

Market structure changes

From the early eighties the bond markets in Europe consisted of a two-speed apparatus loosely joined in the middle. The low-speed part comprised the government debt markets in the separate European countries. The high-speed sector was the eurobond market.

The domestic government bond business moved along slowly and conservatively, until forced to quicken its pace to reflect increased funding requirements and a greater volume of trading activity in secondary markets, most of which was the result of foreign purchases and sales. The run-up to EMU also infused this low-speed sector with new products, trading practices and price transparency, until it was turning over faster than ever.

The high-speed sector was the sophisticated eurobond market, where nothing was regulated and issues and trading strategies had to stand on their own. Increasingly, the most competent issuers and investors were drawn together in this marketplace, and progressively more and more old-fashioned European non-financial corporate issuers joined in. The business grew and soon the major European cities were full of investment bankers seeking to persuade a prospective new client to use the financial markets to lower interest costs. This high-speed sector was price-oriented above all, and geared to supplying the best prices and ideas. Advanced financial technology and communications practices were actively applied.

The result was a significant increase in the rate of disintermediation in the market – the rate at which financing business left the balance sheets of banks and found its way into the markets. In the US, where the bond market began a similar course in the eighties, banks now hold only about a quarter of all financial assets; in Europe the total is still over half. With the effects of competition, however, some of the traditional European banks began to seek new skills and capabilities in order to keep up with the pace, protect their existing client relationships, and indeed attempt to steal others away from their traditional bankers. Others took more defensive measures, such as merging with their competitors to create larger domestic presences, and relied on long-standing relationships, especially with less sophisticated, mid-sized companies, to see them through.

The arrival of the euro, however, altered the European bond markets. The low-speed sector accelerated considerably as a large, liquid bond market in the new currency began to emerge, while the high-speed offshore sector, though not slowing down, was able to attract new business to the larger, more liquid eurobond market, and bring some of its advanced ideas to non-financial companies. Before long, depending on tax and regulatory developments, the old apparatus may be discarded for a larger, single-speed machine that represents the best of both worlds.

In the US, 54 per cent of the bond market in 1998 (excluding tax-advantaged municipal bonds) was represented by the government sector, 41 per cent by the domestic corporate sector, and 5 per cent by the euromarket. In the EU, 46 per cent of the market in 1998 was the EMU-11 government sector, 22 per cent constituted the euro corporate sector. The eurobond portion of EU issuers was another 13 per cent. The non-euro sector was 19 per cent of the total market. So the euro sectors will clearly dominate the market, although the government portion may be less than in the US market. There will be much more competition in the corporate sector, where product and marketing innovations are necessary to get the attention of traditional bank customers (*see* Fig. 3.6).

Supply and demand for funds

As separate national currencies were replaced by the euro, pension funds and other important financial institutions, once restricted to domestic currency investments, became free to invest in assets available within a much wider marketplace. This, of course, has greatly increased the selection and caused them to become better informed in order to choose carefully. The institutions will surely take advantage of this wider investing opportunity to improve investment results, or risk being displaced by more up-to-date competitors. Corporations, too, will see opportunities to reduce their financing costs by using the debt markets.

Disintermediation

Consequently, financial disintermediation on a scale similar to that experienced in the US in the eighties can be expected to occur in Europe as well, and as companies repay their bank debt with the proceeds of bond issues. The markets will become increasingly attractive and user-friendly to issuers. A 1997 Merrill Lynch study suggested that if only 5 per cent of outstanding bank loans to European non-financial corporations were converted into capital market assets, outstanding European corporate debt would practically triple, resulting in a total of $800 billion–900 billion outstanding. The Bank

Fig 3.6 Market structure of US and European bond markets, September 1998 (US$bn)

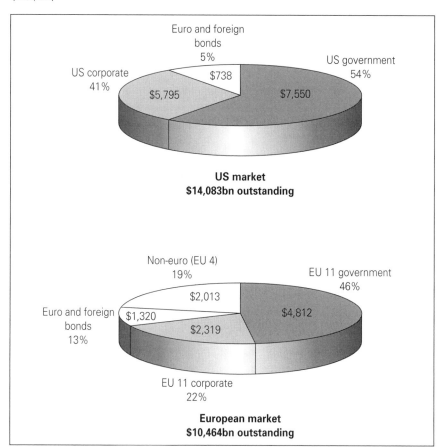

for International Settlements takes a more aggressive view, assuming as much as one-third of all corporate bank loans will be securitized once the euro is firmly in place. This could result in new money flows into the corporate bond market of approximately $2,000 billion.[8] Such flows have the power to change a great deal of traditional practice.

Shrinking foreign exchange

Clearly with the single currency, the large intra-European foreign exchange business is lost to the banking community, although some of the lost revenue may be regained by an increased volume of trading in euros against other currencies – those of the EMU-4 and of the rest of the world, especially the dollar and the yen. Other costs will be incurred to introduce and maintain the euro, and it will be a while before we know how these costs and benefits balance out. Meanwhile, other market effects have already been felt that suggest that the overall foreign exchange market has shrunk because of EMU.

The BIS reported in 1997 that implied exchange rates calculated out to ten years forward, based on yields on interest rate swaps, indicated that the currencies of a number of European countries were expected to be stable against the DM. It also reported that the volatility of many intra-European exchange rates declined significantly during 1996 – the implied volatility in the French franc/DM averaged 2 per cent in 1996 compared with 7 per cent in April 1995 – and foreign exchange volume diminished as a result. These factors suggested to the BIS that approximately 10 per cent of the foreign exchange market (based on its 1995 survey of foreign exchange trading in 26 countries) could disappear with the advent of the euro.[9]

A market shrinkage of this proportion would have several effects on market participants. First, foreign exchange trading opportunities for banks, already squeezed by reduced volatility and efficiency-enhancing developments such as electronic trading, would be reduced further, driving some traders and market-makers into new markets. This could significantly increase competition for smaller market players in individual countries (such as Belgium) which had the local market largely to themselves before the introduction of the euro. Second, dealers could be driven to expand their business in riskier, or higher-margin areas, such as trading derivatives or trading the euro against emerging market currencies. This too might be disadvantageous to smaller, national players without experience or an international infrastructure. The BIS estimated that such displaced business might represent more than one-third of the volume of the intra-European trading that disappeared with the euro.[10]

Currency trading between the prospective EMU currencies contracted from 13 per cent to 6 per cent of global foreign exchange turnover between 1995 and 1998. According to the BIS, the dollar remained the dominant vehicle currency in international finance, appearing in 94 per cent of global currency transactions in spot and forward foreign exchange contracts, while the euro was being used in about half of all foreign exchange dealings in the euro-zone countries, with its future as a transaction currency dependent on its perceived value as a reserve, investment and reference currency.[11]

Effects on money markets

In converting their currencies into euros, the 11 euro-zone countries automatically established a large and liquid market in the new currency, generating an interest by non-Europeans in holding euros. This will hold if EMU conducts monetary policy in a credible manner so as to provide the new currency with low volatility relative to its predecessors. Several portfolio shifts might be expected. Non-participating European (EMU-4) and non-European central banks will invest a portion of their reserves in euro-denominated investments. Moreover, major European institutional fund managers will adjust their portfolios to reflect the investment outlook that the euro-denominated instruments present to them. There is already some concern that the euro may be significantly less inflation-proof than the now departed DM, and that such a concern may generate higher rates, on the one hand, or greater demand for non-euro (such as Swiss Franc) investments, on the other. Some economists, however, believe that the euro may emerge as a better long-term reserve asset than either the DM or the French franc. Accordingly, many investors, including non-Europeans (especially from the US and the Far East) should take up euro positions as a part of their overall portfolio diversification efforts. To them, a larger, more liquid market in euro-denominated securities than in the fragmented markets they replaced should be welcome.

Moreover, the European Central Bank has absorbed all the reserves of the 11 euro-zone countries (for all EU members, reserves excluding gold totalled $370 billion in December 1996, far more than those of Japan or the US). Even after netting EMU-11 member countries' holdings of other members' currencies, this development could lead to substantial excess reserves. What is to be done with the surplus?[12] Unless it can be returned to the countries in the form of a cash distribution, the expectation is that the conservative European Central Bank will hang on to it to provide a fund to stabilize the euro against the dollar and the yen. Might this mean a much more active intervention policy on the part of the new central bank, which would push euro rates below their equilibrium level? Any interventionist activity would also be of great interest to international foreign exchange speculators who are inclined to take the opposite side of the market from government operators. The fall in the euro from $1.17 to $1.00 in 1999, however, suggested a non-interventionist ECB policy stance.

Bond market effects

Despite the many uncertainties associated with EMU, there are some things that appear to be fairly predictable. When the conversion process is complete, it will formalize the existence of the world's second largest bond market after the US, about two-thirds of which will be denominated in euros. The new bond market will be segmented into at least three parts:

● the *eurobond* €-sector for issues by international institutions such as agencies of the EU and the World Bank, and perhaps some major multinational corporations whose currency composition is European or global (e.g. Nestlé, Unilever, Shell). These will be issued free of withholding taxes and in bearer form as previous eurobonds were;

● the *euro-sovereign* sector for issues by the EMU-11 governments and major national private corporations. These bonds replace domestic bonds in the participating countries, and retire outstanding domestic-currency denominated bonds;

● issues in non-euro currencies, including new bonds issued by the EMU-4 opt-out countries and old bonds still outstanding in non-euro currencies, including eurodollar bonds, presently the market's largest component.

The first segment of euro-denominated bonds (which is not expected to be a large one because of the limited number of supranational issuers) will trade in the market on the basis of the creditworthiness of the issuer and liquidity alone. As there is no benchmark reference for direct EU obligations denominated in euros, comparable to Treasury securities in the US, the market will have to establish a pricing regime for such issues, perhaps by comparing the offering yields with currency-swapped US Treasury bonds. On 1 February 1997, the European Investment Bank (EIB) issued €1 billion (equivalent to $1.18 billion) of bonds due in 2004. Payment for the bonds, and payments of interest and principal until January, were in ECU, after which time all payments were denominated in euros. The issue, known in the market as the first 'euro-eurobond', was three times oversubscribed.[13]

The second segment, which is expected to be by far the largest, combining both national government and non-government issuers in a single category, will discriminate between EMU-11 countries and trade at prices reflecting creditworthiness, liquidity and sovereign considerations. This means the market (like the US municipal bond market) will impose a risk premium relative to a base rate (presumably agencies of the EU or possibly German or French sovereign issues) for euro issues of different sovereign and most corporate credits. The premium will reflect the market's valuation of national fiscal policies and economic performance, and the liquidity available in bonds from such issuers. Under these conditions there is considerable potential for spread differentials and volatility among bond issues.[14]

In fact, the market made such distinctions in choosing between EU member country debt issues (which range in credit ratings from Aaa to Baa1) by applying a yield differential. In early April 1998, for example, well before the euro-denominated bonds were traded on their own, yield differentials on long-term bonds (after adjusting for duration differences) that reflected country/credit distinctions were clearly visible. The differentials were relatively modest in size. German bond yields were one or two basis points lower than the French, Italian bond yields were about 20 basis points higher than the French. Figure 3.7 shows the fitted yield spreads between large liquid European sovereign bonds on which Fig. 3.5 is based.

Sophisticated US and Japanese investors may not see much difference in the euro pricings from that in which they invested prior to conversion, although the rate differentials are likely to be somewhat different. Also, prior to the euro they could invest in European securities on either a currency hedged or unhedged basis. Subsequent to the euro, this is still true but the difference in unhedged returns associated with particular countries will appear partly in terms of the euro exposure and partly as a result of the intra-euro-11 sovereign yield differentials.

Those seeking financing in the markets will continue to compete for money – as, for example, when different European governments consider issuing eurodollar bonds, or when US municipalities seek dollar financing in the US markets. For the foreseeable future, such competition will continue to rely mainly on country or company credit ratings, trading market liquidity, innovation in tapping particular market opportunities, and market timing to achieve lower rates. Indeed, modest yield differentials between comparable issuers in euro will provide something for portfolio managers to work with in demonstrating their skills.

There will also be new classes of fixed-income securities and plenty of scope for financial innovation. One example is the market for asset-backed securities, which has been one of the most dynamic on the US financial scene for almost 30 years. Securities backed by pools of mortgages, motor loans, consumer credits and other asset classes add value by making otherwise illiquid assets liquid and greatly broadening the pool of potential investors, both domestically and globally. Such asset-backed structures can be tailored to the needs of particular kinds of investors. They can greatly add to financial market efficiency, to the mutual benefit of ultimate borrowers and investors as well as the various kinds of financial intermediaries involved. With the exception of the German *Pfandbriefe*, asset-backed securities have traditionally made little headway in Europe (*see* Fig. 3.8). This is because of the fragmentation of the national markets, regulatory and taxation barriers, and an absence of large institutional investors in search of attractive asset classes. If securitization has value in the US, it will have value in Europe, and a rapid growth of the market in response to the advent of the euro-zone can be expected.

Fig 3.7 Large liquid bonds in 10–30-year sector

Forward to 1 January 1999

Bond type	Coupon	Maturity	Issue size (millions)	Currency	Issue size (ECU, millions)	Price	Yield	Mod price duration	Fitted yield
OAT	8.5	25-Oct-19	61,328	FRF	9,216	138.87	5.35	11.38	5.355
OAT	8.5	25-Apr-23	87,952	FRF	13,216	141.12	5.41	12.33	5.413
OAT	6	25-Oct-25	61,771	FRF	9,282	107.34	5.47	13.73	5.471
OAT	5.5	25-Apr-29	19,977	FRF	3,002	100.02	5.5	14.7	5.496
OAT(E)	8.25	25-Apr-22	1,500	ECU	1,500	136.41	5.45	12.09	5.401
BUND	6.25	04-Jan-24	20,000	DEM	10,076	110.97	5.44	13.2	5.45
BUND	6.5	04-Jul-27	22,000	DEM	11,084	114.69	5.47	13.91	5.473
BUND	5.63	04-Jan-28	18,000	DEM	9,068	102.11	5.48	14.38	5.49
BTP	9	01-Nov-23	21,737,000	ITL	11,108	146.06	5.63	11.93	5.408
BTP	7.25	01-Nov-26	18,310,000	ITL	9,357	123.33	5.66	13.06	5.455
BTP	6.5	01-Nov-27	18,236,000	ITL	9,319	113.12	5.65	13.53	5.471
DSL	7.5	15-Jan-23	18,162	NLG	8,119	127.43	5.43	12.52	5.422
DSL	5.5	15-Jan-28	4,000	NLG	1,788	100.25	5.48	14.45	5.493
OLO31	5.5	28-Mar-28	49,710	BEF	1,214	99.01	5.57	14.4	5.491
BONOS	6	31-Jan-29	333,556	ESP	1,980	105.23	5.6	14.34	5.485
BONOSE	6	31-Jan-29	1,000	ECU	1,000	104.80	5.63	14.3	5.485

Source: Goldman Sachs & Co., April 1998

Fig 3.8 Total securitization market ($bn outstanding)

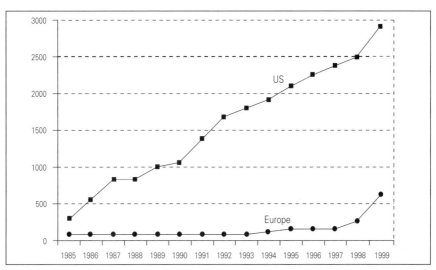

Source: Citibank, CS First Boston (1985–95 data); Moody's (1996–9 YTD data)

In the longer term, the effectiveness and transparency of EMU may lead to a further convergence of fiscal policies, so that no one country within the EU would have a significant advantage over other countries. To the extent that this would mean freer and more open markets, and a retreat from the traditional European mixed economy social policies and political attitudes, it could mean an increase in productivity for the EU region, and an upward revaluation of its securities.[15] There is no certainty that this will occur. However, based on what might be expected in terms of bond market developments, there is some support for the proposition – posed by the EU itself[16] and many euro advocates – that the changes will increase market integration within the EU, lower overall costs of capital, and result in more efficient bond auctions by governments. This would be welcome news to all users of financial markets and services.

The revolution

The coming of a revolution in which one vast, single currency marketplace replaces a dozen or more small, backward and underutilized national markets has been much proclaimed. EMU supporters believe such a revolution would enable European governments and corporations, at long last, to harvest some of the promised financial benefits of the single marketplace. The idea, in which 15 or more highly individualized European countries would voluntarily surrender their treasured financial sovereignty to create a stronger economic unity based on a deregulated single marketplace, was almost impossible to believe when it first surfaced in the mid-eighties. But it survived all forms of attack and debate, and its time has come. The great European financial revolution is about to occur. Or is it?

Like many other aspects of EMU, those affecting financial markets, especially fixed-income securities, have been discounted by the market. The revolution, in many ways, has already taken place because people and institutions have changed in anticipation of a different future, one which is increasingly being accepted and taken for granted. Market professionals are no longer arguing with each other over the merits of EMU or the euro. They instead do their best to make the necessary adjustments to a market environment shaped by EMU and the euro. Most adjustments have probably already taken place – in asset prices, in market mechanisms and, mainly, in anticipating what the financial markets will be like so that firms can participate in them effectively. There are those who still oppose EMU, and they are not few or unimportant, but until the market begins to sense that their power is increasing and that the direction of events is changing, it will proceed towards a future based on the 11 member countries and the potential for expansion – a new currency and a huge market potential for those who have adapted to the environment.

Rethinking the future

Probably the first step a financial firm must take is deciding what sort of role it wants to play in the euro-denominated markets. Clearly, continuing the old-fashioned bond and foreign exchange businesses in one's own country is not going to be possible. The Dutch banks, for example, have suffered the loss of the guilder foreign exchange business, and the sale of guilder bonds to their customers will not be the same. The Dutch role in the wholesale finance market of the EMU-11 will be minuscule unless Dutch financial firms take the necessary steps to change entirely what they do and find a niche that they can fill effectively. Indeed, among the 10,000 or so banks operating in Europe, many of which have been used to a modest amount of recurring wholesale financing business, only a relative handful will be in a position to take advantage of the opportunities in fixed-income securities offered by the euro-zone.

Among that handful, of course, will be the major EMU-11 banks that have already begun to prepare for the new marketplace. Less clear will be the role sought by larger banks in the EMU-4 and non-EU countries, whose involvement in EMU is less direct. Some will inevitably withdraw, preferring to concentrate on retail opportunities in their own markets or in speciality product areas. Others, mainly the US-style investment banks and some of their European rivals, will see the opportunities in EMU much as a small boy with a new lawnmower sees a field of tall grass. For quick-adapting firms which have in fact been adjusting for several years, the opportunities are considerable.

Adjustments

The first adjustment is to the wider fixed-income marketplace, in which the bond markets of Italy, France and Spain must be understood as well as the German market. This requires information and training of personnel to enable companies to operate in those countries' markets. There is also a series of technical adjustments to be made – adapting information and transaction systems to handle euros, collecting computerized market price data for a variety of instruments previously not followed very closely, developing bond market research capabilities to offer to investing clients as a guide to market-making, etc. There is also a need to develop capabilities in the derivatives markets (swaps, futures and options) in support of trading activities. Companies need to hire and train more people interested in and capable of finding the special opportunities in the markets that are yet to develop.

These adjustments are considerable. Starting from scratch, they can take four or five years to complete. Unfortunately for those firms just beginning, many of their competitors began their preparations several years ago, and will be hard to overtake.

Opportunities

A fixed-income department of a financial firm surely must see opportunities in selling bonds to institutional customers inside and outside the EMU-11. Salesmen need to talk to customers about realigning their portfolios, providing market information about the different government and corporate issuers, and offering bond swaps and trades. Trading desks will be rethinking market-making opportunities in euro-sovereigns, euro-euros and in non-euro EMU-4 paper. Arbitrage opportunities will be pursued, for clients and firms' own accounts. New issues and government bond auctions will be followed closely. Proprietary trading opportunities will emerge for many firms interested in using the evolving euro market, much as the US Treasury securities market is used for placing large, fully leveraged interest and exchange rate bets.

In the corporate sector, companies will be offered a wide variety of financing opportunities that will increasingly displace bank borrowing. Large, publicly held companies are already well advanced along this track, but state-owned businesses and smaller companies will get a lot of attention from aggressive, marketing-oriented investment banks hoping to complete an opportunistic transaction, gain new clients and improve their market share.

Mostly, however, the fixed-income service provider will have to become exceptionally market sensitive – to know what's happening to markets all around the world, to 'know the flows', as the traders put it. Otherwise it is difficult to pick the next market move, which may be the basis for a quick offer to, say, DaimlerChrysler to purchase €500 million of its 15-year bonds. The flows come from all over the world – the US, Japan, the Middle East, Switzerland, and many lesser areas for short periods of activity. Knowing the flows requires being in touch with the world's biggest investors, and having the technology to comprehend and communicate the information and turn it into profitable opportunities, just a step or two ahead of the next guy. These are the characteristics of big and efficient markets, such as the US Treasury market, which until recently have not been typical of fixed-income markets in Europe. But they are evolving in this direction and present comparable opportunities to successful participants.

Nevertheless, to be a successful participant means acquiring talent and adopting professional standards in the fixed-income area that are fully state of the art. Those who fail to develop these capabilities and still choose to compete will be in danger of extinction. Those who choose to opt out of this newer, tougher market will have to replace the business somewhere else – if they can.

NOTES

[1] Recollections of Peter Spira, former vice chairman of S.G. Warburg, who handled the Autostrade issue for the firm. From his privately published memoirs, *Ladders and Snakes*, 1997.

[2] *Euromoney* magazine (1963–86).

[3] Hayes, Samuel L. and Hubbard, Philip H. (1990) *Investment Banking, a Tale of Three Cities*, Cambridge, MA: Harvard Business School Press.

[4] BIS, Triennial Central Bank Survey of Foreign Exchange and Derivatives Markets, conducted in April 1998, published in May 1999.

[5] Schatz, Eric (1997) 'The size and structure of the world bond market 1997', Merrill Lynch, Pierce, Fenner & Smith Inc., September, p. 14.

[6] Goldman, Sachs & Co. (1998) 'Global government bond markets: second quarter outlook', April, pp. 9–10.

[7] Schatz, Eric (1997) 'The size and structure of the world bond market 1997', Merrill Lynch, Pierce, Fenner & Smith Inc., September, p. 14.

[8] Schatz, Eric, op. cit. and Schinasi and Prati (1997) 'European monetary union and international capital markets: structural implications and risks', Bank for International Settlements.

[9] Bank for International Settlements (1997) Annual Report, pp. 80–1.

[10] Ibid., pp. 81–3.

[11] Bank for International Settlements (1998) Annual Report, Basle: BIS, 1999.

[12] 'The euro and the dollar' (1997) The Economist, 19 October.

[13] Adams, Richard (1997) 'Boost for EMU as $1.18 billion bond is sold in euros', Financial Times, 2 February.

[14] Fox, Mark (1996) 'The shape of the future euro market', Lehman Brothers, 15 August. The author acknowledges that the US municipal market is frequently referred to as a good model for the euromarket. But he notes that the US municipal market is different because the issuers are within a single sovereign state and have operated as a single currency area for a long time and therefore the euromarket may operate somewhat differently. Also, most US municipal issues are sold free of US tax liability on income, which means that most investors are individuals, not institutions.

[15] See also Fisher, Andrew (1997) 'European bourses may get lift on back of EMU', Financial Times, 15 April. This article refers also to an interesting study by Alexander Schraeder of Bayerische Vereinsbank.

[16] European Commission, Green Paper on the Practical Arrangements for the Introduction of the Single Currency, Brussels, 31 May 1995, pp. 10–15.

Equities, markets and exchanges

Until the mid-eighties, European equity markets remained in the backwater of international finance. Very few shares traded outside their home countries, and not many traded actively within them. There were some attractive multinational corporate stocks, such as Shell and Unilever, that traded in London and in Amsterdam and in the US in the form of American Depositary Receipts (ADRs) but these were mainly of interest to arbitrageurs and a few sophisticated institutional investors. Those European equities that existed were mainly available on the London Stock Exchange. Of all publicly traded companies in Europe in 1985 (combined market capitalization of $850 billion), approximately half were British. At that time, US corporations comprised 50 per cent of the world's equity market capitalization, followed by Japanese (21 per cent), and European corporations (18 per cent). The capitalization of so-called emerging market equity securities was less than 4 per cent of the world total.

The UK market had the benefit of a long tradition of stock trading in London and a practice of investing major portions of pension and mutual fund assets in equity securities, but probably fewer than a dozen UK companies were known to investors outside the country. In the rest of Europe, companies were controlled by family groups, banks and insurance companies, by the government, and by small groups of powerful insiders. Exchanges did not offer much liquidity, or convenient settlement and delivery, and investment information was scarce. Few financial professionals made active markets in European stocks, or promoted their ideas with research. Insider trading was not illegal, and many corporate executives and others 'in the know' took liberal advantage of opportunities that the general public never heard about. This was the way the markets had been for a century, and those who did not care for it could take their business elsewhere.

Since the mid-eighties, however, a great deal has happened to change the environment for equities in Europe, i.e. the number of companies that are publicly traded, the exchanges their shares are traded on, the regulatory arrangements, and the nature and nationality of the competitors. By the end of 1998, European equity market capitalization had increased more than seven-fold to $7,656 billion, or 28 per cent of the world total. The UK's share of total European market capitalization dropped to 26 per cent, while Germany's increased to 14 per cent. The US share of global market capitalization remained at 49 per cent, while Japan's fell sharply from more than 20 per cent to 9.1 per cent (*see* Fig. 4.1).

Fig 4.1 World equity market capitalization (market value in US$bn)

	US	Japan	Europe[1]	EU 11	EU 15	Emerging market	World total
1985	2,325	910	925	444	825	115	4,667
(%)	(49.8)	(19.5)	(19.8)	(9.5)	(17.7)	(2.5)	(100.0)
1998	13,451	2,496	7,656	4,160	6,911	1,908	27,462
(%)	(49.0)	(9.1)	(27.9)	(15.1)	(25.2)	(6.9)	(100.0)
Growth % 1985/1998	478.5	174.3	727.7	836.9	737.7	1,559.1	488.4

[1]Europe = EU-15 plus Switzerland and Norway

Source: IFC

The modernization of European equity markets

The regeneration of the European equity markets began in the early eighties, largely as a by-product of the important series of economic reforms which were just beginning to be introduced. Margaret Thatcher was one of the first to initiate reforms that made a difference. Her measures in Britain, aimed at reducing the power of the government and the trade unions in the private sector and introducing free market measures, were watched carefully by others in Europe also suffering from 'eurosclerosis'. Thatcher cut taxes, removed exchange controls, introduced tough measures to reduce union power, took control of troublesome socialist municipal governments, introduced the first efforts at financial reform in 100 years, and began the long march towards the privatization of state-owned enterprises. These included the bulk of national investments in power, telephones, heavy manufacturing, oil and gas, transportation, and other important (but significantly underper-forming) industry sectors. Early on, these reforms appeared to be successful, and before long an appetite to effect similar measures developed in France, Germany and other parts of the EU, leading to the Single Market Act in 1985.

Market liberalization and deregulation

On 1 May 1975, the New York Stock Exchange (NYSE) abolished fixed commission rates. This much-resisted event, called 'Mayday', generated a number of fundamental changes in the way equity markets operated all over the world. The basic principle was that a stock exchange could not operate as a private club with rules that prevented market access by non-members and required minimum, non-negotiable per-share commission rates, irrespective of trading volume.

As institutional trading grew in the US during the sixties, many large investors began to complain about high commissions and their inability to recover these by becoming members of the stock exchange. The SEC and the antitrust division of the US Justice Department took an interest in the issue, and ultimately forced the NYSE to rescind its minimum commission rules, allow foreign brokerage firms to become members, and include non-members on its board of directors. Immediately after these rule changes, institutional commission rates plummeted (these are down to less than 5 per cent of pre-Mayday levels on large institutional transactions) and many firms failed or were required to reorganize to improve their competitive capabilities. In response to such pressures, the NYSE member firms introduced many innova-tions, and provided much more extensive and more valuable services to customers, thereby dramatically improving the quality and efficiency of the markets.

In 1975, the daily trading volume on the NYSE, which accounted for 85 per cent of all shares traded in the US, was 18.6 million shares, annual market turnover was valued at $127 billion, and the market capitalization of listed companies was $134 billion. By 1985, daily trading volume averaged 109 million shares, annual market turnover was $997 billion, and market capital-ization was $2,325 billion. By 1995, the development of electronic, screen-based markets such as Nasdaq, had increased regional and off-exchange trading. These reduced the NYSE share of total US equity trading to about 50 per cent.[1] At the end of 1995, combined trading on the fully competitive US markets aggregated $6,859 billion, more than 50 times what it had been before the market reforms were introduced 20 years before.

'Big Bang'

The Mayday effect was not lost on other countries. In the late seventies, the Labour government in Britain had instituted a lawsuit against the London Stock Exchange (LSE) alleging that its club-like operations were in restraint of trade. The Conservative government of Mrs Thatcher inherited this lawsuit, and settled it with the Exchange in 1983. Under the terms of the settlement, the LSE agreed that by 27 October 1986 it would abolish membership restrictions and the requirement that members act only in a 'single capacity', i.e. either as a 'jobber', or dealer, or as a broker, but not as both. This settlement seemed innocent enough, but it fundamentally changed the economics of the UK securities business, and led in 1986 to what the British press called the 'Big Bang', a transformation of the equity market in the UK. As a result of the Big Bang, 19 of the 20 leading brokers, and all the top jobbers, sought refuge in the arms of friendly mergers. In the new universe created by the Big Bang, any qualified firm (including commercial and merchant banks and foreign firms) could join the LSE, firms could act as both brokers and dealers (as in New York), and commission rates were fully negotiable.

And other reforms ...

The Bank of England, then responsible for overseeing capital markets, wanted to take advantage of the changes to improve the efficiency of securities markets in the UK (especially for government securities, and in anticipation of large privatization issues). It also wanted to firm up London's position as Europe's most active financial centre. Its contribution to the 'reregulation' of London financial markets was establishing new capital requirements for market-making in government and corporate debt securities, and in equities. Parliament also passed a landmark, omnibus securities regulation bill, the Financial Services Act of 1986, to set up an institutional framework for securities market regulation.

As a consequence, trading volume in the UK more than doubled in the first year. Commissions were slashed, and as many of the British brokers and dealers merged into stronger groups, competition increased greatly and large integrated securities firms, such as S.G. Warburg, BZW, Merrill Lynch and Goldman Sachs, increased their market share. The benefits of the reforms, as in the early days after Mayday in New York, were seen to flow mainly to the users of securities market services, at the expense of the providers of such services. The competitive pressures caused by the Big Bang were heightened after the worldwide stock market crash of 19 October 1987.

... *Spread within Europe*

The rest of Europe was very mindful of the market changes in London. By this time, preparations were under way for the implementation of the Single Market Act – which would take effect at the end of 1992 – and the EU was in the process of promulgating directives for the conduct of banking and other financial services. Liberalization to accommodate greater competition was the key to the EU reforms, and in all countries some form of financial market deregulation occurred. Extensive changes were set in motion in France, Germany, Italy and Switzerland, though they were far less comprehensive than in Brirain.

In general, within a few years of the Big Bang settlement, the principles of freer competition, open access and negotiated commissions were adopted (at least in significant measure) by almost all countries in Europe in which important stock exchanges existed. This wide acceptance of competitive and regulatory best practice reflected a degree of procedural convergence that had not occurred before, one which has become increasingly difficult for individual countries to oppose. This is because market forces could now create alternative trading venues to one that was blocked by local regulation. If Britain imposed a stamp tax on stock trading, for example, then much of the LSE trading business could be conducted somewhere else, e.g. in New York where over-the-counter market-makers can quote tax-free prices to UK investors. Rather than lose its stock market business to New York, the UK would be more likely to drop such a stamp tax.

Moreover, countries now lobby other countries to offer reciprocal access to financial service markets or risk denial of such access to those markets by nationals of their country. For example, if the Swiss denied access to the Zurich Stock Exchange to brokers from the UK, they would run the risk of having access to the various London markets denied to Swiss banks and brokers. Between market forces and political pressures, it has become extremely difficult for any country to drag its feet indefinitely in opposition to the emerging global standard of stock market reforms.[2]

Privatizations and new issues

During the nineties powerful forces on both the supply and demand side shaped equity markets in Europe. The supply of equity securities was vastly increased by the continuing flow of privatization stock issues, in which large European state-owned enterprises undertook initial public offerings of common stock (*see* Chapter 6). Many of these issues, such as the sale of

British Petroleum stock by the British government in 1987 and the sale of Deutsche Telekom shares in 1996 (each valued at $13 billion), required massive efforts to create the necessary investor demand. It was a huge undertaking to educate the investing public on the merits of the shares, and to develop institutional demand for the offerings from investors in the home country and abroad. International syndicates were formed to underwrite and place one-third to one-half of the issue. These syndicates educated institutional investors all over the world about the opportunities associated with privatization issues, and other issues as well. Since 1985, more than $100 billion of privatization issues have been sold by the British government alone, and nearly as much has been offered by other European governments.

Privatization also required the European markets to develop the infrastructure to be able to underwrite, distribute, research and trade the securities actively in secondary markets. Once in place, the investment banks and brokers that supplied most of this infrastructure began to call on existing private sector corporations to offer their services to those companies wanting to sell securities, or to develop an active trading market in them. In many parts of Europe, especially in countries with little history of capital market activity such as Germany, companies needing money, or seeking to sell out, had little alternative but to approach their relationship bank for an investment. Now these companies have a viable alternative to issue shares in the market, and many, especially in Germany, have taken advantage of it.

In addition to privatization issues, the enhanced equity markets were eager to take on conventional initial public offerings of companies seeking to raise new money for an early-stage business, or to liquidate the shareholding of a seasoned partner wishing to withdraw capital. Many continental European companies began to appreciate the advantages and benefits of becoming stand-alone public companies, and took steps to go public on established exchanges or in the smaller-company markets established for entrepreneurial ventures. In June 1998, Alstom, the Anglo-French engineering group, became a public corporation valued at $7.7 billion by selling 8 per cent of its shares to the public, 2 per cent to its employees, and reserving 1 per cent for stock option programmes.

The annual volume of all new international equity issues has risen from less than $2 billion in 1985 to more than $69 billion in 1998 (*see* Fig. 4.2).

In 1999, 'international equity' new issues as reported by Thomson Financial Securities Data were an astonishing $159 billion – more than double the year before.

Fig 4.2 Value of international equity offerings (US$bn)

Year	Common stock	Preferred stock	Total equity
1983	0.1	0.0	0.1
1984	0.4	0.0	0.4
1985	1.9	0.0	1.9
1986	10.2	1.8	12.0
1987	12.5	1.2	13.8
1988	5.4	2.9	8.3
1989	8.9	1.2	10.1
1990	7.9	0.3	8.2
1991	11.7	0.9	12.6
1992	12.3	1.4	13.7
1993	18.7	0.9	19.6
1994	25.1	0.9	26.0
1995	22.2	1.0	23.2
1996	38.5	6.6	45.1
1997	59.8	3.9	63.7
1998	64.2	4.8	69.0

Source: 1998 Securities Industry Factbook

Pension funds

On the demand side, much of the new money flowing into the international equity market has been from pension funds, the total value of which at the end of 1997 was estimated to be $9,700 billion, approximately one-third of all global assets under management. European pension assets totalled almost $2,200 billion in 1997, 23 per cent of all pension assets, but less than half of the $5,760 billion of North American pension assets that accounted for 59 per cent of total pension assets. The annual growth in pension assets over the previous five years, in both Europe and North America, was 10 per cent. Pension funds in the UK accounted for about half of the European total. Because the countries of continental Europe have relied on pay-as-you-go social security systems which have been inadequate for their needs, continental Europe has only one-sixth the per-capita pension funding of North America, although it is beginning to close the gap. Several countries, including Italy, France and Spain, have been driven to legislate programmes to supplement eroding social security systems with tax-advantaged corporate and individual defined contribution schemes.[3] This issue is discussed in detail in Chapter 8.

Cross-border investments of European pension funds averaged about 20 per cent of all pension assets in 1997 (27 per cent for UK funds, and approximately 12 per cent for those in the rest of Europe), totalling approximately $440 billion. During the subsequent five years, InterSec Research Corp.

estimates that total cross-border investments of pension funds will nearly double, to $2,300 billion by 2002, of which $1,035 billion would be from US pension funds, $457 billion from the UK, $340 billion from Japan, and $449 billion from 'other countries'. Of US pension funds, approximately 10 per cent have committed to cross-border investments (83 per cent of which were invested in equities). By 2002, InterSec expects more than $1,000 billion of US cross-border investments by pension funds. Of this, $815 billion will be in equity investments, of which Europe should receive a share of approximately 30 per cent if weighted by share of global market capitalization.[4] Such forecasts suggest that of the approximately $1,000 billion in cross-border asset growth between 1997 and 2002, somewhere between $200 billion and $300 billion will be newly invested in the equity markets in Europe (see Fig. 4.3).

Fig 4.3 World pension assets 1992/1997/2002

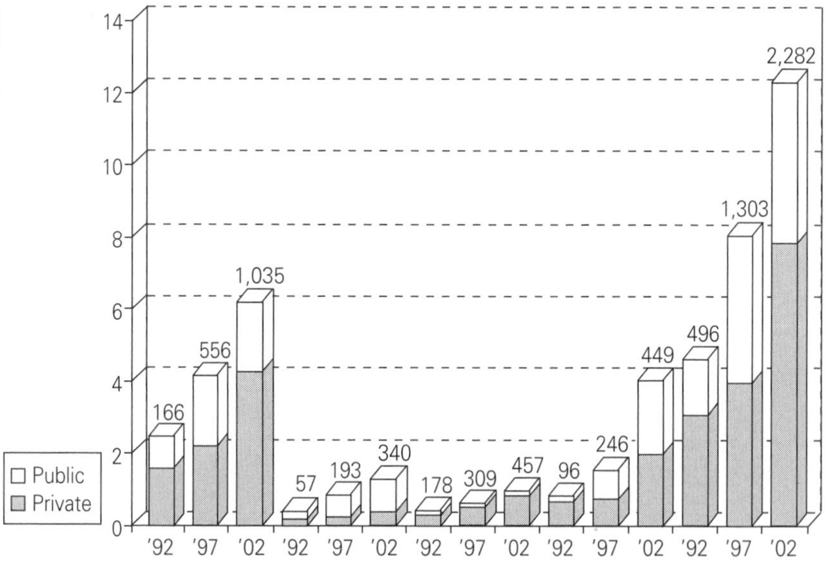

	US			Japan			UK			Other			Total		
Cross-border as % of total	5%	10%	14%	7%	17%	21%	28%	27%	28%	8%	12%	14%	8%	13%	17%
Avg. annual growth five years ended		27%	13%		28%	12%		12%	8%		21%	13%		21%	12%

Source: InterSec Research Corp.

Trading and market-making

Trading markets in international equity securities in Europe have improved steadily since the Big Bang. Before then, and indeed for some years since, the level of trading activity in the home markets, especially in continental Europe, was often limited and offered poor liquidity to investors. The ADR market in New York was useful for some stocks, mainly British, Japanese and Canadian, but prices were still set in the home market, and gradually US institutional investors shifted their business there. A few multinational companies were listed on the NYSE and the Tokyo Stock Exchange (more were listed on the LSE) but trading volume in the foreign markets was rarely significant compared with the home market. Frequently foreign companies chose not to list on the NYSE because of the expense and the awkward disclosure requirements associated with becoming a SEC 'reporting company'. Instead, many companies passively allowed their shares to be traded on Nasdaq or in over-the-counter markets by firms specializing in international stocks.

Arbitrage beginnings

For years, the principal international trading activity was foreign stock arbitrage, in which one would buy an ADR of, say, a Dutch stock and simultaneously sell the number of underlying shares represented by the ADR in Amsterdam. Doing this profitably meant mastering the details. The purchase in dollars after commissions had to be less than the proceeds of the sale of the shares, after commissions and transfer expenses, and after the foreign exchange costs of converting back into dollars. Such arbitrage activities kept prices of international shares around the world in line with their home market values.

Block trading

After the Big Bang, shares began to be traded in large blocks to accommodate institutional investors, mainly those from the US and the UK. These investors were starting to accumulate positions in the UK and other European stocks, and wanted to do so in volume, without causing the market prices to rise because of their heavy buying activity. US brokers in London began to offer the same services to purchasers of European shares as they did to customers of US shares (often the customers were the same) and block trading was soon common in Europe as a competitive action. Before long, all of London was competing for large blocks of European shares at very low commissions, and the business became difficult, although eventually the market settled, until block trading began to penetrate the continental markets as well.

Improved information flows

Advances in information and communications technology have been essential to the growth in the international equities markets. Market information of all types is now available internationally through newspapers, screens and contact with brokers. Securities can be traded internationally in most European countries with a high degree of reliance on trouble-free payment and delivery, which was rarely the case before 1980 in trading outside the US, the UK, Japan and Canada. It is now possible to receive a reliable quote on virtually any stock whose home market is one of the major financial centres, from just about anywhere, on the telephone or over the Internet. Quotes are also available for securities from many other countries on very short notice.

The computerization of national markets such as Britain, France, Switzerland and Germany has introduced a variety of technological capabilities for screen trading, futures and options transactions and paperless trading that did not exist before the Big Bang. These have linked international marketplaces, making possible a level of trading volume expansion and liquidity that probably could not otherwise have occurred.

With these developments has come a large increase in the number of trained professionals who provide the many services needed to sustain a growing market. These include providing investment research for an increasing number of companies from an increasing number of countries, and block trading and portfolio insurance services. In addition, indexing and other services are available to investment companies and mutual funds, and there is an increasing use of derivative securities for customer risk management programmes. Internal and back-office capabilities include firm-wide risk exposure management and hedging functions, optimum financing of trading positions, improved payment and settlement activities, and more efficient record-keeping, as well as management control and information services.

Market-making

With foreign membership available on exchanges in North America, Europe and the Far East, it is possible for participating firms to be active market-makers in US, European and Asian stocks around the clock. Such firms are able to balance orders from around the world, not just from their home market. They are also able to limit their market-making activities to stocks for which they see international demand, and yet not find themselves in the position of being a market-maker for all-comers, as some national dealers feel they must do. Major firms' commitment to dealing in international equities is substantial and is reflected in the number of personnel in research, trading, sales coverage, systems and back-office and foreign exchange that major US, British and other firms have added. A large increase in market infrastructure has occurred which not only makes it possible to improve services, but also provides competitive energy to the market for human capital as all these new employees seek to advance their careers.

An example of the enhanced market-making capabilities that the increase in European financial infrastructure and skills development has made possible was the placement by J.P. Morgan in November 1997 of 20 million shares of Bayerische Vereinsbank AG. The transaction was valued at $1.1 billion and assisted a large shareholder of one of Germany's leading banks, which had announced an $18 billion merger with Bayerische Hypo-und-Wechsel Bank to form the country's second largest bank. The issue was placed around the world (though mainly in Europe) despite volatile stock markets and the fact that German regulators were considering an investigation of the merger on competition grounds.[5]

Stock buy-backs

In the late nineties, changes in tax law increasingly permitted European companies to participate in stock buy-back programmes. Buy-backs had been in common use for a long time in the US as a form of financial restructuring. They permitted companies to improve shareholder returns by reducing capital and doing so fairly to all stockholders by purchasing the shares in the open market. But the change took some years to catch on. In 1997, European companies announced $13 billion of buy-backs, an amount that increased sharply in 1998 to $50 billion, and was expected in early 1999 to double during that year. Initially, the largest, most sophisticated European companies such as Siemens, Veba and Schering in Germany, and Crédit Lyonnais and Paribas in France, were the most involved in share buy-backs, but as the practice became more familiar, more companies adopted it.

Soaring trading volume

The result of these developments has been a substantial increase in the value of worldwide equity trading activities, which increased from $1,646 billion in 1985 to more than $22,000 billion in 1998 (see Fig. 4.4).

The increase in new-issue volume has also done a great deal to stimulate secondary market activity in all the EU member countries, and to provide opportunities for broker-dealers, several of which now maintain research coverage and trading facilities in more than 100 different European stocks.

Fig 4.4 Global value of shares traded (market value in US$bn)

	US	Japan	Europe[1]	EU-11	EU-15	Emerging market	World total
1985	997	383	205	123	203	45	1,646
(%)	(60.6)	(23.3)	(12.5)	(7.5)	(12.3)	(2.7)	(100.0)
1998	13,148	949	5,722	3,671	5,042	1,957	22,874
(%)	(57.5)	(4.1)	(25.0)	(16.0)	(22.0)	(8.6)	(100.0)
Growth % 1985/1996	1,218.8	147.8	2,691.2	2,884.6	2,383.7	4,248.9	1,289.7

[1]Europe = EU-15 plus Switzerland and Norway

Source: IFC

In 1998, the value of trading in all European stocks was approximately $5,700 billion, or 25 per cent of the world total (with the value of German shares traded substantially exceeding that of British shares), second behind the US with a trading value market share of 57 per cent, and well ahead of Japan's 4 per cent. By contrast, in 1985 – the year before the Big Bang – the US market share was 61 per cent, Japan's was 23 per cent and all of Europe's was approximately 13 per cent. Since 1985, the growth in value of shares traded has been significantly higher in Germany, France and the smaller countries in Europe than in the US or in the world as a whole. Indeed, in the decade after the Big Bang, the value of European equity trading increased more than ten-fold.

European investors, especially mutual funds and banks investing customer funds, have also been active traders in US and Japanese securities. In 1985, gross transactions in US equities by European investors was $82.5 billion, or 40 per cent of intra-European trading, and in 1996 gross transactions were $589 billion, or 24 per cent – indicating that Europeans were preferring European shares to those from the US.[6]

European exchanges

The improvement in access to market-making for international shares is also very important. In London, increasing interest in continental European stocks on the part of British, US and Japanese institutional investors has caused many London-based market-makers to offer French, German, Dutch, Italian and Swiss shares through the LSE's Stock Exchange Automated Quotation (SEAQ) system. Accordingly, many European shares are now listed in London. SEAQ is an electronic trading system similar to Nasdaq. It has claimed to handle as much as three-quarters of all trading in blue-chip shares of companies based in Holland, half those in France and Italy, and a quarter of those corporations based in Germany. These figures, however, are subject to some double counting due to inter-dealer purchases and sales. They are also subject to increasing competitive efforts by the continental European countries to re-attract the business to their markets.[7] Approximately half of the total trading volume on the LSE is now derived from trading in non-UK shares.

The SEAQ system has benefited from being the first European electronic trading system in place and from being located at the London hub of European institutional trading activity, where the US presence is greatly felt. Still, it has some disadvantages. It depends on local market prices for its activities, and it is subject to certain non-transparent LSE market-making practices for large blocks of securities which detract from market efficiency. Its settlement practices are somewhat less modern than those of the newer continental exchanges. It is not inconceivable, therefore, that some trading in European stocks could migrate to other, more competitive marketplaces. For the moment, however, the massive English-speaking trading infrastructure, the regulatory environment and the relative size of the London market compared with other European markets all indicate a continuing advantage for market-makers to remain in London.

This situation has of course encouraged continental European markets to accelerate internal reforms to consolidate local and regional exchanges into a single, modernized national market. The task has been completed in Germany and Switzerland, countries with a legacy of exchanges located in principal cities. The effort has been to concentrate on the market's technical architecture to optimize efficiencies and to encourage innovations and increased competitive activity to recapture market share of equity trading in Europe. Futures and options exchanges have also been opened in Paris, Frankfurt and Zurich, and more recently in Madrid and Milan, and equity-based derivatives are rapidly increasing in usage. New market developments and innovations in New York or London are often copied quickly in these other markets and trading volumes are rising.

While competition between London and the other markets continues, the ultimate EU goal is a single, integrated European market, at least for professional investors. As a result, as the new era of the euro began in January 1999 so did a pan-European trading alliance between the LSE and the Deutsche Börse (the two largest exchanges in Europe, with more than 50 per cent of all European trading between them). This alliance, which was to provide reciprocal access and execution, was ultimately not successful, however. Nevertheless, the exchanges of Europe are increasingly becoming wired into a single pan-European infrastructure. Figure 4.5 shows total European equity market turnover by stock exchanges for 1998.

Fig 4.5 European stock exchange turnover in 1998 (Total European turnover: £4.9 trillion. Total US turnover: £13.0 trillion)

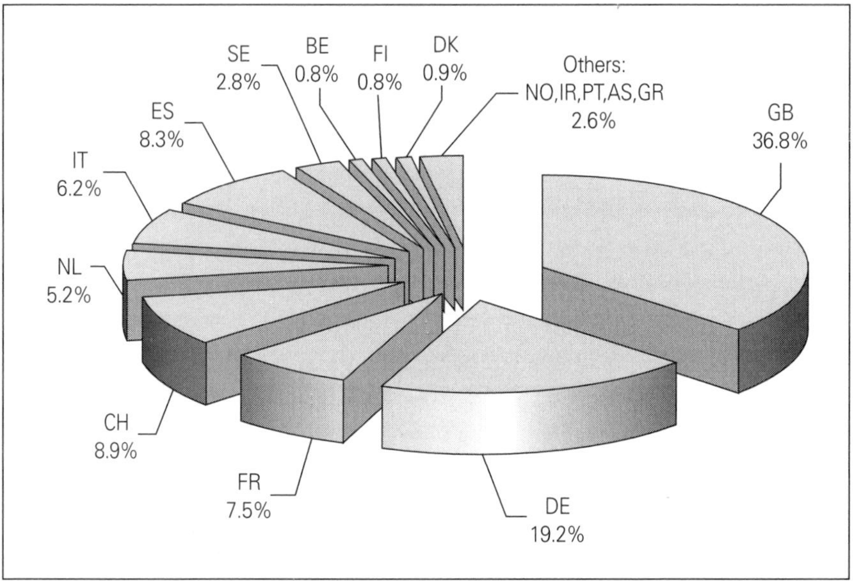

SE 2.8%   BE 0.8%   FI 0.8%   DK 0.9%   Others: NO,IR,PT,AS,GR 2.6%   GB 36.8%
ES 8.3%
IT 6.2%
NL 5.2%
CH 8.9%
FR 7.5%
DE 19.2%

Source: London Stock Exchange 1999

Changing investor behaviour

Participation in international equity portfolios is a comparatively new development for US and Japanese investors, at least in the post-World War II period, but it is not new for Europeans. For many years the most international of all investors were the Swiss banks, which had long attracted foreign 'safekeeping' funds. In Switzerland there was very little to invest in, however, so the banks had to look for suitable investment opportunities abroad. During the sixties and seventies, Swiss banks were the principal foreign investors in US stocks. Subsequently they became substantial investors in Japanese stocks as well. Similar to the Swiss banks in international orientation were banks and investment companies in Holland, Belgium and Luxembourg. In few of these countries were there sufficient good domestic investment opportunities.

Just behind the Swiss as international investors were the British, who have a long history of overseas portfolio investment. Until 1979, Britain had been subject to exchange controls that required that a premium be paid for foreign currency to be used for investment outside the country. Most other countries in Europe had similar foreign exchange regulations, although these were successively abolished. Once the exchange controls were lifted in the UK, there was a substantial increase in overseas investment, mostly in the US and Japan. Institutional investors in the UK have since greatly increased their activities abroad and now hold and trade substantial volumes of international securities of all types.

More recently, US and Japanese institutional investors have entered into active programmes for investing in international equities. As a result, the international pool of funds participating in equities has greatly increased and has become 'institutionalized' (much as the US equity markets were in the sixties), being managed by internationally sophisticated, professional money managers, most of whom are based in London (*see* Fig. 4.6). Moreover, as non-US markets have become more active and attracted more attention from investors outside their own countries, they have grown in relative importance. Gradually, share prices in the countries with less developed markets have risen to international norms.

Fig 4.6 Where the money is managed

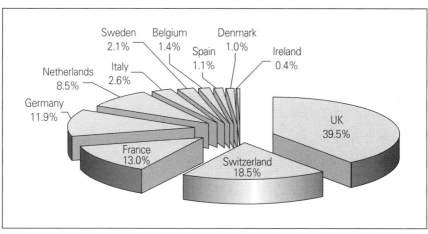

Source: Institutional Investor

International application of modern portfolio theory

During the sixties, a number of academic economists began to develop the basis for what is now known as modern portfolio theory. The theory was based on the idea that the marketplace is, in essence, 'efficient', and price setting instantly reflects information received by market participants. It also maintained that 'risk' in individual securities could be measured relative to the market as a whole and investors should look at risk and returns in the context of their whole portfolio. This led to further development of the theory of portfolio diversification to secure optimal returns, and gradually investors began to act on the advice. But before this could make much difference to the market as a whole, the market had to become more institutionalized, i.e. it had to consist predominantly of institutional money managers dealing with large portfolios in a competitive context in which their published returns would be important and carefully monitored. The larger the influence of such investors, the more efficient the marketplace would be, thereby confirming further the value of application of the investment theories.

Diversification itself was nothing new. What was different was the use of correlations of the returns of individual stocks with the market as a whole. Optimum diversification could be achieved only if the components of the portfolio had imperfect co-movements with one another and in terms of their expected sensitivity to changes in the values of the market.

Diligent investors soon discovered that internationally diversified portfolios (in which investments in different economies around the world would be less than perfectly correlated with each other) had the potential to produce the best overall risk-adjusted portfolio returns. In the international markets for debt securities, a relatively high degree of correlation exists – yields adjusted for currency, maturity and ratings are linked across the principal financial centres. This is not true in equity securities, where correlation between the S&P500 index and foreign market indices can be relatively low. There remain enough differences between individual equity markets that integration and correlation has been modest, as shown in Fig. 4.7. This is because stocks represent different economic values in different countries, and indeed are valued differently in terms of price-earnings ratios and other common measures.

For the international benefits of modern portfolio theory to become reality it had to be possible to identify and trade in a significant number of international stocks. That meant reliable information about foreign stocks and satisfactory market liquidity had to be available. As these investment conditions improved, especially in European and Japanese markets, many institutional investors began to apply what they had learned about theories of portfolio diversification to stocks in other countries.

Figure 4.8 shows the annualized returns on a range of different internationally diversified portfolios (ranging from 0 per cent to 100 per cent invested in the Goldman Sachs/FT global index) for the 20 years as at April 1999. These data indicate that a prudent pension fund manager, for example,

Fig 4.7 Equity market correlation matrix: returns of local indices – latest 250 trading days

	Australia	Austria	Belgium	Canada	Denmark	Finland	France	Germany	Hong Kong	Ireland	Italy	Japan	Malaysia	Mexico	Netherlands	New Zealand	Norway	Singapore	South Africa	Spain	Sweden	Switzerland	United Kingdom	United States
Australia	1.00																							
Austria	0.35	1.00																						
Belgium	0.36	0.58	1.00																					
Canada	0.19	0.32	0.39	1.00																				
Denmark	0.34	0.57	0.60	0.35	1.00																			
Finland	0.36	0.57	0.64	0.60	0.65	1.00																		
France	0.35	0.64	0.79	0.40	0.67	0.74	1.00																	
Germany	0.33	0.65	0.74	0.49	0.69	0.73	0.84	1.00																
Hong Kong	0.53	0.36	0.32	0.43	0.33	0.41	0.33	0.42	1.00															
Ireland	0.40	0.49	0.60	0.21	0.52	0.61	0.64	0.60	0.31	1.00														
Italy	0.33	0.55	0.68	0.45	0.62	0.68	0.82	0.75	0.35	0.54	1.00													
Japan	0.52	0.33	0.31	0.20	0.28	0.34	0.32	0.30	0.35	0.37	0.33	1.00												
Malaysia	0.37	0.25	0.21	0.04	0.20	0.21	0.16	0.19	0.35	0.14	0.18	0.28	1.00											
Mexico	0.28	0.24	0.27	0.50	0.22	0.33	0.36	0.31	0.21	0.22	0.36	0.19	0.12	1.00										
Netherlands	0.32	0.61	0.78	0.39	0.67	0.72	0.85	0.84	0.36	0.61	0.78	0.29	0.19	0.31	1.00									
New Zealand	0.43	0.25	0.34	0.12	0.27	0.27	0.28	0.29	0.32	0.34	0.25	0.24	0.20	0.14	0.31	1.00								
Norway	0.38	0.62	0.54	0.35	0.63	0.65	0.65	0.69	0.39	0.56	0.62	0.31	0.21	0.31	0.65	0.24	1.00							
Singapore	0.52	0.30	0.28	0.19	0.22	0.33	0.31	0.32	0.65	0.34	0.30	0.39	0.35	0.20	0.30	0.39	0.34	1.00						
South Africa	0.44	0.56	0.42	0.32	0.47	0.44	0.52	0.52	0.53	0.40	0.45	0.35	0.28	0.31	0.49	0.33	0.55	0.43	1.00					
Spain	0.31	0.60	0.68	0.51	0.63	0.62	0.81	0.75	0.31	0.53	0.80	0.23	0.11	0.38	0.77	0.26	0.57	0.27	0.50	1.00				
Sweden	0.28	0.57	0.66	0.43	0.60	0.71	0.76	0.71	0.35	0.60	0.72	0.33	0.18	0.28	0.71	0.23	0.63	0.26	0.49	0.66	1.00			
Switzerland	0.34	0.59	0.74	0.51	0.64	0.71	0.85	0.80	0.34	0.64	0.81	0.28	0.20	0.37	0.83	0.25	0.64	0.27	0.48	0.77	0.73	1.00		
United Kingdom	0.42	0.59	0.68	0.41	0.61	0.69	0.81	0.77	0.47	0.64	0.75	0.39	0.32	0.36	0.80	0.29	0.64	0.39	0.53	0.69	0.71	0.80	1.00	
United States	0.13	0.21	0.30	0.76	0.26	0.39	0.44	0.39	0.15	0.28	0.40	0.13	-0.09	0.54	0.32	0.10	0.29	0.15	0.21	0.43	0.36	0.42	0.37	1.00

Source: Goldman Sachs, FT/S&P – Actuaries World Indices, April 1999

might conclude that a balance of about 30 per cent foreign shares (invested in the GS/FT index) and 70 per cent in the S&P500 index would produce a safer and more profitable allocation of assets than if all were invested in the domestic market. It was not long before fund managers in Europe and the US began to appreciate these considerations and to rebalance their portfolios with more international stocks.

Fig 4.8 Portfolio of US and foreign stocks, December 1985 to April 1999*

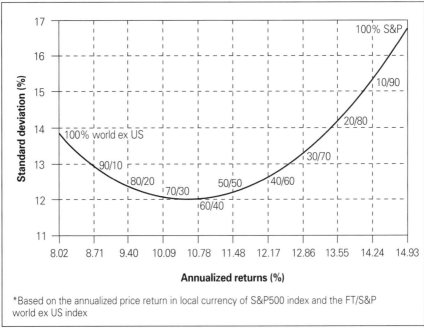

*Based on the annualized price return in local currency of S&P500 index and the FT/S&P world ex US index

Source: Goldman, Sachs & Co.

Because of a better understanding across all financial centres of modern portfolio concepts, and the as yet small amounts of foreign portfolio investment holding as a percentage of total investments (about 13 per cent for pension funds worldwide in 1997, up from 8 per cent in 1992),[8] it is reasonable to expect increases in foreign investment to continue for some years. InterSec Research Corp. estimates that pensions will invest 17 per cent of their assets cross-border by 2002.

On the other hand, as European markets have become more closely linked with the progress towards EMU, and as cross-border equity trading becomes increasingly important, pricing mechanisms have converged. The circulation of high-quality securities research reports, the linking of trading infrastructures around the world, and the increased acceptance of non-home country

European investments to European investors in anticipation of EMU, has already caused this convergence to become apparent.

Venture capital and private equity investments

For a modern capital market to function fully and completely, it must provide a venue for the offering of new issues of securities, a trading environment for outstanding securities, and a mechanism for carrying out mergers and acquisitions. In addition, it must provide an environment for small and start-up companies to obtain investment capital. At the end of the 20th century, only one capital market – the US – offered all these features. The European markets, after several years of powerful development in capital market activity, offered all but one – the environment for small companies to get financing.

This environment, often referred to as the market for venture capital, was slow in developing in Europe. According to *Risk Capital*, an April 1998 report of the Commission of European Communities, this tardiness was the result of institutional and cultural barriers that were unique to Europe. First among these was the lack of interest in high-risk investments on the part of pension funds (which regarded such investments as imprudent), and restrictions on the sale of high-risk mutual funds to the public. Further barriers were the inability to list small or young companies on major stock exchanges, and the continuing existence of governmental programmes that discouraged entrepreneurs from taking risks. Perhaps most important was the general idea that risk-taking was dangerous and therefore should be left to large corporations or governments best able to endure the consequences of failure.

The barriers, the report said, should be removed, with the assistance of governmental actions if necessary, because risk capital was an important key to job creation and economic growth in Europe. This conclusion was based on a careful study of the US experience, in which companies benefiting from venture capital were seen to have experienced employment growth of nearly 30 per cent in the period 1989–93 compared with a 2–3 per cent loss of jobs among the US's 500 largest companies. A comparable study of a much smaller number of European companies enjoying access to venture capital revealed similar results. The importance of job creation being what it was in Europe in the late nineties, the policy implications to the EU were clear. It was necessary to do what could be done to stimulate the flow of venture capital in Europe, and the *Risk Capital* document outlined a number of barrier-breaking initiatives aimed at doing so. These initiatives were welcomed, but market forces were at work even as the report was being written.

Private equity investments in Europe

By the late nineties the concept of 'private equity' investments – any form of equity investment made through a 'private placement', in which (in almost all cases) the company receiving the investment was not yet a public company – had crossed the Atlantic. These include a variety of high-risk 'alternative asset classes', such as start-up financing for informal 'angel' investments (wealthy individuals backing new business ideas) and traditional venture capital investments, later-stage financing, and financing for leveraged buyouts, and certain real estate investments. Sources of capital for such investments come from private equity investment funds or limited partnerships, investments undertaken directly by sophisticated investors, such as investment banks, and a variety of informal arrangements involving wealthy individuals.

According to the European Private Equity and Venture Capital Association (EVCA), 1997 and 1998 were years of explosive growth, with total private equity investment increasing 42 per cent to € 9.6 billion in 1997.[9] In 1998, investments increased 51 per cent to € 14.5 billion. The European private equity portfolio (at cost, net of divestments) was € 45.5 billion at the end of 1998. Since 1984, Europe's private equity industry has invested more than € 81.3 billion in 50,000 companies. In 1998, investors divested € 7.0 billion of private equity investments, mainly through mergers or acquisitions. However, approximately $3.7 billion of investments at cost were recovered through initial public offerings and € 1.5 billion (at cost) was written off.[10]

Based on a 1998 survey, the European Venture Capital Association reported that approximately 51 per cent of investments went to leveraged buyouts, 37.5 per cent to finance second- or later-stage investments, and only 11.4 per cent to start-ups and seed capital investments. The start-up investments, however, had increased by 60 per cent from the previous year, more than any of the other categories.

Sources of venture capital in Europe

In 1997, the EVCA published preliminary results of its first pan-European 'International Investment Benchmarks Report'. This was a pilot survey of about half of the 202 established private equity funds (managing € 14 billion) that were identified in 1996. Multi-country funds amounted to 6.1 billion, UK funds € 5.8 billion (the UK accounted for 106 of the funds identified),

4 • EQUITIES, MARKETS AND EXCHANGES

French funds €1.2 billion, and funds from Spain, Germany, Italy and the Netherlands each accounting for less than €250 million. In 1998, the European private equity market attracted approximately €20 billion in new capital for funds (compared with €7.9 billion in 1996). In 1997, deal value increased in the UK by 49 per cent to €4.4 billion, and in Germany by 85 per cent to €1.3 billion. In France, deal value rose 41 per cent to €1.3 billion.

Overall returns for European private equity investments were estimated in 1997 at 18.6 per cent since inception (based on cumulative returns net of management fees). Generalist private equity funds showed the best average returns (19.4 per cent) and early-stage investments the worst (5.7 per cent) in the EVCA survey, which covered investments made during 1996. Buyout investments, which attracted the bulk of investment over the survey period, returned an average of 17.6 per cent. Upper quartile performance was better for start-ups at 27.2 per cent, compared with all private equity investment returns of 29.1 per cent. For the three years ended 31 December 1996, however, an investment in a European stock index fund would have returned 12.5 per cent per annum.

Whereas European private equity investments can be clearly identified, the investors participating in them cannot. A number of investment funds have been organized by European investment managers, principally from the UK, but now also including multinational European-based financial institutions such as Deutsche Bank (with Morgan Grenfell and Bankers Trust), Credit Suisse First Boston, and UBS (now including Swiss Bank Corp., S.G. Warburg and Dillon Read). Some of these funds involve only the firm's proprietary investments. Most, however, are aimed at the investment clients, who are asked to pay high US-style fees (typically an annual management fee of 2.5 per cent and a 20 per cent carried interest in capital gains) for the opportunity to invest alongside sophisticated players in high-potential private equity investments.

Institutional investors in Europe, still cautious and not fully committed to the US idea of alternative investment classes, have not been strong participants in this market. So the fund managers have turned instead to their wealthy individual clients in the US and elsewhere, and to pension funds, endowments and foundations, which in 1997 had commitments to alternative investments of $91 billion. These US investors seek alternative investments to increase their overall risk-adjusted portfolio returns. Because these asset classes are not closely tied to stock market returns, they are able to contribute significant portfolio diversification. In 1997, leveraged buyouts and venture capital investments in the US accounted for about 72 per cent of all of such alternative investments.

International private equity investments, including investments in Asia and other areas outside Europe, are regarded as a separate category of alternative investments for US investors, and in 1997 this category was the fastest growing, increasing by 60 per cent to 9.3 per cent ($8.5 billion) of total commitments. Approximately 41 per cent ($4 billion) of this was invested in Western Europe. Thus US pension and other tax-free investors were contributing about a quarter of all new investments in European private equities.

The Americans were attracted to international venture investments because they believed the US market for alternative investments was getting too crowded, and there was 'too much money chasing too few good quality deals'.

During 1997 and 1998, the declining prospects in Asia and many emerging markets caused a shift in focus to emphasize Europe.[11] European fund managers rushed to the US to solicit new business, but the activity also attracted the attention of US fund managers. During 1998, a number of private equity specialists opened offices in Europe and began seeking investment opportunities in competition with US investment banks and other investors, such as GE Capital Corp., already established in the sector. Corporations also became significant investors in European private equities in 1997, accounting for about 11 per cent ($2.9 billion), an eight-fold increase over the previous year. In mid-1998, a $1.3 billion investment agreement was reached between American International Group, an insurance company, and the Blackstone Group, an alternative investment specialist, in which a significant portion of their joint investments would be in global private equities.

Start-ups and venture capital investments

Traditional US-style start-up financing is rare in Europe. Investors prefer more fully developed companies with a track record, or at least an investment in which some collateral is available, as in a buyout. Start-ups have been the province of large corporations and government-backed venture-investing enterprises such as 3i in the UK. By contrast, in the US most of the start-up financing for new ventures come from the entrepreneur, his friends and family, and from angels. The formal venture capital (VC) investor usually participates only at a later stage, unless the entrepreneur is someone well known to the firm and the idea is one the investors can easily envision.

In addition, many entrepreneurs decide to team up with large manufacturing corporations which may offer more attractive financial terms than VC investors and which hope to take over the company if it performs well. Microsoft, for example, invests in a large number of computer technology companies in order to keep track of developments and learn from them and to be able to acquire the best of the group if it wants to.

The VC market in the US has moved along the risk spectrum to favour investments in companies which are already functioning and need a modest sum to tide them over to the point where they can go public. Such investments can be profitable for the VC investors, since their money is tied up for only two or three years (instead of five to seven) and the probability of an IPO exit is higher than usual. These investors, however, are finding it increasingly difficult to attract the quality of deals they want because of the competition from so many new private equity investors, so they are beginning to look to Europe for opportunities.

Furthermore, Europe is trying hard to develop better support for smaller companies. High-tech investment (especially in information sciences and health care) opportunities in Germany and Britain are attracting start-up capital. In Germany, during 1996–7 start-up financings tripled and represented 15 per cent of private equity financing. In all of Europe combined, start-up financing represented about 7 per cent of private equity financing.

Leveraged buyouts

During the nineties, the principal form of risk capital investment by Europeans was the management buyout, which came in a variety of forms. Such investments in MBOs or other forms of corporate restructuring dominated the risk capital investment scene, especially once divestitures of businesses no longer considered 'core' became popular. In 1997, according to the EVCA, the number of buyouts increased 19 per cent to 464, with a value of €20 billion, almost twice the 1996 amount. A Salomon Smith Barney study put the number of deals and the volume of transactions in 1997 a bit higher, at approximately 500 transactions worth €36 billion. The 1998 total was 520 deals worth €38 billion, despite a sharp drop-off in the fourth quarter of 1998 while markets were recovering from shocks taken earlier in the year. About half the deals and the volume they accounted for were represented by management buyouts in the UK.[12]

US leveraged buyout specialists have been active investors in European deals, despite some disappointing results in the eighties when they were thought to have rushed into a new market without understanding it. Like other private equity investors, the US firms were looking for 'less efficient markets', as Joseph Rice of Clayton Dubilier, a US leveraged buyout firm, put it, where better returns could be made. These firms were thought to be sitting on as much as $100 billion of uninvested and unleveraged funds in late 1998. Several large funds, including KKR – which manages a $6 billion LBO fund in the US – promised to invest 20–30 per cent in European deals, and some managers are planning Europe-only funds.[13]

Buyouts exceed venture capital and later-stage equity investments for several reasons. They are largely financed with debt, and for those deals that qualify as creditworthy, banks and junk bond investors are willing to supply substantial amounts of financing. Buyouts have been taking place for more than 20 years, and for at least 15 years in Europe, and there is a track record for returns available to institutional investors. Buyout managers, originally housed in the UK, have spread out into continental Europe, looking for opportunities which they increasingly find with larger industrial concerns seeking to shed businesses that are no longer considered strategically important. Restructuring is popular on the continent, and corporate divestitures are fairly commonplace. Many of the early LBO professionals and fund managers have migrated, by choice or by merger, to other employers, which has spread the know-how around. Deutsche Bank, for example, is in the business by virtue of its acquisitions of Morgan Grenfell, Bankers Trust and Alex. Brown. In December 1998, Morgan Grenfell Private Equity announced a $657 million purchase of Coral Group, Britain's third largest chain of betting shops, which it hopes to take public in a few years. Even Japan's Nomura Securities has been an active investor in European deals, mainly in pubs and hotels.

For buyouts and other forms of private equity investments to develop fully, there has to be an active market for small company stock issues so that investments can be 'harvested' through initial public offerings of shares. In the US this function is largely performed by Nasdaq, a screen-traded electronic market for smaller companies established in 1971. In 1998, 5,500 companies with an aggregate market capitalization of $2,000 billion were listed on the Nasdaq market. This market hosted more than 250 initial public offerings during the year, more than 70 per cent of all IPOs in the US.

New stock markets for small European companies

Two new markets for dealing in small company securities have been established in the past few years. Easdaq, a Brussels-based pan-European version of Nasdaq, and Euro.NM, a network of European stock markets for growth companies.

Easdaq is the combined product of the European Venture Capital Association and the members of the European Association of Securities Dealers (EASD). EVCA established a need in Europe to furnish a marketplace for new growth companies and exit opportunities for investors in private equity investments, and EASD organized the securities dealers' community to create the market in 1994. The following year, 26 founding members formed the market in Belgium, with membership open to securities dealers from all countries. At the end of 1998, Easdaq had 140 members from 16 European countries and the US, and 38 listed companies with a market capitalization of about $14 billion.[14]

Following in Easdaq's tracks came the London Stock Exchange's effort to create a special market for smaller capitalization companies, the Alternative Investment Market, or AIM, which was established in 1996 as a successor to London's unlisted securities market. At the end of 1998, Easdaq represented 28 per cent of European small-company market capitalization and 13 per cent of turnover; AIM had 15 per cent of market capitalization and 7 per cent of turnover. All the rest of the Europe's small-company market capitalization and trading was accounted for by a rapidly growing, German-dominated new markets consortium called the Euro-NM.

In mid-1999 Euro.NM had joined eight member organizations (Frankfurt's Neuer Markt, the Nouveau Marché in Paris, the growth company markets of the Netherlands and Belgium, the Borsa Italiana, and smaller company markets in Sweden, Denmark and Switzerland). London's AIM was considered too big to join. The markets are still very small compared to their US counterpart, but they are expanding their listing and trading volume significantly. The Euro.NM grabbed the major share of European new growth company issues in 1998, and at 31 December 1998 the Euro.NM had 165 listings with a total market capitalization of $33 billion, before the markets from Italy, Sweden, Denmark and Switzerland were included.[15]

Other signs of change

The increased private equity investment activity of the late nineties appears to have more to it than simple bull market support. The volume of transactions, especially on the continent, appears to be delivering a message of encouragement to entrepreneurs and to companies attempting to restructure their activities by divesting peripheral operations. There has also been a developing market for family-owned businesses to sell out to financial entrepreneurs, who have traditionally been in short supply in Europe. In fact, the earliest LBOs in the US were transactions in which financial entrepreneurs invested in family-owned corporations that were neither suitable for a public offering nor were good candidates for sale to a larger corporation.

Government policies, at the national and the EU level, are becoming more favourable to financing entrepreneurial activities, and to removing perceived barriers to the development of a robust venture capital market. One of the principal barriers is the fragmentation of the markets for risky investments throughout Europe. The European Commission is stressing a pan-European approach to market building, which should be more effective in the environment of the common currency after 1999.

The new approach will rely on several interrelated features:

- the pan-European markets such as Easdaq and Euro.NM will be supported;
- various EU institutions are participating in efforts to encourage venture capital activity: the European Investment Fund is investing in venture capital deals, the European Commission is considering a risk-capital initiative, and the European Investment Bank has developed a European technology facility;
- efforts are under way to create an appropriate regulatory framework that will permit the sale of risky investment vehicles (including venture capital funds, buyout funds and other funds for illiquid instruments) throughout Europe;
- the regulatory framework protecting pension funds and insurance assets from investment in risky securities is being re-examined;
- complex taxation issues (taxes on capital gains, allowable deductions, taxation of stock options, etc.) are to be re-examined by the Commission in an effort to remove barriers to innovation and the development of risk capital pools.[16]

Moreover, the Commission promises efforts to encourage the formation of small and medium-sized business enterprises, to improve the human resources available for venture capital, and to address cultural barriers that impede increased venture investing. It is not clear what any of these mean, nor is it clear that changing such practices is the work of government. Market forces should contribute significantly to making these changes.

The most promising development for the future of European venture capital remains the huge aggregation of funds and talent being assembled by skilled US investors for application to Europe. Hundreds of billions of dollars may be available at the beginning of the 21st century for risky investments in Europe. Of course, the success of such investing will depend on the ability of the US investors to adapt their notions of opportunity and their operating practices to European conditions. This is something that skilled US financial firms have done in investment banking, trading, investment management and almost all other financial fields. The US, being more experienced and risk-oriented among global investors, will, as it has in other capital market areas, start with an advantage in the struggle for gaining market leadership. The US approach to all business efforts in Europe is to hire bright Europeans, train them, and then unleash them on the market. Many of these individuals later leave the firms that trained them to build their own businesses, independently or under the roof of a major European financial enterprise. The important thing is not who does the work to establish a risk capital market in Europe but that a market gets established. This is under way.

After 2000

The preceding sections described the real revolution that has been taking place in the equity markets in the EU since the early eighties. Virtually every aspect of the marketplace has been changed – in many cases radically – and operating practices and conditions resemble those of the US more closely than ever. Cross-border equity investments, including the sale of new issues, secondary market transactions and mergers and acquisitions, account for approximately 25 per cent of global investments in equities. Despite considerable progress in increasing equity market activity, Europe still lags well behind the US in equity market capitalization per unit of GDP – a proxy measure for equity market utilization as a function of overall economic activity (*see* Fig. 4.9). Nevertheless, for all the reasons given in the preceding section, Europe is catching up rapidly.

Cross-border funds flows

EMU should have the same effect of increasing intra-European cross-border funds flows in equities as it is having in debt securities. Home country preferences, dictated by some regulators and conservative investment managers, may disappear once the threat of foreign exchange losses is removed. Increasingly practitioners will become accustomed to thinking along Euro or EU rather than national boundaries. Initially this may be most pronounced among the 11 euro-zone countries.

Fig 4.9 Equity market capitalization (Market value in US$bn)

	US	Japan	Europe[1]
1985			
Market capitalization	$2,325	$910	$925
GDP	$3,947	$1,328	$2,813
Ratio	58.9%	68.5%	32.9%
1998			
Market capitalization	$13,451	$2,496	$7,656
GDP	$8,179	$3,797	$8,769
Ratio	164.5%	65.7%	87.3%
Compound annual growth (%)			
1985–98	8.2%	–0.3%	7.8%

[1]Europe = EU-15 plus Switzerland and Norway

*Sources: IFC, Emerging Stock Market Factbook for the market capitalization;
World Bank, 'World Development Report', for 1985 GDP; OECD for 1998 GDP*

Restructuring effects

A major factor influencing cross-border equity flows is the considerable restructuring of industrial Europe. The principal goal of this effort, echoing the goals of US corporations in the eighties, has been to improve the economic performance of corporations – their competitiveness and profitability for shareholders. These efforts to improve performance have already been applied to many European conglomerates and industrial manufacturing companies, state-owned enterprises and regulated industries such as banking and insurance.

Restructuring through mergers (Chapter 5) and privatizations (Chapter 6) involves cross-border funds flows, especially when the buyer and seller are from different countries, but also when the acquired company is partly owned by foreigners. Subsequent efforts to restructure that company may involve changes in management, product lines, asset holdings and capital structure. To the extent that restructuring companies are successful, they tend to attract a new set of shareholders, especially those capable of appreciating the effect of these steps on market valuation. Such new shareholders often include sophisticated foreign investors and fund managers. The restructuring effort may also attract the attention of market observers and strategists and research analysts, resulting in an upgrade in the public appeal of the company and further investment from outside the country. From 1985 to 1999, $2,300 billion in transaction value of mergers and corporate reorganizations was reported within Europe (and many additional transactions were not reported). Approximately 10–15 per cent of these were European cross-border deals.

Privatizations have had a similar effect on cross-border funds flows. Large issues have created enormous numbers of new stockholders and liquid secondary trading markets which especially appeal to large foreign investors. After privatization, the newly freed company may seek acquisitions, or divestitures, or direct investments in neighbouring countries. Because of the company's size relative to others in the country, its stock may become part of the national market index, causing passive index fund investors to buy and sell shares regularly.

Competitive effects

Increased competition for stock exchange business will continue to intensify the efforts by the respective firms to service investor and corporate clients. Continental European exchanges have begun to compete with London's SEAQ International for the institutional business in actively traded stocks in Germany, France and Switzerland. These efforts will increase the level and quantity of professional services available in the equity marketplace, bolster trading activity, and in general lead to closer integration of the intra-European market for equity securities.

Such efforts will, as they did in the US during the sixties and seventies, lead to growing participation in the markets by institutional investors, and more intense competition between those seeking to service them. It will also leave the institutions themselves increasingly exposed to the pressures of investment performance. This means the investors will have to attempt to improve their performance by insisting on high standards of professional skills that deliver exceptional returns. These investors will favour growing or restructuring companies and will be forced to give up historical investment ties to underperforming companies. They will no longer look for their investments on a national basis, but will look for the best companies in Europe in particular industries.

Continuing market integration

The euro-denominated stock markets have become the world's second largest in terms of market capitalization and trading volume. The EMU-15 plus Switzerland is even larger, representing market capitalization and trading volume levels that are 57 per cent and 44 per cent respectively of those of the

US, and 307 per cent and 603 per cent of Japan's. However, this new European market is distributed over 11 different stock markets that with few exceptions will continue to have a high national concentration. For those looking for currency diversification as well, there are also the markets in the UK, Sweden, Denmark, Norway and Switzerland.

As investors become more familiar with the euro, fungibility may be created between stocks from different countries that has not yet fully developed. There has been an increase in the correlation in stock market returns between the European countries, caused by growing European cross-border trade, portfolio investment and acquisitions, and this correlation may rise further as a result of the market integrating effects of EMU. This may be seen in one sense as a negative development that could reduce investment activity by some asset holders seeking diversification under the protocols of modern portfolio theory. On the other hand, to the extent that market liquidity increases as a result of growing fungibility, trading and investment activity on the part of large EMU institutions (especially pension funds) should also increase. As fungibility increases, markets begin to cohere as if they were under a single trading and regulatory regime such as that in the US. This could create substantial advantages to investors in the European market. Among these could be substantial increases in block-trading activity, indexing, investor services and discounts, shareholder activism that promotes improved corporate governance, and antifraud enforcement. Such advantages should contribute significantly to improvements in operating and competitive conditions of the European stock markets.

Competitive dynamics

Virtually all major European banks and brokerage firms offering equity market services have shared similar competitive constraints. Frequently, their equity market activities have been supplementary to their principal mission of providing retail banking or money management services. In addition, as prominent national players they have been expected to be service providers and market-makers for all brokerage clients and company shares in their home countries. Most have been tied to their national market so extensively that they have been unable to develop equal capabilities in neighbouring countries that, in aggregate, now constitute the new euro-enhanced marketplace for all Europe. Few banks have mastered the skills and managerial requirements common among leading equity houses in the US and the UK.

These are increasingly in demand in Europe as the new single currency equity market develops more competitive characteristics.

Such competitive constraints will severely limit the ability of most European banks and brokers to claim their 'natural' share of the new market. Competitive leadership will pass to those with the greatest capabilities and appetite for success from those who have long held dominant positions in the national markets by virtue of their size, relationships and traditional influence. The market is wide open for serious competitive effort from almost anyone.

Equity market services

The European equity market differs from the debt market in a few significant ways. It is much less a market in financial 'commodities' in which instruments vary by maturity and credit rating but otherwise are much the same and trade in large volumes at low spreads. Most fixed-income profits are made from market-making and proprietary position-taking. In equities, however, significant position-taking is not necessary if the firm's distribution capabilities are adequate. A firm's expertise in equities can lead to close relationships with corporate clients for whom the stock price, and who owns the shares, is of great importance. Such relationships can lead to fee-producing advisory roles in mergers and acquisitions and a variety of other investment banking services. In addition, the ability to operate in the equity market as an institutional broker on a large scale connects the firm with pension and mutual funds and other important institutional investors.

The full range of equity market services is extensive. Only a few firms are likely to be able to enter the market with such an array of products and activities. Most will develop a selection of activities that are appropriate for their capabilities.

Institutional equity services

Institutions vary from aggressive hedge funds seeking the newest information, the most clever trading ideas and the most aggressive execution services, to traditionally conservative pension funds and insurance companies that require a lot of hand-holding and follow-on service. Yet institutions on the whole are becoming increasingly knowledgeable about the markets and demand top-class research and execution services. Their view of the investment world is not confined to their own country, or just to the new

Europe, but to the world as a whole, and the services they require are becoming increasingly global in scope.

Retail equity services

These range from traditional private banking and discretionary money management services for 'high net worth' individuals and families, to traditional brokerage services, including new services for those seeking discount brokerage and Internet-based execution capabilities. Increasingly, securities firms are creating and/or distributing mass-market mutual funds to accommodate customer requirements and to provide the firms with products that can be sold in several countries.

Custody services

Many firms have begun to focus on custody services as a separate line of business related to the brokerage industry. Institutions and individuals need to retain custody of the securities they own somewhere. Having such securities presents the custodian with the opportunity to offer additional services to the client or to other firms. These services include holding cash balances as deposits (for which a below-market interest rate is paid enabling the custodian to earn a small but risk-free net interest profit), lending securities held to broker-dealers, collecting coupon payments on bearer securities, making transfers, handling foreign exchange and dealing with corporate events such as stock splits and mergers. Some firms add a variety of portfolio advisory and estate planning services for larger customers.

To provide such services, firms must have advanced computer systems to manage large volumes of transactions for relatively small transaction charges. In the US, a number of brokerage firms have entered into this business in competition with commercial banks that have traditionally provided the service. Custody services are also increasingly important to mutual fund management companies.

Reaching the pan-European market

Although many European firms have developed the beginnings of a line of products and services suitable for competing in the new European equity market, few have addressed the question of how to market these services to the entire pan-European marketplace.

Partly, this is because of the extreme labour intensity of the retail brokerage business, in which, despite modern technology and new forms of electronic communications, securities are sold, not bought. That is, salesmen must cover the accounts, offer ideas and press their clients for decisions. Passive marketing is not sufficient. Thus, to take a brokerage business that is successful in France, where a leading firm may still be relatively small by pan-European standards, and roll its business out into Germany and Italy would involve implementation problems beyond the capability of almost all such firms. These problems would include setting up numerous branch offices in leading cities, staffing and training employees for these offices, and developing products suitable for the preferences of German and Italian investors. The undertaking would involve capital outlays, management time and opportunity costs, and in the end might not work. Most firms have taken the view that if some other firm wants to do all the work to become a pan-European player, they will be happy to be acquired by them, but otherwise they are better off sticking to what they have always done – working in the local market.

Indeed, there is no equivalent among the European firms of a widespread retail services business such as Merrill Lynch. The large universal banks have emphasized management of client funds, and have developed little distribution beyond their discretionary clients. The large mutual fund managers use local brokers to distribute their products. The main investment banks restrict their business to institutional investors and high net worth customers. Merrill Lynch, of course, operates throughout Europe and offers a variety of retail brokerage, mutual fund, money management and custodial services to its many clients. Even its US counterparts have so far made little effort to offer retail services in the pan-European market, and will take years to develop them should they decide to do so, in some cases no doubt through local strategic alliances.

Best practices and strategic models for the equity business

Merrill Lynch's approach is a combination of steady, gradual progress towards a strategic vision of pan-European market dominance, and quick-moving opportunism. The former is illustrated by Merrill's efforts to develop its present array of 25 offices in 15 European countries that began in the early sixties. The latter is shown by its moves to acquire Mercury Asset Management, which manages pension funds and mutual funds, and Smith New Court, a major UK trading house. Merrill's retail prominence is balanced by its leadership in the wholesale finance business, one of the few firms in the world to achieve both. It has the managerial capacity to execute plans that would embarrass other firms, plans such as rapidly rolling out its US expertise into an emerging global marketplace (with much importance attached to Europe) for all its financial services – retail and wholesale.

Other US firms are making significant efforts to transfer their skill base into Europe to gain a prominent share of the market. Mostly these efforts have been focused on the wholesale market – block trading, new issues (especially large privatization issues) and asset management services. Morgan Stanley, Goldman Sachs and Citigroup's Salomon Smith Barney have gained some distinction in these areas, but two of these firms have changed themselves through bold acquisition strategies. Morgan Stanley, now part of the Morgan Stanley Dean Witter group, will emphasize retail market activities to a greater extent than before. Salomon Brothers, having first merged with Smith Barney, the US's second largest retail broker, and then with global retail banking giant Citicorp, represents a huge, new type of potential competitor – one that is capable of combining broad retail brokerage, consumer banking services and investment banking in one entity.

These US market development efforts have been effective in putting their businesses into all parts of Europe. In 1999, for example, US firms held the top three positions among bookrunners for international equity issues, accounting between them for 43.1 per cent of the market (*see* Fig. 4.10).

Fig 4.10 International equity top 10 bookrunners (ranked by amount 1 January to 12 December 1999)

Rank	Managing bank	Proceeds ($m)	%	No. of deals	Fees ($m)
1	Morgan Stanley Dean Witter	24,923.5	18.0	89	701.7
2	Goldman Sachs	17,695.7	12.8	89	624.0
3	Merrill Lynch	17,089.1	12.3	121	725.4
4	Crédit Suisse First Boston	8,110.6	5.9	75	228.5
5	Warburg Dillon Read	7,318.8	5.3	49	154.8
6	JP Morgan	6,615.0	4.8	17	188.5
7	Deutsche Banc Alex. Brown	6,573.2	4.7	58	105.4
8	Lehman Brothers	5,479.1	4.0	51	144.3
9	Group Salomon Smith Barney	5,132.0	3.7	40	194.5
10	ABN Amro	4,496.5	3.3	37	55.8

Source: IFR Securities Data, 12 December 1999

Other strategic approaches depend on association with insurance firms, which also have retail sales forces and pan-European distribution, and are substantial investors in all financial products. The Crédit Suisse Group, combining the investment banking skills of CS First Boston with the private banking business of Crédit Suisse and the significant insurance market share of Winterthur, is one example of a potentially powerful, pan-European 'Alfinanz' group in formation. ING and its Dutch insurance counterpart Ahold are two others. The French group AXA, combining large European insurance interests with those of the Equitable Group in the US, appears to be another potential European competitor approaching the retail market from the insurance end. The Equitable Group owns a controlling interest in US investment bank Donaldson, Lufkin & Jenrette (DJL) and money manager Alliance Capital Management.

Another approach to this market is through the private banking sector, as UBS perhaps best demonstrates. This bank, which combined two of the three leading Swiss banks, dominates global private banking, with assets under management in 1998 of nearly $1,000 billion. The bank also owns UBS-Brinson, a US fund manager with a significant institutional market share, and the Warburg Dillon Read investment bank. The challenge to this bank, which it shares with Citigroup, will be to manage the transition into one effective competitive force without stumbling over the managerial problems associated with integration of different firms into a single one, and controlling effectively operations of such a large scale.

For a different type of model, many European firms of lesser size or ambition than those mentioned might prefer to consider the history of an unusual US firm that created a successful place for itself in the equities market without relying on acquisitions to do so. DLJ was organized in the early sixties by three young men interested in tapping into the rapidly developing institutional equities market. As in Europe today, the pension and mutual fund sectors were emerging for the first time to become the central focal point of the market for equities. This market required new services, especially, the DLJ founders thought, high-quality investment research. The firm was organized to supply such research, in exchange for brokerage orders, and quickly developed a name for itself because few other firms were making similar efforts at the time. Later, DLJ decided to found a pension fund manager, Alliance Capital, which subsequently developed an equally strong business in mutual funds. DLJ also established an investment banking business, but fearing competition from the major firms serving the country's largest companies, it focused instead on middle-sized companies seeking initial public offerings, venture capital financing, and mergers and acquisitions. It also set up investment funds specializing in smaller growth companies, which it marketed successfully to institutional clients. DLJ directed all its energies into the sectors it selected for itself – ones that its skills and expertise could service effectively – and built new businesses to fit into and complement the original business.

DLJ was sold to the Equitable in 1985, and a controlling interest in the Equitable was sold to AXA in 1992. The firm went public again in 1995, and in 1999 had a market capitalization of $5.5 billion. It never tried to establish a leading market share for any reason other than to make money for its shareholders. It avoided sectors of the market in which it felt its competitive capabilities were limited. It relied on its ability to attract the talent necessary to conceive new businesses and to create interrelated services that others were not providing. It was a success in 'going it alone' and building its business from within.

In many ways the DLJ example is a better model for most European banks seeking a role in the new market for equities in Europe without giving up control of their future than that of the firms that have created large enterprises by merger. But the new pan-European market is still being formed, and there is room for many different strategic efforts.

NOTES

[1] New York Stock Exchange Fact Books.

[2] Portions of the text for this chapter are taken from Chapter 11, 'International Equity Securities' in Smith and Walter's *Global Banking*, Oxford University Press, 1997.

[3] InterSec Research Corp., unpublished memorandum to clients, 24 April 1998.

[4] Ibid.

[5] *Investment Dealers' Digest*, 10 November 1997.

[6] Data regarding market capitalization and value of shares traded are from *Securities Industry Fact Book 1998*.

[7] 'Too many trading places', *The Economist*, 19 June 1993.

[8] Ibid.

[9] The European Private Equity and Venture Capital Association was formed in 1983 by 43 founding members. In 1997 it had 410 members from 30 countries.

[10] Jury, Jennifer (1998) 'European private equity sees boom in 1997', *IAC Industry Express*, Securities Data Publishing, 22 June 1998.

[11] Report on Alternative Investing, Goldman, Sachs & Co. and Frank Russell Capital, Inc., November 1997.

[12] Paschelles, Mitchell (1998) 'US buyout firms search for deals in Europe', *The Wall Street Journal*, 30 December. Smy, Lucy (1998) 'MBO market falls sharply in final quarter', *Financial Times*, 3 December.

[13] Pachelles, op. cit.

[14] http://www.easd.com/easd.htm

[15] Boland, Vincent (1998) 'Three more countries to join Euro.NM', *Financial Times*, 18 December.

[16] Commission of the European Communities, 'Risk capital, a key to job creation in the European Union', April 1998.

Mergers and acquisitions

The decision in 1985 to pursue the path towards the single market caused many changes in the structure, organization and business strategies of European corporations. If the single market was to occur, and the industrial globalization that precipitated it was to continue, European corporations with more than a local or regional business would have to rethink their futures in the light of this significant regulatory change. Should they expand into other parts of Europe, now so accessible, to increase market share? Or should they consolidate with a local competitor to create a more formidable presence in their traditional market that could fight off incursions into their territory? On the other hand, should they assume that energy and funds expended in this direction would be a waste – the benefits of the single market not being worth the investment – and the company's time and effort would be better spent just sticking to its traditional business?

Growing competitive pressures were also a reason to consider strategy shifts. Should a company develop a stronger North American or Asian base to protect itself from the competitive and technological exertions of the US and Japan, or to capitalize on opportunities available in those markets but not at home? In the US during the eighties, corporations responded to market pressures to improve their competitive positions and returns to shareholders by a large-scale immersion in restructuring. This was in part a code word for an involuntary change of management, initiated by other corporations or takeover specialists that promised shareholders improved results (or a significant cash premium to buy them out). Restructuring was also, in part, a code word for internal reform initiated by existing management, possibly to forestall a takeover, in order to achieve the same improved results for shareholders. In the US the medium for effecting such changes is the 'market for corporate control' or the merger and acquisition market. This market, like the mergers market in the UK, is open, easily accessed and regulated with the objective of providing a level playing field for all participants, 'raiders' as well as 'entrenched management' groups.

Merger booms

During the eighties, more than $1,500 billion of mergers or other corporate recombinations took place in the US. These involved more than 40,000 companies, and constituted one of four merger 'booms' during the 20th century. (After a lull at the end of the eighties and in the early nineties, the boom has continued, so there has either been one 20-year boom from 1980–2000 or two ten-year booms; it's the reader's choice.) Previous US merger booms in the 1900s, the twenties and the sixties enabled the US corporate sector to respond rapidly to changes in industrial economics, technology and finance throughout the century. Thus public companies were about as efficient as they could be, according to standards of the times, in terms of returns to shareholders and other performance criteria.

Many observers note that this continuous 'marking to market' of the corporate sector provides the US with a comparative advantage in competing with companies from other countries. Others disagree, regretting the 'short-term' strategic views of US companies and lamenting that takeover pressure clouds their vision and prevents companies from making suitable long-term investments to assure competitive performance. This view is generally advanced by supporters of German and Japanese companies, which have been immune to challenges for control due to the governance structure of their corporations. It was more loudly expressed at the beginning of the nineties than at the end when US companies appeared to be leading the world in productivity, market share, technological development and on returns to shareholders. Systems of corporate governance and control are further discussed in Chapter 7.

The need to consider the competitive performance of individual European countries, and whether they would be better off joined together into a more competitive and open single marketplace, drew attention to the competitive characteristics of European corporations. Many corporate executives in Europe came to believe that the developments offered opportunities not only to improve their company's global or regional strategic positions, but also to improve their performance. They believed that those succeeding in making the opportunities work for the company would be entitled to great rewards, and the time to get started was early on, when other companies were still unprepared.

European mergers before 2000

Thus the first European merger boom began in the late eighties, and it continues today. After all, Europe had never had such a boom and the forest was heavy with corporate 'underbrush', or targets for restructuring that needed to be cleared away.

By 1999, the reported value of all global merger and acquisitions transactions was more than $1,600 billion. Half of this was accounted for by transactions within the US, still the world's most prolific merger market. But the other half represented transactions by non-US corporations: US cross-border deals amounted to $303 billion, and transactions entirely outside the US totalled $867 billion, almost all of which were transactions involving European companies. By comparison, in 1989, all European transactions, including cross-border deals, were $204 billion. It is worth noting that US domestic merger volume had never exceeded $500 billion before 1998.

The structure of international M&A deal flows

Between 1985 and 1999 the pattern of worldwide M&A activity – broadly defined to include mergers, acquisitions, tender offers, purchases of stakes, divestitures and leveraged buy-outs – changed considerably. Transactions entirely within the US peaked in 1988, then declined sharply to a level of one-third the peak volume just five years later. US cross-border transactions, and transactions entirely outside the US also declined after 1989 and 1990 respectively, but much less rapidly. Following 1993, however, the US and the world markets recovered and began rising steadily to reach the 1999 level of $1,689.6 billion of completed transactions.[1]

The action moves to Europe

Figure 5.1 shows combined M&A activities on a worldwide basis for the period 1985–99, when approximately 81,500 transactions with a market value of $9,258 billion were completed. For another 87,000 transactions, no pricing information was reported. Of the valued transactions, approximately 45 per cent were transactions between US companies. Nearly $3,638 billion, or 39 per cent, were transactions entirely outside the US, i.e. in which only non-US companies (or non-US subsidiaries of US companies) were involved, and $1,397 billion, or 15 per cent, were cross-border transactions in which US parent companies acted as buyers and sellers with non-US counterparts.

Fig 5.1 Volume of completed international merger and corporate transactions, US 1985–99

Year	Domestic US		Cross-border						Outside US		Global total	
			Buyer US		Seller US		Total cross-border					
	No.	$m	No.	$m	No.	$m	No.	$m	No.	$m	No.	$m
1985	815 (88)*	192,294	30 (79)	4,034	99 (122)	11,898	129 (201)	15,932	166 (124)	24,842	1,110 (413)	233,068
1986	1,205 (1,369)	200,913	46 (78)	2,672	212 (177)	36,658	258 (255)	39,331	347 (307)	54,597	1,810 (1,931)	294,841
1987	1,357 (1,409)	203,936	62 (142)	8,551	227 (173)	41,662	289 (315)	50,213	797 (560)	96,177	2,443 (2,284)	350,326
1988	1,642 (1,370)	293,194	91 (164)	7,309	324 (226)	70,817	415 (390)	77,856	1,664 (1,015)	140,331	3,721 (2,775)	511,381
1989	2,005 (1,969)	250,096	157 (250)	25,136	456 (293)	60,449	613 (543)	85,585	2,048 (1,817)	227,824	4,666 (4,329)	563,505
1990	1,741 (2,448)	124,874	154 (267)	16,604	453 (378)	56,350	607 (645)	72,954	2,218 (1,936)	236,187	4,566 (5,029)	434,016
1991	1,795 (2,050)	108,464	209 (327)	13,376	318 (266)	27,159	527 (593)	40,535	2,564 (3,894)	202,397	4,886 (6,537)	351,396
1992	2,173 (2,035)	119,264	249 (310)	14,991	263 (158)	18,513	512 (468)	33,505	2,348 (3,339)	163,769	5,033 (5,842)	316,539
1993	2,011 (1,855)	101,068	212 (366)	13,696	224 (134)	21,215	436 (500)	34,911	2,448 (2,989)	125,755	4,895 (5,344)	261,734
1994	2,898 (2,319)	199,784	284 (455)	19,089	319 (192)	39,299	603 (647)	58,388	2,867 (3,347)	148,738	6,368 (6,313)	406,910
1995	2,822 (3,002)	218,545	370 (578)	38,111	328 (223)	68,391	698 (801)	106,502	3,235 (4,054)	227,762	6,755 (7,857)	552,808
1996	3,495 (3,324)	330,667	409 (634)	34,354	350 (265)	50,111	759 (899)	84,465	3,395 (3,681)	298,607	7,649 (7,904)	713,739
1997	3,601 (3,573)	448,288	475 (599)	54,909	423 (272)	47,034	898 (871)	101,943	3,871 (3,069)	388,311	8,371 (7,513)	978,542
1998	3,669 (4,166)	801,832	656 (863)	111,303	433 (339)	180,850	1,089 (1,202)	292,153	4,697 (4,824)	505,623	9,455 (10,192)	1,599,609
1999	3,072 (4,114)	588,728	569 (897)	104,722	536 (448)	198,687	1,105 (1,345)	303,409	5,578 (7,428)	797,512	9,755 (12,887)	1,689,649
Totals	**34,301 (35,091)**	**4,181,946**	**3,973 (6,009)**	**468,588**	**4,965 (3,666)**	**929,093**	**8,938 (9,675)**	**1,397,681**	**38,243 (42,384)**	**3,638,432**	**81,483 (87,150)**	**9,258,060**

Source: Thomson Financial Securities Data Company.

* Numbers in brackets denote additional deals for which no values were available.

The predominance of US to US transactions obscures important changes abroad. Whereas the value of US domestic transactions in 1999 was $589, down from a high of $802 billion in 1998, about four times the volume of such transactions in 1985, US cross-border transactions have grown much more rapidly. Transactions in which US corporations were sellers to non-US buyers were more than 16 times larger in 1999 than in 1985. US buyer transactions were 26 times in 1999 what they were in 1985. Deals completed outside the US grew by a factor of 32 between 1985 and 1999. Similarly, these transactions declined less than domestic US transactions during the downturn period 1989–95.

Industry sectors involved

The completed acquisitions data have also been broken down by Standard Industrial Classification (SIC) codes identifying the primary business of firms on both sides of each transaction. Figures 5.2 and 5.3 show European M&A deals from 1985 to 1999 valued at $50 million or more by major industry category of the firm undertaking the transaction (Fig. 5.2) and of the target (Fig. 5.3). Industries most heavily involved in European M&A transactions included banks and financial services, telecommunications, electric, gas and water distribution, and food products.

Fig 5.2 Rankings of industry groups of US and European buyers 1985–99

Acquiring industry	US acquirer			European acquirer		
	Rank	Rank value ($m)	No. of deals	Rank	Rank value ($m)	No. of deals
Advertising Services	50	11,911.3	645	47	8022.0	678
Aerospace and Aircraft	19	96,384.3	409	34	23,037.1	222
Agriculture, Forestry and Fishing	51	8,706.1	333	45	9,249.3	355
Air Transportation and Shipping	43	31,594.7	323	36	19,540.8	369
Amusement and Recreation Services	41	35,041.7	508	48	7,431.0	328
Business Services	8	174,710.3	7,745	13	76,694.3	4,496
Chemicals and Allied Products	9	156,004.4	1,636	4	216,609.1	1,929
Commercial Banks, Bank Holding Companies	2	589,524.5	5,369	2	407,257.0	3,537
Communications Equipment	24	72,295.6	920	19	42,229.0	565
Computer and Office Equipment	18	98,294.8	1,459	49	5,919.8	401
Construction Firms	48	17,213.6	797	31	23,316.4	1,620
Credit Institutions	16	101,645.1	728	39	17,145.9	384
Drugs	11	130,630.9	1,246	10	111,603.5	912
Educational Services	60	1,384.4	137	58	560.5	67
Electric, Gas and Water Distribution	6	240,137.6	1,243	6	178,860.7	1,142
Electronic and Electrical Equipment	10	133,070.2	2,284	14	72,808.0	1,855
Food and Kindred Products	12	120,310.0	1,740	8	159,836.7	3,404
Health Services	15	103,320.6	3,090	51	4,522.9	377
Holding Companies, Except Banks	53	4,851.0	58	37	19,529.3	368
Hotels and Casinos	31	59,795.8	658	32	23,253.8	646
Insurance	5	300,646.1	2,516	3	285,843.0	2,273
Investment & Commodity Firms, Dealers, Exchanges	1	1,306,774.4	16,647	1	638,607.8	14,389
Leather and Leather Products	56	3,241.8	99	24	30,753.1	241
Legal Services	61	259.1	87	61	1.4	163
Machinery	17	99,435.6	2,153	22	37,832.3	2,389
Measuring, Medical, Photo Equipment; Clocks	13	112,336.4	2,792	21	38,253.7	1,015
Metal and Metal Products	20	84,043.4	1,835	9	111,802.7	2,655
Mining	33	48,953.0	633	23	32,287.7	439
Miscellaneous Manufacturing	36	46,399.1	564	53	3,157.0	370
Miscellaneous Retail Trade	39	42,326.7	1,504	26	28,203.2	883
Miscellaneous Services	45	22,948.9	66	59	126.3	48
Motion Picture Production and Distribution	30	59,804.7	602	46	8,511.2	291
Oil and Gas; Petroleum Refining	4	329,961.0	2,864	7	164,861.7	1,129
Other Financial	59	1,452.7	102	35	20,594.5	60
Paper and Allied Products	22	79,389.5	682	17	48,122.1	975
Personal Services	52	6,858.9	235	56	1,780.0	145
Prepackaged Software	23	72,617.3	2,212	44	10,471.1	920
Printing, Publishing and Allied Services	21	82,902.2	2,223	12	83,919.4	2,483
Public Administration	58	1,553.2	74	43	11,792.5	227
Radio and Television Broadcasting Stations	7	238,942.1	1,774	40	16,461.1	473
Real Estate; Mortgage Bankers and Brokers	38	43,067.7	1,324	16	64,045.3	1,619
Repair Services	49	13,907.7	263	55	1,920.4	209

Fig 5.2 *cont.*

Acquiring industry	US acquirer			European acquirer		
	Rank	*Rank value ($m)*	*No. of deals*	*Rank*	*Rank value ($m)*	*No. of deals*
Retail Trade-Eating and Drinking Places	47	20,166.7	647	30	23,480.7	553
Retail Trade-Food Stores	32	57,472.5	295	20	38,312.0	581
Retail Trade-General Merchandise and Apparel	26	68,407.0	450	33	23,166.5	489
Retail Trade-Home Furnishings	55	3,956.6	216	52	3,917.7	202
Rubber and Miscellaneous Plastic Products	46	20,220.3	769	29	25,018.0	931
Sanitary Services	28	62,248.8	862	50	4,875.4	300
Savings and Loans, Mutual Savings Banks	25	69,229.4	1,971	54	2,078.6	10
Soaps, Cosmetics and Personal-Care Products	37	43,255.3	377	38	19,447.2	367
Social Services	57	1,815.8	95	60	67.4	13
Stone, Clay, Glass and Concrete Products	40	40,255.5	601	15	70,041.7	1,635
Telecommunications	3	518,481.3	1,826	5	196,909.2	764
Textile and Apparel Products	42	32,606.1	793	42	14,644.7	1,208
Tobacco Products	34	48,503.3	74	27	28,101.7	99
Transportation and Shipping (except air)	29	60,076.5	1,185	18	47,142.9	2,287
Transportation Equipment	14	110,917.4	988	11	94,788.0	1,155
Unknown	54	4,593.0	230	57	580.8	108
Wholesale Trade-Durable Goods	35	48,288.8	2,269	28	25,885.6	2,237
Wholesale Trade-Nondurable Goods	27	62,769.5	1,571	25	30,453.0	1,554
Wood Products, Furniture and Fixtures	44	30,053.8	640	41	15,253.8	627
Industry totals		**6,487,965.6**	**88,438**		**3,730,938.9**	**72,171**

Source: Thomson Financial Securities Data Company

Fig 5.3 Rankings of industry groups of US and European sellers 1985–99

Target industry	US target			European target		
	Rank	Rank value ($m)	No. of deals	Rank	Rank value ($m)	No. of deals
Commercial Banks, Bank Holding Companies	1	597,731.6	4,196	1	386,078.0	2,352
Telecommunications	2	535,203.1	1,738	3	205,126.1	806
Radio and Television Broadcasting Stations	3	416,196.9	2,113	19	49,769.6	891
Oil and Gas; Petroleum Refining	4	400,631.4	3,098	8	121,547.2	1,183
Business Services	5	354,502.1	9,429	11	96,031.9	6,676
Insurance	6	264,314.4	2,438	2	232,825.2	1,917
Investment & Commodity Firms, Dealers, Exchanges	7	196,069.8	2,747	9	120,370.9	3,713
Electric, Gas and Water Distribution	8	194,253.7	968	4	186,898.0	1,030
Chemicals and Allied Products	9	186,327.7	1,668	7	126,215.9	1,941
Measuring, Medical, Photo Equipment; Clocks	10	182,111.4	3,051	29	36,735.8	1,469
Food and Kindred Products	11	173,492.4	1,863	5	174,580.2	3,986
Health Services	12	169,154.9	3,499	49	9,817.9	522
Electronic and Electrical Equipment	13	167,139.5	2,510	12	83,194.3	2,204
Drugs	14	163,815.8	1,292	6	131,702.0	948
Real Estate; Mortgage Bankers and Brokers	15	150,234.3	3,283	10	117,146.1	2,637
Hotels and Casinos	16	141,813.7	1,312	23	41,809.9	1,086
Credit Institutions	17	136,560.9	752	37	20,545.9	382
Transportation Equipment	18	134,597.3	929	14	75,970.4	1,538
Machinery	19	133,966.7	2,389	18	52,751.8	3,132
Communications Equipment	20	131,385.4	1,070	30	32,329.6	680
Printing, Publishing and Allied Services	21	125,551.5	2,338	17	63,507.5	2,806
Computer and Office Equipment	22	124,514.9	1,394	50	9,567.7	529
Metal and Metal Products	23	106,970.7	2,372	13	83,039.0	3,127
Motion Picture Production and Distribution	24	106,152.4	721	51	8,257.9	423
Prepackaged Software	25	104,390.6	3,029	40	15,678.7	1,469
Savings and Loans, Mutual Savings Banks	26	103,408.0	2,968	57	540.8	10
Transportation and Shipping (except air)	27	102,533.0	1,494	16	64,644.8	3,065
Retail Trade-General Merchandise and Apparel	28	99,380.8	635	26	39,380.7	592
Retail Trade-Food Stores	29	91,464.4	546	22	43,718.1	687
Paper and Allied Products	30	91,019.7	648	15	67,258.4	1,170
Miscellaneous Retail Trade	31	79,009.6	2,027	28	37,201.6	1,549
Wholesale Trade-Nondurable Goods	32	76,154.8	1,731	31	31,400.1	2,087
Aerospace and Aircraft	33	72,396.0	356	42	15,130.1	268
Mining	34	71,540.4	760	35	27,237.8	533
Wholesale Trade-Durable Goods	35	60,601.7	3,024	25	41,485.9	3,404
Retail Trade-Eating and Drinking Places	36	56,904.2	935	24	41,756.9	813
Textile and Apparel Products	37	56,265.2	1,057	36	24,052.4	1,748
Stone, Clay, Glass and Concrete Products	38	55,349.1	643	20	46,851.8	1,534
Rubber and Miscellaneous Plastic Products	39	54,893.9	1,057	34	27,329.6	1,249

Fig 5.3 *cont.*

	US target			European target		
Target industry	*Rank*	*Rank value ($m)*	*No. of deals*	*Rank*	*Rank value ($m)*	*No. of deals*
Sanitary Services	40	53,661.2	825	44	11,959.7	398
Tobacco Products	41	50,108.2	54	27	38,106.3	87
Air Transportation and Shipping	42	43,801.1	399	33	27,505.0	549
Soaps, Cosmetics and Personal-Care Products	43	38,898.2	400	38	19,508.2	406
Repair Services	44	33,432.1	460	46	10,617.1	498
Amusement and Recreation Services	45	32,371.7	778	39	19,321.5	647
Wood Products, Furniture and Fixtures	46	30,222.3	747	41	15,417.9	986
Advertising Services	47	28,532.7	582	47	10,593.4	740
Agriculture, Forestry and Fishing	48	23,008.4	453	43	12,605.1	545
Miscellaneous Manufacturing	49	22,158.8	694	45	10,811.0	650
Construction Firms	50	21,214.2	1,074	21	46,095.1	2,015
Retail Trade-Home Furnishings	51	12,248.0	423	48	10,396.5	364
Personal Services	52	6,431.6	236	52	8,221.8	182
Leather and Leather Products	53	6,038.4	145	53	7,720.2	263
Holding Companies, Except Banks	54	4,448.2	34	32	31,199.4	178
Miscellaneous Services	55	4,424.1	71	59	358.1	65
Other Financial	56	4,264.5	143	55	3,601.7	53
Social Services	57	3,067.3	153	60	321.4	36
Educational Services	58	2,640.4	199	56	647.6	129
Public Administration	59	2,041.0	69	54	6,346.6	100
Unknown	60	555.6	63	58	401.5	35
Legal Services	61	380.2	105	62	57.2	159
Nonclassifiable Establishments	62	44.0	2	61	78.0	17
Industry totals		**6,891,995.9**	**86,189**		**3,281,376.4**	**75,258**

Source: Thomson Financial Securities Data Company

Figure 5.4 shows that the industry segments so far subject to restructuring through M&A transactions in the EU correlate significantly with those involved in M&A activity in the US during the same period. This is not surprising as the underlying economic forces affected these newly globalized industries in similar ways on both sides of the Atlantic.

Fig 5.4 Spearman rank correlation of US and European industries participating in M&A transactions[1]

		Buyer's industry	Seller's industry
	r	0.7803	0.7719
No. of deals	N	(62)	(62)
	p (b)	0.0000	0.0000
	r	0.6818	0.7862
$ volume	N	(62)	(62)
	p (b)	0.0000	0.0000

(a) Correlations are based on the number of transactions and the dollar volume of US and European industry groups.
(b) One-tailed significance.

European merger premiums

Whereas merger premiums (the percentage premium that the merger price represents relative to the last sale price before the merger announcement) of transactions in the US have been declining since 1989, due mainly to a shift from cash to stock deals, European merger premiums have been increasing slightly. In 1998, the median premium paid on a European transaction was 31 per cent (up from 25 per cent in 1996) and on hostile or contested deals the premium was in the 46–50 per cent range. In the US in 1998, the median premium was 28 per cent (also 28 per cent in 1996), down from 39 per cent in 1992. The variation in premiums within the wide European market, from the UK to Italy to Sweden, not all of which are equally developed merger marketplaces, mainly explains the higher European median.[2]

Cross-border transactions

During the period 1985–99, cross-border transactions accounted for 25 per cent of M&A transactions involving US corporations, and 66 per cent of these deals were inward investments, most of which involved European buyers. Clearly, European corporations were not interested only in the EU internal market. For many years they had recognized the importance of deploying more of their business activities into the US, where the domestic economy had been expanding rapidly, the dollar had declined sharply after 1985, and fears of possible protectionism interrupting market access through imports were rising. During the eighties, European and Japanese companies began to increase direct investment in the US, which was then the world's largest market for most industrial and consumer products. In this respect, European corporations were acting in a manner similar to that of US companies during the fifties and sixties when a high level of *de novo* investment and acquisition took place in Europe to shore up US market positions and competitive capabilities there. US companies remain the largest direct investors in other countries, and maintain about 25 per cent of their manufacturing capability outside the US.

US cross-border transactions have included numerous large transactions in which European corporations acquired control of an important US corporation. Among these were Daimler-Benz's $40 billion merger with Chrysler Corp., announced in May 1998, and British Petroleum's $48 billion deal with Amoco a few months later, which in turn was followed by BP's attempted acquisition of Atlantic Richfield announced in 1999.

On other occasions, European corporations acquired the outstanding minority interests in their majority-owned US subsidiaries. In 1970, British Petroleum exchanged certain Alaskan oil production interests for an increasing share interest in the Standard Oil Company (Sohio), which reached 53 per cent in 1978. In 1987, BP decided to acquire the remaining 47 per cent through a $7.9 billion tender offer to shareholders. Similar acquisitions of minority interests have been undertaken by Royal Dutch Shell and N.V. Philips Gloeilampenfabrieken, the large Dutch electronics concern. The UK's Midland Bank acquired the 43 per cent interest in Crocker National Bank that it did not own preparatory to selling the whole of Crocker to Wells Fargo in 1986. In addition, of course, many smaller acquisitions took place, many of which involved US companies that were for sale and looked with their advisers to international names among possible buyers.

There were also divestitures of companies that no longer suited their foreign owners. Imperial Group, a UK tobacco company, which acquired Howard Johnson's in 1980, sold it in 1985. BAT Industries, another large UK tobacco, retailing and insurance concern, acquired Gimbels department stores in 1973, and sold it in 1986. Later, under attack from corporate raider Sir James Goldsmith, BAT sold the rest of its retailing businesses, to focus only on tobacco and insurance. In 1998, BAT sold its insurance businesses to Zurich Insurance. The international aspects of the merger and acquisition business thus involve both the buying and selling of companies, big and small.

Intra-European transactions

Of the transactions entirely outside the US between 1985 and 1999, approximately 62 per cent were intra-European deals, of which transactions entirely within the UK (the largest component of intra-European deals) accounted for about 30 per cent. European corporations have been active on three fronts – in domestic mergers and consolidations, intra-European cross-border transactions, and transactions in the US. Figure 5.5 shows the value of completed international merger and corporate transactions for Europe during 1985–99. Figure 5.6 shows the volume of completed Intra-European M&A transactions by country. This illustrates the concentration of activity within domestic markets in the UK, France and Italy, the countries with the most open (or least closed) M&A markets. It also shows the rising importance of European cross-border transactions, especially by German companies. Some of Europe's largest deals in the late nineties were attempts by large industrial and financial concerns to grow outside their home European markets. Such deals included those attempted by Vodaphone-Airtouch (Fa Mannesmann), Deutsche Telecom (for Telecom Italia), Zeneca Group (AB Astra) and Hoechst (for Rhone Poulenc Life Sciences).

The remainder of the non-US transactions have been, in descending order of transaction value, intra-Canadian, intra-Australian and intra-Asian (including a comparatively small but growing activity in Japan). In aggregate, transactions not involving US corporations grew to approximately 58 per cent of the worldwide total in 1991, up from about 11 per cent in 1985, before dropping back to 32 per cent of the worldwide total in 1998 then rising again to 47 per cent in 1999. Non-US and US cross-border transactions, i.e. international transactions from the point of view of US investment bankers, grew from 17 per cent of worldwide transactions in 1985 to 65 per cent in 1999.

Characteristics of European M&A transactions

Several broad economic and political forces accelerated European merger transactions during the nineties. These included globalization effects on industrial competitive structures, integration of financial markets and the free flow of capital across borders, aggressive privatization policies, and the movement towards the single European market and, ultimately, EMU. More recently, the collapse of the communist powers in Eastern Europe and the effort to bring these countries into a general European capitalistic society, as well as a perverse, low-growth, high-unemployment economic environment throughout Europe, has created great pressures for improved competitive performance and efficiency. Clearly these forces, in aggregate, have become extremely powerful; perhaps so powerful as to be irresistible, by even the long entrenched practices and attitudes about corporate control and governance that have existed in Europe for generations.

Fig. 5.5 Value of completed international merger and corporate transactions, Europe 1985–99

Year	Intra-Europe No.	Intra-Europe $m	Cross-border European buyer No.	European buyer $m	European seller No.	European seller $m	Total cross-border No.	Total cross-border $m
1985	84 (62)*	11,508.4	51 (47)	6,335.3	32 (64)	2,511.3	83 (111)	8,846.6
1986	219 (184)	20,692.6	119 (85)	19,642.8	55 (58)	15,747.3	174 (143)	35,390.1
1987	581 (351)	54,852.0	142 (102)	28,123.6	81 (131)	13,259.0	223 (233)	41,382.6
1988	1,252 (728)	86,430.3	235 (164)	37,623.6	145 (174)	17,020.5	380 (338)	54,644.1
1989	1,507 (1,211)	130,115.7	316 (206)	39,120.7	225 (317)	35,150.8	541 (523)	74,271.5
1990	1,440 (1,191)	127,225.9	274 (219)	46,841.6	310 (361)	50,897.9	584 (580)	97,739.5
1991	1,430 (2,926)	117,248.5	220 (202)	21,445.8	316 (406)	32,346.5	536 (608)	53,792.3
1992	1,462 (2,667)	91,022.0	179 (116)	8,201.6	274 (328)	34,825.2	453 (444)	43,026.8
1993	1,290 (2,100)	59,946.1	183 (150)	12,519.1	247 (391)	20,446.7	430 (541)	32,965.8
1994	1,538 (2,335)	85,586.5	241 (163)	30,836.3	292 (445)	26,265.9	533 (608)	57,102.2
1995	1,686 (2,655)	151,763.3	302 (253)	41,195.0	296 (467)	31,165.0	598 (214)	72,360.0
1996	1,677 (2,109)	193,257.8	313 (291)	48,685.1	306 (472)	24,505.3	619 (763)	73,190.4
1997	1,959 (1,795)	242,448.6	345 (223)	45,451.0	381 (432)	33,085.5	726 (655)	78,536.5
1998	2,467 (3,048)	305,851.3	470 (376)	191,741.3	534 (689)	99,616.0	1,004.0 (1,065.0)	291,357.3
1999	3,266 (5,320)	575,528	585 (508)	216,610.6	466 (679)	75,379.9	1,051.0 (1,187.0)	291,990.5
Totals	**21,858 (28,682)**	**2,253,477**	**3,975 (3,105)**	**794,373**	**3,960 (4,480)**	**512,223**	**7,935 (7,585)**	**1,306,596**

Source: Thomson Financial Securities Data Company

* Numbers in brackets denote additional deals for which no values were available.

Fig 5.6 Volume of completed intra-European M&A transactions by country, 1985–99

Country of buyer	Year	Country of seller					Totals buyer
		UK	France	Italy	Germany	Other European	
	1985	9,186.2	0.0	0.0	0.0	12.2	9,198.4
	1986	12,806.4	23.8	0.0	1.0	80.4	12,911.6
	1987	33,500.1	302.6	125.9	341.4	576.3	34,846.3
	1988	42,890.3	1,213.5	409.1	369.7	1,158.4	46,041.0
	1989	55,799.6	1,221.8	305.7	344.6	3,289.9	60,961.6
	1990	27,549.1	2,597.4	115.1	1,245.9	4,054.5	35,562.0
	1991	30,689.0	624.4	39.5	316.5	1,526.7	33,196.1
UK	1992	17,250.8	1,141.8	402.4	796.4	10,558.6	30,150.0
	1993	20,536.1	5,318.2	46.4	516.1	1,219.0	27,635.8
	1994	22,127.0	4,508.0	83.0	542.0	3,723.0	30,983.0
	1995	68,943.2	1,924.6	433.3	2,995.3	3,417.9	77,714.3
	1996	57,794.8	871.6	273.0	405.1	4,250.7	65,591.2
	1997	67,260.2	3,950.8	199.5	1,454.7	1,632.1	89,187.3
	1998	89,490.2	6,773.8	400.4	3,069.7	7,474.4	107,208.5
	1999	124,814.0	2,820.1	1,058.7	2,227.0	23,298.6	154,218.4
	1985	0.0	10.7	0.0	0.0	0.0	10.7
	1986	5.9	1,285.7	520.9	0.0	32.1	1,844.6
	1987	316.6	1,958.9	343.3	0.0	0.0	2,618.8
	1988	3,209.6	7,716.3	428.7	310.2	1,392.5	13,057.3
	1989	5,727.5	15,906.5	837.3	2,044.8	4,296.7	28,812.8
	1990	3,195.0	12,648.4	3,380.9	502.9	4,548.4	24,275.6
	1991	621.3	17,005.5	1,627.8	5,437.1	3,118.4	27,810.1
France	1992	211.3	9,696.5	406.8	2,454.8	4,053.2	16,822.6
	1993	39.5	6,646.6	288.6	217.1	673.8	7,865.6
	1994	840.0	9,352.0	39.0	15.0	703.0	10,949.0
	1995	2,254.3	9,971.8	143.0	237.7	1,790.0	14,396.8
	1996	912.9	31,359.0	0.0	13.5	5,343.7	39,625.1
	1997	6,845.7	40,340.1	929.7	2,846.7	3,237.8	54,200.0
	1998	5,149.5	24,900.9	7.6	186.0	11,521.6	41,765.6
	1999	4,074.6	43,332.3	298.5	25,803.7	16,265.0	89,774.1
	1985	16.8	0.0	165.0	0.0	0.0	181.8
	1986	0.0	0.0	1,1994	129.0	0.0	1,328.4
	1987	0.0	20.4	8,039.9	0.0	1,050.8	9,111.1
	1988	0.0	504.9	1,509.6	429.3	887.7	3,331.5
	1989	7.9	294.4	8,523.6	180.6	0.0	9,006.5
	1990	68.6	602.8	15,752.9	772.3	518.8	17,715.4
	1991	71.9	335.1	4,415.4	356.1	536.9	5,715.4
Italy	1992	10.6	2,279.3	4,589.9	747.6	308.2	7,935.6
	1993	0.0	156.5	2,535.8	2.3	102.9	2,797.5
	1994	0.0	281.0	7,542.0	54.0	1,475.0	9,352.0
	1995	189.4	103.5	4,972.0	299.1	575.1	6,139.1
	1996	2.3	419.2	11,794.3	0.0	225.6	14,437.4
	1997	0.0	397.6	22,758.9	24.7	2,669.6	25,849.9
	1998	0.0	539.9	29,158.7	288.6	272.9	30,260.1
	1999	264.8	200.2	96,898.1	924.6	2,775.7	101,063.4

Fig 5.6 *cont.*

Country of buyer	Year	Country of seller					Totals buyer
		UK	France	Italy	Germany	Other European	
Germany	1985	0.0	0.0	0.0	898.5	445.0	1,343.5
	1986	425.0	0.3	887.4	980.0	0.0	2,292.7
	1987	167.0	414.8	0.0	452.8	0.0	1,034.6
	1988	59.2	154.0	866.1	2,518.7	39.6	3,637.6
	1989	2,378.4	1,341.3	37.5	2,649.4	1,466.0	7,872.6
	1990	1,499.7	2.2	53.2	2,101.5	1,341.9	4,998.5
	1991	456.7	8.5	0.0	13,697.8	1,242.0	15,405.0
	1992	986.5	10.5	39.0	7,157.3	1,511.3	9,704.6
	1993	167.1	458.6	0.0	3,401.6	1,796.3	5,823.6
	1994	11.0	1,350.0	470.0	5,893.0	877.0	8,601.0
	1995	4,226.7	3.4	341.7	3,476.6	3,069.3	11,117.7
	1996	943.6	196.2	521.7	3,184.6	4,708.1	11,550.2
	1997	2,753.7	557.8	49.3	18,975.4	7,472.9	29,809.1
	1998	1,490.5	2,076.5	614.1	12,841.0	5,442.8	22,464.9
	1999	47,770.8	1,122.4	8,581.8	19,428.5	7,084.2	83,987.7
Other European	1985	268.5	0.0	0.0	0.0	505.5	774.0
	1986	828.6	0.0	0.0	0.0	1,486.7	2,315.3
	1987	574.9	188.9	26.8	239.0	6,211.6	7,241.2
	1988	7,540.9	1,028.6	2,098.7	0.0	9,694.7	20,362.9
	1989	2,074.3	4,040.7	158.9	902.5	16,285.7	23,462.1
	1990	7,245.7	1,285.1	436.9	2,794.8	32,911.9	44,674.4
	1991	2,730.7	838.2	529.5	651.6	30,371.9	35,121.9
	1992	1,845.4	4,087.4	272.3	196.2	20,007.9	26,409.2
	1993	775.4	207.2	1,956.6	327.6	12,556.8	15,823.6
	1994	1,669.0	3,934.0	9.0	1,390.0	16,130.0	23,132.0
	1995	6,085.0	313.4	321.6	4,206.7	31,566.4	42,493.1
	1996	6,252.5	3,479.9	175.4	2,472.9	58,530.9	72,907.6
	1997	1,801.8	1,601.0	161.7	2,045.1	61,456.8	67,066.4
	1998	10,712.4	35,884.1	31,418.9	19,936.5	207,899.4	305,851.3
	1999	35,240.0	20,672.4	1,629.4	13,939.3	150,383.4	221,864.5
Totals seller	1985	9,471.5	10.7	165.0	898.5	962.7	11,508.4
	1986	14,065.9	1,309.8	2,607.7	1,110.0	1,599.2	20,692.6
	1987	34,558.6	2,885.6	8,535.9	1,033.2	7,838.7	54,852.0
	1988	53,700.0	10,617.3	5,312.2	3,627.9	13,172.9	86,430.3
	1989	65,987.7	22,804.7	9,863.0	6,121.9	25,338.3	130,115.6
	1990	39,558.1	17,135.9	19,739.0	7,417.4	43,375.5	127,225.9
	1991	34,569.6	18,811.7	6,612.2	20,459.1	36,795.9	117,248.5
	1992	20,304.6	17,215.5	5,710.4	11,352.3	36,439.2	91,022.0
	1993	21,518.1	12,787.1	4,827.4	4,464.7	16,348.8	59,946.1
	1994	24,647.0	19,425.0	8,143.0	7,894.0	22,908.0	83,017.0
	1995	81,698.6	12,316.7	6,211.6	11,215.4	40,418.7	151,861.0
	1996	65,906.1	36,325.9	12,764.4	6,076.1	73,059.0	196,127.5
	1997	78,661.4	46,847.3	24,099.1	25,346.6	76,469.2	266,112.7
	1998	106,842.6	70,175.2	61,599.7	36,321.8	232,611.1	507,550.4
	1999	212,164.2	68,147.4	108,466.5	62,323.1	199,806.9	650,908.1

Source: Thomson Financial Securities Data Company

These practices and attitudes have centred on close control of corporations, non-market valuation of shares to be transferred, effecting control through minority positions in a large network of stakeholdings, and resistance to hostile takeovers, leveraged buyouts and the advice of independent advisers. Now, after several years of observation, we can conclude that the market forces have inculcated changes into the European marketplace – changes that appear to be irreversible. These have been accompanied by a variety of regulatory reforms in national markets and at the EU level that will increase the efficiency of the marketplace. As this process continues, in ten years or so it may not be possible to describe especially distinctive characteristics of the market for corporate control in continental Europe compared with the US or Britain. As these characteristics exist, however, we shall examine them briefly.

Minority stakeholdings

Figure 5.7 compares partial ownership positions (stakes) as a percentage of all completed M&A transactions in the US, the UK and the rest of Europe for the period 1985–99. Compared with the US, stakeholding transactions were approximately twice as prevalent in transactions involving non-UK European corporations, indicating a uniquely European *modus operandi*. European companies appear to favour stakes for several reasons, including the concept of forging a strategic alliance for a common purpose – offensive or defensive – without giving up their independence. An example was Generalli's $700 million equity swap with Commerzbank in November 1998. Generalli already held a 66 per cent stake in Aachener and Muenchener Insurance, which may have had use for a German banking partner.

Some companies are also attracted to the idea that a gradual commitment to a final arrangement is wiser, cheaper and reversible, and because in many situations a substantial minority stakeholding can assure *de facto* control of a company. In the US, by comparison, acquirers are motivated by tax, accounting and legal reasons to prefer 100 per cent ownership. The US practice of minority shareholder litigation and class action suits makes the elimination of minority interests especially important to many companies, although these companies often recognize that when in Rome, Brussels, Lyon or Dusseldorf, it may be acceptable to abide by local customs.

Some academic observers have suggested that lengthy European liaisons and courtships, or trial marriages, may lead to full mergers that prove to be more lasting and beneficial than some of the more impulsive, opportunistic US acquisitions which often appear to fail in delivering expected benefits.

Fig 5.7 Partial ownership positions as a percentage of all completed US and European M&A transactions 1985–99[1,2,3]

Year	US seller[4]	European seller[5]		Intra-European deal[6]	
		UK	*Rest of Europe*	*UK-UK*	*Europe-Europe*
1985	6.30%	14.21%	25.13%	5.09%	25.59%
1986	17.12%	7.15%	38.14%	6.51%	39.05%
1987	15.09%	37.01%	8.12%	28.12%	7.96%
1988	11.77%	24.03%	42.25%	12.58%	42.72%
1989	25.50%	25.53%	34.76%	30.02%	34.13%
1990	13.82%	22.20%	20.74%	20.91%	17.57%
1991	11.53%	38.84%	25.33%	20.58%	20.99%
1992	7.62%	41.42%	31.98%	41.97%	29.17%
1993	11.15%	9.78%	54.15%	7.02%	49.58%
1994	14.33%	24.92%	48.84%	24.33%	54.97%
1995	16.75%	18.67%	55.93%	11.43%	61.51%
1996	12.92%	18.85%	30.77%	14.73%	28.24%
1997	17.49%	8.47%	25.10%	10.36%	44.05%
1998	8.72%	23.31%	52.99%	18.62%	54.27%
1999	12.77%	18.32%	59.66%	24.86%	65.39%
Average	**13.53%**	**22.18%**	**36.93%**	**18.48%**	**38.35%**

[1] Partial ownership positions involve open or privately negotiated stake purchases of stock or assets
[2] Data include only completed transactions. Data are classified according to announcement date of a transaction, not taking into consideration when a transaction is completed
[3] Percentage values denote the fraction of total volume that involves partial stakes
[4] Completed partial stakes as a percentage of total volume of completed transactions in which the seller was a US company
[5] Completed partial stakes as a percentage of total volume of completed transactions in which the seller was a company from the UK or the rest of Europe
[6] Completed partial stakes as a percentage of total volume of completed intra-European transactions in which the seller was a company from the UK or the rest of Europe

Source: Thomson Financial Securities Data Company

This may be the case, but there are many reasons for not preferring a minority stake to a 100 per cent purchase. In many situations, for example, the seller of the stake wants above all to preserve a *status quo*, which is in fact economically inefficient. For example, a strategic alliance involving a 10 per cent cross-shareholding between two competing companies from different countries may appear shrewd and desirable when announced but may not produce the intended synergies. Each company may find itself within a few years unable to influence policies in the allied company and even in serious competition with it.

In 1992, shareholders of the Belgian company Wagon-Lits issued a minority shareholder law suit against the French group Accord to block a below-market transfer of control. Increasing investment in companies such as Wagon-Lits by powerful institutional investors from the UK or the US makes these types of challenges more likely in the future.

Leveraged buyouts

As recently as 1985, leveraged buyouts began to appear in Europe, especially in the UK, where they appeared in two forms: management buyouts, in which existing management would receive financing sufficient to purchase the company from its owner, usually a large company no longer wanting the business; or management buy-ins, ('MBIs') in which new management and investors would take over a company on a highly leveraged basis. The inspiration for these transactions came from the US where the LBO boom reached its peak in 1988 (the year of the RJR Nabisco deal) and 31 per cent of all completed US transactions were LBOs. Figure 5.8 compares LBO activity in the US with that in the UK and on the continent for 1985–99. It clearly shows much more activity in the US (where public financing of LBOs through the sale of junk bonds was available) during the late eighties than elsewhere, after which this activity declined sharply. It also shows more than a trivial amount of LBO trans-

Fig 5.8 Leverage buyouts as a percentage of all completed US and European M&A transactions 1985–99[1,2,3]

Year	US seller[4]	European seller[5]		Intra-European deal[6]	
		UK	Rest of Europe	UK	Rest of Europe
1985	13.43%	4.45%	0.00%	8.70%	0.00%
1986	16.45%	1.67%	0.85%	3.83%	0.00%
1987	19.73%	7.84%	0.72%	9.92%	7.60%
1988	31.10%	8.00%	3.67%	12.09%	4.29%
1989	11.18%	8.94%	3.18%	14.53%	3.52%
1990	6.60%	4.64%	2.21%	11.05%	2.33%
1991	4.56%	5.67%	5.19%	8.54%	5.81%
1992	6.60%	6.78%	1.91%	14.96%	2.15%
1993	5.37%	9.13%	1.61%	7.86%	1.67%
1994	2.97%	8.69%	0.83%	9.99%	0.83%
1995	1.40%	5.43%	1.03%	7.20%	1.27%
1996	0.28%	5.22%	0.40%	5.77%	0.36%
1997	1.30%	7.84%	1.29%	14.60%	2.64%
1998	0.40%	4.70%	1.69%	8.06%	1.25%
1999	1.34%	9.29%	2.07%	15.22%	1.19%

[1] Leverage buyout is defined as a transaction in which an investor group, investor or investor / LBO firm acquires a company, taking on an extraordinary amount of debt, with plans to repay the debt with funds generated from the company or with revenue earned by selling off the newly acquired company's assets
[2] Data include only completed transactions. Data are classified according to announcement date of a transaction, not taking into consideration when a transaction is completed
[3] Percentage values denote the fraction of total volume that involves LBOs
[4] Completed LBOs as a percentage of total volume of completed transactions in which the seller was a US company
[5] Completed LBOs as a percentage of total volume of completed transactions in which the seller was a company from the UK or the rest of Europe
[6] Completed LBOs as a percentage of total volume of completed intra-European transactions in which the seller was a company from the UK or the rest of Europe

Source: Thomson Financial Securities Data Company

actions occurring in Europe between 1987 and 1999, as divestitures increased, and funds were made available to financial entrepreneurs.

Hostile takeovers

Takeover attempts made directly to shareholders that are opposed by management are called hostile offers. In the early eighties, when hostile offers again became highly visible in the US and Britain, there was little ambiguity as to whether an offer was hostile or not. Management usually criticized the offer as disruptive and undervalued, those on the other side pointed to management failures that had depressed the value of the company's shares. In both the US and Britain, hostile offers were fairly common – in a market dominated by independent financial institutions, such struggles for corporate control are often needed to decide conflicts that arise between a company's managers and its owners.

During the eighties, however, defence measures evolved and various different ways to protect shareholders against undervalued offers emerged. It was no longer normal for management to complain about a bid it did not like; instead management was sent looking for viable alternatives or into negotiations with the potential acquirer to improve the terms. This resulted in the difference between hostile and friendly offers becoming obscured. By the end of the eighties, it became clear that a friendly offer was one that was immediately declared such by the target company, and all other offers were 'unsolicited' or 'non-friendly' offers. Figure 5.9 shows unsolicited or non-friendly takeover offers as a percentage of all completed offers in the US, the UK and in the rest of Europe for 1985–99.

The figure also shows the periodically extensive use of unsolicited offers in Britain, where permitted defensive manoeuvres are more limited than in the US, and a significant incidence of unsolicited offers in the rest of Europe. Only completed deals are included. A number of unsuccessful unsolicited offers, such as the attempt on Navigation-Mixte by Paribas (France) in 1989, Sandoz's effort to acquire Schering A.G. in 1990 (Switzerland and Germany respectively), Pirelli's celebrated effort to take over Continental A.G. (Italy and Germany respectively) in 1991–2, and BK Vision's attempt to secure control of Union Bank of Switzerland in 1995–7, are not included. Nor are the very large intra-European hostile transactions for Gucci, Telecom Italia, Société Générale/Banque Paribas and Mannesmann that were pending in the autumn of 1999.

Prior to the eighties, hostile offers were virtually unheard of in continental Europe, where markets were not dominated by institutions and concentrated holdings among insiders was the norm. This began to change during the

Fig 5.9 Unsolicited or non-friendly offers as a percentage of all completed US and European M&A transactions 1985–99[1,2,3]

Year	United States						United Kingdom						Rest of Europe[8]	
	US Domestic[4]		Cross Border[5]				UK Domestic[6]		Rest of Europe[7]					
			US buyer		US seller				UK buyer		UK seller			
	No.	%	No.	%	No.	%	No.	%	No.	%	No.	%	No.	%
1985	385	22.3	10	5.9	24	11.2	12	14.6	1	14.3	2	18.2	13	12.1
1986	456	17.7	17	7.8	39	10.6	29	11.1	2	12.5	3	13.0	12	6.7
1987	691	25.0	21	7.1	70	15.8	57	9.2	3	5.7	6	15.0	30	8.2
1988	598	19.8	35	8.5	50	8.0	100	8.1	5	2.6	19	17.1	85	10.4
1989	833	20.9	47	7.6	79	9.3	415	27.2	11	4.4	36	23.1	119	8.9
1990	1,010	24.0	27	4.3	52	6.1	252	20.5	6	2.8	27	15.3	134	7.9
1991	748	19.3	59	8.5	25	4.2	130	12.7	6	2.9	15	11.5	332	7.5
1992	600	14.1	54	7.3	33	7.0	75	8.0	4	2.2	11	10.4	332	8.0
1993	572	12.4	46	5.8	40	8.3	88	8.8	8	4.5	5	5.3	404	12.0
1994	746	14.4	61	6.9	56	10.1	88	8.0	7	3.6	5	6.3	407	13.2
1995	777	14.2	54	22.1	65	44.8	78	34.3	8	2.1	5	6.2	222	21.9
1996	1,027	15.1	72	6.9	63	10.2	62	5.4	13	6.6	3	3.3	290	12.4
1997	519	7.2	40	3.7	48	6.9	51	3.5	13	5.3	3	2.9	185	9.4
1998	478	6.1	89	5.9	27	3.5	60	3.1	10	3.4	10	5.7	296	3.8
1999	302	4.2	98	6.7	31	3.2	73	3.3	19	5.0	22	8.5	879	11.5
Average	**649**	**15.77**	**49**	**7.66**	**42**	**10.61**	**105**	**11.85**	**8**	**5.19**	**10**	**10.78**	**249**	**10.26**

[1] Hostile offers are defined as those transactions in which the acquiring company proceeds with its offer against the wishes of the target company's management
[2] Data include only completed transactions. Data are classified according to announcement date of a transaction, not taking into consideration when a transaction is completed
[3] Percentage values denote the fraction of total deals that involve partial stakes
[4] Completed hostile deals as a percentage of total deals of completed transactions in which the buyer and seller was a US company
[5] Completed hostile deals as a percentage of total deals of completed transactions in which the buyer and seller was a US company and the counterpart a non-US company
[6] Completed hostile deals as a percentage of total deals of completed transactions in which the buyer and seller was a company from the UK
[7] Completed hostile deals as a percentage of total deals of completed transactions in which the buyer and seller was a company from the UK and the counterpart a continental European company
[8] Completed hostile deals as a percentage of total deals of completed transactions in which the buyer and seller was a continental European company

Source: Thomson Financial Securities Data Company

eighties, as institutional holdings increased, markets improved, trading volume increased and financial professionals from Britain and the US became interested in the European scene.

The end of 1993 saw many highly visible hostile takeover attempts launched in France, Italy, Sweden, Germany, Denmark, Spain, Ireland, Portugal and Switzerland. Such efforts included the attack on Société Générale de Belgique by the Italian industrialist Carlo de Benedetti in 1987, various struggles for control of Montedison in Italy, the takeover of Feldmuhle-Nobel by the Flick brothers in Germany in 1989, Nestlé and Indosuez's joint effort to take over Perrier, and Krupp's acquisition of Hoesch Steel. De Benedetti's effort demonstrated that Belgium had far fewer legal barriers to takeover than had been assumed, and that the fact that the 'right' people might own a corporation did not prevent takeovers.

After this and some of the other early European hostile deals by well established companies, attitudes began to change: attention was paid to the performance of target companies and the management teams that led them, to the position of minority shareholders in change of control situations, to the rules affecting disclosure of share accumulations and restrictions on voting shares acquired by unwelcome holders. In 1991, the Amsterdam Stock Exchange limited the number of barriers to hostile takeovers that Dutch companies had relied on for years, and in 1992 it issued a warning to 20 listed companies that had not complied. Later that year the chief of Germany's leading fund management company, a subsidiary of the Deutsche Bank, called for a code of practice to permit and regulate contested takeovers in Germany. There have been similar actions in other parts of Europe. Hostile deals, though once shunned and thought of as out of step in Europe, have become quite familiar and accounted for 11.5 per cent of all deals completed in Europe in 1999 outside the UK.

Converging regulations

Since the Single Market Act and the various efforts at financial market reforms in most of the principal European countries, the EU and its member countries have tried to devise a common set of takeover rules and procedures. In general, there are two approaches to choose from, but as yet no EU directive on takeover policy has emerged as the methods are quite different. One approach – the British model – involves a set of rules designed to protect minority shareholders from unfair transactions. This system depends on full disclosure and proceeding according to established rules. The other system – sometimes called the German model, though many other countries follow similar practices – protects the rights of major shareholders, such as banks and insurance companies, to act paternalistically and responsibly, though not always visibly, in the interest of all shareholders. Market forces are eroding the viability of the German model, but the Germans are still working towards a compromise between the two systems.

Regulations that affect takeovers are numerous. These include antitrust regulations, securities laws, and regulations relating to fraudulent practice, e.g. required disclosures, trading restrictions (such as insider trading) and prohibitions against making false markets. There are also rules, codes and established procedures prescribed by stock exchanges or self-regulatory bodies that may or may not be supported by enforcement powers. These various tiers of regulation can be imposed at national as well as at the EU level. Until a few years ago, they were vastly different from one another, creating a confusing and often uneven playing field for participants. There have been efforts to harmonize regulations, but progress has been modest, though efforts continue.

Regulation at the EU level has been confined to the antitrust sector. There are two governing principles in effect: one, that of 'subsidiarity' (a concept of EU governance that extends into all aspects of the common market), which provides that the EU will make no decision on issues that can equally well be decided nationally, and the other, that of 'compatibility with the common market', which restricts EU actions to matters affecting the whole of the EU. The EU regulations that were passed in 1990 provide:

- that only deals involving combined worldwide sale of € 5 billion ($5.7 billion) or two or more companies with EU sales of € 250 million will be reviewed by the EU's 'merger task force';
- the merger task force must report within one month after announcement whether it believes the deal is compatible with the common market;
- if it reports doubts, it has four months to resolve them and either approve the deal, block it or insist on modifications.

After eight years of operation, the 100-person staff of the merger task force had reviewed more than 600 transactions, but had blocked only a handful, and then on terms which allowed the transaction to continue if the companies involved sold off certain overlapping assets.

At the national levels, regulatory bodies such as Britain's Competition Commission and Germany's Cartel Office rule on deals below € 5 billion in size, and are required by national regulations to consider mainly national competitive effects. These bodies usually decide within a few weeks of an announced transaction whether they see a competition problem. If so, a more extensive review, taking as long as six months, is undertaken before the deal can be completed. During this period the bid is usually withdrawn, to be reinstated after the review if the buyer decides to go ahead. Growth in transactions involving companies with operations in several national jurisdictions has meant that often companies have had to seek many different approvals to complete the deal. In 1997, the EU attempted to alleviate the problem of this inefficient and expensive process by allowing companies having to face several national merger control regimes to instead be reviewed at the EU level. EU officials expect this change in the rules to increase their caseload tenfold.

In terms of securities laws, there are also considerable differences. Under the British system, all share accumulations above a threshold of 1 per cent of outstanding shares have to be announced to the market. Once a bidder accumulates 30 per cent of the stock of the target it is obliged to make an offer to the rest of the shareholders at the same price. Once a bid is announced, certain time schedules must be adhered to. The intent is to create a level playing field on which neither bidder nor defender would have any kind of advantage over the other and the market could decide the outcome on a fair and unimpeded basis. To referee the conduct on the playing field, the British system relies on the Takeover Panel, a non-government body staffed by professionals seconded from their firms and a small permanent staff. The panel has issued rules (the Takeover Code) which must be observed, previously only at penalty of sanction but now legally enforceable by the government. The panel has the power to rule on disputes as they occur and its decision is binding. Lawsuits are only rarely involved. The process is generally regarded as flexible, timely, fair and efficient. Though different in many details from takeover procedures in the US, which rely mainly on court actions in the state of incorporation of the defending company, the basic principles and objectives are very similar. Moves to accommodate the Anglo-Saxon model have been made in France and a few other countries, and are the basis of the draft European Takeover Directive, which requires a passage of laws and special courts to regulate mergers. The British, in particular, think this could be cumbersome.

Mergers in the financial services industry

Mergers and acquisition transactions within the financial services industry – that is, between and among banks, insurance companies, securities firms and asset managers, and including partial ownership acquisitions – have been extraordinarily active since 1985. Over half by value of all global M&A transactions in the period 1985–99 have involved this diverse, far-flung and rapidly changing industry. In 1985, the industry accounted for 25 per cent of global M&A activity (25 per cent in the US as well) but by 1998 it accounted for more than 35 per cent of US activity and 67 per cent of non-US transactions. In total, more than $7,100 billion of financial services transactions took place during that period, of which approximately $1,240 billion involved banks, insurance companies and securities firms (*see* Figs 5.10 and 5.11).

Among the $10,200 of transactions involving banks, insurance companies and securities firms (all components of the modern universal bank), nearly half of the transactions involved commercial banks acquiring other commercial banks. Banking deals together with insurance companies acquiring other insurance companies, and securities firms acquiring other securities firms, accounted for 76 per cent of transactions during the period 1985–99. Only 24 per cent of the deal flow involved acquisitions of different types of businesses.

Drivers of change

Before 1985, both the US and Europe surely had a surplus of banks, with about 15,000 in the US and approximately 10,000 in Europe. Both environments had long believed that banks were special entities and had to be not only regulated but also protected to ensure their solvency. The protection ran mainly to restrictions on competition from banks in other parts of the continental scene, and from non-banking enterprises. Efficiency, which could result in lower-cost services to the banks' customers, was of less concern than stability and solvency. To doubly ensure that this would be so, some countries, especially France and Italy, cloaked the major banks in government-controlled ownership. All banks were, in effect, public utilities. To a somewhat lesser degree, so were the insurance companies.

This began to change during the eighties, a sad decade for banks in which most experienced huge losses from mismatched assets and liabilities, and from non-performing domestic and international loans, many of which were made in a careless manner. Banks in the US and Europe had to undergo a long period of internal restructuring in order to emerge in the early nineties as significant competitors once again. During the recovery period many weak banks were merged into stronger ones, for which protective barriers had to be set aside. Banks changed management and business strategies, cut costs and 'downsized' significantly. New management teams began to look at their strategic destiny differently – no longer would banks attempt to offer all their

Fig 5.10 Completed global M&A transactions 1985–98 (US$bn – thousands of transactions)

	1985				1999				1985–99 (15 years)			
	$ value (%)		No. (%)		$ value (%)		No. (%)		$ value (%)		No. (%)	
US domestic												
All industries	192.5	(82.5)	0.9	(59.3)	608.4	(35.3)	7.2	(31.6)	5,714.9	(48.5)	77.2	(39.1)
All financial services	47.9	(82.3)	0.7	(77.7)	308.5	(25.3)	3.5	(29.7)	3,313.1	(46.3)	40.3	(39.5)
US cross-border												
All industries	15.7	(6.8)	0.3	(21.7)	311.0	(18.0)	2.4	(10.5)	1,488.7	(12.6)	20.4	(10.3)
All financial services	6.3	(10.8)	0.3	(8.6)	91.4	(7.5)	0.8	(6.8)	475.8	(6.7)	6.9	(6.8)
Non-US												
All industries	24.8	(10.7)	0.3	(19.0)	806.4	(46.7)	13.2	(57.9)	4,582.4	(38.9)	99.9	(50.6)
All financial services	4.0	(6.9)	0.1	(8.6)	821.2	(67.3)	7.5	(63.6)	3,364.7	(47.0)	54.7	(53.7)
Total												
All industries	233.0	(100.0)	1.5	(100.0)	1,725.8	(100.0)	22.8	(100.0)	11,786.0	(100.0)	197.5	(100.0)
All financial services	58.2	(100.0)	0.9	(100.0)	1,221.1	(100.0)	11.8	(100.0)	7,153.6	(100.0)	101.9	(100.0)

Source: Thomson Financial Securities Data Company; author calculations

Fig 5.11 Intensity of financial services M&A activity 1985–98

Dollar value of financial services industry M&A transactions as a percentage of global total	1985	1998	14 years
US domestic	86.0	55.9	47.8
US cross-border	3.4	6.1	6.9
Non-US	10.6	38.0	45.3
Financial Services as a percentage of global M&A activity	**25.0**	**46.0**	**44.6**

Source: Thomson Financial Securities Data Company

services all over the world. Instead they would cut back on less-promising products and services and concentrate on their basic businesses, offering retail services in their home region.

Some banks in Europe preferred to combine with other large banks in their own countries to present a more formidable presence there, probably influenced by both the EU's Second Banking Directive, which permitted banks to operate anywhere in Europe, and by the Basle Agreement, which provided for new rules on bank capital adequacy to which all European governments, the US and Japan had subscribed. This agreement required all banks to have the same minimum amount of capital to assure their financial stability, making it possible for competition between them to shift to the quality and cost of their services. Banks believed they had to be bigger to withstand competitive assaults from other banks in their home markets, and to be able to launch successful competitive attacks of their own into their neighbours' markets.

As a result a process of substantial consolidation within European countries began in Italy, Spain, Holland, Switzerland and Scandinavia. Some of the most important of these consolidations since 1995 have included BNP and both Société Générale and Banque Paribas ($37 billion), UBS and Swiss Bank Corp. ($23 billion), Lloyds Bank and TSB ($15.5 billion), Banco Santander and Banco Central Hispano ($11.6 billion), Unicredito and Credito Italiano ($11 billion), and Bayerishe Vereinsbank and Bayerishe Hypo bank ($7 billion).

Restructuring

But mergers into bigger players was not all. Restructuring of basic businesses became the next major theme. This involved reorganizing branch networks, closing marginal ones and upgrading the services offered; shifting the mix of businesses, mainly to favour consumer loans and credit cards; and restructuring wholesale and investment banking businesses to become more competitive with independent, integrated securities firms. The banks also began to look for more ways to effect expense controls, to increase fee businesses and to enter non-banking businesses such as insurance and asset management.

Larger banks acquiring smaller enterprises and attempting to lower costs and streamline products and services have effected some of the latter activities. Crédit Suisse was been actively restructuring itself with acquisitions of (the minority interest) Crédit Suisse First Boston, Volksbank, and Winterthur insurance. Swiss Bank Corp., its cross-town rival, has also been active in changing its business through major acquisitions of O'Connor Group (derivatives), S.G. Warburg, Brinson Partners (institutional asset managers), Dillon Read, and most significantly by engineering a merger with (and control of) a weakened Union Bank of Switzerland. Other banks have put forward more cautious programmes for expanding into new skill areas through mergers – ABN Amro and ING (both created from large mergers in Holland), Société Générale and Dresdner Bank by acquiring securities firms, all of which were cross-border transactions.

Other firms have attempted to effect their restructuring through dispositions of businesses rather than acquisitions. Crédit Lyonnais, after several years pursuing an unsuccessful policy of acquiring banks and industrial companies to make itself into a *banque industrial*, has, under new management, tried to unwind some of these transactions by selling them off. The big Germans, Deutsche, Dresdner and Allianz, frequently describe the reduction of their industrial holdings as long-term policy. In 1997, the largest British banks, Barclays and National Westminster, divested most of their investment banking and brokerage businesses, having failed to make an adequate return in them over the preceding decade.

Cross-border banking

After a number of years of struggling with difficult acquisitions in the US, a number of European banks decided to withdraw, and sold their US businesses. Others, of course, took a different approach. Swiss Bank acquired the US investment bank Dillon Read, and Deutsche Bank, after attempting for a long time to build its own investment banking in the US, acquired Bankers Trust in 1999 for $10 billion. In retail and private banking, HSBC Holdings, which already owned Marine Midland bank in the US, acquired Republic New York Corp. and its affiliates from financier Edmund Safra for $10 billion. HSBC also acquired a 70 per cent interest in a distressed Seoul Bank and invested more than $1 billion in Latin American banking paper in 1997 when such paper was very inexpensive.

Insurance too

Because of the positive effects of the restructuring efforts among banks in Europe, the once sleepy insurance industry also began to reshape itself, fearing perhaps the competitive powers of banks to enter their business. The industry started to take shareholder value seriously and commenced a series of major reorganizations.

Germany's Allianz is the largest insurance company in Europe. Its returns on equity have been improving as a result of a large internal restructuring effort, and by intra-European expansion. In early 1998 it acquired France's third largest insurer, Assurances Générales de France, after defeating a hostile takeover effort by Italy's Assicurazioni Generale. The second largest insurance company is AXA-UAP, a French group that combined with and owns a controlling interest in the Equitable Group in New York (which in turn controls money manager Alliance Capital and investment banker Donaldson Lufkin Jenrette). AXA also announced a $5.6 billion acquisition of Guardian Royal Exchange in January 1999.

Third largest is the Zurich Group, which acquired BAT Group's insurance interests (Eagle Star in the UK, and Farmers Group in the US) in 1998, creating a $35 billion market capitalization company. Before that deal Zurich had acquired two big US money managers, Kemper, and Scudder, Stevens & Clark, as well as Threadneedle Asset Management in London.

European insurance industry mergers have also occurred within less powerful groups and in other countries. In the UK, Commercial Union merged with General Accident ($22.5 billion), and Royal Insurance merged with Sun Alliance. AEGON, the Dutch insurance group, acquired Transamerica ($10 billion) and Providan ($3 billion). Also important were acquisitions of insurance companies by banks (Winterthur by Crédit Suisse, $10 billion) and of banks by insurers (Generale Bank by Fortis, $14 billion; Banque Bruxelles Lambert by ING, $5 billion).

The outlook

All indicators suggest that the future will consist of more of the same. Within the EU countries, continued emphasis on restructuring and shareholder value, increasing financial market capabilities and activity, and a growing number of public companies resulting from privatizations and initial public offerings all argue for more merger and acquisition transactions, within individual countries and across borders within Europe. The number of companies seeking restructuring and reorganization will increase substantially as the EU incorporates more of Eastern Europe. By comparison, in the US the wave of merger activity may be dependent on adapting to technology and regulation in particular industries, and on extremely ebullient financial markets, and in due course will dampen out. Most US public companies have undergone some form of restructuring over the past 15 years, and there are fewer and fewer with low market values or in need of further restructuring. In Europe, on the other hand, only a relatively small number of companies have undergone restructuring and there is an abundant supply.

Some European industries, such as financial services, will benefit also from the single currency. For the first time, all a bank's products and services can be offered around the continent in the same currency. As most European banking and insurance companies are predominantly retail in orientation, the coming to life of the euro will mean that a firm's entire product range can be sold in other countries in Europe. To penetrate the market in such countries requires patience, either while the firm attempts to build from scratch its vehicle from which to compete, or to acquire a firm that could begin to handle its products right away. It seems almost inevitable that among the strong national players reinforced by mergers over the past 10–15 years there will be several seeking to expand further – into the new Europe – and they will rely increasingly on cross-border transactions to do so.

Competing in the M&A business

In 1997, merger and acquisition transactions involving European companies were valued at $333 billion; in 1999, the figure increased to $867 billion. Most of the transactions of more than $500 million involved one or more financial advisers on each side. These advisers offered assistance in valuing the companies and assessing alternative courses of action, as well as tactical advice and recommendations on the expected responses of target companies or other bidders, and opinions as to the probable reaction of the stock market to particular transactions. They also shared their global market knowledge with their clients in thinking through which companies might wish to compete to acquire a particular business. They offered to field teams of competent experts for as long as the transaction lasted. The European companies on their own could have carried out few of these services. Equally, few of the services could have been carried out by a company's local bank or by more than a few of the major firms involved in global mergers and acquisitions. In 1999, six of the ten most active firms in M&A deals involving European targets were US based or had evolved from US roots. The top two advisers were Morgan Stanley Dean Witter and Goldman Sachs, both of

Fig 5.12 European M&A adviser rankings, 1998

Rank	Adviser	Rank value ($m)	Market share	No. of deals
1	Morgan Stanley Dean Witter	526,160.1	43.0	132
2	Goldman Sachs	518,660.2	42.4	96
3	Merrill Lynch	467,558.7	38.2	106
4	JP Morgan	353,321.8	28.9	81
5	Warburg Dillon Read	284,102.6	23.2	115
6	Crédit Suisse First Boston	255,045.2	20.8	111
7	Lazard Houses	208,763.0	17.1	98
8	Deutsche Banc	205,049.3	16.8	87
9	Dresdner KB	131,768.5	10.8	71
10	Rothschild	130,190.8	10.6	155
11	BNP Paribas	110,310.9	9.0	84
12	Lehman Brothers	106,181.3	8.7	62
13	Credit Agricole Indosuez	62,353.5	5.1	12
14	Donaldson, Lufkin & V Jenrette	56,328.6	4.6	56
15	Mediobanca	52,023.1	4.3	8
	Industry totals	**1,224,033.0**	**100.0**	**12,553**

Source: Thomson Financial Securities Data Company

which reported merger fees on European deals of almost $100 million for 1999 (*see* Fig. 5.12).

The US and British firms that have succeeded so well in carving out a significant market share in the European mergers business have done so by demonstrating their skills and value-added in a long string of transactions. The firms were trained in these services in New York and London, but began to export them into Europe in the early eighties. Continental European banks had little experience with mergers (there were very few acquisitions) and possessed no trained staff capable of working on transactions deals in which international parties might be involved. The US and Britain marketed their unique skills (and highlighted the European banks' lack of them) throughout the continent. Gradually they received mandates for deals, then more. According to Richard Sapp, then head of European M&A at Goldman Sachs: 'We are seeing the breakdown of the historic networks where local advisers had captive clients. The larger and more complex the deal, the more likely it is that a client will turn to the big investment banks.' At the same time, however, Michael Zaoui, Sapp's counterpart at Morgan Stanley, said: 'There is also a strong push by the commercial banks into our advisory business, but [we] are putting up strong resistance.'[3]

Included in this resistance is the increasing willingness of investment banks to provide bridge financing for the deals, and to come up with original ideas and strategies for getting companies to go along with (or to avoid) proposals, and to secure higher prices for target companies. This takes know-how, experience and training to put into effect. The US has earned a place in mergers and acquisitions in Europe, and has trained and developed many talented European executives in the art of M&A. Equally, the larger European banks are hiring experienced mergers executives from New York and London, to train and organize their teams. There is room for several players in the business, but the competition is increasing and when that happens, fees begin to decline.

NOTES

[1] Parts of this chapter are taken from Smith, Roy C. and Walter, Ingo (1997) *Global Banking*, New York, Oxford University Press.

[2] J.P. Morgan Securities Ltd. Merger and Acquisitions Analysis Policy Group, 27 January 1999.

[3] Davies, Simon and Graham, George (1998) 'Europe's M&A bonanza', *Financial Times*, 18 November 1998.

CHAPTER 6

Privatization

Privatization has become a key dimension of the world capital markets over the past two decades, and Europe has been the global leader in transferring state-owned productive assets in both manufacturing and service industries to the private sector. In part, this is because the state has historically taken a major direct role in the economy of most European countries, rooted in the great depression of the thirties and World War II. The Depression shifted many productive assets to state ownership or control as failing enterprises were taken over by governments or by banks which later came under government control. The war left the new German government with large legacy stakes in the economy – both at the federal and state levels – in companies such as Veba, Lufthansa and Volkswagen, while virtually all Eastern European enterprise ended up in state hands. Elsewhere, strong socialist tendencies in the UK, *dirigiste* tendencies in France, and some of both in Italy and other European countries increased still further the degree of state participation in economies from the late forties until well into the seventies. Perhaps the last major expansion of state control in Europe was the nationalization of the banks in France at the outset of the Mitterrand administration in 1981. But the pendulum had already begun to swing the other way.

By the early eighties the state accounted directly and indirectly for perhaps half of GDP in the European economies. Direct government involvement in commercial activities was substantial in many of them, so that governments owned large amounts of assets that could be sold as privatization began to take hold as a global phenomenon. As a result of these privatizations, the share of state-owned enterprises (SOEs) in the GDP of OECD (Organization for Economic Co-operation and Development) countries declined from about 10 per cent in the mid-seventies to about 7 per cent in the late eighties and perhaps 5 per cent at the end of the nineties. In all, governments raised almost $670 billion by direct sales and public share offerings between 1977 and 1998. In the OECD countries during the nineties, primary and secondary privatization share offerings accounted for more than 55 per cent of all equity offerings in Europe, and in countries such as Italy and Spain they accounted for more than 70 per cent of stock market capitalization by 1998.[1]

The great debate

There has always been a lively intellectual debate in Europe and elsewhere about the kinds of activities that properly belong in the public sector and the private sector. With the organization of economies by means of central planning and command structures increasingly discredited – and assessments of cumulative damage surpassing even the expectations of the most vociferous critics – one long-standing model of economic organization progressively lost its appeal. Countries that followed it (voluntarily or not) searched for alternatives. 'Market-orientation' became the key, but itself encompassed a broad array of more or less subtle historical and contemporary gradations. It is arguable that the role the market played in the economic renaissance 'success stories' of West Germany or Japan in the forties and fifties, South Korea or Singapore in the sixties and seventies, Hong Kong or Chile in the eighties, and perhaps Mexico or China in the nineties, is more distinguishable by differences than similarities. And in the Eastern Europe of the nineties the search often seemed to progress under conditions of crisis and chaos.

In the seventies and eighties, some two hundred years after his death, Adam Smith's ideas began to dominate more strongly than ever the debate on the proper organization of economic activity. The 'invisible hand' guides people, seeking to improve their well-being and helping to produce the greatest good for the greatest number through the allocation of labour, capital and intellectual and natural resources in the most efficient way. Smith predicated his positions on the idea of free markets and perfect competition, in which many relatively small players interact, with none sufficiently powerful to affect prices and competition. He was silent as to who would regulate competition, and how, so as to achieve this ideal competitive condition. The interaction of the market would provide for individual success and failure – the winners would indeed win, and the losers lose. However eagerly one wanted to be a winner, fear of being a loser would affect economic behaviour. The aim was to have an economic system with a level playing field that would optimize results for society, thereby maximizing economic welfare, growth and opportunity.

The world described by Smith and his disciples such as Walter Bageot, Alfred Marshall, Joseph Schumpeter, Friedrich Hayek, Milton Friedman and Ayn Rand, became increasingly compelling, repeatedly beating off challenges from alternative visions of society ranging from that of the Fabian socialists of the 19th century, to those of the Fascists and Marxists of the 20th century. Even milder forms of government planning and control, such as French intervention in the private sector and the much-touted Swedish welfare state, eventually lost much of their appeal or began to sink under their own weight. Challenger after challenger was discarded as unworkable.

Perhaps there was a lesson here, to do with human nature. The free market that Adam Smith described seemed to be the one form of economic organization that most closely aligned with what people really perceived as being in their own interests. Even when an alternative system was imposed for a long time, as was Marxism-Leninism over a large part of the world for well over half a century, the invisible hand crept in again through black markets, mini-capitalism, work-minimizing behaviour and a host of other ways now thoroughly familiar in the history of Soviet-style command economies. Despite all the excitement surrounding the 'transformation economies' of Eastern Europe and the 'emerging markets' of Latin America and Asia, little more was involved than the invisible hand being allowed more room to apply its touch. The ideas of even the most modern writers on business affairs, running the gamut from 'new' models of competitive advantage for companies and countries and 'new' trade theory, to the 'new' ideas of core competencies of corporations, usually end up on closer examination to be little more than old wine in new bottles – essentially vintage Adam Smith repackaged and retailed to a broader market.

If the invisible hand so dominates the landscape of economic ideas, then government intervention should be calibrated against its market impact in the cold light of how people are most likely to respond, not according to some social thinker's ideas about how they *ought* to respond. Any such intervention needs to be tested as to whether it is effective in making the market work more efficiently or, if it is not (which is usually the case) whether it works with market incentives or against them – and ultimately whether the social gains achieved by the intervention outweigh the loss in market efficiency. Where free markets have been permitted they have left powerful performance benchmarks behind, and recent history certainly suggests that policies that deviate too far from them are doomed to eventual failure. Indeed some have argued that what is good for free-market capitalism is ultimately good for society – that every other system that has been tried has fared less well. Still, even the most free market-oriented countries have chains of social and economic policies that constrain overly aggressive market behaviour. In this sense, the political process, democratic or otherwise, invariably comes up with ways of guiding the economic process in the direction of results that depart (sometimes significantly) from what would happen under totally free market conditions. The need for such forms of government guidance is to be found in the failure of market mechanisms to produce socially acceptable results.

That the notion of state-owned enterprises as a viable tool of government intervention increasingly appeared to be a relic of the failed economic models of the past – and a bad fit with the growing dominance of free market thinking – is hardly surprising. Even in the early postwar years debate focused on what kinds of activities should fall into the government domain, and it is a debate that continues to this day. Increasingly, private ownership became the default solution, albeit sometimes with a significant degree of government regulation. SOEs had to justify their existence based on a lack of better alternatives, a position that became increasingly untenable across a broad spectrum of economic activities.

What kinds of activities properly belong in the public sector? The concept of 'public goods' helps provide some guidance. There are certain things the free market is not good at providing – things whose value is hard to identify and to allocate among beneficiaries in rough proportion to the benefits received, even as others (as free riders) are able to enjoy them without sharing in their cost. National defence, public parks, the survival of endangered species, and public safety are possible examples. Others, ranging from education and hospitals to airports, roads and postal services are often subject to debate. Vigorous discussion has developed in many countries about the efficacy of market-based solutions to such problems as environmental pollution and maintenance of fisheries – solutions that are 'incentive-compatible' and confer on resource users ownership rights that make it clearly in their own interests to maintain that resource on a sustainable basis. So even though the market demonstrates some weaknesses when costs and benefits cannot easily be allocated, it can nevertheless be used to provide cost-effective solutions for social problems involving public goods. On the whole, however, public goods provide a durable rationale for government inter-vention to allocate costs and benefits of shared resources effectively. But only, of course, to a point beyond which economic efficiency will suffer unacceptably.

A related issue involved industries with natural monopolies, such as water supply, where privatization could lead to abuse of monopoly power. Propo-nents of privatization argue that watchful and vigorous government regulation provides an adequate safeguard, so privatization can provide the benefits of improved efficiency without the costs of monopolization.

As thinking on public goods and natural monopolies has evolved alongside the more general thrust towards market-based solutions to problems of resource allocation and economic growth, together with the catalytic effects of technological change, the line between public and private ownership has shifted towards the latter, sometimes at dramatic speed.

Historically, SOEs have been particularly prominent in banking, telecommunications, postal services, electricity and gas utilities, airlines, railways, defence-related manufacturing, banking and certain strategic industries such as coal and steel. In many cases private-sector activity has existed alongside SOEs for extended periods of time, and even after SOEs have been transferred to the private sector the government may continue to hold an equity stake.

First on the list for transfer from the public to the private sector may be primary and manufacturing activities in industries such as mining, agribusiness, automobiles, steel, pharmaceuticals and the like. Next are commercial services such as airlines, broadcasting, road haulage and other forms of transport, as well as financial services. Then come parts of the economic infrastructure such as electric power, water and sewage systems, telecommunications, rail lines, roads, tunnels and bridges, airports and air traffic control systems. And there is the 'social infrastructure', comprising such often controversial elements as hospitals and schools, security services and even the criminal justice system. The consensus has emerged that the state ought to be confined to a limited range of core economic activities that have strong public-good characteristics – although wide variations in thinking on this among countries is not surprising.

Why privatize?

With the philosophical and political debate on the allocation of economic functions between the private and government sectors providing the context, the arguments for privatization are clear. They are:

● to raise revenue for the state through sale proceeds or to staunch the financial drain arising from direct and indirect subsidies of inefficient SOEs. This financial objective may be politically controversial, since the government gives up a potential stream of earnings in favour of current sale proceeds, but gains from not having to give future subsidies. Which is larger, on a present-value basis, can be the subject of lively debate. The financial arguments are given additional weight in the European context by a strongly anti-subsidy stance taken by EU competition authorities in industries such as air transport and banking, as well as the budgetary commitments under the Maastricht Treaty;

● to promote economic efficiency in the internal operations of the affected enterprises. The poor performance of many SOEs has been widely documented in studies comparing their cost and efficiency levels with private sector companies in the seventies and early eighties, and later confirmed in studies of pre- and post-privatization performance differentials. The potential for substantial efficiency gains through privatization is no longer a contested notion;

● to reduce government interference and politically-based distortions in the economy and, with it, reduce the potential for corruption, cronyism and perverse effects on income distribution;

● to encourage competition and market-based discipline in the affected industries, particularly when those industries are themselves becoming global;

● to encourage wide share ownership among the general population, both directly and through retirement accounts and mutual funds, and thereby develop a broad and deep financial market that will serve as an efficient and dynamic allocator of capital. Liquid capital markets and performance-driven institutional asset managers, in turn, help assure effective corporate governance and management attention to shareholder value;

● to respond effectively to globalization of industries and international consolidation which includes cross-border M&A activity and various types of joint ventures and strategic alliances in industries such as telecommunications and air transport. Arguably, privatization is necessary to fully develop effective business strategies in dynamic sectors of the global economy.

Various academic studies have shown that managers of SOEs have little incentive to improve quality and service, cut costs or innovate; and only in rare cases when such considerations are unimportant does public ownership involve relatively low costs. Moreover, politicians use SOEs to reward political supporters through mispricing of products, investments in low-value projects, cross-subsidization, overstaffing, suboptimum plant location and the like.[2] So privatization almost invariably brings significant gains in performance. Nor are alternatives such as reduced subsidies and deregulation effective substitutes for the kinds of performance improvements that can be obtained through private ownership.[3]

Studies of privatization show how significant performance improvements can be. A recent survey of 15 such studies covering several thousand privatizations in more than 50 countries concluded that performance of SOEs compared poorly with comparable private sector firms, and improved dramatically after privatization in terms of efficiency and profitability, as well as increased capital spending and reduced leverage. And even where employment was reduced, there was a disproportionate improvement in labour performance and (arguably) an increase in employment opportunities in other sectors of the economy.[4]

Privatization activity tends to have different phases depending on the industry involved. SOEs already operating in what are competitive commercial markets tend to be sold early. Public utility and telecoms privatizations tend to occur somewhat later and sometimes require substantial restructuring prior to sale, as well as the implementation of a viable regulatory framework to govern critical infrastructure activities newly allocated to the private sector. By far the greatest amount of privatization in the latter category is in telecoms, where dramatic technological change as well as industry globalization has strengthened the conventional arguments for privatization.

Privatization can assume disproportionate importance in the banking sector due to its central role in capital allocation and the payments mechanism, as well as in monitoring and governance of non-financial enterprises. In many countries, state-controlled banks have exerted a strong influence over non-financial businesses through credit rationing and non-arm's length lending. Indeed, in some countries control of banks has been conferred on borrowing enterprises. In the absence of strong sensible regulation and adequate credit analysis this is often a recipe for disaster. Privatization sales to the public via major institutional investors such as pension funds and mutual funds, on the other hand, tend to encourage the shift from a governance system based on large, stable shareholdings to one based on portfolio fluidity and emphasis on shareholder value.

Patterns of privatization in the EU

The development of privatization can be divided into three activity zones:

- privatization in the countries that are members of the Organization for Economic Co-operation and Development, i.e. the developed market economy countries of Europe, North America, Japan, Australia and New Zealand, with the later addition of Turkey, Mexico, South Korea, Poland, the Czech Republic and Hungary;

- privatization in countries in Eastern Europe and Asia undergoing the transition to market-based systems (including those later joining the OECD);

- privatization in non-OECD developing countries.

Much attention has been focused on privatization in non-OECD transition economies because it was key to successful launch of a market-based economic system, and in the emerging market countries because privatization promised important gains in the efficiency of resource allocation and the rate of economic growth. Indeed, during the late eighties there was far more privatization in emerging market countries than in OECD countries, usually under the tutelage of the IMF and World Bank as being central to economic stabilization and development, and for the requisite degree of economic discipline. And in the early nineties all eyes were on Eastern Europe, where efforts ranged from successful mass privatizations in Poland and eastern Germany (under the Treuhandanstalt, the East German privatization agency) to botched efforts in Russia marked by corruption, manipulation and failure to carry out accompanying legal, regulatory and fiscal reforms.

The focus here is on privatization in the OECD countries and, specifically, in the members of the EU and the euro-zone. As Fig. 6.1 shows, between 1990–8 the bulk of this activity, as measured by privatization proceeds to the government, occurred in OECD countries – $485 billion out of a global total of $698 billion (69 per cent) – although this was lower than the OECD share of combined global GDP. The EU accounted for $301 billion in privatization proceeds during this period. Figure 6.2 gives a breakdown by country of privatization activity from 1990 to 1998. Overall, global privatization reached a peak of $153.8 billion in 1997 and declined to $114.5 billion in 1998, due mainly to the financial crisis in Asia and the emerging markets.

European privatization after World War II began in Germany under the Adenauer government, with the 1961 sale of the state's majority stake in Volkswagen to the public. Placement of shares with small investors was

Fig 6.1 Global amounts raised from privatization (US$bn)

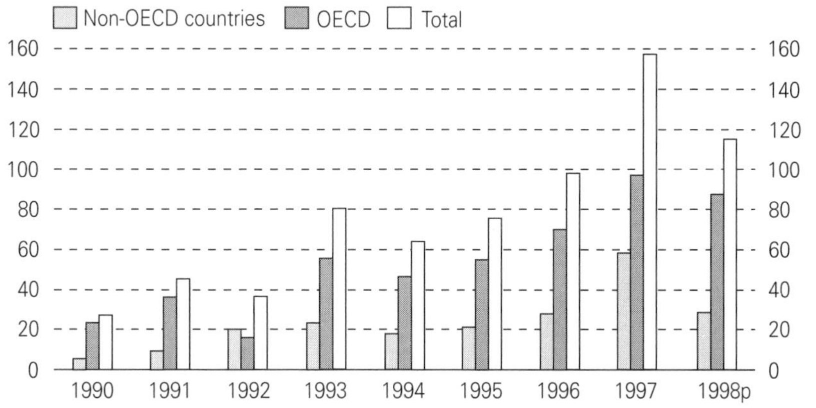

| | Non-OECD countries | OECD | Total |

p: provisional.

Sources: OECD based on national statistics; World Bank; Warburg Dillon Read; IFR Securities (as from 1997)

emphasized. This was followed in 1965 with the sale of Veba. In both cases, subsequent poor performance of the German stock market soured the public's attitude to equities and the government was forced into shareholder bailouts.[5]

It was almost 20 years after the initial German efforts that the first massive privatization programme was launched by the government of Margaret Thatcher in Britain, which in turn had far-reaching effects on redefining the appropriate role of the state in economic activities in Europe and beyond. The first major transaction was that of British Telecom in 1984, a highly successful public offering, followed by massive privatizations of British Airways, British Petroleum, British Airports Authority (BAA), British Rail, Cable & Wireless and British Aerospace. All involved share sales to institutional and retail share-holders in the UK and abroad, and reduced the proportion of SOEs in the UK economy from over 10 per cent of GDP in 1978 to virtually zero when the Conservatives left office in 1997. Virtually all the privatized firms became highly efficient and vibrant domestic and often global competitors in their respective sectors. Privatization undoubtedly played a key role in transforming the British economy from the butt of jokes in the seventies to arguably the most dynamic in Europe at the end of the nineties. A broad political consensus has been reached in the UK, with Labour shifting its position from bitter opposition to privatization and threats of renationalizations in the early days of the Thatcher initiative to strong support of what had been achieved by the time the Blair administration took office.

Fig 6.2 Country breakdown of global amount raised from privatization (US$m)

	1990	1991	1992	1993	1994	1995	1996	1997	1998
Australia	19	1,042	1,893	2,057	1,841	8,089	9,052	16,815	7,146
Austria	32	48	49	142	700	1,035	1,251	2,020	2,935
Belgium	–	–	–	956	549	2,681	1,222	1,562	1,467
Canada[2]	1,504	808	1,249	755	490	3,998	1,770	–	11
Czech Republic[3]	–	–	–	–	1,077	1,205	994	442	469
Denmark	644	–	–	122	229	10	366	45	4,502
Finland	–	–	–	229	1,166	363	911	835	1,999
France	–	–	–	12,160	5,479	4,136	5,099	8,189	13,467
Germany[4]	–	325	–	435	240	–	13,228	1,125	364
Greece	–	–	–	35	73	44	558	1,395	3,892
Hungary	38	470	720	1,842	1,017	3,813	1,157	1,966	353
Iceland	–	–	21	10	2	6	–	4	129
Ireland	–	515	70	274	–	157	293	–	–
Italy[5]	–	–	–	1,943	6,493	7,434	6,265	27,719	13,619
Japan	–	–	–	15,919	13,773	–	6,379	4,009	6,641
Korea	–	–	–	817	2,435	480	1,866	539	600
Luxembourg	–	–	–	–	–	–	–	–	–
Mexico	3,122	10,757	6,859	2,503	766	167	73	2,690	995
Netherlands	716	179	–	780	3,766	3,993	1,239	831	335
New Zealand	3,895	17	967	630	29	264	1,839	–	441
Norway	73	–	–	–	118	521	660	35	28
Portugal	1,192	1,198	2,326	500	1,132	2,425	3,011	4,968	4,271
Poland	23	23	238	245	385	714	749	2,179	2,020
Spain	172	–	820	3,223	1,458	2,941	2,679	12,522	11,618
Sweden	–	–	378	252	2,313	852	785	1,055	172
Switzerland	–	–	–	–	–	–	–	–	4,426
Turkey	486	244	423	546	412	515	292	466	1,009
United Kingdom[6]	12,906	21,825	604	8,523	1,341	6,691	7,610	4,544	–
United States	–	–	–	–	–	–	–	–	3,100
Total OECD	**24,822**	**37,451**	**16,617**	**54,898**	**47,284**	**52,534**	**69,348**	**95,955**	**86,009**
of which: EU15	15,662	24,090	4,247	29,573	24,940	32,765	44,518	66,812	58,641
Other countries[7]	5,078	10,413	19,845	23,976	18,111	21,115	27,911	57,827	28,533
Global total	**29,900**	**47,864**	**36,462**	**78,874**	**65,395**	**73,649**	**97,259**	**153,782**	**114,542**

– Nil or insignificant.
[1] The amounts shown are gross proceeds from privatization. These do not necessarily correspond to the net amount available to the government. The figures are on a calendar year basis and they may not add up to published budget figures
[2] There were no federal privatizations in 1997. Provincial data are currently not available
[3] The cumulative amount for 1991–3 is US$2,240 million
[4] Up to 1997 information on trade sales is not available
[5] Including convertible bond issue (INA) of US$2,055 million in 1996 and indirect privatizations raising US$2,658 million in 1996 and US$2,620 million in 1997
[6] Debt sales amounting for years 1990–7 (fiscal years) to: £5,347 million, £7,924 million, £8,189 million, £5,453 million, £6,429 million, £2,439 million, £4,500 million respectively
[7] Source for 1990–6 is World Bank and Warburg Dillon Read, from 1997 source is IFR Securities

Source: National statistics unless otherwise indicated

France embarked on an ambitious programme of privatization under the government of Prime Minister Jacques Chirac in 1986, which saw the privatization of 22 companies worth $12 billion in the following two years, a process that was halted (but not reversed) by the socialists in 1988. Privatization was resumed by the Balladur government in 1993 and continued under the Jospin government, often with spectacular successes such as the $7.1 billion France Telecom IPO in 1997. French privatization proceeds averaged over $7 billion annually during 1994–8, almost twice the amount in Germany during this period.

As Fig. 6.2 shows, Spain and Portugal undertook sizeable privatizations in 1997 and 1998, with Italy engaging in SOE sales of well over $60 billion during 1994–8. The Nordic countries and Greece, on the other hand, lagged behind much of the rest of Europe. In terms of industries, Fig. 6.3 shows how the pattern has evolved throughout the OECD in the nineties, with the most intense activity in the telecommunications, financial services, transport and public utilities sectors.

The EU share of global privatizations has increased steadily as Commission directives have mandated market liberalization and reductions in subsidies, and as the Maastricht fiscal targets have placed a premium on raising government revenues and limiting spending. During 1998 alone, Italy undertook a public issue of BNL (Banca Nazionale del Lavoro) shares for $4.6 billion, as well as the fourth tranche of privatization of ENI (Ente Nazionale Industriale, a major Italian industrial holding company) begun in 1995. France did a $7 billion secondary offering of France Telecom shares, in addition to the sale of 2 per cent to Deutsche Telekom to cement a strategic alliance between them. There were also insurance and banking offerings such as those by CNP Assurances and GAN. Spain raised over $24 billion in privatization revenue in 1997 and 1998 through sales of shares in telecoms, Argentaria Bank, the Endesa power group and Tabacalera, the tobacco company. Portugal undertook secondary offerings of EDP electricity, BRISA, the motorway toll operator, and Cimpor cement companies. Finland sold a 22.2 per cent stake in Sonara telecoms and a 15 per cent stake in Fortum, the electricity company. Austria undertook its largest privatization in the form of a 25 per cent share offer in Telekom Austria for $2.33 billion. Figure 6.3 shows the main sectors involved in OECD privatizations during 1990–8.

In contrast to Europe, where SOEs have traditionally played a much more important role, US privatizations have been few and far between. In 1998 the government carried out a $3.1 billion IPO of US Enrichment Corporation, which produces 75 per cent of US nuclear fuel. The previous privatization occurred ten years earlier with the sale of Conrail, which had resulted from a

Fig 6.3 Privatizations in OECD countries by main sector (US$bn)

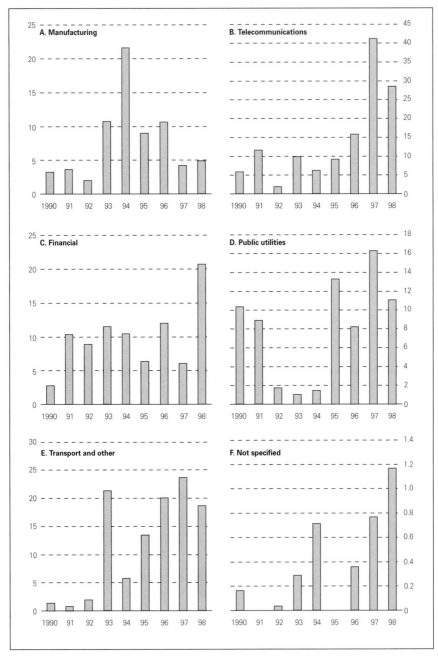

Source: OECD based on national statistics, World Bank and Warburg Dillon Read

government merger and takeover of the bankrupt New York Central and Pennsylvania Railroads. A lot of US privatization activity occurs at the state and local level through contracting out services in sectors ranging from refuse disposal to prison management. The type of large infrastructure holdings that have been prominently involved in privatizations in Europe and emerging markets today remain in public hands in the US, both directly and through special public agencies. These include ports, airports, power generation, roads and the postal system. Paradoxically, a country that prides itself on market orientation lags behind in privatization.

Figure 6.4 depicts the 1998 market value, sales and profits of the 34 largest publicly-traded privatized companies in the world, each having a market capitalization of at least $15 billion. The table shows where each ranks in the global top 1,000 companies according to *Business Week,* as well as where each firm ranks in its own country. Note in particular the number of French and German companies on the list. In 1998, 75 of the top 1,000 global companies in terms of market value were privatized firms, amounting to a capitalization of about $1.7 trillion in mid-1998 – roughly 10 per cent of the top 1,000 total and over 20 per cent of the non-US total.[6]

The privatization process

Successful privatization requires, first and foremost, a strong political commitment to carry the process through systematically, expeditiously and fairly. This has to be based on some combination of political consensus and strong political leadership. In many cases, privatization will face opposition from entrenched members of the existing management concerned about losing their positions, from labour groups concerned about job losses in subsequent business restructuring, or from local interest groups and linked industries that might be adversely affected by a change in ownership. Formid-able minefields are often put in the way by such opponents, and it takes per-severence and political commitment to get through them. Political opponents are often eager to use the issues raised in the privatization debate for political advantage, and are capable of putting legislative hurdles in the path of the process. Political preoccupation with the privatization process rather than the outcome is often among opposing factors, as are excessive demands for second opinions and timidity among public officials who may be held personally or politically accountable for any problems.

Besides an underlying political commitment, established privatization

Fig 6.4 Market value, sales and profits of the 34 largest publicly traded privatized firms

Company	Country	Global 1000 rank	Country rank	Market value US$m	Total sales US$m	Total profits US$m
Nippon Telegraph & Telephone	Japan	8	1	130,911	63,665	1,081
British Petroleum	United Kingdom	26	2	85,283	70,870	4,600
Deutsche Telekom	Germany	32	2	73,640	37,891	1,853
British Telecommunications	United Kingdom	40	6	66,261	25,504	3,307
ENI	Italy	57	1	56,424	34,551	2,913
France Telecom	France	59	1	56,011	26,197	2,484
Telecom Italia	Italy	67	2	51,301	24,372	1,963
Telefónica	Spain	78	1	45,854	15,617	1,256
Total	France	127	6	38,345	31,939	1,272
Elf Acquitaine	France	91	2	38,123	42,507	1,702
Gazprom	Russia	128	1	32,906	20,462	1,456
Telebras	Brazil	129	1	32,759	13,739	3,390
VEBA	Germany	116	10	32,686	42,667	1,576
Volkswagen	Germany	122	11	30,938	63,521	749
Telstra	Australia	130	1	30,278	9,668	1,608
Koninklijke PTT Nederland	Netherlands	150	7	26,420	7,590	1,339
Cable & Wireless	United Kingdom	156	17	25,601	11,417	1,194
Endesa	Spain	164	4	24,950	8,475	1,102
Singapore Telecommunications	Singapore	189	1	21,499	2,952	1,127
Hong Kong Telecommunications	Hong Kong	190	1	21,440	4,522	2,197
China Telecom	China	199	1	20,676	1,871	599
BG	United Kingdom	204	21	20,246	7,012	820
Rhône-Poulenc	France	207	10	20,122	15,042	571
Telefonos de Mexico	Mexico	209	1	19,999	6,873	1,455
Commonwealth Bank	Australia	211	3	19,828	NA	1,391
Société Générale	France	216	12	19,548	NA	1,021
East Japan Railways	Japan	221	18	18,995	18,142	510
Banque Nationale de Paris	France	231	15	18,214	NA	997
Compagnie de Saint-Gobain	France	239	16	17,603	17,898	939
Repsol	Spain	256	5	16,694	21,208	833
Paribas	France	261	17	16,327	NA	1,099
Credito Italiano	Italy	265	6	16,113	NA	274
British Aerospace	United Kingdom	266	27	15,918	11,850	695
Electricidade de Portugal	Portugal	268	1	15,785	3,132	510

These firms are from a companion 'Top 100 emerging-market companies' in the same issue, and subsequent rankings are adjusted to reflect their inclusion in the Global 1,000 list

This table details the stock market value, total sales and total profits – in millions of US dollars (translated at the contemporaneous exchange rate) – of the 34 publicly-traded privatized firms worth at least US$15 billion as of 28 May 1998. Market value is calculated as the stock price times the latest available number of shares outstanding. Firms are classified as privatized if any shares of a state-owned enterprise have been sold to private investors through a public share offering, even if the government still retains a majority of the company's outstanding shares. The issues are described in an appendix to this paper. Information is from Morgan Stanley Capital International, as reported in 'The Business Week Global 1,000,' *Business Week*, 13 July 1998, pp. 52–92. Global 1,000 rank refers to the company's global ranking based on market valuation, while country rank refers to the company's relative position among those firms from their country on the Global 1,000 list.

guidelines and timetables are important. First, there has to be a solid legal basis for privatization that will stand up under possible court challenge.[7] Then there should be a pre-announced plan or high-level directive as the basis for a commitment to carry through the process on a fixed schedule to on-time completion that cannot easily be changed. Guidelines should be transparent and demonstrably fair, including objective selection criteria for possible private-sector buyers, investment bankers, consultants, tax advisers, account-ants and auditors, and legal advisers who form the infrastructure or 'facili-tators' of the privatization process. All this requires dedicated and motivated public officials and the commitment of substantial amounts of time and resources.

Important to the process is the preparation of SOEs for privatization. A key issue is whether the business should be restructured first, while under public ownership, in order to maximize investor interest and achieve the highest possible price for the government, or whether it should be sold to investors at a low price, letting the new management do the restructuring. The arguments are complex. Restructuring while under state ownership is likely to meet strong opposition from those affected, especially the workers, and may therefore prove ineffective – if restructuring were easy to carry out, it might have been done earlier by the existing management. On the other hand, an enterprise that is a basket case will command a very low price which, if it is far below book value, can prompt political charges of a 'giveaway'. And there are possible long-term liabilities involving environmental and health issues that the new owners may not want to take on and which may require some sort of government guarantee.

A good example of the complex nature of these problems is Air France, which went through massive government subsidies to the consternation of the airline's private sector competitors and the EU competition authorities, as well as the earnest restructuring efforts of two teams of top managers, before it was deemed ready for partial privatization by the socialist government in 1999. Along the way, even the employees did not want shares in a business that seemed uncompetitive in a rapidly changing industry – and with a continued majority shareholding by the state – in return for wage concessions demanded by management. By the time a successful IPO occurred in 1999, however, Air France had become a substantially more competitive airline.

Evaluating the condition of an SOE is often complex and difficult. A set of books has to be built that means something in the real world, and the government has to accept a realistic 'fair value' concept that reflects the economic worth of the enterprise which may well be below book value. The value of disposals of peripheral activities has to be established, as does the competitive stand-alone viability of the enterprise. There are a number of valuation techniques that can be used, none of which may be precisely suited to the situation. Appropriate discount rates need to be used, and a host of complex tax and other regulations must be considered, including the appropriate role of foreign direct and portfolio investors in the privatization process.

Post-privatization regulation in infrastructure activities and public utilities needs to tread a fine line between over- and under-regulation, and prevent co-opting of the regulators by the newly privatized enterprises. In some cases regulatory forbearance, exclusivity and protectionism has been incorporated into privatization programmes in order to maximize the price to the government. Such 'sweetheart' deals, of course, come at the expense of consumers who overpay in the future to underwrite government revenues and assure excess profits for the privatized firms. Sales to strategic buyers who are in a strong bargaining position tend to be especially vulnerable to such pressures. Proper regulation involves clear separation between regulatory and commercial functions, a high level of regulatory independence, commitment to phasing in competition where possible, and co-ordination between competition authorities, industry-specific regulators and self-regulatory organizations. It also involves interregional co-ordination in federal states, appropriate modelling of rates of return and the use of price caps, possible universal service requirements, and the use of periodic reviews and regulatory sunset clauses.[8]

Also important is the state of development of the domestic capital market, its legal infrastructure and the size of the SOE to be privatized. Capital market development and privatization are interdependent, with privatization often making major contributions to the breadth and depth of capital markets and the state of the markets; at the same time, the appetite of retail and institutional investor pools determines the size and structuring of initial and secondary privatization offerings. A well-developed capital market makes an important contribution to the transparency and credibility of the privatization process.

Figure 6.5 shows the alternative approaches to privatization. The principal techniques are:

● *Trade sales.* This involves selling the SOE to a firm or group of investors who will manage the business after privatization. The buyer is usually a domestic or foreign corporation with a strategic interest in the business to be privatized. Firms privatized through trade sales are often small and unsuitable for privatization via share offers. Besides asset stripping, a domestic or foreign bidder in a trade sale might be interested only in the real estate involved, or in closing the former SOE in order to reduce the degree of competition.

● *Leveraged and management buyouts.* An alternative to selling control of an SOE to a buyer already active in the business is to sell shares to an

Fig 6.5 Alternative privatization methods

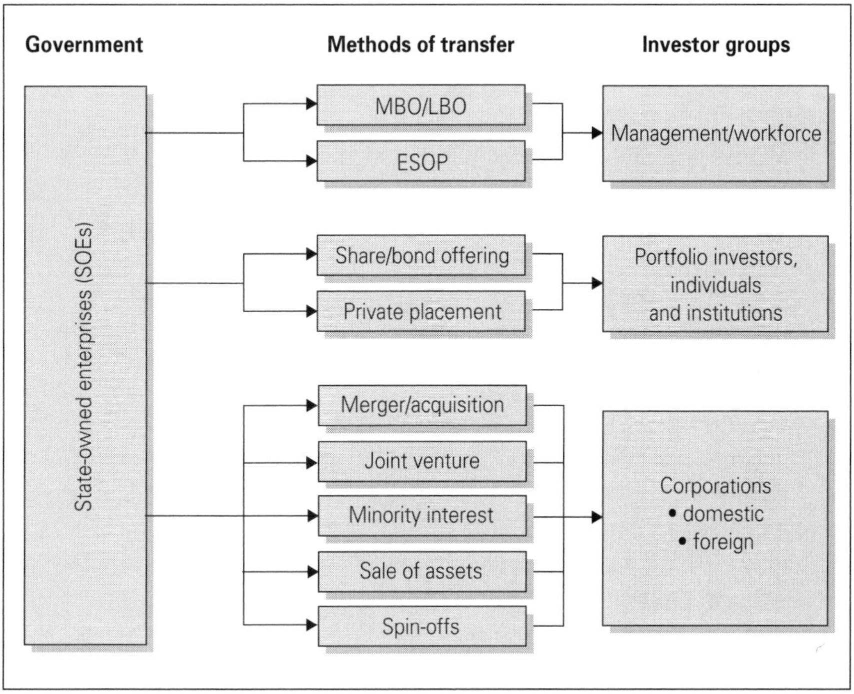

Source: J.P. Morgan

investment fund controlled by outsiders or by existing managers who see potential in the privatized company and are willing to put up capital to realize it, sometimes on a leveraged basis. The advantage is that LBO or MBO investors have a strong personal interest in restructuring the SOE and maximizing its value over a relatively short period, often with an exit strategy of selling the improved firm for a significantly higher price. They are therefore likely to want to get on with the job and to be intolerant of delays in the restructuring process. Governments, on the other hand, may be suspicious of asset stripping and liquidation motives among LBO or MBO investors, and of the high political fallout that may result.

● *Initial and secondary public offerings.* Shares may be offered to the public in an IPO or an SEO. Among the government's decisions, with advice from an experienced investment bank, will be the appropriate price – one that will attract broad investor interest and is low enough so that shares will trade strongly in the aftermarket. The extent to which a sizeable allocation of shares will be reserved for domestic retail investors has to be decided, as well as the terms on which they will be able to buy. These decisions may have important political as well as financial consequences. In OECD countries in recent years a large proportion of share sales have gone to retail investors, encouraged by a range of incentives such as discounts, bonus shares based on a holding period and guarantees against stock price declines. There is also the issue of institutional distribution, including allocations to various investment banking intermediaries, the structure of the underwriting syndicate, and international tranches to be distributed to foreign institutional and retail portfolio investors. Because IPOs tend to be underpriced, these decisions have to be well justified, transparent and fairly executed in the likely scramble among prospective investors.

- *Private placements.* In addition to, or in place of, initial public offerings, shares in privatized enterprises may be sold in large blocks to institutional investors such as insurance companies, pension funds, mutual funds or other large pools of capital. The reason might be to focus ownership on fiduciaries who will maintain large, stable and possibly strategic stakes in the company, thereby improving post-privatization corporate governance in comparison with absence of control implicit in widely dispersed and fragmented stakes, where management is accountable to no one. Among private-placement buyers might be a domestic or foreign firm with a strategic interest and capable of providing managerial and technical expertise, possibly with a view to increasing its stake.

- *Voucher privatizations.* In some cases, especially in some Eastern European countries, vouchers that can be exchanged for shares in SOEs to be privatized have been given to citizens without charge or sold at a nominal price. These vouchers become 'currency' for acquiring newly issued shares at ratios that depend on the perceived prospects of each privatized firm, or they can be sold beforehand in a secondary voucher market that usually develops quickly and enables the initial voucher holders to trade in for cash. The vouchers usually end up in the hands of large investors, who use them to acquire significant stakes in newly privatized firms. While voucher privatization has advantages – notably the formation of control groups capable of demanding management accountability and exercising effective corporate governance – in practice it has been largely discredited due to corruption, favouritism and inefficiency.

- *Sale of shares to employees.* The government's objective may be the allocation of significant ownership stakes to employees of the SOE to be privatized. The justification may be that employees have contributed materially to the value of the firm and therefore deserve a stake in its ownership, or that employees as owners may improve performance and make the privatized firm more attractive to outside investors. In some cases employee share ownership plans (ESOPs) are used to hold employee shares collectively instead of individual share allocations, and to prevent 'flipping' by employees. On the other hand, employee shareholdings may increase the difficulty of restructuring the enterprise, much of which is likely to involve layoffs and personnel changes. In a comprehensive study of privatizations during 1977–98, on average 8.5 per cent of shares were reserved for employees in IPOs and 4.8 per cent in SEOs.

● *Leases, asset sales and management contracts.* Alternatives to shifting ownership to new investors include leasing and operating concessions. For example, a build-operate-transfer contract may involve the sale to a private company of a concession to undertake an infrastructure project like a bridge or tunnel and to operate it on a commercial basis for perhaps 30 years, after which the project reverts to the government at no cost. Or a facility such as a resort or motorway restaurant chain may be leased to a private operator for a fixed period against mutually agreeable performance requirements and financial terms. Or an SOE may be placed under a management contract with a private operator who has the necessary expertise. Such approaches may be useful where there is no legal basis for transfers to private ownership, or where such a transfer is politically difficult.

Selecting among alternative privatization methods depends on:

● the economic and political objectives of the seller
● the types of buyers targeted
● the capabilities of the domestic financial market and access to external capital markets
● the capabilities of local investors and eligibility of foreign participants in the privatization process
● the condition of the SOE itself
● whether the legal entity is to be privatized or only the assets sold
● legal and tax implications.

Important decisions include share allocation and the degree of underpricing, whether a tender offer, book-building or fixed-price offer should be used and, if the latter, at what point the offer price should be fixed. In fact, governments seem to rely almost exclusively on fixed-price offerings, even though a competitive tender offer could raise more revenue. And while governments typically tend to give up operational control in privatizations via share offers, they tend to retain veto power through the corporate charter with regard to choice of the CEO, maximum allowable foreign shareholdings, and by retention of a 'golden share' which enables them to block certain corporate action. In the case of trade sales there have to be clear bidding rules and criteria for selecting winning bidders.

A comprehensive analysis of 630 privatizations via share offers in 59 countries from 1977 to 1997, comprising 417 IPOs and 213 SEOs, shows a mean underpricing of 34.1 per cent for IPOs and 9.4 per cent for SEOs – 85 per cent of the IPOs and 61 per cent of the SEOs were sold at a fixed price. The analysis shows that the mean all-in expense for the privatizing govern-ments was only 4.4 per cent, presumably due to low selling costs attributable to deliberate underpricing.[9]

Over the long term, investors likewise tend to gain by taking part in privat-ization issues. One recent global study shows that privatizations outperform both local and international stock market indices over one-year holding periods for IPOs, with even greater returns over three- and five-year holding periods.[10] While country risk considerations in some cases doubtless pushed up these returns, other research tends to show that the country risk premium declines with time.[11]

Other research suggests that mass SOE privatization using vouchers or share distribution to domestic mutual funds appears to be a method necessi-tated by a lack of properly functioning capital markets and eligible private bidders, often used for political motives and almost impossible to execute without serious irregularities and insider appropriation of control of the best parts.[12]

As Fig. 6.6 shows, IPOs and SEOs have dominated privatizations in OECD countries during the nineties, accounting for perhaps 60 per cent of the cumulative total. This is indicative of the level of investor interest, the state of development of the domestic and international capital markets, and governments' interest in cultivating broad and deep equity markets as an important factor in future economic growth. Second in importance have been trade sales to domestic and foreign firms – with sales to the latter rising in importance as barriers to foreign direct investment have fallen.

All other types of privatizations such as MBOs, sales of shares to employees, asset sales, leases and management contracts have been of minor importance in OECD countries, in contrast to their significance in some emerging market and transition economies. Whereas privatizations via share offerings dominate in OECD countries, trade sales to strategic investors dominate elsewhere due mainly to the more limited development of the investor base in local capital markets.

Fig 6.6 Privatizations in OECD countries by type of transaction (US$bn)

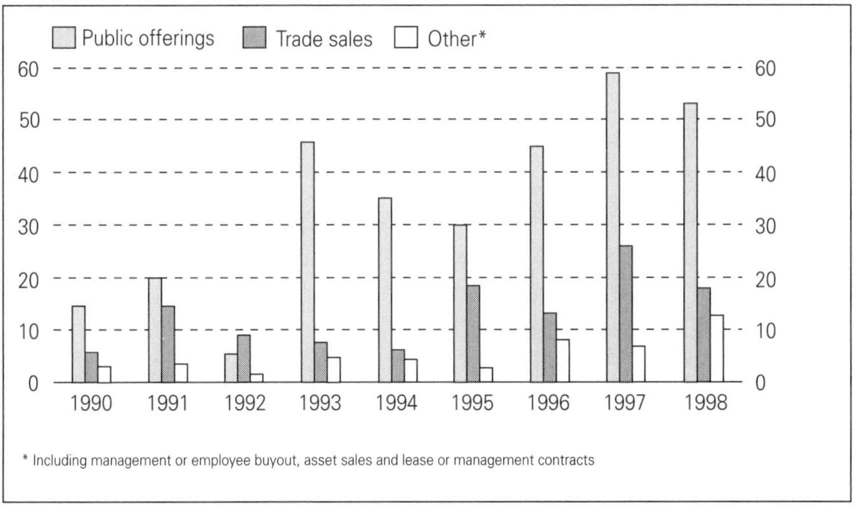
Public offerings
Trade sales
Other*
60
50
40
30
20
10
0
1990
1991
1992
1993
1994
1995
1996
1997
1998
* Including management or employee buyout, asset sales and lease or management contracts

Sources: OECD based on national statistics, World Bank and Warburg Dillon Read

Figure 6.7 shows the 49 largest share offerings in history, either through initial public offerings or seasoned equity offerings, of which 41 were privatization offerings, three were demutualizations (Halifax Building Society, Autoliv Sverige and Norwich Union) and four were private issues (Conoco, Wellcome PLC, Alsthom and Lucent Technologies). The 18 largest share offerings in history, and 33 of the 38 largest thus far, have all been privatizations, with 18 of them raising over $7 billion each.[13]

Fig 6.7 The world's 49 largest share offerings

Date	Company	Country	Amount ($m)	IPO/SEO
Nov 87	Nippon Telegraph & Telephone	Japan	40,260	SEO
Oct 88	Nippon Telegraph & Telephone	Japan	22,400	SEO
Oct 98	NTT DoCoMo	Japan	18,000	IPO
Oct 97	Telecom Italia	Italy	15,500	SEO
Feb 87	Nippon Telegraph & Telephone	Japan	15,097	IPO
Nov 96	Deutsche Telekom	Germany	13,300	IPO
Oct 87	British Petroleum	United Kingdom	12,430	SEO
Nov 97	Telstra	Australia	10,530	IPO
Dec 90	Regional electricity companies[a]	United Kingdom	9,995	IPO
Dec 91	British Telecom	United Kingdom	9,927	SEO
Dec 89	UK water authorities[a]	United Kingdom	8,679	IPO
Nov 98	Sonora [Telecom Finland]	Finland	8,400	IPO
Dec 86	British Gas	United Kingdom	8,012	IPO
Jun 98	Endesa	Spain	8,000	SEO
Jul 97	ENI	Italy	7,800	SEO

Fig 6.7 *cont.*

Date	Company	Country	Amount ($m)	IPO/SEO
Jul 93	British Telecom	United Kingdom	7,360	SEO
Oct 93	Japan Railroad East	Japan	7,312	IPO
Oct 97	France Telecom	France	7,080	IPO
Feb 94	Elf Acquitane	France	6,823	SEO
Jun 97	*Halifax Building Society*	*United Kingdom*	*6,813*	*IPO*
Jun 98	ENI	Italy	6,740	SEO
Oct 98	Swisscom	Switzerland	6,000	IPO
May 94	*Autoliv Sverige*	*Sweden*	*5,818*	*IPO*
Oct 96	ENI	Italy	5,864	SEO
Oct 93	Banque Nationale de Paris	France	4,920	IPO
Nov 84	British Telecom	United Kingdom	4,763	IPO
Jun 97	*Norwich Union*	*United Kingdom*	*4,722*	*IPO*
Dec 87	Japan Air Lines	Japan	4,645	IPO
Dec 88	British Steel	United Kingdom	4,645	IPO
Oct 97	Endesa	Spain	4,500	SEO
Oct 98	*Conoco*	*United States*	*4,400*	*IPO*
Oct 96	Japan Railroad West	Japan	4,400	IPO
Feb 97	Telefónica	Spain	4,360	SEO
May 91	Hydro-Electric, Scottish Power[a]	United Kingdom	4,313	IPO
Jul 92	*Wellcome PLC*	*United Kingdom*	*4,118*	*IPO*
Oct 97	China Telecom	China (HK)	4,000	IPO
Jul 95	Usinor Sacilor	France	3,930	IPO
Nov 95	ENI	Italy	3,907	IPO
Jun 94	Koninklijke PTT Nederland	Netherlands	3,868	IPO
Jun 98	*Alstom*	*UK/France*	*3,720*	*IPO*
Mar 95	National Power, PowerGen Ltd[a]	United Kingdom	3,657	IPO
Jun 87	Société Générale	France	3,577	IPO
Oct 95	Koninklijke PTT Nederland	Netherlands	3,514	SEO
Jun 88	Pohang Iron and Steel	Korea	3,400	IPO
Sep 94	Japan Tobacco	Japan	3,400	IPO
Apr 94	Union des Assurances de Paris	France	3,250	SEO
Jul 96	Commonwealth Bank	Australia	3,100	SEO
Jun 94	Istituto Nazionale de Assicurazioni	Italy	3,100	IPO
Apr 96	*Lucent Technologies*	*United States*	*3,025*	*IPO*

[a] Indicates a group offering of multiple companies that trade separately after the IPO

This table details the 42 largest public and seven largest private sector share offerings in financial history, up to November 1998. Offers are reported in nominal amounts (not inflation-adjusted), and are translated into millions of US dollars ($m) using the contemporaneous exchange rate. *Private sector offerings* are presented in bold, italicized type, while share issue privatizations (SIPs) ae presented in normal typeface. An initial public offering is indicated as an IPO, while a seasoned equity offering is designated an SEO, although only the private sector offerings were actually capital-raising events (SIPs were almost exclusively secondary offerings of shares held by the national government). Amounts reported for SIP offerings are taken from an appendix to this paper, and are recorded as described in the *Financial Times* at the time of the issue (or as detailed in the *Privatisation International* database if a definitive amount was not reported at the time of issuance). Private sector offering amounts are as reported in the Thompson Financial *Securities Data Corporation* datafile in August 1998, updated through November 1998 from secondary sources.

Figure 6.8 shows the extent to which retail investors have participated in OECD privatizations through public offerings in the nineties, accounting for well over half the cumulative total – significantly more than institutional

Fig 6.8 Public offerings in OECD countries by type of buyer

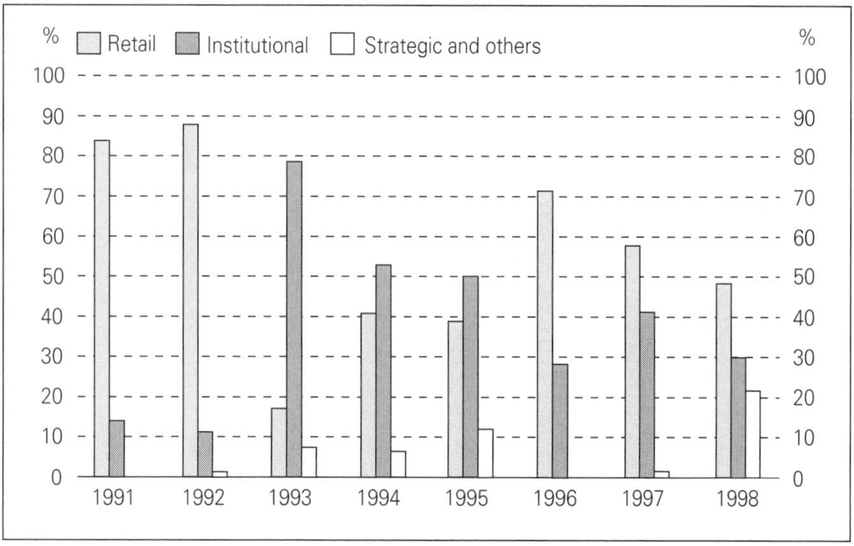

Sources: OECD based on national statistics, World Bank and Warburg Dillon Read

investors. Of course, retail investors often 'flip' their shares quite soon after an underpriced public offering, and the shares have subsequently ended up in large institutional portfolios.

A final question is the extent to which foreign investors should be included as eligible buyers in privatizations. There are strong arguments against limits to foreign participation. The more eligible buyers, the stronger the demand and the higher the share price and revenue for the government is likely to be. Foreign participation with its wider investor base encourages broader interest in the privatized company, and may help it meet its financial needs in the future. Foreign strategic investors can provide managerial and technical expertise, and their deep pockets help post-privatization restructuring, improved competitiveness and easier access to foreign markets.

An example of successful participation by a foreign strategic investor is that of Volkswagen in Skoda in the Czech Republic, involving not only acqui-sition of a highly cost-effective manufacturing base but also leveraging the Skoda brand as part of Volkswagen's global portfolio. An example of a less successful acquisition is Spanish airline Iberia's stake in Aerolineas Argentinas, a venture beset by financial and operational problems. There was also the abortive strategic alliance in the automotive business between privately-owned Volvo and state-owned Renault, regarded by opponents as back-door nationalization of Volvo, whose car division was ultimately acquired in 1998 by the Ford Motor Company.

Figure 6.9 shows resident and non-resident investors in both public offerings and trade sales in OECD countries during the nineties. Note the growing predominance of resident investors in privatization share issues over the period, reflecting strong local interest and the emergence of an 'equity culture' in many of the countries concerned – together with government preference for local strategic investors. As expected, foreign participation was

Fig 6.9 Privatizations in OECD countries by residence of buyer

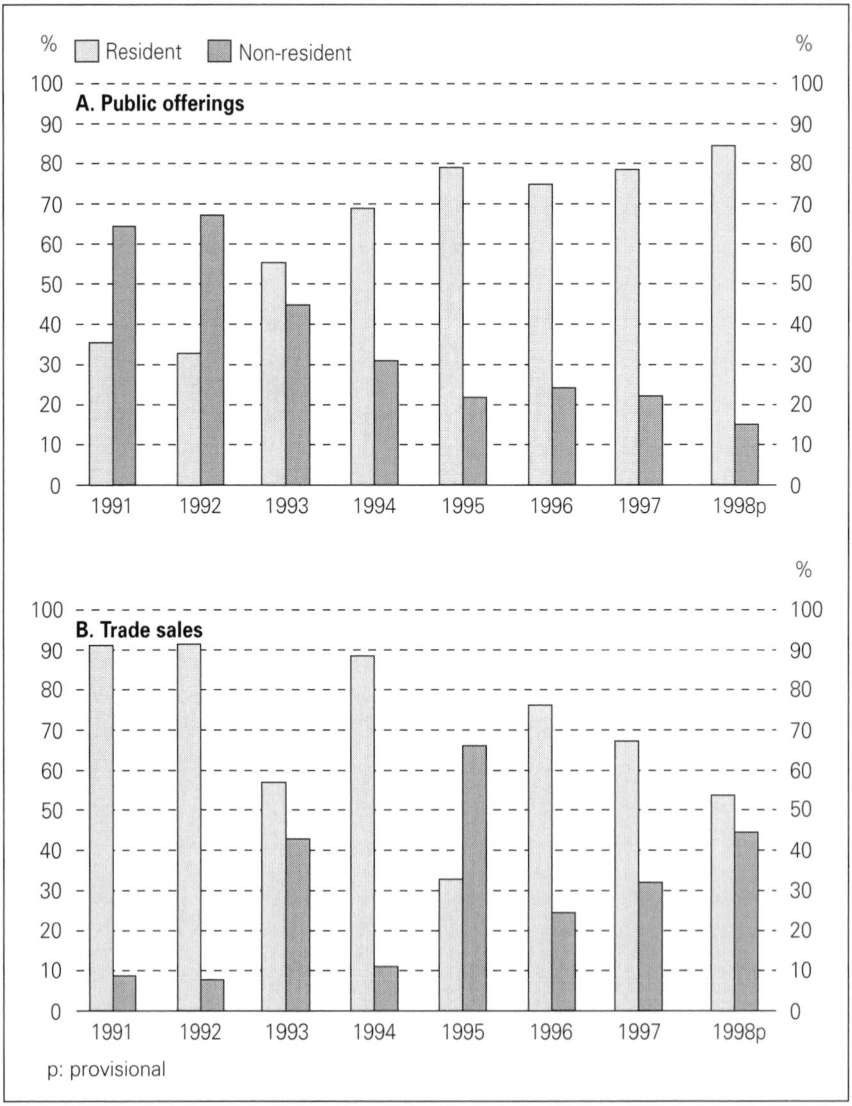

Sources: OECD based on national statistics, World Bank and Warburg Dillon Read

much stronger in the case of trade sales, where the benefits of involvement by a competitive foreign party are likely to have high incremental value for the privatized enterprise. In a comprehensive study of privatizations between 1977 and 1998, on average 28.4 per cent of shares were allocated to foreign investors in IPOs and 35.9 per cent in SEOs, with most large public offerings specifically targeting the US market through American Depository Receipts (ADRs) – with shares thereby gaining in liquidity both in the US and home markets.[14]

Figure 6.10 depicts the key elements of the privatization process. At the centre are the facilitators or intermediaries. These include investment banks which:

● represent the government or potential buyers in negotiations;

● conduct valuations and co-ordinate due diligence;

● underwrite initial or secondary public equity offerings and distribute the securities to target investors;

● arrange financing.

Fig 6.10 Key elements in the privatization process

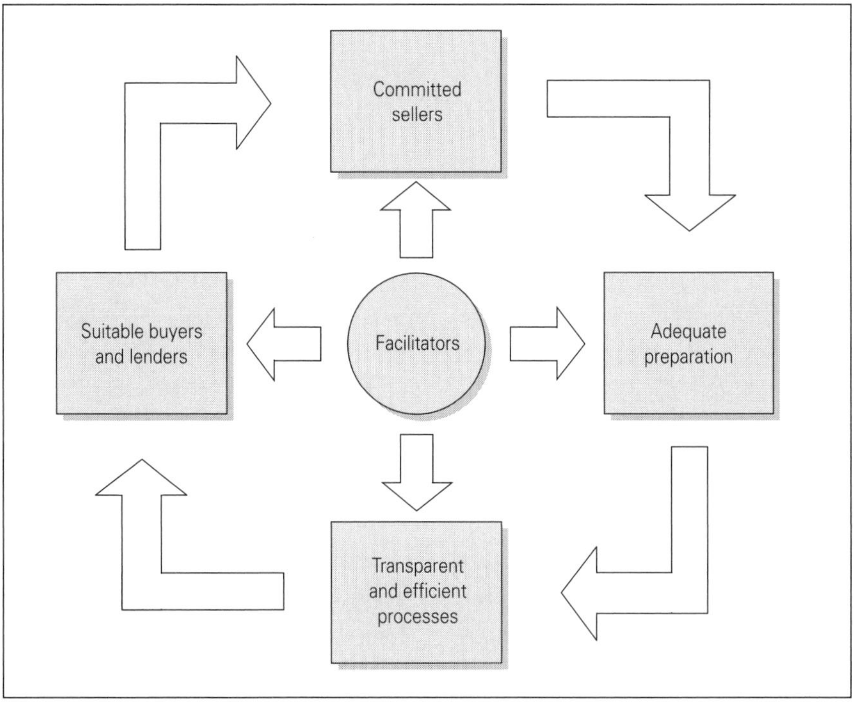

Source: J.P. Morgan

They also include the accountants, lawyers and tax specialists involved in the privatization process, as well as commercial bankers arranging and providing any bank financing required. In the end, successful privatization always involves a balance of multiple objectives. There must be tangible gains for the government as well as for the private investors. The privatized firm has to be competitively viable and profitable on a stand-alone basis – i.e. it has to be able to survive in the private sector without government subsidies, protection or other competitive distortions.

Privatization and investment banking competition in the euro-zone

There are few aspects of investment banking that are more attractive than privatization, both with respect to the available advisory assignments and the securities underwriting opportunities that may be involved in the sometimes massive initial and secondary public offerings. There are several more or less distinct roles that investment banks may play in the privatization process, though they may often overlap.

Government advisers and representation

Important functions for advisers to the government include building a positive image of the SOE to be privatized, preparing sales documents and road-shows, approaching prospective investors and prospective lenders, creating fall-back plans in case bids are inadequate, and educating prospective buyers on alternative acquisition structures. Advisers also have to maintain a constructive stance with potential buyers, including co-ordinated monitoring of contacts and avoidance of favouritism, with all inquiries referred to the adviser. Throughout, a high degree of confidentiality has to be maintained, and press coverage, which is often politicized, has to be carefully handled.

Based on a thorough understanding of the SOE's business, a review of current market data and the banker's own experience, the investment banking adviser to the government must conduct thorough due diligence in order to value the SOE, and advise on the probable selling price range in either a trade sale, public offering or other share distribution. In discussions with privatization officials, it must advise on a strategy that optimizes the government's financial, economic and other objectives, which may involve any of the alternatives discussed earlier. If the privatization is to be undertaken, the investment bank must:

- prepare material describing the company, based on information supplied by the SOE and developed during the due diligence process, that emphasizes the points of value to a buyer, but is also fair and objective in all respects;

- control the process of distributing information to prospective buyers or the market, and provide opportunities for buyers or securities analysts and institutional investors to ask questions about the business, meet management, and conduct their own due diligence.

The investment bank's expertise and track record in executing and financing privatizations is critical, as is the professional standing of its research team covering the industry in question. In the case of a trade sale, the principal functions of the privatization adviser are to:

- analyze a list of possible buyers, including those furnished by the government and existing SOE management – as well as LBO, MBO and/or employee investors, where appropriate and consistent with government objectives – to determine the most likely buyers and the ability of each to obtain financing for the transaction;

- explain how the identified buyers would go about making an evaluation of the company, and, in the case of publicly-traded private sector buyers, what the impact of the privatization acquisition would be on the financial statements and stock price;

- contact potential buyers at decision-making level and serve from that point forward as the exclusive contact for potential buyers;

- construct a bidding process so as to create an auction-like situation aimed at getting the highest price for the seller (or to maximize any other factors that may be important;

- advise on the financing structure of the transaction in order to get the maximum advantage for both sides;

- ensure that all important non-financial terms are settled at an early stage, and see that post-privatization documentation flows smoothly.

This process is fairly straightforward. For larger privatizations a number of domestic and perhaps international names will be included on the list of prospective buyers. These the banker will contact at the appropriate level after a shortlist has been approved by the government. In all transactions, the banker's work is complemented by that of lawyers, accountants, tax experts, and other advisers selected by the government. It is the banker, however, who leads the team.

In the case of an IPO or SEO the investment banking adviser to the government must be capable of:

- designing a distribution strategy that will maximize proceeds for the government and place shares strategically to assure adequate market liquidity and research coverage in the future;

- broad distribution of sales publicity to potential investors, and assembling a syndicate capable of efficiently underwriting the sale of securities to targeted groups of investors domestically and perhaps globally. Here the investment bank's research credibility and the ability of its sales force are of central importance in winning mandates;

- carrying through a pricing exercise through bookbuilding or a fixed-price offer that promises to achieve the government's pricing objectives and a successful share distribution;

- underwriting and distributing the securities and providing strong after-market liquidity support and research coverage.

Advice and representation for buyers

Buyer activity in privatizations usually begin in one of two ways. The buyer may have already identified a prospective privatization and retains an investment banker to assist in executing the transaction, or in confirming the valuation placed on the prospective purchase. Alternatively, the investment banker may approach a potential buyer about a privatization and is retained to pursue it. Historically, some international corporations disliked the idea of a competitive auction process in acquiring an SOE and preferred direct, off-market, one-to-one negotiations. But sellers and their bankers had a vested interest in promoting aggressive bidding. Inexperienced international buyers would sometimes balk at these procedures, or bid too low to win. Usually, however, when an international company has been through the process unsuccessfully once or twice, it adapts and does much better the next time. When representing a buyer, a banker will perform the following tasks:

- conduct a thorough review based on all publicly available information and that provided by the privatization authorities about the SOE and its subsidiaries, if any. Advise as to the probable price range necessary to acquire the SOE, bearing in mind the advice that would be given to the government by the privatization adviser;

- advise as to the likelihood of the government's receptiveness to an invitation to enter discussions aimed at a purchase, how privatization officials will react when made aware of the client's interest, and what the government will consider to be its options and what actions it is likely to take;

- advise on the initial approach to the government, the value to be suggested, and steps for following up the approach;
- evaluate tactical options and a fallback position with the client, and play the role of the government's adviser in simulated negotiations, devising tactics accordingly;
- prepare recommendations on the financial structure of the transaction, and how the buyer should best proceed to arrange financing. Advise also on the probable reaction of the stock market and rating agencies to the buyer's purchase of the privatized enterprise if this is considered relevant;
- function as a continuous liaison between client and the government and its bankers, looking for and heading off problems through to completion of the deal; also advise on any changing tactical situation and responses to communications from the government or other bidders;
- assist in arranging long-term financing for the privatization purchase and in selling any assets that are not to be retained.

Figures 6.11 and 6.12 depict the relative success that investment banks have had in the privatization business in relation to IPOs and SEOs. The league tables differ markedly from the overall wholesale rankings presented in Chapter 9. In the case of IPOs, note, for example, the strong positions of IMI Capital Markets and Mediobanca in Italy, Paribas, BNP and Société Générale in France, and other local investment banks in Spain and Portugal, while the league table for SEOs conforms much more closely to that for wholesale banking in general. Privatization is at its root a very local business with strong political links. But the need to obtain the best possible acquirer and price in a trade sale, or strongest possible distribution in share sales, requires firms with broad and sometimes global reach.

For investment bankers themselves, few sources of revenue are more attractive than the kinds of fees that can be earned in privatization transactions. They put their firm's skills and knowledge to work without necessarily committing its capital, and the fees – commensurate with the value-added of the service – are usually considerable. Like the M&A business generally, privatization work has become globalized. The agents and brokers who are capable of providing advice and guidance to their governments or buyer clients, and governments seeking to use the marketplace in privatization IPOs and SEOs, are the bankers with the infrastructure, the trained personnel and the contacts with the worldwide corporate and financial market community.

Fig 6.11 Advisers on privatization IPOs 1985–99 (full credit to bookrunner, equal credit if joint)

	Proceeds ($m)	Rank	Market share	Number of issues
Goldman Sachs	16,949.5	1	10.1	45
IMI Capital Markets	12,358.1	2	7.4	15
Warburg Dillon Read	10,901.4	3	6.5	43
Dresdner Kleinwort Benson	9,797.5	4	5.9	12
Paribas	9,466.0	5	5.7	18
Mediobanca	8,594.2	6	5.1	5
Merrill Lynch	8,351.4	7	5.0	46
Crédit Suisse First Boston	7,279.2	8	4.4	32
Morgan Stanley Dean Witter	5,012.9	9	3.0	20
Société Générale	4,358.6	10	2.6	3
Banque Nationale de Paris	4,054.1	11	2.4	8
Banco Portugues Investimento	4,026.1	12	2.4	6
Argentaria Bolsa	3,539.8	13	2.1	10
ABN AMRO	3,270.5	14	2.0	9
Banco Central Hispanoamericano	3,211.8	15	1.9	10
J.B. Were & Son	3,127.3	16	1.9	2
J.P. Morgan	2,582.2	17	1.5	6
Daiwa Securities	2,498.4	18	1.5	7
Santander Investment	1,985.4	19	1.2	8
China International Capital Co.	1,982.5	20	1.2	4
Banco Bilbao Vizcaya	1,942.0	21	1.2	10
Lazard Houses	1,931.8	22	1.2	3
Lehman Brothers	1,708.2	23	1.0	10
Underwriter(s) unspecified	1,548.8		0.9	6
Not available	2,478.8		1.5	2
Industry totals	**167,217.8**	**–**	**100.0**	**488**

As of April 1999

Source: Thomson Financial Securities Data Company

Privatization continues to be an active business for investment bankers, although ultimately whatever can reasonably be transferred to the private sector will have been. Europe has been the scene of considerable privatization action because of the historically large role of SOEs in many countries. Some, such as the UK, are basically 'sold out'. Others, such as Italy and France, have a long way to go and will remain attractive arenas for investment banks for some years to come.

Fig 6.12 Advisers on privatization SEOs 1985–99 (full credit to bookrunner, equal credit if joint)

	Proceeds ($m)	Rank	Market share	Number of issues
Crédit Suisse First Boston	79,798.3	1	17.3	183
Warburg Dillon Read	65,286.2	2	14.1	122
Salomon Smith Barney	60,425.3	3	13.1	101
Morgan Stanley Dean Witter	59,671.7	4	12.9	76
J.P. Morgan	51,484.0	5	11.1	95
Deutsche Bank	48,125.4	6	10.4	108
Goldman Sachs	47,489.3	7	10.3	68
Rothschild Group	38,464.9	8	8.3	91
Lehman Brothers	37,217.0	9	8.1	47
Merrill Lynch	32,569.5	10	7.0	64
Dresdner Kleinwort Benson	28,819.9	11	6.2	54
KPMG	21,522.5	12	4.7	73
Schroder Group	19,141.9	13	4.1	46
PricewaterhouseCoopers	17,584.1	14	3.8	109
Barclays Capital	17,410.8	15	3.8	44
Lazard Houses	15,322.9	16	3.3	37
ING Barings	13,029.8	17	2.8	29
Maxima Consultoria	12,172.2	18	2.6	9
Banco Brascan	11,732.9	19	2.5	11
Paribas	10,947.3	20	2.4	36
Chase Manhattan Corporation	10,352.9	21	2.2	30
HSBC	9,162.8	22	2.0	52
BES Investimentos	9,081.5	23	2.0	3
Flemings	8,202.1	24	1.8	25
Banque Nationale de Paris	8,122.0	25	1.8	15
Deals with adviser	360,208	–	77.9	1,362
Deals without adviser	102,191	–	22.1	3,574
Industry totals	**462,399**	**–**	**100.0**	**4,936**

Source: Thomson Financial Securities Data Company

NOTES

[1] For a comprehensive overview of privatization developments *see Privatization Trends*, Paris: OECD, 1999 (annual).

[2] *See*, for example, Hart, Oliver, Schleifer, Andrei and Vishny, Robert W. (1997) 'The proper scope of government: theory and application to prisons,' *Quarterly Journal of Economics*, 112. *See also* Boycko, Maxim, Schleifer, Andrei and Vishny, Robert W. (1996) 'A theory of privatization,' *Economic Journal*, 106.

[3] A good survey of the impacts of privatization is contained in OECD, 'Competition, Privatization and Regulation: Synthesis Note' (1999) Paris: OECD.

[4] Megginson, William L. and Netter, Jeffrey M. (1998) 'From state to market: a survey of empirical studies on privatization', New York Stock Exchange Privatizations Working Paper no. 98–05, December.

[5] Megginson, William L. and Netter, Jeffrey M., op. cit., p. 24.

[6] Megginson and Netter, op. cit., p. 8.

[7] For a survey of the legal infrastructure of privatization in OECD countries *see* 'Comparative overview of privatization policies and institutions in the OECD member countries' (1999) Paris: OECD.

[8] OECD, 'Competition, privatization and regulation: synthesis note', loc. cit.

[9] Jones, Steven, Megginson, William L., Nash, Robert C. and Netter, Jeffrey M. (1999) 'Share issue privatizations as financial means to political and economic ends', *Journal of Financial Economics*.

[10] Megginson, William L., Nash, Robert C., Netter, Jeffrey M. and Schwartz, Adam L. (1998) 'The long-term return to investors in share issue privatizations', University of Georgia Working Paper.

[11] Huibers, Fred and Perrotti, Enrico C. (1998) 'The performance of privatization stocks in emerging markets: the role of political risk', University of Amsterdam Working Paper.

[12] *See*, for example, Boycko, Maxim, Schleifer, Andrei and Vishny, Robert W. (1994) 'Voucher privatization', *Journal of Financial Economics*, 35.

[13] Megginson, William L. and Netter, Jeffrey M. (op. cit.) note that, as of the end of 1998, 27 privatization share issues were larger than the then largest share offering in US history, the $4.4 billion Conoco IPO in October 1998.

[14] Smith, Katherine and Sofianos, George (1997) 'The impact of an NYSE listing on the global trading of non-US stocks', New York Stock Exchange Working Paper.

CHAPTER 7

Evolving patterns of corporate governance and control

A key dimension of financial integration under the euro is the complex relationship between the structure of the financial system, the control of enterprises and the role of the state. The financial system plays a critical role in corporate governance, in determining to whom management reports and the performance standards to which management is held. If Europe is to have a truly integrated financial market under a single currency in which capital is continuously allocated to the most productive uses (and equally important, denied to the least competitive), a uniform approach to corporate control will ultimately have to emerge from the highly divergent systems that have traditionally existed in the national economies now participating in the euro.

As discussed in previous chapters, highly liquid and contestable financial markets will provide corporations throughout the euro-zone with a growing range of opportunities for external financing, lowering the weighted average cost of capital, and improving competitive performance. But those opportunities are likely to go hand in hand with far greater scrutiny of management and workforce performance. Shake-outs, downsizing, management accountability and a sharper focus on shareholder value will thus continue to permeate Europe and accelerate under the euro, providing strong opportunities for the financial advisory functions in investment banking.

In this chapter we focus on how the organization and regulation of the financial system – the role of banks and other types of financial institutions (notably insurance companies and fund management entities such as pension funds discussed in the following chapter) – influences critical dimensions of domestic and international economic performance through the process of corporate control. That is, how the institutional design of the financial system influences the character of the capital-allocation process, national economic performance, and international economic and financial relationships. Following a discussion of alternative financial-industrial control structures, we provide short, stylized comparisons of four quite different approaches that co-exist uneasily in Europe – the Anglo-American, German and French approaches, as well as the Japanese system that has certain attributes reflected in Europe. All of the remaining European approaches are variants of these four models.[1]

Each can be evaluated in terms of how it appears to stand up against a set of performance benchmarks, with the role of financial institutions as the centrepiece of the discussion. Each can be assessed in terms of its implications for structural adjustment, financial integration and market access. Each fundamentally affects the volume and structure of M&A and privatization deal-flow discussed in Chapters 5 and 6. And each has a unique set of implications for investment banking, in terms of capital market access, research, trading, asset management, principal investing and, more generally, the definition and value of client relationships.

Investment banks that have been able to capitalize on traditional corporate governance structures in Europe are having to learn new ways of doing things, even as newcomers are finding clients increasingly open to demonstrated capabilities and new ideas. Ongoing shifts in governance structures, in short, enhance the contestability of the market for investment banking services.

Financial institutions as a central element in corporate control systems

Corporate control has to do with the management of enterprises. In classic assumptions of market capitalism, management is deemed to consistently act in the interest of shareholders to maximize their long-term wealth as measured by equity values. Agency problems, wherein managers' and owners' interests diverge, are not supposed to arise, and managers strive to meet their fiduciary responsibilities to the shareholders in a firm's purchasing and marketing decisions, in selecting investment projects and making financing decisions, in the use of human resources, and in maximizing available economies of scale and scope.[2]

In the real world, of course, agency problems can and do arise, and present one of the most difficult problems in market economies. How these are resolved, therefore, is of great importance. Four stylized models for handling them can be described in terms such as those in Fig. 7.1. All assign central but quite distinct roles to financial institutions. First, each model contains a particular structure of bank relationships with non-financial firms that in turn is related to the comparative importance of earnings retention (self-financing), bank finance and disintermediated finance via capital markets as alternative sources of capital. Second, bank-industry linkages can be examined at the level of equity shareholdings between banks and industrial firms, particularly the holding of stakes in industrial companies by banks. Third, the linkages can be examined at the level of corporate surveillance and control, drawing distinctions between outsider systems – in which control

Fig 7.1 Alternative corporate control structures

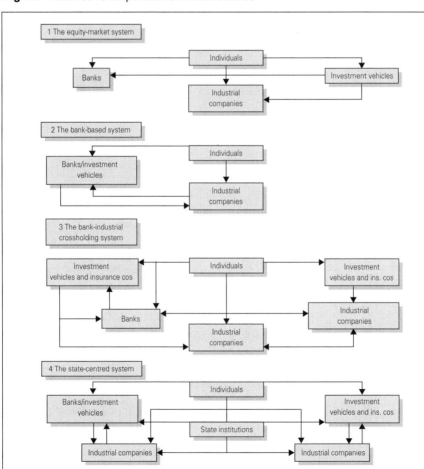

runs directly from shareholders to companies – and insider systems, in which industrial companies and banks have interlocking control structures. Finally, each system profile can be related to some of the informal structures which, in some countries, play as important a role in binding industry and finance together as do the various formal institutional and legal linkages.

The equity market system

In this essentially Anglo-American approach, bank functions are more or less separated legally or managerially between commercial banking and investment banking. The former may provide short-term financing for corporations, but the major source of external financing for firms is the capital market. In the equity market, shares in corporations are held by the public, either directly or through institutional vehicles – insurance companies, mutual funds and pension funds – and are actively traded.

Corporate restructuring, involving the shrinking of the firms' assets or their shifting to alternative uses or locations,[3] tends to be triggered by exploitation of a control premium between the existing market capitalization of a firm and that which an acquirer (whether an industrial company or an active financial investor or managers of one of its business units) perceives and acts upon by initiating a takeover effort designed to unlock shareholder value through management changes. There is a high level of transparency and reliance on public information provided under prevailing accounting and disclosure rules, with systemic surveillance by equity investors and research analysts. Concerns about unwanted takeover efforts continually pressure management to act in the interests of shareholders, many of whom tend to view their shares as put options, i.e. options to sell. The control structure of this essentially outsider-based system is mainly characterized by arm's length financing by commercial lenders or in the debt markets of issues including takeovers and internal corporate restructuring. Investment banks may give strategic and financial advice, and sometimes take debt or equity positions in firms (and occasionally control of them) for their own benefit – the latter with the objective of later resale at a profit.[4]

This model, to operate to maximum effect, assumes that the more powerful stakeholders in the firm (shareholders, workers, managers and customers) regard this process as legitimate. Its central claim to that legitimacy resides in an assertion that, everything else being equal, it is the most efficient approach to maximizing wealth. Its supporters also argue that free markets are most compatible with democracy as a system of limited government. If, for instance, financial markets are free to allocate funds to the most efficient rather than the most politically influential users of capital, then the returns for the investors will be higher than if some of them use their vote to extract rents from less remunerative, but politically determined, investments. Labour market legislation in particular has to be supportive, so that labour forces may be shrunk or shifted in task or location with the minimum of friction. The model also presupposes that government will not prove an easy target for corporate lobbies seeking to avoid restructuring or takeovers through access to the public purse as a less demanding source of funds. Government's major task is to provide the regulatory and legal structure within which open capital markets may function, and to supply a social safety net for those in need. Not least, this Anglo-American approach assumes that the two kings of the corporate roost are shareholders and customers – if other types of financial systems in world markets have different priorities, benefiting other interests, they will eventually be forced to adapt or to lose market share to rivals focusing firmly on consumer and shareholder interests.

The bank-based system

The bank-based system of corporate control is often associated with Germany, among others, where the rules of the game have traditionally enabled banks to take deposits, extend loans to firms and issue securities in capital markets as part of a tight relationship with clients. In this system, significant equity stakes in non-financial companies are held by banks and by investment companies run by banks, who act as both commercial and investment bankers to their clients. With large equity as well as debt exposures, banks take on a vital monitoring role in the management of corporations, including active boardroom participation and guidance with the benefit of non-public (*inside*) information. Insurance companies may hold significant stakes in banks and non-financial companies, which in turn may also hold shares in insurance companies. The public holds shares in both banks and corporations, but these shares tend to be ceded by individual owners to the banks to vote with on the grounds that the banks have superior and often privileged information about corporate policy and performance.

Markets for corporate equity and debt tend to be relatively poorly developed in bank-based systems, with large investor holdings of public-sector bonds as opposed to corporate bonds or stocks. The investing public in such a system tends to be risk averse, preferring predictability and reliability to a high degree of transparency and the 'surprises' that come with it. This attitude is reciprocated by management who invite patient investors to hold shares in their firms in return for long-term gains as the firms expand, rather than higher dividends now and the freedom to redeploy assets which could deprive management of resources needed for investment. Financial disclosure tends to be relatively limited as accounts are drawn up essentially to meet tax and reporting obligations rather than to inform a shareholding public. The amount of shares available on the market is small, so trading may be comparatively thin and volatile as investors at home and abroad move in and out of the limited supply.

The bank-based system tends to be embedded in a regime which buttresses its legitimacy.[5] Regulatory bodies are supported by framework laws, which provide ample discretion for both regulators and the market operators in the relevant sectors of the financial system to adapt to changing circumstances and market processes, with the central bank giving priority to maintaining the value of the currency rather than detailed regulatory concerns. It requires banks and other financial institutions to maintain provisions and capital reserves, and places limits on exposures to credit risk. Semi-detached banking and insurance companies, in effect, police the financial system.

Figure 7.2 is a partial representation of the traditional German bank-based system. Note the extensive equity linkages between the banking, insurance and non-financial corporate sectors.

In the German insurance sector, Allianz AG has been one of the largest institutional shareholders in industrial and other financial companies with 21.7 per cent ownership of shares of Dresdner Bank AG, 5 per cent of Deutsche Bank AG and 17.4 per cent of HypoVereinsbank in banking, 25 per cent of Munich Re in insurance, 10.4 per cent of BASF in chemicals, 10.1 per cent of RWE in the utilities sector, 10.1 per cent of Schering in pharmaceuticals, among others, even as 25 per cent of its own shares were owned by Munich Re, 10 per cent by Dresdner Bank, 9.3 per cent by Deutsche Bank and 6.8 per cent by HypoVereinsbank at the end of 1999.[6] As in the case of bank shareholdings in industry, Allianz's holdings stemmed in part from a poorly developed German equity market which forced it into plough insurance reserves into large positions in individual companies, currency marching rules which prevented broad-gauge international diversification of its asset portfolio, and a punitive 53 per cent tax payable on capital gains in Germany.

The bank-based system personalizes many of the market functions performed by impersonal capital markets, so that trust is an essential ingredient of relations among its insider élites. Bankers play a central 'co-ordinating' function through their positions on corporate supervisory boards,[7] their close relations with the central bank, their role in dominating the bond markets, their administration of fiduciary shares in annual general meetings, and their provision of multiple services to clients.

Fig 7.2 The traditional German shareholding structure

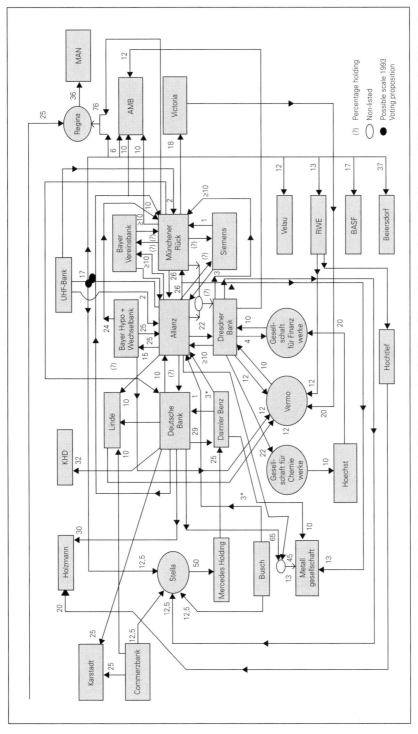

Source: Professor E. Wenger, University of Würzburg, reproduced in M. Adams, Anborung I. Macht von Banken und Versicherungen – Wettbewerb im Finanzdienstleistungssektor, 8 December 1993, Deutscher Bundestag, Ausschuss für Wirtschaft

This role, however, is shared with other bodies, such as trade unions, local or central government officials, and managers in their capacity as stakeholders in corporations. Bankers are not, therefore, left alone to carry the burden of public acclaim or hostility through fluctuating corporate performance. Above all, they are guardians of a stable, property-holding democracy which has co-opted trade unions through their representatives' positions on works councils and on corporate supervisory boards.[8]

The bank industry crossholding system

The crossholding system is rooted in close collaboration between government bureaucrats, corporate managers and politicians who share a common aim to attain acceptable economic growth and high employment in part through abundant low-cost capital. As corporations develop under this system, they seek stable shareholders who are sufficiently patient to enable managers to recover investments in the development of products and processes, and in a stable labour force.[9] Corporations prefer other corporations as shareholders because they share similar concerns. If bank-industrial crossholdings are pervasive, the banks tend to be most comfortable when the corporations in which they hold stakes rely mainly on their own resources. The financial system as a whole must be prepared to deal with the consequences of large trade surpluses, which flow from joint corporate interest in market shares.

Domestic inflationary pressures have to be kept in check through rapid recycling of funds earned from exports. This entails the building up of portfolio investments in external markets. Revaluations of the currency from exports and investment income abroad may be delayed by further external portfolio investments, as well as by corporate direct investments abroad as domestic production costs continue to rise relative to other locations around the world.

The bank-industrial crossholding system is perhaps best embodied in Japan's *keiretsu* (*see below*), where non-financial corporations as well as banks hold significant stakes in each other as well as seats on each other's boards. These links may complement close domestic supplier–customer relationships, with dependability and co-operation often dominating price in transactions. The central paradox of such a bank-industrial crossholding system in the past was that it sought to limit foreign ownership and market access, while requiring open markets for corporate assets in other countries alongside open access for exports.

The state-led financial market system

The role of government and the structure of the financial system, in turn, may be related. A more interventionist role for the state may be facilitated or hindered by the kind of banking structure that exists.[10] The more universal the banking system and the closer the bank-industry control linkages, the easier it tends to be for government to implement activist industrial policy and the more tempted it will be to apply it.[11]

France is perhaps the historical reference point for the state-led financial market system, as characterized in Fig. 7.3.[12] The Ministry of Finance has tradi-tionally been the dominant focus for savers and borrowers as it regulates the domestic capital market both directly and indirectly. Deposit-taking institutions place surplus funds in the capital markets, to be taken up in significant volume by public sector institutions which lend them to specific industries, such as housing, agriculture and energy, or for regional investments. Both lending and borrowing institutions fall under the tutelage of the Ministry of Finance, which formally draws up investment priorities through elaborate consultations with trade associations recorded in The Plan (the French economic master plan issued periodically by the government) as well as through negotiations with the Ministry of Industry or in response to requests filtered through the political parties.

Officials in the Ministry of Finance enjoy prestige through their position in the state hierarchy, and because of the value of their contacts across the extensive state sector to those seeking access to them.

As resources of personnel and time are scarce, such a state-centred admin-istrative mechanism at the heart of the national financial system tends to lead to a queue. Organizations with close contacts and claims on the loyalties of public officials – such as state-controlled economic enterprises or large private firms – get served first. Small and medium-sized firms are nudged aside, so their representatives join one of the political armies fighting for privileged access to the state's resources through elections. The regular cycle of local, regional or national elections in part becomes a contest between competing industrial coalitions for the keys to public finance.

It is not just financial resources that flow through the hands of public officials. Patronage does too, in the form of appointments to the management and boards of state enterprises or large private enterprises in receipt of state benefits. Public officials compete among themselves, through their own organizations and to a lesser extent through their proclamations of party political fealty. Their legitimacy derives from a claim to act in the public interest. Yet the state institutions whose resources they deploy directly or

Fig 7.3 Selected French crossholdings 1998

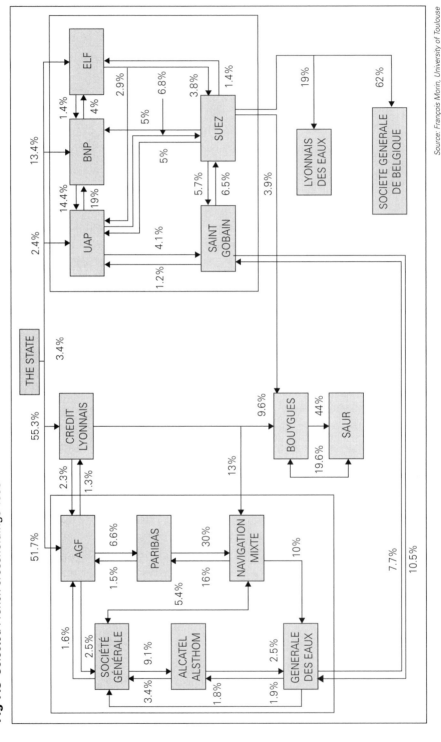

Source: François Morin, University of Toulouse

indirectly may expand their stakes in business enterprises, extending the potential for public patronage.

Indeed, a cynic could argue that state-led systems have a built-in vested interest in nationalizing private enterprise in order to expand the reach of public officials, and then of privatizing the assets in exchange for key positions in management or on the boards of companies. Ownership of these is less significant to public officials than the fact they remain on the career circuit, and that they stay within the bounds of what is in effect a political market for economic control. Such a market extends throughout the multiple levels of government, as local mayors become businessmen and bankers for their communities through resources obtained under the political process. Ultimately, the state can see its role as acting in the public interest erode as it merges into the surrounding maze of non-transparent political markets.

The role of public officials

The role of public officials in the corporate control process in the four systems described here range from *laissez faire* to active participation in a political market for resources of all types. At one extreme, public officials set the macro-economic policy, competition policy and international trade policy under which enterprises operate, and essentially all other industrial outcomes are left to markets. These outcomes are considered legitimate precisely because impersonal forces are at work in what is essentially a rule-based system. Quite simply, the argument runs, corporate restructuring is called for when market forces decree it. At the other extreme, public officials become fully fledged participants in the market process. Their involvement on behalf of the state may be through full or partial government ownership of corporations, public stakes in financial institutions with major influence on investment or lending decisions, influence on credit allocation through the process of bank regulation and supervision, or some combination of these. The nature of the corporate control structure and bank-industry linkages thus may have a significant bearing on the willingness and ability of public officials to affect industrial outcomes.

The role of public officials and the structure of the financial system are closely related. Where finance ministry officials may have inherited a rigid and compartmentalized national financial system, they may feel obliged to discharge some of the functions of a market. In a decentralized federal state, regulators and public officials are more likely to carry out a variety of related but disjointed or competing functions. A centralized state is likely to have highly centralized markets to finance its various activities. A federal state is likely to find the regions well organized to defend local interests, including local financial institutions standing up against centralizing tendencies of the country's political or financial capital. Appointments, patronage and budgetary allocations may be either central or local in origin, just as implicit state or mutualist guarantees of particular financial institutions – no matter what kind of explicit ownership and control structure exists – may originate from the centre or the regions. In the last analysis, the financial system provides the arteries of the state's resource flows. Politics and markets are inseparable.

In this regard, too, the euro-zone is likely to take on a decentralized, federalist character as countries become 'regions' from a financial markets perspective, each with strong financial institutions and powerful command over financial resources. This is likely to loosen corporate governance structures in the euro-zone and gradually limit the role of the state to one of setting the broad policy parameters within which corporations and financial markets operate.

Patterns of convergence and divergence

The discussion of the four government-bank-industry models can be summarized within the European context as traditionally exemplified by the UK, Germany and France, as follows.

First, the large UK industrial firm is semi-detached from banks and other types of financial institutions, and maintains an arm's length relationship with government. Financing is largely done through the capital markets, with short-term needs satisfied through commercial paper programmes, longer-term debt through straight or structured bond issues and medium-term note programmes, and equity through public issues or private placements. Bank relationships continue to exist and can be very important, often through backstop credit lines, but the relationship is between arm's length buyer and seller, with closer monitoring and control only in cases of difficulty. Corporate control is exercised through the takeover market on the basis of outside information, with bank roles limited to financing bids or corporate restructurings. The government role is normally even more arm's length, with a focus on setting ground rules considered to be in the public interest. Relations between government, banks and industry are sometimes antagonistic.

Second, the German approach has traditionally centred on close bank-industry relationships, with financing needs met by earnings and bank support. Bank roles, furthermore, extend beyond credit to stock ownership, share voting and board membership.[13] Capital allocation and restructuring of enterprises is undertaken mainly based on inside information, and unwanted takeovers have traditionally been rare. Mergers and acquisitions have tended to be carried out mainly by *Hausbanken*, whose importance is amplified by the large role played by *Mittelstand* firms in the German economy – medium-sized, usually specialized companies whose shares tend to be closely held, often by members of the founding family. Capital markets are relatively poorly developed in both corporate debt and equity. Although state (*Länder*) governments can play an important role in bank ownership and control, relations between the federal government and both industrial firms and banks are mainly arm's length, with some exceptions in public sector shareholdings.

Third, the French approach involves a strong government role through national ownership of major banks and corporations, as well as government central savings institutions such as the Caisse de Depôts et Consignations. Financing of enterprises involves a mixture of bank credits and capital market issues, domestic as well as international, on the part of both private and public sector firms. Formal channels of government influence exercised through the Ministry of Finance are supplemented by informal channels centred on the *Grandes Écoles* (the government-run educational establishments for the elite). The government generally appoints the heads of state-owned companies.

The market for corporate control operates on the basis of both public and private information. There have been a number of takeover battles, but the Ministry of Finance has often played a determining role in the outcome. Privately-owned *Banques d'Affaires* have been active in ownership and corporate restructuring, although the state sought to shape the structure of French industry through public ownership and influence.

Perhaps the closest European parallels to Japan's corporate crossholding approach have been Belgium and Italy as well as Portugal and Spain, where inter-firm boundaries themselves have sometimes become blurred, and banks and financial holding companies have traditionally played a central role and provided corporate guidance, co-ordination and financing. In most cases there are strong formal and informal links which run from the government, through the respective ministries, to both the financial and real sectors of the economy. Restructuring tends to be done on the basis of inside information by drawing on these business-banking-government ties, and the open market for corporate control erupts only rarely. There are few battles as byzantine as the 1990 fight for control of Société Générale de Belgique – a Belgian holding company with far-reaching industrial and financial interests, which accounts for a significant share of Belgian economic activity – after a hostile approach engineered by Carlo de Benedetti, the Italian industrialist. The same was true in the case of the 1998 battle for control of the Generale Bank between ABN-AMRO, the Dutch universal bank, and Fortis, the Belgian-Dutch financial conglomerate, with plenty of political influence to try to forge a 'Belgian solution'. And there are few financial institutions as powerful or Machiavellian in their national markets as Mediobanca in Italy, the dominant merchant bank in the country, without whose involvement very little restructuring among major corporations has been carried out.

Still, things change, as was shown by the battle for Gucci between new-style French entrepreneurs François Pinault (of Yves Saint Laurent) and Bernard Arnault (of LVMH), part of the global trend towards consolidation in the luxury goods industry. Likewise, the contest between Olivetti and Deutsche Telekom for Telecom Italia, discussed at the beginning of this book; the long-running fight by Banque Nationale de Paris to break up an agreed merger between Paribas and Société Générale; and the competing efforts by Banco Santander Central Hispanoamericano (BSCH) of Spain and Banco Comercial Portugués (BCP) to gain control of the Champalimaud financial group in Portugal – which in the end pitted the Portugese government against EU competition authorities and was won ultimately by BSCH. All these battles occurred in 1999. In addition, there was the $158 billion hostile acquisition of Mannesman A.G. by Vodafone-Airtouch PLC, which was fought almost entirely on Anglo-American type rules and ultimately succeeded in early 2000 – the largest M&A deal in history. The virus of market-driven changes in corporate control, once it takes hold, is hard to stop.

Figure 7.4 (*overleaf*) summarizes some of the corporate governance conditions that exist in three of the systems discussed here. Note that the so-called Anglo-American approaches are different in detail even though they are both dominated by financial market-driven outsider systems. Similarly, the traditional German and Japanese bank-based insider approaches are different from one another in many respects. The critical differences lie in the legal conditions under which banks, insurance companies and various types of fiduciaries may control shares, the comparative pattern of ownership and agency relationships, and the variety of board structures.

Comparative performance issues

Given the dramatically different historical characteristics of the British, German and French approaches to government-bank-industry linkages and their variants in other EU countries – benchmarked against the US and Japanese systems – it is not at all surprising that there has been continuing debate about the degree to which these differences have been responsible for the performance of European national economies during various chapters of their economic and financial histories. The arguments have been part of the economic policy scene for many years. Not least important is whether the governance structure of government-bank-industry links has anything to do with performance in global competition and the flow of international investment.

In the UK (and in the US) there was a debate especially during the sixties and seventies about whether the unguided rule of the market and outsider-based corporate control systems were indeed the key to superior national economic performance: had corporate control systems which are perceived (rightly or wrongly) to be significantly more interventionist outperformed the market-based systems? In the nineties the pendulum had swung the other way, with both the German and French (and indeed Japanese) approaches coming under increasing scrutiny for lack of transparency, flexibility and creativity in a dynamic global economy. And some of the emerging market 'insider' systems modelled on the Japanese approach, notably in South Korea, arguably contributed materially to the severity of the Asian financial crisis in the late nineties.

In order to reach a conclusion on this central issue, one would have to define carefully the term 'economic performance' as some multi-dimensional composite of real economic growth – as determined mainly by the quantitative and qualitative development of the labour force, physical capital formation, and technological change, as well as long-term unemployment, shifts in the terms of international trade, and other familiar measures. Even if one could agree that one approach has been demonstrably superior to another, one would still have to test it on the economy in question and see how things *might have gone* if the approach had been different.

In the UK, admiration of the German economy has often centred on the perceived differences in corporate governance. This usually involves heated discussions about:

● the contribution of (or damage caused by) corporate takeovers;
● the proper role of mutual funds and pension funds in corporate governance;

Fig 7.4 Comparative attributes of corporate control

Institutional ownership	US	UK	Germany	Japan
Banks	Stock ownership prohibited or requires prior approval of FRB and must be passive. *Source*: Glass-Steagall and BHC Act (repeated in 1999)	Bank of England may discourage ownership on prudential grounds. Capital adequacy rules discourage large stakes	No restrictions, apart from some generous prudential rule	Prior to 1987, banks could hold up to 10 per cent of firm's stock. After 1987, can hold up to 5 per cent. *Source*: Anti-Monopoly Act
Life insurance companies	Can hold up to 2 per cent of assets in a single company's securities. Can hold up to 20 per cent of assets in equities. *Source*: NY Insurance Law	Self-imposed limits on fund assets invested in one company, stemming from fiduciary requirements of liquidity	No restrictions	Can hold up to 10 per cent of firm's stock. *Source*: Anti-Monopoly Act
Other insurers	Control of non-insurance company prohibited. *Source*: NY Insurance Law		No restrictions	Can hold up to 10 per cent of firm's stock. *Source*: Anti-Monopoly Act
Mutual funds	Tax penalties and regulatory restrictions if own 10 per cent of firm's stock. *Sourced*: Investment Company Act, IRS	Cannot take large stakes in firms. *Source*: Financial Services Act 1986	No restrictions	No restrictions
Pension funds	Must diversify. *Source*: ERISA	Self-imposed limits on fund assets invested in one company, stemming from fiduciary requirement for liquidity	No restrictions	No restrictions
Effective method of board appointment	By invitation of CEO	By invitation of CEO	50 per cent of board elected by shareholders, the rest by employees. CEO may not be a member	By invitation of CEO

Fig 7.4 cont

Institutional ownership	US	UK	Germany	Japan
Method of appointment of chairman of the board	Selected by board	Selected by board	Elected by shareholder/employee representatives. Usually a shareholder representative	Selected by board
CEO and chairman of the board are the same person?	Frequently	Frequently	Never	Frequently
Sources of information	Management	Management	Zero	Management. Informally, president's club members of stakeholder firms
Ratio of management directors to total	High	High	Always (management board)	High
Presence of large shareholders on board	Rarely	Rarely	Always (supervisory board)	Sometimes
Presence of banks on board	Rarely	Rarely	Frequently	Sometimes
General	Securities and Exchange Commission filing required for 5 per cent ownership. Antitrust laws prohibiting vertical restraints. Insider trading laws discourage active shareholding. Creditor in control of firm liable to subordination of its loans. *Source:* bankruptcy case law			Regulatory filing required for 25 per cent ownership
Ownership pattern (%)				
Individuals	30–35	22	29	3
Financial institutions as agents	55–62	13	57	3
Financial institutions as principals	2	39	1	36
Non-financial corporations	7	25	3	42
Foreign	0	4	6	14
Government		0	4	5

Source: Theodor Baums, University of Osnabrück, 1994

- the role of insurance companies and other types of institutional investors such as financial holding companies;
- management and/or employee holdings of equity stakes in their own firms;
- the nature of executive compensation schemes, inter-company equity links and strategic alliances;
- the appropriate control function of banks and other financial institutions.[14]

The continuing debate on the optimum system of enterprise governance, together with pressure for change in virtually all industrial countries, suggests we are still some way from resolving these matters.

The idea that the German-style *Hausbank* shareholding and proxy voting systems impart pre-emptive adjustment and stability to industrial firms is based on the view that markets are short-sighted (dynamically inefficient) and that placing a significant degree of corporate governance in the hands of bankers will achieve greater social welfare over the long term. This view is supported to some degree by financial theoreticians, who have argued there may be a lot of benefit in resolving information asymmetries when the bank is both an equity insider and a creditor.

Some observers[15] have argued that past success of the German and Japanese economies is partly due to direct equity links and main-bank relationships. For example, it has been argued that, while lending makes a bank a privileged insider to a firm, the control of ownership stakes makes it even more of an insider than if it remained just a privileged creditor.[16] As a result, a bank can exercise greater control over the degree of risk of projects chosen by the firm. Full insider status internalizes and perfects information flows from the firm to the bank, allowing the bank to make more efficient and timely financing decisions. Therefore, German-type organizational structures in which banks hold both debt and equity stakes in client firms can be seen as creating an internal (but informal) capital market between bank and firm. However, others have been unable to reject the hypothesis that universal banks better support the long-term financial strategies of non-financial companies than do financial systems based on capital markets.[17]

There is also the problem of endemic conflicts of interest due to the breadth of the banks' involvement in corporate affairs and the absence of internal controls. Some of the issues examined in detail,[18] especially in the German model, have been the conflicts between the fiduciary responsibilities of a bank and its role as an investment banker, between its interest in completing an

M&A transaction and its obligation to a target company that is (or has been) a client, between the profitability of actively managing investment portfolios and its fiduciary responsibilities to asset-holders, and between its interests as an investor in, and lender to, the same firm. Indeed, it may be that conflicts of interest which arise in serving various clients increase with the breadth of activities of a financial services firm. Economists generally rely on adverse reputation effects and on legal and regulatory sanctions to check the incentives to exploit such conflicts,[19] and some observers point out that larger customers will in any case turn away from banks that are not as competitive as services from non-affiliated banks, thereby limiting potential conflicts.[20]

There is the further argument that large banks inevitably will not be permitted to fail due to the social cost, and that they therefore have an artificial advantage in competing with institutions that have no such access to implied state support. The failure of separately incorporated non-bank affiliates of these too-big-to-fail banks (possibly industrial companies) may lead to a safety net being brought into play, resulting in unfair advantages in financing costs and the possibility of public bailouts. And the market may effectively stretch the safety net under the affiliates as well. Counter arguments take the view that a broader range of activities increases the inherent diversification and stability of the financial institution, and therefore decreases the likelihood that the safety net will come into play.[21]

Beyond corporate control issues, German *Hausbank*-type links, and to a lesser extent the French state-centred approach, may have had an adverse bearing on the historical development of each country's financial markets compared with the Anglo-American system, with possibly large costs due to inefficiencies in the financial intermediation process. The interests of institutions with strong links to their clients are rarely fertile ground for innovations that compete with financial services already being offered, and possibly contribute to an erosion of the bank-client relationship itself. In view of this, market-oriented financial systems are often credited with greater efficiency, greater innovation and dynamism, superior resistance to inherent conflicts of interests among the various stakeholders involved, and (through better transparency) less susceptibility to major uncorrected industrial blunders.

There is also the issue of politically excessive concentration of economic influence. Control of large blocks of stock in industrial companies by banks, investment companies, insurance companies or other industrial concerns is sometimes considered capable of influencing the national economy in ways that run counter to the public interest. Examples often cited include the role in the US economy of banking houses such as J.P. Morgan during the twenties, and the more recent role of Germany's *Grossbanken* and insurers. Counter arguments generally refer to the vigour and sophistication of antitrust enforcement in many countries, including members of the European Union.

Finally, there is the argument that universal banks, through their dominance of client relationships and presumed degree of economic influence, have the ability to suborn the political process and set in motion action that shifts the balance of risks and returns in their favour. This may include favourable tax legislation, access to government guarantees, and antitrust exemptions. Counter arguments focus on the fact that special interest pressures from other types of financial firms (e.g. savings institutions) or sectors of the real economy (e.g. farmers) are no less capable of co-opting the political process, and that the root of any such problem may therefore lie in the political process itself.

Transition in financial systems

The different types of EU corporate governance described here are embedded in their specific national financial systems. Each was structured by idiosyncratic founding circumstances – different points of departure imprinted their own mark on their evolution. Interactions between institutions in the market process or relations between firms and financial institutions were always evolving, but at greater or lesser degrees of speed or intensity. There were four broad sources of change, whose relative importance varied with time.

First, national societies in each of the countries participating in the euro were transformed as their economies developed. Financial systems were affected by the growth in incomes and expanding volumes of savings. An ever larger proportion of their populations entrusted their assets to financial institutions, which had often been created for specific social groups, such as farm populations, industrial workers or small enterprises. As the occupation structures changed, the original functions and weight of farm, co-operative or mutual banks altered too.

Second, national 'policy communities' were subject to evolution as well, alongside enduring features such as the role of the bureaucrats and the products of the French *Grandes Écoles*. In some countries, the structure of government remained stable whereas in France, for example, considerable financial autonomy was delegated after 1970, and particularly after 1982, to the regions and departments. Within the 'policy communities', changes in the relative weighting of different types of financial institution were common to all, but the reasons for the rise of some institutions and the decline of others were often idiosyncratic. In the UK, for instance, commercial banks dominated about 80 per cent of the deposit market in the twenties, but held a market share of under 30 per cent by the late seventies. In France, by contrast, the top ten banks have consistently captured about 90 per cent of the market as measured by deposits.

Third, the style of public policy varied considerably, both over time and between the countries. In all countries, the financial disaster of 1929–31 undermined the legitimacy of capitalism, leading to a general sidelining of securities markets and a high degree of formal regulation. After the war, the particular circumstances of each country conditioned style and language of public policy for nearly four decades. The ideas behind the economic programme of the French National Council of Resistance were predominantly Marxist, for example, favourable to extensive nationalization and dismissive of a bourgeoisie widely blamed for the stagnation of the thirties. In Germany, by contrast, the language of public policy was consistently expressed in terms of the 'social market economy', whereby government regulators set the legal parameters within which market processes could evolve. In the sixties, however, the content of Germany's style altered, as elsewhere, to incorporate prevalent ideas on the benefits to economic growth of stimulative fiscal policies. These in turn promoted the expansion of government bond markets, with far-reaching implications for financial systems.

Fourth, international or global forces impinged more or less simultaneously on all EU countries, but the content and timing of reactions to them remained very different. All countries were affected both by flows and structures in the world political economy. The flows included variations in the prevailing climate of diplomatic or military relations between the major powers, the rapid growth of international trade and the operations of multinational corporations, developments in financial markets and relations between the major-currency countries, and in global communications. They were also conditioned by the structure of the global political economy whose four components – security, production, finance and information – fashion the constraints within which organizations may exert discretion.[22]

The evolution of different types of corporate governance and financial systems may also be traced by means of literature on the political dynamics of regime change. Political transitions have been defined as the interval between one regime and another.[23] Adapting this scheme to financial systems, the familiar sequence runs through a pre-transition (or preparatory) phase, a decision phase and a consolidation phase.[24]

The pre-transition phase can be characterized by such factors as inflation, bank exposure and corporate bankruptcies, inadequate control over monetary aggregates and credit, an intellectual battle of ideas among economists and within the media, and an increasing vulnerability of the currency or the domestic financial system to external sources of disturbance. The decision phase is shaped by the actions of leaders who seek to regain control over the financial system by altering it. In the period under discussion for the three EU countries, efforts to regain control have focused on the organization of securities markets – a clear indication of how significant state financing has become. This phase is characterized by a contest between contending parties over the rules of the game which are to prevail in the new regime, and the appropriate means to be applied. The moderates offer one set of proposals, which are not *a priori* doomed to failure. If they fail, a reign of the radicals begins, and the transition moves away from mere regime change to a revolution from above. The consolidation or habituation phase involves a 'joint learning process' about the procedures of the new regime, where competition in markets and between systems evolves along more pragmatic channels, and the procedures of the new regime gradually acquire the features of an old regime. This phase may last for an indefinite period depending on whether the regime's norms, procedures or performance are compatible with changing conditions. If they are compatible, consolidation continues. If they are not, either consolidation is accelerated to confront a common challenge or the regime, system and market process moves towards breakdown.

Evolution along such a political trajectory is not preordained, any more than the weighting of forces driving change remains constant. Developments may accelerate, stagnate or take unexpected turns as EU financial markets simultaneously converge, compete, cross-penetrate and subvert each other as they adapt yet strive to stay distinct. Moreover, the regulatory authorities responsible for financial markets are always seeking to learn from their own past, and from others' considered failures or successes. The process of selective emulation or rejection is a key feature of policy change, just as defensive measures to protect or offensive measures to project financial market arrangements are key components of the battle between the systems.

Corporate governance in the euro-zone

The EU has thus been home to several competing types of corporate governance control, three of which we have discussed in this chapter. They have differed in several important and interrelated ways:

- the sourcing of debt and equity financing for enterprises;
- the role of financial institutions in the process of corporate control and economic restructuring of business firms;
- the role of the state regulator, and as a source of capital and in the exercise of corporate governance.

Assessment of the comparative performance of different industry-bank-government models is basically impossible, due both to the complexity and essentially political definition of the dependent variable as well as tracking measurable performance attributes under different model assumptions – either longitudinally for a single country or cross-sectionally among countries.

In a 1995 report by the Centre for European Policy Studies (CEPS) a set of draft guidelines was proposed which suggested that, for all European companies:

- shareholders should determine which rights are attached to their shares, and should in principle be entitled to one vote per share;
- shareholders' basic rights should include the appointment and removal of board members and auditors, approval of the dividend, approval of bylaws and creation of new shares;
- corporate boards should be responsible for sound management of the company, and should include a sufficient number of outside directors who are highly qualified and experienced;
- all information given to the market should be provided in a way that respects equal treatment of shareholders;
- boards should make sure that an objective and clear relationship is maintained with the auditors. In view of their position on the board, outside directors should take a special responsibility in overseeing the audit.

This is, of course, a policy proposal along the rhetorical lines of the financial area covered by the euro as distinguished from a factual description of those markets. However, signs abound that financial liberalization and the wider use of securities markets by continental European corporations, together with increasingly performance-oriented portfolio management on the part of mutual funds, insurance companies and other institutional investors, have led to a surprisingly rapid shift away from bank finance and a weakening of tight industry-bank relationships. There are now unprecedented, unwanted takeover attempts in continental Europe through acquisition of shareholdings by unaffiliated (sometimes foreign) investors.[25]

Easing of bank activity limits in the UK and US is allowing them to play a larger role in industrial restructuring transactions, and to exploit some of the information and relationship advantages they have as lenders. Gradual convergence of Anglo-American-style capital-market orientation and Euro-Japanese-style bank-firm links may be expected to test the relative merits of outsider and insider systems – that is, the importance of information asymmetries against the free market's capability of allocating and pricing capital both within and across national frontiers.[26]

The possible outcomes of convergence are many. Germany could move broadly from bank-based to capital market-based. Large firms could move rapidly to the capital-market model, thereby diversifying the nature and type of financing and governance within the German corporate community, even as it remains mainly bank-based for *Mittelstand* firms. That would require the evolution of a large primary and secondary equity market, with major implications for corporate governance and for labour market or fiscal policy. Indeed, late in 1998 Deutsche Bank announced it would transfer its industrial portfolio to DB Investor – *see* Fig. 7.5 – a holding company whose assets are to be actively managed for shareholder value and, not coincidentally, setting Deutsche Bank free to pursue a more independent course in corporate and investment banking. Finally, a government proposal in early 2000 to scrap the capital gains tax on long-term institutional shareholdings signalled a much more fluid shareholding structure in the future and immediately boosted share prices.

The speed with which the German approach to corporate governance has moved in the direction of the capital-markets approach has surprised many, as have battles for corporate control such as Pirelli-Continental in 1996, Krupp-Thyssen in 1997 and Vodafone-AirTouch-Mannesmann in 1999–2000. Not all succeeded, but the impact on the pace and market-orientation of industrial restructuring was palpable. In part, this was due to a new generation of German industrial leaders more comfortable with letting shareholders decide governance outcomes, large blocks of shares in German companies residing in the hands of foreign institutions in the absence of major German funded pension pools, German companies who themselves have made important acquisitions abroad and need to play by market-oriented rules, as well as the elimination of currency-matching of assets and liabilities for insurance companies with the advent of the euro. Politician's protestations against shareholder-driven industrial outcomes notwithstanding, 'It is wrong for governments to intervene in takeover bids, friendly or unfriendly. National flags should not play a crucial role any more.'[27]

Meanwhile, stylized France could move from state-led to a capital market-

Fig 7.5 Holdings of DB Investor, December 1988[1]

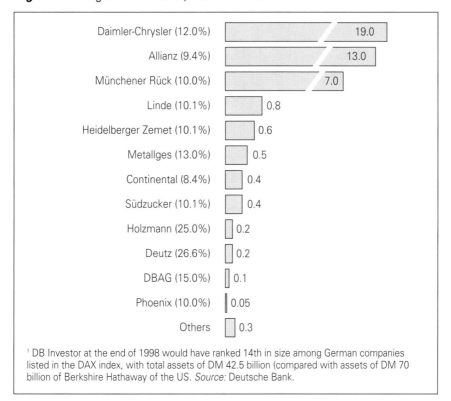

Daimler-Chrysler (12.0%) — 19.0
Allianz (9.4%) — 13.0
Münchener Rück (10.0%) — 7.0
Linde (10.1%) — 0.8
Heidelberger Zemet (10.1%) — 0.6
Metallges (13.0%) — 0.5
Continental (8.4%) — 0.4
Südzucker (10.1%) — 0.4
Holzmann (25.0%) — 0.2
Deutz (26.6%) — 0.2
DBAG (15.0%) — 0.1
Phoenix (10.0%) — 0.05
Others — 0.3

[1] DB Investor at the end of 1998 would have ranked 14th in size among German companies listed in the DAX index, with total assets of DM 42.5 billion (compared with assets of DM 70 billion of Berkshire Hathaway of the US. *Source:* Deutsche Bank.

based system, possibly much more dramatically than in Germany, but stay bank-based for the *petites et moyennes* enterprises, and at the same time remain state-led in its guidance of markets and corporate control. The Anglo-American system may itself move towards a more bank-based or institutional investor-based system as shareholdings are increasingly concentrated in massive mutual fund and pension fund asset pools that have difficulty selling shares in underperforming companies and are prompted to take a more activist role in corporate governance. They would do so along with mutual funds and limited partnerships specifically set up to take such a position where significant capital gains can be achieved by triggering corporate restructurings.

Contestable corporate control and market efficiency

If the market for corporate control is to be an integral part of an efficient capital allocation process, then 'control premiums' – the difference between what shares in a company are worth in the market and what they could be worth under optimum capital allocation circumstances – should be at a minimum. That is, management consistently acts in the best interests of its shareholders, so that other parties are unlikely to be able to achieve significant additional value should they be able to take over the company. One indicator of control premiums and their development over time is the difference between the price paid for a company's shares in a merger or acquisition and the market price five business days after the initial offer for the shares is made. Figure 7.6 shows this premium has in fact declined in the US over the years – i.e. the US market for corporate control has indeed become more efficient.[28] The European bid premium has been somewhat higher than in the US in recent years (35 per cent versus 30 per cent in 1998), and has perhaps been less prone to erosion. As expected, bid premiums on hostile transactions in the US during the period 1988–98 have been significantly higher than agreed transactions (60 per cent versus 31.6 per cent) and for Europe during 1998 this was true as well (51 per cent versus 30 per cent).

Fig 7.6 Median control premiums paid for US firms, 1988–98*

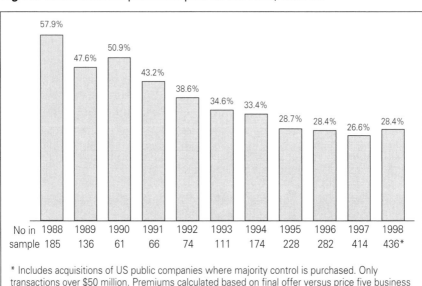

* Includes acquisitions of US public companies where majority control is purchased. Only transactions over $50 million. Premiums calculated based on final offer versus price five business days prior to initial offer.

Source: J.P. Morgan

The European takeover market that developed in the late nineties, often on a cross-border, hostile basis – for example, ABN-AMRO-Generale Bank-Fortis, Olivetti-Telecom Italia-Deutsche Telekom, Vodafone AirTouch-

Mannesmann, Coca-Cola-Orangina and Gucci-LVMH Moët Hennessy Louis Vuitton-Pinault Printemps Redoute – brought into sharp relief the inconsistencies in the pattern of European takeover laws. Some countries maintained takeover-friendly rules, such as the UK, while others have been decidedly unfriendly, such as the Netherlands and France. Some of the differences include the following:

- In the UK, once an acquirer reaches a 30 per cent shareholding a full offer must be made, 'final' offers are final, and takeover disputes are resolved by the Takeover Panel and cannot be appealed to the courts.
- In France, the threshold at which a full offer has to be made is a 33 per cent shareholding, defensive measures can be launched during a bid, and regulatory actions can be appealed to the courts.
- In Germany the takeover code is voluntary, and companies can choose whether or not to subject themselves to it.
- In Italy there are several limits on defences a target company can use to thwart a takeover bid.
- In the Netherlands companies can use a broad range of takeover defences during a bid, and companies are never obliged to make a full offer to all shareholders, leaving minorities with basically no rights.
- In Spain a company can avail itself of a broad range of defences before a takeover bid, but a much more limited set of options after a bid has been launched, and offers do not have to be extended to all shareholders.
- In Switzerland a panolpy of takeover defences is allowed before and after a bid, and a buyer can force minorities to sell only after it has achieved 98 per cent voting control of the target.

The need for a pan-European takeover code has become increasingly evident, although an EU draft code was deadlocked in a dispute among member countries. Its absence helped impede serious industrial restructuring, distorted capital investment and harmed shareholders even as it triggered frictions between national governments – and arguably had an adverse effect on the euro itself. With national sovereignty looming so large in takeover rules, even the broad outlines of a consistent set of regulations remain exceedingly fuzzy.[29]

In the end, there is little question today that the 'battle of the systems' will be won by the Anglo-American approach to corporate governance, perhaps modified by an as yet to be defined role exercised by institutional investors acting as fiduciaries driven by portfolio performance in a highly competitive environment, as discussed in the next chapter. The reasons have to do with:

● increasingly competitive, liquid and transparent equity markets covered by the euro;

● growing cross-border investments seeking higher returns and improved portfolio allocation which have little patience for corporate underperformance;

● banks and insurance companies increasingly under pressure to perform, where long-term holdings in non-financial companies may not be a good way to compete with more performance driven rivals;

● the growing role of US and UK institutional investors in European capital markets seeking the kind of superior returns that may come with economic restructuring in the region;

● the increasing acceptability of market-driven corporate moves to force changes in strategy, disposition of peripheral operations, declaration of special dividends and share repurchases, improvements in operating efficiency, and other actions to enhance shareholder value.

In all these areas the euro is sure to serve as a catalyst in accelerating and amplifying developments that globalization of markets has already set in motion.

NOTES

[1] For a detailed discussion, *see* Story, Jonathan and Walter, Ingo (1997) *The Political Economy of Financial Integration in Europe*, Manchester: Manchester University Press; and Cambridge: MIT Press.

[2] Walter, Ingo (1993) *The Battle of the Systems*, Kiel: Institut für Weltwirtschaft.

[3] *See* Ergas, Henry (1986) 'Does technology matter?', Centre for European Policy Studies, Brussels.

[4] Rybczynski, T.N. (1989) 'Corporate restructuring', *National Westminster Bank Review*, August.

[5] Röller, Wolfgang (1990) 'Die Macht der Banken', *Zeitschrift für das Gesamte Kreditwesen*, 1 January.

[6] Plender, John (1999) 'Rhineland, USA', *Financial Times*, 7 December.

[7] Schonfield, Andrew (1965) *Modern Capitalism: The Changing Balance of Public and Private Power*, New York: Oxford University Press, p. 253.

[8] Baums, Theodor (1996) 'Universal banks and investment companies in Germany', in Saunders, Anthony and Walter, Ingo (eds) (1996) *Financial System Design*, Oak Park, Ill.: Irwin-Professional.

[9] Prowse, S.D. (1990) 'Institutional investment patterns and corporate financial behavior in the US and Japan', Board of Governors of the Federal Reserve System, Working Paper, January.

[10] Herring, Richard J. and Santomero, A.M. (1990) 'The corporate structure of financial conglomerates', *Journal of Financial Services Research,* December.

[11] Dermine, Jean (ed.) (1990) *European Banking After 1992,* Oxford: Basil Blackwell.

[12] Zysman, John (1983) *Governments, Markets and Growth: financial systems and policies of industrial change,* Oxford: Martin Robertson, pp. 99–169.

[13] Edwards, James and Fischer, Klaus (1994) *Banks, Finance and Investment in Germany,* Cambridge: Cambridge University Press.

[14] Cable, J. (1985) 'Capital market information and industrial performance: the role of West German banks', *The Economic Journal,* pp. 118–32.

[15] Cable, J. (1985) 'Capital market information and industrial performance: the role of West German banks', *The Economic Journal,* pp. 118–32; Sheard, P. (1989) 'The main bank system and corporate monitoring and control in Japan', *Journal of Commercial Banking and Organization*; and Kim, S.B. (1990) 'Modus operandi of lenders-cum-shareholder banks', Federal Reserve Bank of San Francisco, *mimeo,* September.

[16] Walter, Ingo (1985) (ed.), *Deregulating Wall Street,* New York: John Wiley & Sons. *See also* Smith, Roy C. and Walter, Ingo (1992) 'Bank-industry linkages: models for Eastern European restructuring', paper presented at a SUERF conference on 'The New Europe: evolving economic and financial systems in East and West', Berlin, Germany, 8–10 October.

[17] Steinherr, Alfred and Huveneers, Christian (1992) 'On the performance of differently regulated financial institutions: some empirical evidence', Université Catholique de Louvain, Working Paper (*mimeo*), February.

[18] Saunders, 'The Separation of Banking and Commerce', New York University Salomon Center Working Paper (*mimeo*), September 1990.

[19] Krümmel, Hans-Jakob (1980) 'German universal banking scrutinized', *Journal of Banking and Finance,* March.

[20] Smith, Roy C. (1994) *Comeback,* Boston: Harvard Business School Press.

[21] Jensen, Michael and Ruback, Richard (1983) 'The market for corporate control: the scientific evidence', *Journal of Financial Economics,* 11 April.

[22] Strange, Susan (1988) *States and Markets,* London: Pinter.

[23] O'Donnell, G. and Schmitter, P. (1986) *Transitions From Authoritarian Rule: tentative conclusions about uncertain democracies,* Baltimore: Johns Hopkins University Press.

[24] Rustow, D. 'Transitions to democracy: towards a dynamic model', *Comparative Politics,* 22 (3).

[25] Walter, Ingo and Smith, Roy C. (1989) *Investment Banking in Europe: restructuring for the 1990s,* Oxford: Basil Blackwell.

[26] Walter, Ingo (ed.) (1994) *Reforming Japan's Securities Markets,* Homewood, Ill.: Business One/Irwin.

[27] Schulte-Nölle, Henning, CEO of Allianz AG as quoted in Plender, John (1999) 'Rhineland, USA', *Financial Times,* 7 December.

[28] Estrich, Rick Mergers & Acquisitions Policy Group, J.P. Morgan Securities, Inc.

[29] Raghavan, Anita and Kamm, Thomas (1999) 'Pressure grows to unify Europe's takeover laws', *Wall Street Journal,* 13 December.

CHAPTER 8

The ongoing revolution in asset management

The institutional asset management industry is likely to be one of the largest and most dynamic segments of the European and global financial services industry in the years ahead. As of March 1999, the global total of assets under management was estimated at close to $50 trillion, comprising some $9.5 trillion in pension fund assets, about $11 trillion in mutual fund assets, $7.6 trillion in fiduciary assets controlled by insurance companies, $14.4 trillion in onshore private client assets and perhaps $7.2 trillion in offshore assets of high net-worth clients.[1] Not only will this already massive industry experience substantial growth in comparison with other parts of the financial services sector, but cross-border volume – both regional and global – is likely to take an increasing share of that activity. Much of the action will be centred in Europe, which has lagged well behind the US in institutional asset management and where many of the global pension problems are to be found. In turn, the rapid growth of performance-oriented managed asset pools will alter the European financial landscape – including traditional approaches to corporate control.

Within this high-growth context, asset management attracts competitors from an extraordinarily broad range of strategic groups – commercial and universal banks, investment banks, trust companies, insurance companies, private banks, captive and independent pension fund managers, mutual fund companies, and various types of specialist firms. This rich array of contenders, marked by very different starting points, competitive resources and strategic objectives, is likely to make the market for institutional asset management a highly competitive one even with substantial predicted growth.

The underlying driving forces in the market for institutional asset management are well understood. They include:

- a continued broad-based trend towards professional management of discretionary household assets in the form of mutual funds or unit trusts and other types of collective investment vehicles – a development that has perhaps run much of its course in some national financial systems but has only begun in others;

- the recognition that most government-sponsored pension systems, many of which were created wholly or partially on a pay-as-you-go basis, have become fundamentally untenable under demographic projections that appear virtually certain to materialize, and must be progressively replaced by asset pools that will bring the kinds of returns necessary to meet the needs of growing numbers of longer-living retirees;

- partial replacement of traditional defined benefit public and private sector pension programmes backed by assets contributed by employers and employees – due to pressure of evolving demographics, rising administrative costs, and shifts in risk allocation – by a variety of defined contribution schemes;

- reallocation of portfolios that have – for regulatory, tax or institutional reasons – become overweight domestic financial instruments (notably fixed-income securities), towards a greater role for equities and non-domestic asset classes. These not only promise higher returns but may also reduce the beneficiaries' exposure to risk due to portfolio diversification across both asset classes and economic and financial environments that are less than perfectly correlated in terms of total investment returns.

The growth implied by the first three of these factors, combined with the asset allocation shifts implied by the fourth, will tend to drive the dynamics and competitive structure of the global institutional asset management industry in the years ahead.

The euro carries with it a number of important implications for the industry. It will have an impact on total asset returns and the potential for international portfolio diversification, for example by eliminating national currencies, interest rate differentials and divergent monetary policies within the region covered by a common currency. It has given rise to a whole new class of government securities denominated in euros that are broadly equivalent to municipals in the US context. These securities are rated, priced and distributed to increasingly dominant, performance-driven institutional asset managers, and will have to compete with an expanding array of euro-denominated corporate bonds, asset-backed securities, equities and other investment alternatives available to institutional investors in a single capital market that will eventually rival that of the US in both size and competitive structure.

These forces will, in turn, enhance European financial market liquidity, transparency, performance orientation and benchmarking standards by which both asset managers and issuers are assessed. And it will shift competitive relationships among universal banks, full-service investment banks, specialist and generalist fund management companies, insurance companies and other players in the asset management business, including highly experienced non-domestic competitors in various national markets that were previously sheltered from foreign competition.

This chapter assesses the three principal sectors of the asset management industry – mutual funds, pension funds and private clients – as well as foundations, endowments, central bank reserves and other large financial pools requiring institutional asset management services. In each case, the European experience is compared with that of the US as well as, where appropriate, Japan and certain emerging market countries. This is followed by a discussion about the competitive structure, conduct and performance of the asset management industry. Finally, the European dimensions of the issue considered in each section of the paper are brought together in an assessment of the impact of institutional asset management on the European capital market.

Asset management in a financial intermediation framework

The asset management services in focus here are depicted in Fig. 8.1, as follows:

● First, retail clients have the option of placing funds directly with financial institutions such as banks or by purchasing securities from retail sales forces of broker-dealers, possibly with the help of fee-based financial advisers. Alternatively, retail investors can have their funds professionally managed by buying shares in mutual funds or unit trusts (again possibly with the help of advisers), which in turn buy securities from the institutional sales desks of broker-dealers (and from time to time maintain balances with banks).

Fig 8.1 Organization of institutional asset management functions

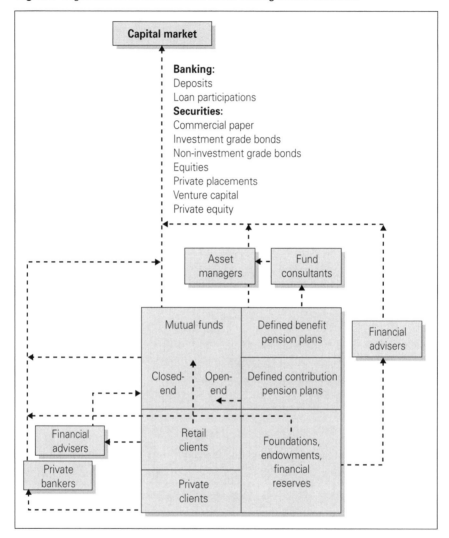

- Second, as in Fig. 8.1, private clients are broken out as a separate segment of the asset management market, and are usually serviced by private bankers who bundle asset management with various other services such as tax planning, estates and trusts. They place assets directly into financial instruments, commingled managed asset pools, or sometimes publicly-available mutual funds and unit trusts.

- Third, foundations, endowments and financial reserves held by non-financial companies, institutions and governments can rely on in-house investment expertise to purchase securities directly from the institutional sales desks of banks or securities broker-dealers, use financial advisers to help them build efficient portfolios, or place funds with open-end or closed-end mutual funds.

● Fourth, pension funds take two principal forms, those guaranteeing a level of benefits and those aimed at building beneficiary assets from which a pension will be drawn (see below). Defined benefit pension funds can buy securities directly in the market or place funds with banks, trust companies or other types of asset managers, often aided by fund consultants who advise pension trustees on performance and asset allocation styles. Defined contribution pension programmes may operate in a similar way if they are managed in-house, creating proprietary asset pools, and in addition (or alternatively) provide participants with the option to purchase shares in publicly-available mutual funds.

The structure of the asset management industry encompasses a number of overlaps among the four types of asset pools to the point where they are sometimes difficult to distinguish. For example, there is a strong linkage between defined contribution pension funds and the mutual fund industry. There is a similar but perhaps more limited linkage between private client assets and mutual funds, on the one hand, and pension funds on the other. This is particularly the case for lower levels of private client business (in terms of assets managed), which is often commingled with mass-marketed mutual funds, and pension benefits awarded to high-income executives, which in effect become part of high net-worth portfolios.

Mutual funds

As in the US, the mutual fund industry in Europe has enjoyed rapid growth during the nineties, although there are wide differences among national financial markets in its pace of development, in the composition of the assets under management, and in the nature of mutual fund marketing and distribution. The pattern of development in Europe has also differed significantly from that of the US, where at the end of 1999 there were more than 6,000 mutual funds (and over 4,500 equity mutual funds) available to the public – more than the number of stocks listed on the New York Stock Exchange. Average annual growth was in excess of 20 per cent between 1975 and 1999, with almost $4 trillion of assets under management in the funds at the end of

1997 (about 13 per cent of household net financial wealth, more than that of life insurance companies and about equal to the total assets of commercial banks).[2] Much of the growth is also attributable to the use of mutual funds for retirement savings, capturing roughly 17 per cent of US retirement assets in 1998 (*see below*). Similar dynamics are expected in Europe under economic monetary union, but with a number of significant differences.

Figure 8.2 shows the distribution of mutual fund assets in terms of market capitalization and asset allocation at the end of 1998 in Europe and the US. The US accounted for slightly over half the assets under management, with Europe about 31 per cent and Japan 9 per cent of the total.[3] Within Europe, France had the top position in 1997 with 29 per cent, followed by Germany with 17 per cent, the UK with 12 per cent and Switzerland with 11 per cent. In Europe, mutual funds and unit trusts were roughly evenly split between money market funds, fixed-income funds and equity funds, but this masks the wide inter-country differences shown in Fig. 8.3. The French market has been dominated by money market funds, in part due to tax advantages, while the British market is virtually monopolized by equity funds. At the same time, fixed-income funds take a disproportionate share of the market in other European countries, notably Germany, reflecting both traditional investor preferences and the limited state of development of national equity markets in the countries concerned.

Fig 8.2 Comparative domestic mutual fund assets by investment type, 1998 (US$bn)

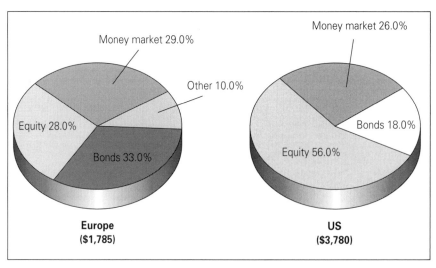

Source: EFID; Lipper Analytical Services International; Goldman Sachs

Fig 8.3 Mutual funds: total assets under management in major European markets, end of 1997

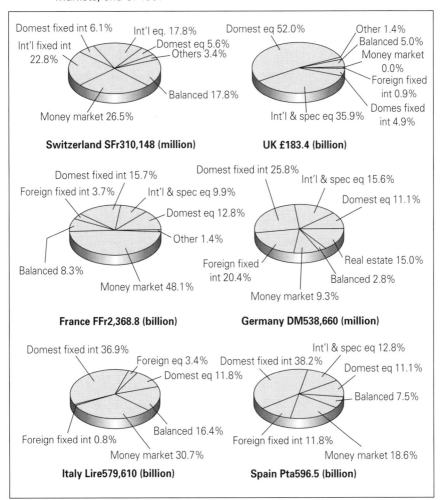

In the US, on the other hand, mutual funds were traditionally invested mainly in equities – in 1975, over 82 per cent of the fund assets under management were allocated to equities and a mere 10 per cent and 8 per cent to bonds and money market instruments respectively. By 1985 this picture had changed completely, with the equity component declining to 24 per cent and money market funds capturing 49 per cent, due both to poor stock market performance in the seventies and early eighties, and to the substitution of money market mutual funds for bank savings products by households searching for higher yields at a time when banks continued to be limited by interest rate regulation on deposits. By 1998 the US pattern of mutual fund investments had shifted yet again, with equities accounting for 49 per cent of the total, money market funds 26 per cent, and bond funds 25 per cent.[4]

Mutual fund distribution

There are also wide differences among countries in how mutual funds are distributed; these differences, in turn, are linked to comparative mutual fund growth and structure. As shown in Fig. 8.4, the main method of distribution of European mutual funds is through bank branches in countries such as Germany (80 per cent), France (70 per cent) and Spain (61 per cent), with UK distribution concentrated among independent advisers and Italian distribution roughly split between bank branches and independent sales forces. The dominance of universal banks, savings banks and co-operative banks as financial intermediaries in most of the continental European countries explains the high concentration of mutual fund distribution via bank branch networks.[5] One major exception to bank-based fund distribution was Robeco, a Dutch asset management company, which was highly successful in penetrating the retail market, only to be taken over by Rabobank after a brief joint venture to market each other's products.

In contrast, US mutual fund distribution has been concentrated through full service broker-dealers which maintain large retail sales forces capable of penetrating the household sector and which are compensated mainly on the basis of commissions earned on assets under management (AUM). In recent years, discount brokers and e-brokers have made substantial inroads into mutual fund distribution, compensating for reduced sales effort and limited investment advice by lower fees and expenses. Insurance agents account for 11 per cent of US mutual fund distribution, focusing on mutual funds with an insurance wrapper such as fixed and variable annuities and guaranteed investment contracts (GICs). Bank branches have played a limited role in the US due to the legacy of regulatory constraints, accounting for a relatively small 8 per cent distribution share – restrictions finally scrapped in 1999.

A key question is how mutual funds will be distributed in the future European unified financial market. Distribution without advice will clearly be most efficient over the Internet or other on-line interfaces with the retail client. This means that transaction services can be separated from investment advice, both functionally and in terms of pricing. Advice can be delivered only in part in disembodied form, with value-added depending partly on interpretive information on investments and partly on personal counselling that the client must be willing to pay for. With this advice increasingly likely to

Fig 8.4 Estimated mutual fund market share by distribution channel in major markets, 1996

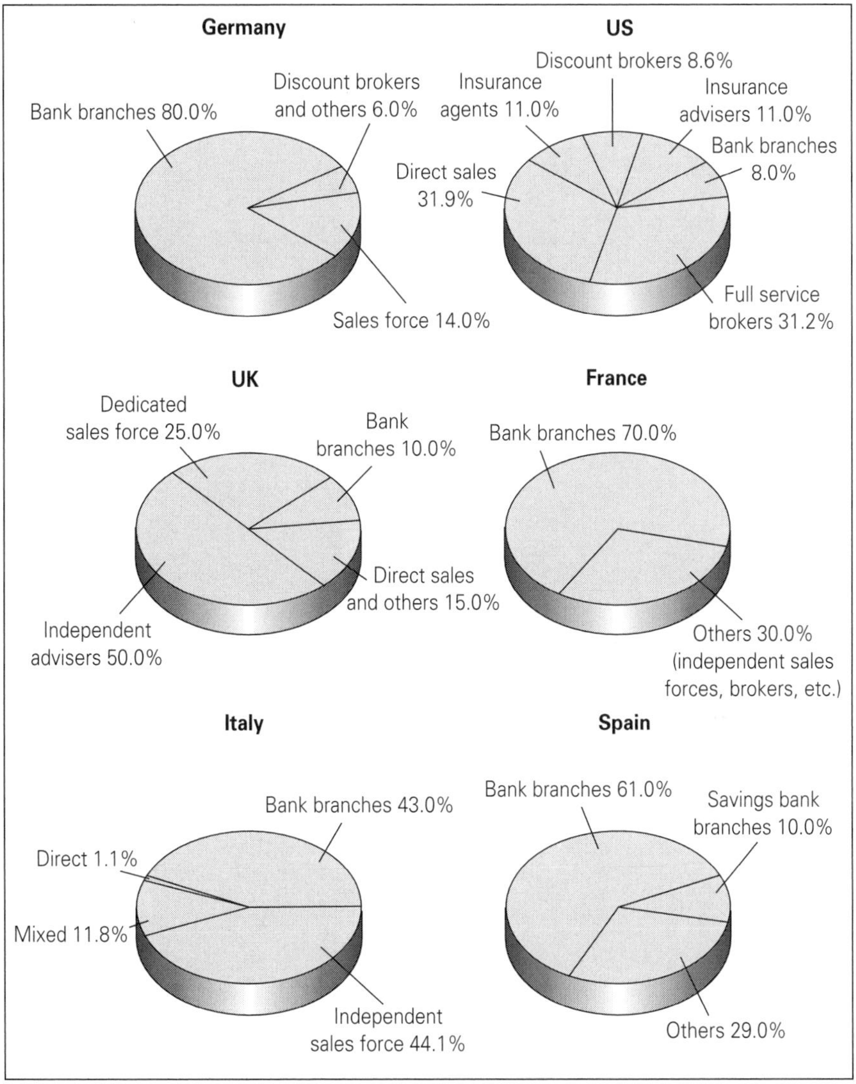

Germany
- Bank branches 80.0%
- Discount brokers and others 6.0%
- Insurance agents 11.0%
- Sales force 14.0%

US
- Discount brokers 8.6%
- Insurance advisers 11.0%
- Bank branches 8.0%
- Direct sales 31.9%
- Full service brokers 31.2%

UK
- Dedicated sales force 25.0%
- Bank branches 10.0%
- Direct sales and others 15.0%
- Independent advisers 50.0%

France
- Bank branches 70.0%
- Others 30.0% (independent sales forces, brokers, etc.)

Italy
- Bank branches 43.0%
- Direct 1.1%
- Mixed 11.8%
- Independent sales force 44.1%

Spain
- Bank branches 61.0%
- Savings bank branches 10.0%
- Others 29.0%

Source: EFID, Banca Fideuram, Investment Company Institute, Securities Industry Association

come from independent financial planners in many markets, traditional distributors of mutual funds are encroached upon from both sides and have had to react in order to maintain market share.

It is certain that the major US mutual fund companies such as Fidelity and Vanguard will work to penetrate the European bank-based distribution channels that have traditionally prevailed in most countries. So too will US broker-dealers like Merrill Lynch, which acquired the UK's Mercury Asset Management in 1997, Morgan Stanley Dean Witter, discounters such as Charles Schwab, and the Citigroup financial conglomerate as the only US institution with a European presence of sufficient mass to use as perhaps a platform for mutual fund distribution. UK fund managers and insurance companies will try to do the same thing on the continent, even as continental European banks and insurance companies strive to adapt their powerful distribution systems to more effective asset management and mutual fund marketing, and to sharpen their product range and investment performance.

Mutual fund competition

Competition among mutual funds can be among the most intense anywhere in the financial system, increased by the aforementioned analytical services which track performance of funds in terms of risk and return against indices over different holding periods, and assign ratings based on fund performance. These fund rating services are important, because the vast majority of new investments tend to flow into highly rated funds. For example, in the US between 1993 and 1998, about 85 per cent of all new money was allocated to funds rated 4-star or 5-star by Morningstar Inc. These funds captured roughly three-quarters of all mutual fund assets at the end of 1998. In addition, widely read business publications publish regular 'scoreboards' among publicly available mutual funds based on such ratings and, together with specialized investment publications and information distributed over the Internet, have made mutual funds one of the most transparent parts of the retail financial services sector. These developments are mirrored to varying degrees in Europe as well, notably in the UK.

Despite clear warnings that past performance is no assurance of future results, a rise in the performance rankings often brings in a flood of new investments and management company revenues, with the individual asset manager compensated commensurately and sometimes moving on to take charge of larger and more prestigious funds. Conversely, serious performance slippage causes investors to withdraw funds, taking with them a good part of the manager's bonus and maybe his or her job, given that the mutual fund company's revenues are vitally dependent on new investments and total assets under management. With a gradual decline in the level of sophistication of the average investor in many markets – as mutual funds become increasingly mass market retail-oriented and interlinked with pension schemes (*see below*) – performance ratings, name recognition and 'branding' appear to be progressively more important in defining competitive performance in the industry.

Historically, there has been little evidence of increasing market concentration in the mutual fund industry at least in the US. As Fig. 8.5 shows, the largest and smallest long-term funds have gradually eroded the market share of mid-sized funds. Factors that seem to argue for greater industry concentration in the future are economies of scale and brand-name concentration among progressively less sophisticated investors in taxable funds and mutual funds – part of retirement accounts among the enormous number of funds vying for the investors' business.[6] Arguments against further concentration include shifts in performance track records and the role of mutual fund supermarkets and the Internet in distribution, which increase the relative marketing advantage of smaller funds.

Fig 8.5 Mutual fund market share by size of firm, 1988–97

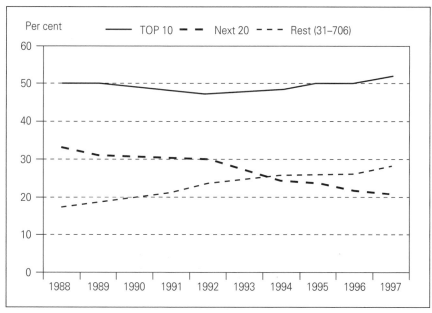

Source: Simfund; Goldman Sachs

In addition to promoting their performance (when favourable), mutual fund companies and securities broker-dealers have aggressively added banking-type services such as checking and cash management accounts, credit cards and overdraft lines. They provide user friendly, integrated account statements and tax reporting. Client contact is based on easy access by telephone, mail and the Internet. Securities firms, meanwhile, have increased their mutual fund activity, presumably with the view that this part of the securities industry is more capable of supporting significant, sustained returns than is wholesale investment banking where competition has become cut-throat, capital-intensive and subject to a high degree of earnings instability. Insurance companies have also considered the mutual fund business to be a strong candidate for strategic development, especially in the face of competition in their traditional annuities business and the cross-links that have emerged in some countries between the pension fund and mutual fund industries. Banks, too, have pushed aggressively into the mutual fund business.

There have been successful examples of direct fund distribution even in heavily bank-dominated European financial systems, such as Direct Anlage in Germany, Virgin Direct in the UK and Cortal Banque (affiliated with BNP-Paribas) in France. Examples of effective cross-border mutual fund distribution include Fidelity of the US and Fleming Flagship of the UK. Such cross-border incursions into idiosyncratic national markets requires high levels of product performance, good service quality and effective distribution techniques that are appropriate to the national environment – either on a stand-alone basis or in joint ventures with local financial firms. This suggests that targeted approaches which provide specific client segments with products superior to those available from traditional vendors is probably the only viable way to develop a pan-European approach to retail asset management.

Competition in the mutual funds business thus covers a rich array of players, ranging from commercial banks and securities broker-dealers to specialized mutual fund companies, discount brokerages, insurance companies and non-financial firms. Such interpenetration of strategic groups, each approaching the business from a different direction, tends to make markets hyper-competitive. This is the likely competitive structure of the mutual fund industry in the future, particularly in large, integrated markets such as the US and – with a common currency – the European Union.

Comparative regulation of mutual funds

In the US, there are strict regulations for companies managing mutual funds sold to the public, and requirements for extensive disclosure of pertinent information. The National Securities Markets Improvement Act of 1996 made the Securities and Exchange Commission responsible for overseeing investment advisers with more than $25 million under management, with state regulators alone responsible for investment advisers dealing with smaller amounts – advisers who had previously been jointly regulated with the SEC. The large investment advisers falling under SEC jurisdiction account for about 95 per cent of US assets under management, although the vast majority of abusive practices and enforcement problems occur among the smaller firms.[7]

Threat of regulatory action and civil liability lawsuits keep the pressure on US mutual fund boards to take seriously their obligations to investors to insure that fund objectives are faithfully carried out. Some fund management companies, however, nominate individuals to serve as directors of sometimes a large number of funds from among those it manages, perhaps raising questions about whether the directors can fulfil all their responsibilities to their investors. Still, if they are thought not to be doing so they can expect legal action from lawyers representing the investors as a class. All this, along with a high level of transparency with regard to performance, ample media coverage of the industry, and vigorous competition among fund managers, means investors have a generally fair and efficient market in which to make their asset choices. The mutual fund business in the US and a number of countries is therefore probably a good example of how regulation and competition can work together to properly serve the retail investor.

In contrast to the US, the rules governing the operation and distribution of mutual funds in Europe have traditionally been highly fragmented, although this will gradually come to an end under the euro in the years ahead. As of the mid eighties, definitions of mutual funds varied from country to country, as did legal status and regulatory provisions. Door-to-door selling was forbidden in Belgium and Luxembourg, for example, and strictly regulated in Germany. In Britain, on the other hand, direct marketing was the norm. Market access to clients varied between heavily restricted to virtually unhindered.

The EU directive governing the operation and sale of mutual funds – Undertakings for the Collective Investment of Transferable Securities (UCITS) – came into force on 1 October 1989 after 15 years of negotiation. It specifies general rules for the kinds of investments that are appropriate for mutual funds and how they should be sold. The regulatory requirements for fund management and certification are left to the home country of the fund management firm, while specific rules governing the adequacy of disclosure and selling practices are left to the respective host countries.[8]

Consequently, mutual funds established and monitored in any EU member country such as Luxembourg – and which are in compliance with UCITS – can be sold without restriction to investors in national financial markets EU-wide, and promoted and advertised through local marketing networks and via direct mail, as long as selling requirements applicable in each country are met. Permissible investment vehicles include conventional equity and fixed-income securities, as well as high-performance 'synthetic' funds based on futures and options not previously permitted in some financial centres such as London. Under UCITS, 90 per cent of mutual fund assets must be invested in publicly traded companies, no more than 5 per cent of the outstanding stock of any company may be owned by a mutual fund, and there are limits on investment funds' borrowing rights. Property funds, commodity funds and money market funds are specifically excluded from UCITS.

European taxation and the mutual fund industry

Unlike those in the EU, US mutual funds have operated in a comparatively coherent tax environment. There is a uniform federal income tax code, which requires mutual fund companies to report all income and capital gains to the Internal Revenue Service (IRS) – normally there is no withholding at source – and individuals to report the same information in annual tax returns, with data reconciliation undertaken by the IRS. Taxable fund income is subject to normal federal income tax rates, while capital gains and losses are recorded as they are incurred in mutual fund trading, with net gains attributed to the mutual fund investor and taxed at the federal capital gains rates. Tax fraud, including the use of offshore accounts to evade tax, is a criminal offence. States and sometimes municipalities tend to tax mutual fund income and capital gains (and sometimes assets) at substantially lower rates. Under the US Constitution the states and the federal government cannot tax each other. So there is a broad range of mutual funds that invest in securities issued by state and local governments with income exempt from federal tax as well as (usually) tax on the income from the states' own securities contained in the portfolio. Similarly, the states do not tax income derived from federal government securities. The US tax environment, while complex, provides the mutual fund industry with opportunities for product development such as tax-efficient funds (e.g. investing in municipals and capital gains-oriented equities) and imposes compliance costs in terms of required reporting of tax both to the IRS and to the investor client.

The European tax environment has been far more heterogeneous by comparison, with the power of tax authorities stopping at the national border and – in the presence in many EU countries of very high tax rates on capital income – widespread tax avoidance and evasion on the part of investors. In the light of intra-EU capital mobility, the euro and the UCITS initiative, of continuing interest has been the narrowing or elimination of intra-EU differentials in taxation of capital income and assets, and the establishment of a coherent tax environment that is considered equitable and resistant to evasion.

In 1988, Germany announced consideration of a 10 per cent withholding tax on interest and dividend income in what became an embarrassing demonstration that such taxes can provoke immediate and massive capital flight. Overall, Bundesbank estimates showed a total long-term capital outflow of $42.8 billion during 1988, even though the 10 per cent withholding tax was only being discussed and had not yet been implemented. That occurred on 1 January, 1989 and triggered further massive capital flight, so that four months later, on 27 April, the German authorities announced that the withholding tax would be abolished on 1 July of that year.

In February 1989, midway through the German tax debacle, the European Commission formally proposed a minimum 15 per cent withholding tax (administered at source) on interest income from investments (bonds and bank deposits) by residents of other EU countries, as well as on eurobonds. Non-EU residents were to be exempt from the withholding tax, as were savings accounts of young people and small savers who were already exempt from taxation in a number of EU countries. Member states were to be free to impose withholding taxes above the 15 per cent floor. Governments could exempt interest income subject to withholding at source from declaration for tax purposes. Also exempted were countries that already applied equal or higher withholding taxes on interest income. Additional aspects of the proposal concerned co-operation in enforcement and exchange of information among EU fiscal authorities. Dividends were omitted from the proposals because they were generally less heavily taxed by EU member countries, and because national income tax systems were thought to capture this type of investment income relatively effectively.[9]

Supporters of abolishing capital income tax differences within the EU – led by France, Belgium, Italy and Spain – argued that tax harmonization was essential if financial market integration was not to lead to widespread tax evasion. All four countries had tax collection systems considered relatively weak in terms of enforcement and widely subject to evasion.

Opponents of the EU tax harmonization initiative, mainly the UK and Luxembourg as well as the Netherlands, argued that tax harmonization was both unnecessary and harmful to the functioning of efficient financial markets, and that substantial investments would subsequently flow out of the EU, especially to Switzerland and other havens. They argued that the proposal failed to recognize that Europe is part of a global financial market and that EU securities returns might have to be raised to levels providing equivalent after-tax yields in order to prevent capital outflows from becoming a serious problem.

After two years of intense debate on the issue, the 15 per cent EU withholding tax proposal finally collapsed in mid-1989 as Germany withdrew its support of the Commission's initiative and shifted to the opposition. The idea of harmonizing EU taxes was quietly shelved, with the finance ministers of member states agreeing to seek alternative means of co-operation and more effective measures against money laundering. Nevertheless, there remained little doubt that greater uniformity in capital income taxation and closer co-operation between EU tax authorities would eventually have to be revived – although harmonization of withholding tax rates and enforcement remained constrained by the possibility of capital flight to low-tax environments outside the EU. At the very least, it was difficult to see how an active EU-wide mutual fund industry could develop under UCITS without a reasonably coherent tax environment.

Meanwhile, Luxembourg has remained the centre of EU tax attention. Funds registered in the country are exempt from local taxation. Investors pay no withholding tax on dividends, and a 1983 law recognized French-type Sociétés d'Investissements à Capital Variable (SICAVs). In March 1988, Luxembourg became the first EU member state to ratify the UCITS in a successful bid to become the functional centre for marketing mutual funds throughout the EU. Jacques Santer, Luxembourg's prime minister at the time and later president of the EU Commission, pointed out that open competition in Europe's financial sector would determine which financial centre won out, but that there were no provisions in EU law for co-operation between tax authorities.[10] But a former EU President Jacques Delors memorably said: 'We will deal with Luxembourg when the time comes.' There seems little doubt that, in the end, he will be right. A financially integrated Europe can no more afford a haven for tax evaders than the US federal government could afford to permit one of the states to declare itself a domestic version of Luxembourg. In 1998 and 1999 the debate resumed with an EU Commission proposal for a 15 per cent withholding tax at source for interest and dividend payments or, alternatively, reporting by the paying entity of any capital income payments to the fiscal authorities of the member state in which the recipient is resident. This proposal moved the EU closer to the US model of a more uniform tax environment for the financial markets and managed asset pools. Still there was no agreement by 2000.

Pension funds

The pension fund market has proved to be one of the fastest growing sectors of the global financial system, and promises to be comparably dynamic in the years ahead. As a result, pension assets have been in the forefront of strategic targeting by all types of financial institutions, including banks, trust companies, broker-dealers, insurance companies, mutual fund companies, and independent asset management firms. Pension assets in 1997 were estimated to amount to $13.7 trillion globally (*see* Fig. 8.6), roughly two-thirds of which covered private sector employees and the rest public sector employees. Total western European pension assets at the end of 1997 had an estimated market value of about $2.2 trillion, with the UK accounting for almost 73 per cent of the total.

Fig 8.6 Global pension assets 1997 ($bn)

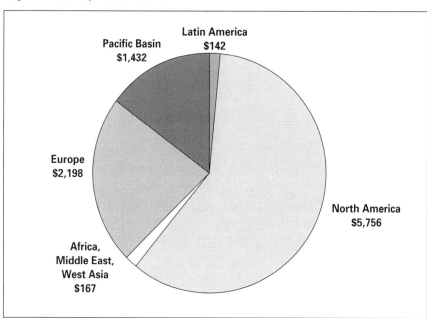

Source: Intersec, 1998

The basis for such projected growth is the demographics of gradually ageing populations, colliding with existing structures for retirement support which in many countries carry heavy political baggage.[11] Politically, it is very difficult to bring these structures up to the standards required for the future, yet it is an inevitability.[12] With a population of some 261 million at the beginning of 1995, the US at that time had accumulated pension pools worth $3.76 trillion. Western Europe, with a population almost twice as large, had accumulated pension assets of only $1.61 trillion. Japan's population and pension accumulations at that time were $125 million and $1.12 trillion respectively.[13] The global epicentre of this problem will thus be the European Union, with profound implications for the size and structure of capital markets, the competitive positioning and performance of financial intermediaries in general and asset managers in particular, and for the systems of corporate governance in the region.[14]

Demographics of dependency

The demographics of the pension fund problem are straightforward. Figure 8.7 depicts data for the so-called 'support ratio' (roughly, those of retirement age as a percentage of those of working age) in OECD countries. Unless there are major unforeseen changes in birth rates, death dates or migration rates, for the EU as a whole the support ratio will have doubled between 1990 and 2040, with the highest support ratios being attained in the Netherlands and Spain, and the lowest in France, Italy and Sweden. While the demographics underlying these projections may be quite reliable, support ratios remain

Fig 8.7 Support ratios for OECD countries (number of people aged 25–59 for each person aged 65+)

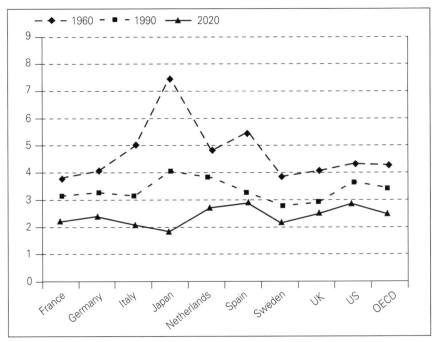

subject to shifts in the ages at which people begin work and retire. Obviously, the longer people remain out of the active labour force (e.g. for purposes of education), the higher the level of sustained unemployment, and the earlier the average retirement age, the higher will be the support ratio. In recent years all these factors have contributed to raising the EU's support ratio, certainly relative to that of the US, although there are early signs that it may eventually stabilize or be reversed under pressure from the realities of the pension issue.

Alternative approaches to old age support

There are basically three ways to provide support for the retired population:

- *Pay-as-you-go (PAYG) programmes.* Pension benefits under this approach are committed by the state based on various formulas – number of years worked and income subject to social charges, for example – and funded by mandatory contributions by those employed (taxes and social charges) that may or may not be specifically earmarked to covering current pension payouts. Under PAYG systems, pension contributions may exceed or fall short of current disbursements. In the former case a 'trust fund' may be set up which, as in the case of US social security, may be invested in government securities. In the latter case, any pension system deficit will tend to be covered out of general tax revenues, government borrowing, or the liquidation of previously accumulated trust fund assets.

- *Defined benefit programmes.* Pension benefits under such programmes are committed to public or private sector employees by their employers, based on actuarial benefit formulas that are part of the employment contract. Defined benefit pension payouts may be linked to the cost of living, adjusted for survivorship, etc., and the funds set aside to support future claims may be contributed solely by the employer or with some level of employee contribution. The pool of assets may be invested in a portfolio of debt and equity securities (possibly including the company's own shares) that are managed in-house or by external fund managers. Depending on the level of contributions and benefit claims, as well as investment performance, defined benefit plans may be overfunded or underfunded. They may thus be tapped by the employer from time to time for general corporate purposes, or they may have to be topped up from the employer's own resources. Defined benefit plans may be insured (e.g. against corporate bankruptcy) either in the private market or by government agencies, and are usually subject to strict regulation.

● *Defined contribution programmes.* Pension fund contributions are made by the employer, the employee or both, into a fund that will ultimately form the basis for pension benefits under defined contribution pension plans. The employee's share in the fund tends to vest after a number of years of employment, and may be managed by the employer or placed with various asset managers under portfolio constraints intended to serve the best interests of the beneficiaries. The employee's responsibility for asset allocation can vary from none at all to virtually full discretion. Employees may, for example, be allowed to select from among a range of approved investment vehicles, notably mutual funds, based on individual risk-return preferences.

Most countries have several types of pension arrangement operating simultaneously – for example, a base-level PAYG system supplemented by state-sponsored or privately-sponsored defined benefit plans, and defined contribution plans sponsored by employers or mandated by the state. As of 1998, 54 countries had defined contribution pension systems of some kind, ranging from nationwide compulsory schemes to funds intended to supplement state-guaranteed pensions.[15] The collision of the aforementioned demographics and heavy reliance by many European countries on PAYG approaches is at the heart of the EU pension problem, and forms the basis for future opportunities in this part of national and global financial systems.[16]

Figure 8.8 shows the percentage of the labour force in various countries covered by occupational pension schemes, with countries such as Italy, Belgium and Spain highly dependent on PAYG state-run pension systems with little asset accumulations, and countries such as the Netherlands, Denmark and the UK having long traditions of defined benefit pension schemes backed by large asset pools. The French system involves a virtually universal state-directed defined benefit scheme which, given the demographics, is heavily under-funded. This is reflected in pension assets per capita and pension assets as a percentage of GDP, shown in the last two columns. Among the EU countries only Denmark, the Netherlands and the UK appear to be in reasonably good shape under this criterion. German companies have traditionally run defined benefit plans, with pension reserves booked within the balance sheets of the employers themselves as opposed to externally managed asset pools, backstopped by a government-mandated pension fund guarantee scheme.[17]

Today's conventional wisdom is that the pension problems centred in European countries with heavy PAYG obligations (*see* Fig. 8.9) will have to be

Fig 8.8 Comparative population and pension assets 1998

Country	Population in millions	Dependency ratio* (%)	Percentage of labour force covered by occupational pension schemes	Value of pension assets ($bn)	Pension assets as a percentage of GDP	Pension assets per capita ($000s)
Belgium	10.2	24.2	5.0	25	11	2.5
Denmark	5.3	22.4	NA	148	84	27.9
Finland	5.1	20.9	NA	40	35	7.9
France	58.0	22.7	80.0	95	7	1.6
Germany	82.0	21.7	65.0	310	14	3.8
Ireland	3.6	19.0	NA	29	42	8.0
Italy	57.4	23.2	5.0	91	7	1.6
Netherlands	15.6	18.8	82.0	502	127	32.2
Norway	4.4	25.0	NA	35	23	7.9
Portugal	9.9	22.4	NA	10	9	1.0
Spain	39.3	23.5	3.0	22	4	0.6
Sweden	8.9	28.6	NA	112	66	16.0
Switzerland	7.1	22.4	92.0	288	117	40.6
UK	59.0	24.6	55.0	1,015	77	17.2
US	270.0	19.7	55.0	5,542	61	20.5

* Population aged 65+ as a proportion of population aged 15–54

Source: William M. Mercer, National Statistical offices

resolved in the foreseeable future, and that there are only a limited number of options:

● Raise mandatory social charges on employees and employers to cover increasing pension obligations under PAYG systems. It is unlikely that any degree of uniformity in the EU can be achieved, given the large inter-country differences in pension schemes and their financing. The competitive effects of the required major increases in employer burdens, especially in a unified market with a common currency, are unlikely to make this a feasible alternative. Saddling employees with additional social contributions in what are already some of the most heavily taxed environments in the world is not likely to be any more palatable.

● Make major reductions in retirement benefits, cutting dramatically into benefit levels. This is unlikely to be any more feasible politically than the first option, especially considering the way many PAYG systems have been positioned – as 'contributions' (not taxes) which would assure a comfortable old age. Taking away something people feel has already been paid for is far more difficult politically than denying them something they never had in the first place. The sensitivity of fiscal reforms to social welfare is illustrated by the fact that just limiting the growth in pension expenditures to the projected rate of economic growth from 2015 onwards would reduce income replacement rates from 45 per cent to 30 per cent over a period of 15 years, leaving those among the elderly without adequate personal resources in relative poverty.

- Significant increases in the retirement age at which individuals are eligible for full PAYG-financed pensions, perhaps to age 70 for those not incapacitated by ill health. This is unlikely to be any more palatable than the previous option, especially in many countries where there has been active pressure to go the other way, i.e. to reduce the age of eligibility for PAYG retirement benefits to 60 or even 55. This is compounded by a chronically high unemployment rate in Europe, which has been widely used as a justification for earlier retirements.

- Major increases in general taxation levels or government borrowing to top up eroding trust funds or finance PAYG benefits on a continuing basis. Again, this is an unlikely alternative due to the economic and competitive consequences of further increases in tax rates, major political resistance, and Maastricht-type fiscal constraints. Furthermore, national states maintaining PAYG systems – under a single currency and without the ability to monetize debt – would have to compete for financing in a unified, rated bond market, which would constrain their ability to run large borrowing programmes on similar lines to those of individual states in the US.

- Major pension reforms to progressively move away from PAYG systems towards defined contribution and defined benefit schemes such as those widely used in the US, Chile, Singapore, Malaysia, the UK, the Netherlands, Denmark and certain other EU countries. Each of these differs in detail, but all involve the creation of large asset pools that are reasonably actuarially sound. Where such asset pools already exist, more attention will have to be focused on investment performance, with a shift away from government bonds towards higher yielding assets in order to help maintain benefit levels.

Given the relatively bleak outlook for most of these alternatives, it seems inevitable that increasing reliance will be placed on the last of these options. The fact that future generations can no longer count on the 'free ride' of the value of benefits exceeding the present value of contributions and social charges as demographics inevitably turn against them – in the presence of clear fiscal constraints facing governments – requires fundamental rethinking of pension arrangements in most OECD countries, notably those of the

Fig 8.9 Estimates of combined pension debt and conventional public debt

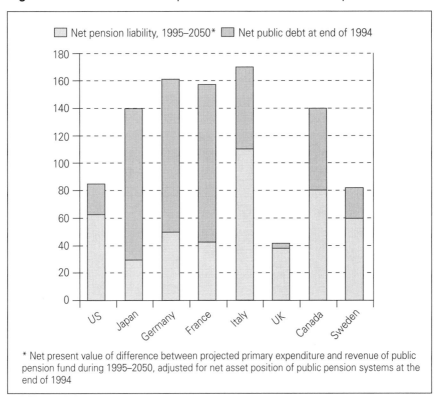

* Net present value of difference between projected primary expenditure and revenue of public pension fund during 1995–2050, adjusted for net asset position of public pension systems at the end of 1994

Source: Chand, Sheetal K. and Jaeger, Albert (1996) Aging Population and Public Pension Schemes, *International Monetary Fund, Occasional Paper no. 147, December. Goldman Sachs*

European Union. Alternatively, the fiscal deficits necessary for unreformed national PAYG pension schemes in those EU countries that are part of a single currency zone would imply higher interest rates across the euro-zone, and/or higher levels of inflation if there is monetization by the European Central Bank of some of the incremental public debt.

Asset allocation and cross-links with mutual funds

Whereas there are wide differences among countries in their reliance on PAYG pension systems and in the degree of demographic and financial pressure to build actuarially viable dedicated asset pools, there are equally wide differences in how those assets have been allocated.

As depicted in Fig. 8.10, the US (not including the Social Security Trust Fund) and the UK have relied quite heavily on domestic equities. The largest

15 pension fund managers in 1997 had about 50 per cent of equity assets invested in passive funds, against about 5 per cent in the case of mutual funds. The share of asset allocation to domestic bonds is highest in Germany and Denmark, followed by Portugal, Switzerland and the Netherlands. Foreign equity holdings are proportionately highest in Ireland, the Netherlands and Belgium (each with small domestic stock markets). Foreign bond holdings play a major role only in the case of Belgium. Equity holdings among European $1.9 trillion in pension assets (mid-1996) varies widely, ranging from 75 per cent of assets in the UK, 42 per cent in Belgium, 34 per cent in the Netherlands, 13 per cent in France, and 11 per cent in Spain. The share of equities in EU pension pools has been growing significantly, from 17.4 per cent in 1992 to 26.0 per cent in 1996 and 30.7 per cent in 1997, at the expense of money market assets and, to a lesser extent, bonds.[18]

Fig 8.10 Comparative pension fund asset allocations

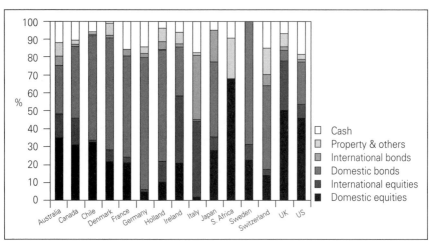

Source: InterSec Securities Corporation, 1997. Date for year-end 1995

Regulations that require pension funds to match the currency of their assets with the currency of their liabilities are redundant in the euro-zone, and this will greatly broaden the equity allocation opportunities for fund trustees. In some cases currency exposure restrictions have made pension fund equity allocations overweight in certain industries (such as petroleum in the Netherlands) due to the importance of a few major companies in national equity market capitalization; the euro, therefore, will permit significantly improved sectoral asset allocation in pension portfolios. This will require large increases in cross-border equity flows in Europe, and the creation of pan-European pension fund performance benchmarks to replace existing national benchmarks.[19]

Taxation remains a major problem in the creation of efficient pension asset allocations in Europe via international portfolio diversification. The reason is that governments often do not provide reciprocal tax exemption for pension assets invested abroad. For example, many countries exempt employee and employer pension contributions and pension fund earnings from tax, and subsequently taxes them at prevailing personal income tax rates when they are distributed on an employee's retirement – although some countries tax retirement income at concessionary rates as well. If part of a retirement fund is invested abroad, however, the host country often treats the assets the same as all other financial assets, and levies taxes on interest, dividends and/or capital gains at regular withholding rates. Such differential tax treatment obviously puts a bias on asset allocation towards domestic investments, and can significantly affect portfolio optimization. Several proposals have been made to deal with this issue. The OECD Model Tax Convention would tax dividend income at 15 per cent, interest income at 10 per cent and capital gains at 0 per cent without regard to the distinction between retirement and non-retirement assets. The US Model Income Tax Convention would tax dividend income of foreign assets at 15 per cent and exempt interest income and capital gains, but would also exempt all income on retirement assets as long as at least half of the participants of the fund were residents of the home country. Ideally, of course, there should be reciprocal exemption from tax for all retirement assets invested internationally, together with reciprocal acceptance of certification of retirement plan qualifications.[20]

The growing role of defined contribution plans in the US has led to strong links between pension funds and mutual funds. Many mutual funds – notably in the equities sector – are strongly influenced by pension inflows. At the end of 1996, more than 35 per cent ($1.2 trillion) of mutual fund assets represented retirement accounts of various types in the US. Some 15 per cent of total retirement assets were invested in mutual funds, up from about 1 per cent in 1980.[21] This is reflected in the structure of the pension fund management industry in the US. The top 25 defined benefit asset managers in 1995 were trust departments of commercial banks, with the top ten averaging discretionary assets of about $150 billion each. There is little evidence of increasing market concentration in the fixed-income part of the trust business, with the top 25 firms controlling 62 per cent of assets in both 1990 and 1995. However, the top-25 market share in the equities segment (which was roughly twice as large) rose from 29 per cent in 1990 to 35 per cent in

1995, presumably due to the importance of performance differentials in attracting assets.[22] Among the top 25 employer-sponsored defined contribution plan fund managers in 1995 three were mutual fund companies, ten were insurance companies, five were banks, one was a broker-dealer, two were diversified financial firms, and four were specialist asset managers.[23] A similar development is likely in the EU, with defined contribution assets in European pension pools rising from 13 per cent ($490 billion) in 1995 to an estimated 19 per cent ($1.42 trillion) in 2000.[24]

Partly as a consequence, European pension funds' use of asset managers has changed significantly over the years. In 1987 banks had a market share of about 95 per cent, while insurance companies and independent fund managers split the rest about evenly. By 1995 independent fund managers had captured over 40 per cent of the market, banks were down to about 55 per cent and insurance companies had the rest. There is also some evidence of increasing pension fund management concentration, at least in the UK, where in 1995 six pension fund managers accounted for about 70 per cent of the market. Of these, five were actively managed funds and one (Barclays Global Investors) specialized in index funds.

Asset management for private clients

One of the largest pools of institutionally-managed assets in the world is associated with high net-worth individuals and families, generally grouped under the heading of 'private banking'. Total funds under management have been variously estimated at up to $25 trillion[25] – significantly exceeding the size of the global pension asset pool – although the confidentiality aspect of private banking makes such estimates little more than educated guesses. Figure 8.11 provides a rough estimate of the location (source) of private wealth. Of this total, perhaps $6 trillion is held offshore by private clients seeking to diversify asset exposures, avoid political and/or economic risk in their home countries, avoid or evade domestic taxation, or obtain protection from financial disclosure under foreign sovereign jurisdiction – including concealment of gains from criminal activities. Europe and Latin America appear to be overrepresented in offshore private client assets as against their respective shares of global private wealth, while North America appears to be underrepresented. Figure 8.12 provides estimates for the destination of offshore private wealth, indicating the disproportionate role of Switzerland and (to a lesser extent) Luxembourg and the UK (including the Isle of Man and the Channel Islands, which are 'semi-detached' for tax purposes).

Fig 8.11 Global private client assets by source region

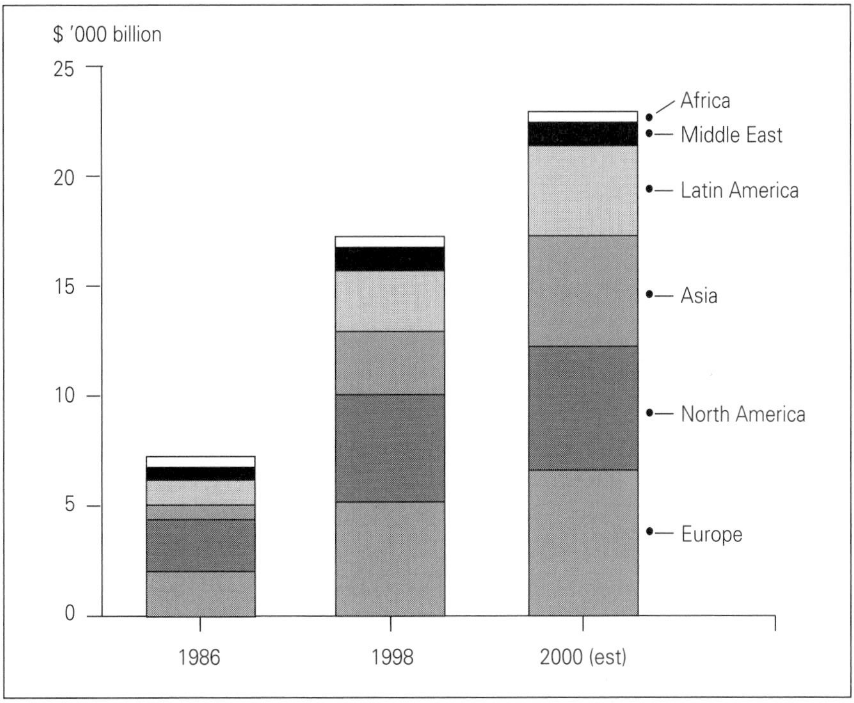

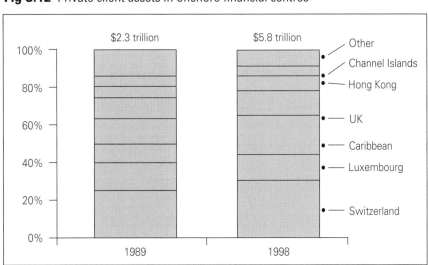

Source: Merrill Lynch, World Wealth Report (New York: Merrill Lynch, April 1999)

Fig 8.12 Private client assets in offshore financial centres

Source: Merrill Lynch, World Wealth Report (New York: Merrill Lynch, April 1999)

Private-client asset allocation objectives

Private clients' asset management objectives are an amalgam of preferences across a number of variables among which liquidity, yield, security, tax-efficiency, confidentiality, and service level are paramount. Each plays a distinctive role.

- *Yield.* The traditional European private banking client was concerned with wealth preservation in the face of antagonistic government policies and fickle asset markets. Clients demanded the utmost in discretion from their private bankers, with whom they maintained lifelong relationships initiated by personal recommendations. Such high net-worth clients have to some degree given way to more active and sophisticated customers. Aware of opportunity costs and often exposed to high marginal tax rates, they consider net after-tax yield to be far more relevant than the security and focus on capital preservation traditionally sought by high net-worth clients. They may prefer gains to accrue in the form of capital appreciation rather than interest or dividend income, and tend to have a much more active response to changes in total rate of return.

- *Security.* The environment faced by high net-worth investors is arguably more stable today than it has been in the past. The probability of revolution, war and expropriation has declined over the years in Europe, North America, the Far East and Latin America. Nevertheless, a large segment of the private banking market remains highly security-conscious. Such clients are generally prepared to trade off yield for stability, safety and capital preservation.

- *Tax efficiency.* Like everyone else, high net-worth clients are highly sensitive to taxation, perhaps more so as cash-strapped politicians target 'the rich' in a constant search for fiscal revenues. International financial markets have traditionally provided plenty of tax-avoidance and tax-evasion opportunities, ranging from offshore tax havens to private banking services able to sidestep even sophisticated efforts to claim the state's share.

- *Confidentiality.* Secrecy is a major factor in private banking – secrecy required for personal reasons, for business reasons, for tax reasons and for legal or political reasons. Confidentiality, in this sense, is a 'product' that is bought and sold as part of the private asset management business through secrecy and statutes on the part of countries and high levels of discretion on the part of financial institutions. The value of this 'product' depends on the probability and consequences of disclosure, and is 'priced' in the form of lower portfolio returns, higher fees, sub-optimum asset allocation, or reduced liquidity as compared with portfolios not driven by confidentiality motives.[26]

● *Service level.* While some of the tales of personal services provided for private banking clients are undoubtedly apocryphal, the 'fringe benefits' offered to high net-worth clients may well influence the choice of and loyalty to a particular financial institution. Such benefits may save time, reduce anxiety, increase efficiency, or make the wealth management process more convenient. Personal service is a way for asset managers to show their full commitment to clients accustomed to high levels of personal service in their daily lives.

The essence of private banking is to identify accurately each client's unique objectives, and to have the flexibility and expertise to satisfy these as fully as possible in a highly competitive marketplace. On the assumption that the vast majority of funds managed by private banking vendors have not been accumulated illegally, the demand for financial secrecy in Europe relates mainly to matters of taxation, and the transfer of funds across borders – something that has long been a concern of virtually all Europeans with assets to preserve. The euro had eliminated the latter motive among participating countries. Tax issues will take longer to address, and will always be a major driver of the international private banking industry, but within the euro-zone they will have to be tackled. As suggested earlier, traditional tax havens will sooner or later be eliminated under fiscal pressure from partner countries, and EU states will eventually harmonize rules regarding personal taxation and disclosure of tax information. The ability to conceal private wealth from tax collectors will diminish within the EU, and with it the 'value' of secrecy as one of the services offered by asset managers. Only Switzerland will remain as a European haven for tax evaders (as distinct from those committing fax fraud as defined under Swiss law).[27]

Competition among private banking firms in Europe is likely to intensify. They will offer increasingly sophisticated products, perhaps at lower cost than private banks have traditionally charged in the past. Some will be offering innovative mutual funds or shares in limited partnerships or other specialized investments. Certainly there will be a profusion of both services and those offering them. And the field of competitive struggle will be in marketing just as much as it is in product development and investment performance. Such competition is bound to lower fees and commissions for private client asset management in Europe, and the strength of European banks' control over their high net-worth clients will be tested.

Restructuring of the asset management industry in Europe

We have noted that various kinds of financial firms have emerged to perform asset-management functions – commercial banks, savings banks, postal savings institutions, savings co-operatives, credit unions, securities firms (full-service firms and various kinds of specialists), insurance companies, finance companies, finance subsidiaries of industrial groups, mutual fund companies, financial advisers and various others. Members of each strategic group compete with each other, as well as with members of other strategic groups. There are two questions. First, what determines competitive advantage to the end investor in operating distribution gateways? Second, what determines competitive advantage in the asset management process itself?

One supposition is that distribution of asset management services is both scope-driven and technology-driven. That is, it can be distributed jointly with other types of financial services, and thereby benefit from cost economies of scope as well as demand economies of scope (cross-selling). This would tend to give retail-oriented financial services firms like commercial and universal banks, life insurance companies and savings institutions a competitive advantage in distribution. At the same time, firms that are more specialized may establish cost-effective distribution of asset management services using proprietary remote-marketing techniques like mail, telephone selling or the Internet, or by 'renting' distribution through the established infrastructures of other financial intermediaries like banks, insurance companies or mutual fund 'supermarkets'. They may also gain access to clients through fund management consultants and financial advisers.

Asset management itself depends heavily on portfolio management skills, as well as economies of scale, and capital investment and technology involved in back-office functions, some of which can be outsourced. Since fiduciary activities must be kept separate from other financial services operations that involve potential conflicts of interest, either through organizational separation or Chinese walls, there are constraints on what can be gained in the way of economies of scope.

Inter-sectoral competition, alongside already vigorous intra-sectoral competition, is what will make asset management one of the most competitive areas of finance, even in the presence of rapid growth in the size of the market for asset management services. Certainly the dynamics of competition for the growing pools of defined benefit and defined contribution pension assets in various parts of the world, and its cross-linkage to the mutual fund business, has led to various strategic initiatives among fund managers. These include mergers, acquisitions and strategic alliances among fund managers themselves, as well as between fund managers, commercial and universal banks, securities broker-dealers, and insurance companies.

This is reflected in Fig. 8.13, which presents the volume and number of mergers and acquisitions involving asset managers, both in total and in open-end mutual funds only, covering the period from 1985 to 1999. About 70 per cent of the total M&A value involved European targets, and British asset managers represented the largest single target group. The predominant buyers were continental European institutions, mainly banks and insurance companies. These data suggest that M&A market action and strategic repositioning substantially reflect the economic driving forces behind the asset management industry's restructuring. Much of that action, both with respect to pension funds and mutual funds, is in western Europe. Market valuations of asset management companies have been quite high in comparison with other types of firms in the financial services industry, reflecting the high quality of earnings.

Fig 8.13 Merger and acquisitions activity in asset management industry 1985–99

Total	Total asset managers	Open-end mutual fund managers
Global target	56,740 (1,489)	14,045 (355)
European target	29,773 (664)	5,134 (175)
US target	15,315 (488)	5,118 (105)
Other target	11,652 (337)	3,793 (75)

Total asset managers	Total	European acquirer	US acquirer
US target	15,315 (488)	3,527 (29)	11,169 (436)
UK target	19,245 (322)	17,840 (275)	346 (21)
Cont. Eur. target	10,528 (342)	9,744 (307)	9 (10)

Open-end Mutual fund managers	Total	European acquirer	US acquirer
US target	5,118 (105)	1,849 (6)	3,227 (96)
UK target	1,386 (33)	1,215 (26)	70 (4)
Cont. Eur. target	3,748 (142)	3,578 (124)	9 (2)

Value of deals in US$m. Number of deals in brackets
Data: Thomson Financial Securities Data Company; author calculations

Besides gaining access to distribution and fund management expertise, the underlying economics of the M&A deal-flow in asset management presumably have to do with the realization of economies of scale and economies of scope, making possible both cost reductions and cross-selling of multiple types of funds, banking and/or insurance services, investment advice, and high-quality research, in a one-stop shopping interface for investors – despite a good deal of evidence that investors are quite happy to shop on their own with low-cost fund managers. Evidence of either economies of scale or economies of scope in this sector is lacking, although the plausibility of scale economies exceeds that for scope economies. In any event, there has been little evidence so far that M&A activity in this sector has led to lower fees and charges to retail investors.[28]

Finally, Fig. 8.14 provides some indication of the relative size of the world's top asset managers in 1999. Overall, countries with traditional reliance on funded pension schemes and mutual funds marketed to retail investors – the US, Japan and the UK – were home to 72 of the top 100 asset managers and 76 per cent of the assets under management.[29] Continental European countries captured only a fourth of the top spots and 22 per cent of the assets, although this is likely to change as PAYG pension programmes increasingly give way to dedicated asset pools, and as financial market integration stimulates a competitive battle among different types of financial institutions for asset management services. Within Europe, 31 per cent of assets are managed in the UK, 20.3 per cent in Switzerland, 16.5 per cent in Germany, 15.6 per cent in France, and 8.4 per cent in the Netherlands, with the balance in Liechtenstein, Denmark, Spain, Belgium, Sweden and Italy.[30]

Institutional asset pools and capital market development

The impact of the euro on European financial markets in the context of the growing role of performance-driven asset managers is likely to run the gamut from the composition of financial assets and the scope available for portfolio diversification, to competition among financial centres and corporate governance.

Composition of financial assets

The role of a burgeoning European asset management industry in promoting disintermediation in an increasingly unified financial market is unlikely to differ much in character from what has occurred in the US, except that its pacing may be quite different under distinctly European tax, institutional and regulatory conditions.

Fig 8.14 Global league table of leading asset managers (assets under management exceeding $100 billion)

Rank as at 1 January 1999	Firm	Country	AUM ($bn)
1	Kampo	Japan	1,685
2	UBS AG[1]	Switzerland	1,167
3	Fidelity Investments	US	773
4	Deutsche Bank Group[2]	Germany	698
5	Groupe AXA[3]	France	672
6	Barclays Global Investors	UK	616
7	Merrill Lynch	US	501
8	State Street Global Advisors	US	493
9	Capital Group Companies	US	424
10	Zurich Group[4]	Switzerland	407
11	Mellon Financial Services	US	401
12	Nippon Life	Japan	383
13	Allianz	Germany	363
14	Equitable Cos.	US	359
15	Morgan Stanley Dean Witter	US	346
16	Citigroup	US	327
17	J.P. Morgan	US	316
18	Putnam Investments	US	294
19	Zenkyoren	Japan	279
20	Vanguard Group	US	276
21	Dai-Ichi Mutual Life	Japan	267
22	TIAA-CREF	US	244
23	Pimco Advisors	US	244
24	Prudential Insurance Co.	US	242
25	Bank of America Corp.	US	234
26	Crédit Suisse Group	Switzerland	231
27	Northern Trust Company	US	226
28	Mitsui Trust and Banking	Japan	225
29	Franklin Group of Funds	US	220
30	Sumitomo Mutual Life	Japan	220
31	Fortis Group	Belgium	219
32	Amvescap	US	217
33	National Westminster Bank[5]	UK	212
34	Wellington Mgmt Co.	US	211
35	Generali Group[6]	Italy	198
36	Schroder Investment Man.	UK	197
37	American Express	US	196
38	Chase Manhattan Corp.	US	190
39	United Asset Mgmt Corp.	US	188
40	BNP Gestions[7]	France	184
41	Goldman Sachs Asset Mgmt	US	181
42	Commercial Union	UK	175
43	Société Générale	France	175
44	First Union Corp.	US	169
45	ING Groep	Netherlands	169
46	Group Caisse des Dépôts	France	168
47	MassMutual	US	157

Fig 8.14 *cont.*

Rank as at 1 January 1999	Firm	Country	AUM ($bn)
48	Aegon NV	Netherlands	156
49	Metropolitan Life	US	154
50	Dresdner Bank Group	Germany	152
51	Lloyds TSB[8]	UK	151
52	Indocar (Crédit Agricole)	France	151
53	Meiji Mutual Life	Japan	150
54	T. Rowe Price Assoc.	US	148
55	Mitsubishi Trust & Bank	Japan	145
56	Hypo Vereinsbank	Germany	140
57	Prudential Corp.[9]	UK	141
58	Sumitomo Trust & Bank	Japan	137
59	Nvest Cos.	US	135
60	BlackRock	US	132
61	Münchner Rückversich	Germany	130
62	Asahi Mutual Life	Japan	129
63	Commerzbank Group	Germany	124
64	BancOne Inv. Advisors	US	122
65	Standard Life	UK	122
66	Daiwa Trust & Banking	Japan	115
67	Yasuda Mutual Life	Japan	114
68	Desjardin-Laurentian	Canada	114
69	Toyo Trust & Banking	Japan	111
70	Janus Capital Corp.	US	108
71	Fleming Investment Mgmt	UK	108
72	Federated Investors	US	107
73	Grupo Intesa	Italy	107
74	John Hancock	US	105
75	Deka Bank	Germany	105
76	Sun Life of Canada	US	105
77	Daiwa Group	Japan	103
78	Sun Life of Canada	Canada	102

[1] Includes Global Asset Management.
[2] Including Bankers Trust Co.
[3] Includes Guardian Royal Exchange.
[4] Including Scudder Kemper Investments.
[5] Includes Legal & General and Gartmore.
[6] Includes Achener & Münchner.
[7] Includes Paribas.
[8] Includes Scottish Widows.
[9] Includes Mutual & General.

Sources: Euromoney, *August 1999 (non-US asset managers) based on InterSec Research Corp. Data.*
Institutional Investor, *July 1999 (US asset managers)*

Europe, with roughly twice the proportion of financial assets on the books of banks and other financial intermediaries than the US, will go through much the same process of financial disintermediation that characterized the US in the seventies and eighties. A recent study suggests that a gradual shift from banking to securities transactions is likely to be accelerated by the euro because the factors that underlie this development – by reducing transactions and information costs (both heavily driven by technology) and making available new products to end-investors – cannot be fully exploited in a fragmented foreign exchange environment, i.e. one characterized by widespread currency-matching rules affecting issuers and investors. This includes a range of financial instruments broadly available in the US that have been unable to reach the critical mass needed for trading efficiency and liquidity in Europe. 'If EMU has the side effect of bringing those assets to the market, then the playing field will tilt a little. If technology shifts the management expenses goal posts as well, then we may be in a new ball game.'[31]

The rise to prominence of institutional asset managers in Europe will also do a great deal to enhance financial market liquidity. Mutual funds – whether part of defined contribution pension schemes or mass-marketed as savings vehicles to the general public – and other types of money managers are so-called 'noise traders' who must buy and sell assets whenever there are net fund purchases or redemptions, in addition to discretionary trades to adjust portfolios. They therefore tend to make a disproportionate contribution to capital market liquidity – mutual funds alone account for the largest share of US equity turnover.

Overall, it is likely that the euro will have a strong growth impact on the asset management industry. Asset managers will be less affected than banks in terms of the cost implications of the euro and will benefit disproportionately from the increased depth and breadth of the European capital market that a single currency implies. At the same time, they will be favoured by the fiscal implications of Maastricht-type criteria, which will place greater pressure on governments to accelerate the transition from PAYG pension schemes to various types of defined contribution programmes.[32]

Portfolio diversification and globalization

Professional fund managers attempt to optimize asset allocation in line with modern investment concepts by taking advantage of the potential for domestic and international portfolio diversification inherent across the range of financial instruments being offered, as well as by using the most efficient (friction-free) available securities markets and infrastructure services. Both dimensions are likely to be affected by European financial integration and a single currency. Under the euro, professional asset managers seeking sources of diversification across less than perfectly correlated exchange rates and interest rates will thus have to look outside the region, while external investors will lose any comparable diversification gains that may have existed within the region. The euro-zone becomes a single market-risk and sovereign-risk 'bucket' from the perspective of portfolio diversification.

There are also likely to be increased correlations across equity markets covered by the euro, representing a continuation of the gradual increases in inter-market correlations that have already been observed.[33] This will force portfolio managers to focus relatively more heavily on diversification strategies involving non-European markets. Despite problems in the nineties, the attraction of emerging market equities may increase due to potentially lower correlations between emerging market stock returns and the major market indices.

In terms of asset classes, we have already noted that the euro will create a new, generic type of fixed-income security that will be very similar to municipal bonds in the US. Since national central banks and the possibility of debt monetization at the national level will disappear in EMU countries, borrowing requirements of national governments will involve rated debt instruments denominated in euros that will be available to institutional investors, with spreads differing among issuing governments based on the market's perceptions of the degree of risk involved. Since currency risk will be eliminated within the EMU region, the focus will be entirely on market risk and credit risk, and such 'euro-munis' will represent a major asset class in institutional fund pools for both EU portfolios, and non-EU portfolios such as those managed in the US and Japan.

Asset managers, shareholder value and corporate governance

Assuming that the rapid advance in prominence of institutional asset managers follows the lines suggested here, the capital markets will increasingly be the major source of external financing for European corporations in the future – as against the traditional, heavy continental European reliance (compared with US and British companies) on bank finance for debt, and bank and corporate long-term shareholdings for equity. Fiduciary asset pools managed against performance benchmarks by mutual funds and pension funds will create increasingly fluid sources of capital for industry, and a fundamental shift in the accountability of management and monitoring of corporate performance in Europe.[34]

In such a system, industrial restructuring will increasingly be triggered by the emergence of a control premium between the existing share price of a corporation and the value that an unaffiliated acquirer (whether an industrial company or an active financial investor) perceives could be unlocked by changes in management strategies or policies. Based on such a perception of corporate underperformance, an investor may purchase a significant block of shares and signal his unhappiness with the company's performance, or perhaps initiate a full takeover bid for the target firm. Institutional asset managers can assume a critical role in such a scenario. They may agree that a control premium does indeed exist and begin purchasing shares themselves, thereby placing still greater pressure on management of the target company.[35]

Even in the absence of a potential acquirer making a company a target, major institutional asset managers who, because of their size or portfolio constraints, find it difficult or impossible to dispose of their ownership interest in a company they feel is performing poorly, can request a meeting with management about the company's strategy, financial performance and realization of shareholder value, and perhaps raise their concerns at annual general meetings. Concerns about unwanted takeover efforts, and institutional investor dissatisfaction, may prompt management to either undertake self-restructuring, seek an acceptable merger partner (a white knight), pay out special dividends or initiate share repurchases, or find other ways to enhance shareholder value and efficiency in the use of capital to preclude the emergence of a control premium and hostile action.

Such a transition – from the traditional continental European corporate governance process with two-tier boards and large, friendly ownership stakes (*noyeux durs*) insulating management from the pressure of external shareholders seeking improved total returns, to a more 'contestable' model along Anglo-American lines – is an important possible consequence of the growing role of professionally managed institutional asset pools. The potential benefits of such developments involve reduced cost of capital through higher share prices, improved access to global financial markets, and a greater capacity for restructuring the European economy in response to changes in technology, market competition and other fundamentals.

Investor-driven, market-based systems such as this will require much higher levels of transparency in corporate accounting and disclosure than has been the norm in most of Europe, together with greater reliance on public information provided by management and systemic surveillance by research analysts working aggressively on behalf of investors. It implies arm's length financing on commercially viable terms by banks and financial markets, with financial institutions active in giving strategic and financial advice and sometimes taking transitional, non-permanent equity positions in (and occasionally control of) corporations in the process of restructuring.

Future directions

There are at least six principal conclusions that can be drawn from the discussion presented in this chapter.

First, the asset management industry in Europe is likely to grow substantially in the years ahead. Institutionalization and professional management of discretionary household assets through mutual funds has begun to take hold in many of the continental European countries that have traditionally been dominated by bank assets. At the same time, demographic and structural pressures in European national pension systems will require strong growth in dedicated financial asset pools as pay-as-you-go systems become increasingly unsupportable fiscally, and alternative means of addressing the problem show themselves to be politically difficult or impossible to implement. There are, however, substantial differences of view as to the timing of these developments within national environments, since pension reform is politically difficult to carry out and the political willingness to do so is difficult to predict. In both mutual funds and pension funds, and their links through participant-influenced defined contribution pension schemes, the centre of global growth is likely to be in Europe.

Proliferation of asset management products, which is already exceedingly high in the US and the UK, will no doubt be equally impressive in the remainder of the EU as financial markets become more fully integrated under the euro. There will be a great deal of jockeying for position and higher levels of concentration, especially in the pension fund sector, that will begin to permeate the mutual fund business through defined contribution plans – given the importance of economies of scale and the role of pension fund consultants. However, as in the US, the role of fund supermarkets, low-cost distribution via the Internet, as well as the very large contingent of universal banks, insurance companies and non-European fund management companies, is likely to prevent market structure from becoming monopolistic to any significant degree.

Fund performance will become a commodity, with few differences among the major players and the majority of actively managed funds underperforming the indices. This implies a competitive playing field that, as in the US, will be heavily conditioned by branding, advertising and distribution channels, which in turn are likely to move gradually away from the traditional dominance of banks in some of the EU markets. All of this implies that asset management fees – historically quite high, particularly in continental Europe – will come under pressure as competition heats up, to the benefit of the individual investors and participants in funded pension plans.

Second, despite the prospects for rapid growth, the structure of the asset management industry is likely to reflect a high degree of contestability. In addition to normal commercial rivalry among established players in the European national markets for asset management services, these same markets are being aggressively targeted by foreign suppliers from other EU countries as well as from outside the EU, notably Switzerland and the US. Moreover asset management (including private banking) is being marked for expansion by virtually every strategic group in the financial services sector – commercial and universal banks, private banks, securities firms, insurance companies, mutual fund companies, financial conglomerates, and financial advisers of various types.

Normally, the addition of new vendors in a given market would be expected to reduce market concentration, increase the degree of competition, and lead to an erosion of margins and trigger a more rapid pace of financial innovation. If the new vendors are from the same basic strategic groups as existing players, the expected outcome would be along conventional lines of intensified intra-industry competition. But if, as in this case, expansion-minded players come from very different strategic groups, the outcome may involve a substantially greater increase in the degree of competition. This is because of potential diversification benefits, possibilities for cross-subsidization and staying-power, and incremental horizontal or vertical integration gains that the player from a 'foreign' strategic group may be able to find. And natural barriers to entry in the asset management industry – which include the need for capital investment in infrastructure (especially in distribution and back-office functions), human resources (especially in portfolio management), technology, and the realization of economies of scale and scope – are not excessively difficult for newcomers to surmount. So the degree of internal, external and inter-sectoral competition in this industry is likely to promote market efficiency for the benefit of the end-users in managing discretionary household assets, pension funds, the wealth of high net-worth individuals, and other types of asset pools in Europe.

Third, the rapid evolution of the European institutional asset management industry will have a major impact on financial markets. The needs of performance-oriented institutional investors will accelerate the triage among competing debt and equity markets in favour of those that can best meet their evolving requirements for liquidity, execution efficiency, transparency, and efficient regulation. In turn, this will influence where firms and public entities choose to issue and trade securities in their search for cost-effective financing and execution. At the same time, the growing presence of institutional investors in European capital markets will greatly increase the degree of liquidity due to their active trading patterns, and create a ready market for new classes of public-sector securities that will emerge under EMU. And it will intensify competitive pressure and enhance opportunities for the sales and trading activities of banks and securities firms, and for the role of product development and research in providing useful investment ideas.

Fourth, cross-border asset allocation will grow disproportionately as a product of institutional investors' search for efficient portfolios through international diversification, although such gains will disappear among those financial markets covered by EMU and will be replaced by sectoral and asset-class diversification. With the euro-zone essentially one 'bucket' with respect to currencies and interest rates, international diversification options will shift to other asset groups, including emerging market debt and equities. Arguably, much of this has already occurred as intra-euro-zone rates converged in anticipation of the euro.

Fifth, the development of a deeper and broader pan-European capital market, spurred by the development of the institutional asset management industry, will fundamentally alter the European market for corporate control into a much more fluid one focused on financial performance and shareholder value. This in turn has the potential of triggering widespread and long overdue European economic restructuring, and creating a much trimmer, more competitive global economic force willing and able to disengage from uncompetitive sectors through the denial of capital, either venture capital or other forms of start-up financing. Such a transformation will hardly be painless, and will depend critically on political will and public support for a more market-driven growth process.

Finally, developments in institutional asset management will pose strategic challenges for the management of universal banks and other traditional European financial institutions in extracting maximum competitive advantage from this high-growth sector – in structuring and motivating their organizations, and in managing the conflicts of interest and professional conduct problems that can arise in asset management and that can easily cause major problems for the value of an institution's competitive franchise. The fact that institutional asset management requires a global perspective, both on the buy side and on the sell side, reinforces the need to achieve a corres-pondingly global market positioning for many financial institutions, although technology and the changing economics of distribution virtually assures the survival of a healthy cohort of asset management boutiques and specialists.

NOTES

[1] This compares with roughly $42 trillion in global bank assets and $55 trillion in global stock and bond market capitalization.

[2] Only a part of US mutual fund growth is attributable to new net investments in this sector of the financial system, of course, with the balance of the growth in assets under management attributable to reinvested earnings and capital gains. So the relative importance of equity funds and the performance of national stock markets is directly linked to observed differences in mutual fund growth patterns among countries and regions.

[3] According to the OECD, personal financial assets in Europe have grown at an average rate of about 11 per cent in the decade up to 1996, compared to about 8 per cent in the US and Japan, with a disproportionately high growth rate of more than 18 per cent in the case of Italy during this period.

[4] Investment Company Institute, *Mutual Fund Fact Book*, Washington, Investment Company Institute, 1998.

[5] For example, German mutual fund distribution is dominated by the major banks, with DWS (Deutsche Bank) controlling a 24 per cent market share, DIT (Dresdner Bank) 14.1 per cent, and ADIG (Commerzbank and the merged Bayerische Hypo and Bayerische Vereinsbank) 21.1 per cent. However, foreign players such as Fidelity of the US and Bank Julius Baer of Switzerland appear to be making significant inroads even as local competitors strive to improve investment performance, increase the range of products available, and enhance their non-European (particularly US) funds marketed to German investors.

[6] One factor that may promote continued fragmentation of the mutual fund industry is that size itself can lead to significant performance problems.

[7] Siwolop, Sana (1997) 'Regulating financial advisers: are the states up to it?', *The New York Times,* 29 June.

[8] For a discussion, *see* Story, Jonathan and Walter, Ingo (1997) *Politics of European Financial Integration*, Manchester: Manchester University Press, and Cambridge: MIT Press.

[9] Levich, Richard and Walter, Ingo (1990) 'Tax-driven regulatory drag and competition among European financial centers', in Siebert, Horst (ed.) *Reforming Capital Income Taxation*, Tübingen: J.C.B. Mohr / Paul Siebeck.

[10] The Economic and Social Council expressed concern that capital be invested in tax free bonds, J.O. No. C. 221/29. The European Parliament also regretted that the EU had not been able to reach an agreement on an EC system of taxation on interest, J.O. No. C. 68/145. 19 March 1990. *See also Les Echos*, 19 June 1990.

[11] There are a number of dissenting opinions with regard to this high-growth scenario, however, some of which suggests that the growth in pension assets may actually decline from the rates achieved in the nineties. These forecasts are based on the presumption that Germany's system of defined benefit plans with limited dedicated external asset pools is basically sound (and carries a high weight in the European total), and that enabling legislation to change PAYG systems like France and Italy will be politically difficult and slow to develop. Davis International Banking Consultants, *Trends in European Asset Management*, New York: Smith Barney, 1996.

[12] For a more detailed discussion, *see* Turner, John and Watanabe, Noriyasu (1995) *Private Pension Policies in Industrialized Countries*, Kalamazoo: W.E. Upjohn Institute for Employment Research.

[13] *Data:* InterSec Research Corporation and Goldman Sachs & Co.

[14] For a discussion, *see* Story, Jonathan and Walter, Ingo (1997) *The Politics of European*

Financial Integration: the battle of the systems, Manchester: Manchester University Press, and Cambridge: MIT Press.

[15] Assets in these funds are expected to grow at a rate of 16 per cent per year outside the US, compared to a US growth rate of 14 per cent, with the fastest growth (24 per cent annually) expected in Latin America and European pension pools growing at a rate of 14 per cent. Overall, global pension pools are likely to grow from $8.5 trillion in 1997 to perhaps $13.5 trillion in 2002. *Data:* InterSec Research Corporation, 1997.

[16] In the US, for example, the PAYG attributes of social security and projections on the evolution of the social security trust fund have been highlighted by a number of commissions to study the problem, and the conclusions have invariably pointed to some combination of increased retirement eligibility, increased social security taxes, increased taxation of social security benefits, and means-testing of benefits so that those who have saved more for retirement on their own would receive smaller benefits or be taxed at higher rates on the benefits they receive. For a survey, *see* Cadette, Walter M. (1997) 'Social security: financing the baby-boom's retirement', The Jerome Levy Economics Institute, Working Paper no. 192, April. *See also* 1994–6 Advisory Council on Social Security, *Report of the 1994–96 Advisory Council on Social Security: Findings and Recommendations* (Washington, DC: US Government Printing Office, 1997).

[17] First Consulting, *European Pensions*, London: AMP Asset Management, 1997.

[18] *Data:* FEFSI, Luxembourg.

[19] Martinson, Jane (1997) 'Management revolution', *Financial Times*, 21 November.

[20] Schott Stevens, Paul (1997) 'Selected issues in international taxation of retirement savings', *Investment Company Institute Perspective*, August.

[21] Reid, Brian and Crumrine, Jean (1996) *Retirement Plan Holdings of Mutual Funds*, Washington, DC: Investment Company Institute, 1997.

[22] *Sources:* J.P. Morgan. US Department of Labour, *Pensions and Investments*, EBRI.

[23] *Source: Pensions and Investments*.

[24] *Data:* Intersec, 1998.

[25] Gemini Consulting, 1997 estimate.

[26] *See* Walter, Ingo (1990) *The Secret Money Market*, New York: HarperCollins.

[27] As long as a decade ago, Dr Marcus Lusser, then President of the Swiss National Bank, conceded the diminishing value of banking secrecy. In his opinion, the strengthening of the EU was bound to weaken Switzerland as a centre for the management of private wealth. He advised bankers in Switzerland to concentrate on the institutional investment management sector. ('Good-bye to complacency', *Financial Times*, 19 December 1988). In conversation, Swiss private bankers appear to agree that upwards of two-thirds of assets of OECD-based private clients under management could disappear if Swiss banks reported assets and income to home-country tax authorities.

[28] Gasparino, Charles (1997) 'Do mutual fund mergers hurt small investors?', *Wall Street Journal*, 8 July.

[29] 'Watson Wyatt World-500', *Pension Age*, September 1996.

[30] *Institutional Investor*.

[31] Bishop, Graham (1997) *Post Emu: bank credit versus capital markets*, London: Salomon Brothers Inc.

[32] For a discussion of the overall capital market effects of EMU, *see* J.P. Morgan (1997) *EMU: impacts on financial markets*, New York: J.P. Morgan.

[33] *See*, for example, Longin, François and Solnik, Bruno (1995) 'Is the correlation of international equity returns constant?' *Journal of International Money and Finance*, vol. 14, no. 1. Portfolio diversification gains tend to be greater across global equity markets than across global

bond markets, where they derive solely from less than perfectly correlated interest rate and exchange rate movements. Moreover, unlike the global bond markets, stocks tend to be more highly differentiated and subject to local trading conditions, although listings on foreign stock exchanges through depository receipts have made some foreign equities considerably more accessible to foreign investors.

[34] For a full discussion, see Sametz, Arnold (1998) *The Power and Influence of Pension and Mutual Funds*, Amsterdam: Kluwer.

[35] For a comparison between traditional market-based and institution-based approaches to corporate control, *see* Story, Jonathan and Walter, Ingo (1997) *The Politics of European Financial Integration*, Manchester: Manchester University Press, and Cambridge: MIT Press.

PART III

Looking ahead

CHAPTER 9

The lie of the land: future competitive parameters

The euro-zone has evolved surprisingly quickly into one of the most attractive and hotly contested financial markets in the world – one that should ultimately function to the great benefit of market users of all types. These comprise issuers such as corporations, governments, institutions and households which regularly tap the financial markets and for which the lower costs of financing associated with a unified financial market will contribute materially to improved performance and, ultimately, economic welfare. There are the savers, too, who stand to benefit from improved returns and better portfolio allocation as markets become more competitive and efficient. Financial intermediaries, both wholesale and retail – banks, asset managers, securities firms, and various types of information-related and transaction-related utilities – provide the various links between these two sets of end-users.

That there are major gains to be had is beyond doubt. So is the mutuality of these gains. Unless everyone stands to benefit, new financial markets or products rarely last long. The key question centres around the allocation of these benefits. The more competitive the euro-zone financial markets turn out to be, the more these gains will ultimately go to the end-users and the thinner will be the pickings for the various financial intermediaries. Specifically from the wholesale banking perspective, will the industry ultimately turn out to be highly profitable for those firms that are active in the market, or will it become so highly competitive that most of the benefits will flow through to the end-users of the financial system – the clients? This is a key question confronting the shareholders of such firms now the time has come to think about the risks and opportunities created by the euro-zone.

There are three questions that need to be answered in any attempt to determine the durability of the opportunities offered to the wholesale banking industry:

● Will the single currency glue that binds the constituent countries together be strong enough to weather the inevitable storms and set the stage for the expected growth in financial transactions volume?

● What will be the competitive structure of the euro-zone financial market, and will it be possible for the industry to earn an attractive and sustainable return for its shareholders?

● What will be the distinguishing characteristics of the winners and losers among the wholesale banking firms that will contest this new market whose precise outlines are hard to discern?

Macro-economic policy and financial market dynamics

Macro-economic developments and policies represent key factors affecting the volume and structure of national and international financial market activity. They form the basis of financial market size and volatility character-istics, and therefore affect:

● investors' behaviour in their efforts to build efficient portfolios

● issuers' behaviour in the search for cost-effective financing

● trading volumes in underlying and derivative markets

● opportunities to supply value-added services for both corporate and investor clients.

Macro-economic policy convergence, in terms of its relationship to financial markets, is particularly important in the context of management of the euro against the dollar and the yen. Currency blocs, in turn, are effectively extended to countries that peg their own currencies to those of the bloc-linked currencies. While there is only limited evidence of the formation of three distinct currency blocs at present, the possibility of such an evolution clearly exists, which raises the question of the degree of convergence both between blocs and with respect to non-bloc countries. Europe's unified voice in future discussion of the global monetary order may, through its enhanced influence and its long-established advocacy of exchange-rate stability, have far-reaching consequences for how currencies are managed – and therefore for risks and opportunities facing investors, issuers and traders in world financial markets. What now seems unthinkable may well become entirely plausible – some of the most dynamic financial market segments may become obsolete, and financial strategies built on the volatility parameters of the past may turn out to be as outdated as the assumption of continued financial stability became some three decades ago under the Bretton Woods system.

Early developments

When the euro was launched on 4 January 1999, regulations on its intro-duction as legal tender came into force. In addition, key financial market elements came into operation:

● the real-time gross settlement (RTGS) of payments in euros under the Target system commenced (this clearance and settlement system for stocks, attempted by the LSE, ultimately failed)

● foreign exchange operations in euros began

● all euro-zone stock exchanges quoted prices and settled in euros

● all new public debt was denominated in euros, with old public debt trading in national currencies at the locked-in rates or redenominated in euros

● corporations were afforded the option of trading and invoicing in national currencies or euros, with retail transactions in either under a 'no compulsion, no prohibition' rule.

New currency was set for introduction in January 2002, to be followed within six months by withdrawal of national currencies from circulation. Everything in the early stages went remarkably smoothly, and fears of an adverse impact on financial markets proved unwarranted. So, in terms of its institutional development, by the beginning of 2000 the EU had come full circle to many of the basic principles enumerated in the so-called Werner Report almost 20 years earlier.[1] But the world had changed. The earlier emphasis on collective pan-European wage setting, incomes policies, indicative planning by the state and Keynesian economic fine-tuning using fiscal policy, had all been superceded by greater reliance on the free market, privatizations and fiscal austerity.

The European Central Bank

In the future, much depends on the functioning of the European Central Bank, which has an executive board and a 17-member governing council, comprising six board members (in charge of day-to-day operations) and the central bank governors from each of the 11 euro-zone countries. The principal function of the governing council is setting monetary policy, with one vote each. In addition, it is intended to assure close policy co-ordination between the ECB and non-member EU monetary authorities.[2] This has not been easy. Indeed, the matter of who was to head the ECB was the subject to bitter debate at a May 1998 meeting of euro-zone heads of state, the culmination of months of wrangling after France proposed Jean-Claude Trichet to replace the consensus candidate, Wim Duisenberg of the Netherlands, who had already been heading the European Monetary Institute. A last-minute face-saving compromise that committed Duisenberg to retire 'of his own free will' after four years of his eight-year term to be replaced by Trichet (serving a full term) launched the ECB on a sour note, particularly on the matter of its future political independence.

The situation the ECB found itself in during its first year of existence was not dissimilar to the awkward but workable US Federal Reserve system in which, ultimately, much of the monetary policy influence has over time gravitated to the chairman of the board of governors. Whether this parallel is eventually sustained remains to be seen. The Fed also has substantial regulatory influence which has grown over time in relation to that of state bank regulators, while in the euro-zone the regulatory function remains entirely with the national authorities.

In one of its first policy actions, the ECB in mid-1998 set minimum reserves for euro-zone credit institutions to be maintained with the central bank, an approach along the lines of that taken by the Bundesbank and the Federal Reserve. Criticism that reserve requirements are anachronistic in modern financial systems were ignored.

A uniform exchange rate and interest rate environment

Although exchange rate targeting appeared to be relegated to the background in ECB policy even as the euro dropped below parity with the dollar before its first year of life had ended, the euro-dollar exchange rate will inevitably remain a major focus of interest, in part because each currency represents a much wider 'zone' of currencies that are either pegged or managed with reference to it. The traditional G-7 in effect becomes the 'G-3' and it should be easier to co-ordinate policies across the three zones – even with a relatively high degree of central bank independence, and secondary importance attached to exchange rate matters in the conduct of monetary policies. Since both the US and the 11 countries of the euro-zone are large economies in which international trade plays a relatively small role, one possibility for policymakers was 'benign neglect' of the external value of the euro. Indeed, despite almost universal predictions of a rise in the euro following its launch, it lost some 17 per cent against the dollar in the first 12 months of trading due mainly to strong US and weak European economic fundamentals.

There was also much discussion about ECB monetary policy targeting – i.e. British-style calibration of interest rates based on forecasts of future inflation, versus German-style targeting of growth in euro monetary aggregates, with most observers predicting some sort of composite targeting leaning towards the monetary aggregates-based approach. In fact, a 'two pillar' strategy seems to have been adopted, the first being a reference value of 4.5 per cent annual growth in the money supply, and the second being a number of economic indicators (wages, prices, business confidence) that gives the ECB some wiggle-room – indeed, the first two ECB interest rate cuts in late 1998 and early 1999 had to do with the second rather than the first pillar. Still, the Maastricht Treaty mandates the ECB to preserve the internal value of the euro above all, and its independence from political pressures is intended to help achieve that.

The initial bias in the euro-zone was towards low interest rates, both to reflect low inflation rates and to combat a relatively weak real economy. Aside from producing initial weakness in the euro, this had the immediate effect of creating buoyant financial markets during the initial post-launch period – which in turn stimulated merger activity and capital-raising generally.

Critics have argued that, in addition to all the policy uncertainty, the operational characteristics of the ECB will make it one of the least transparent central banks in the world, and that this will help assure substantial volatility in the value of the euro. Moreover, monthly publication of minutes of the governing council was rejected as psychologically divisive and likely to encourage political interference from national governments, further reducing transparency (minutes of ECB meetings are embargoed for 30 years). In the early period, contradictory statements from ECB officials were especially unsettling for financial markets, compounded by the continued significant role of the national central banks – unlike the US Federal Reserve system, where power was centralized after major political battles in the fifties between the central bank, the Congress and the Administration. There is also the lack of history, and absence of a consistent pre-euro database as a statistical foundation for policymaking. As one observer noted: 'The euro-zone economy is still something of a mystery. All you can do is zap it with a particular voltage, like Frankenstein, then cross your fingers.'[3]

The international role of the euro

The euro should eventually create a significant competitor to the US in a number of dimensions, especially with the hoped-for structural economic reforms in Europe. The remark by one observer that 'the euro will be to the dollar what Airbus is to Boeing' may (unintentionally) be more appropriate than first seems the case, given some of the intractable management issues facing the two aircraft manufacturers and the two central banks.[4] Others argue that, even in the absence of any major economic upsets, it will take a long time for the euro to become a credible threat to the supremacy of the dollar in global economics and finance. One reason is that institutional rigidities in the euro-zone – continued inflexibility of labour markets, the strong role of the state, the strong culture of social support and entitlements, and resistance to change in corporate governance and to structural adjustment – will be broken down only gradually and will retard Europe's competitive transformation into a more powerful challenger in global markets; and ultimately, this will be reflected in the performance of the two currencies. Counter arguments focus on the so-called Trojan Horse aspects of a single currency, with structural change in all these dimensions already underway and likely to be recognized by many of the adversely affected interest groups only when it is too late.

The prospects are that the euro will – despite its rocky start – eventually come to rival the dollar as a vehicle currency in international trade with, for example, Norway invoicing oil exports in euros instead of dollars in view of its intensive trade with the euro-zone. In 1997, 48 per cent of international trade was invoiced in dollars as against 33 per cent in euro-zone currencies. Similarly, the euro is likely to become a significantly more important reserve currency than the constituent national currencies have been in the past. Of 1998 global central bank reserves, 60 per cent were held in dollars and 26 per cent in the various euro-zone currencies. In contrast, the proportions of the US and the euro-zone in global GDP were roughly equal in 1998. If transactions denomination and central bank reserve holdings start to reflect the relative importance of the two regions in global economic activity, such a shift could be significant for financial markets, although early returns suggest that any such development will take quite a while.

Seigniorage

Not least, the euro could eventually come to challenge the dollar in the seigniorage gains associated with banknotes in circulation – in effect, a banknote in circulation represents an interest-free loan from the public to the issuing central bank. The US had, on average, roughly $450 billion in banknotes in circulation in 1998, implying a seigniorage gain (assuming a 5 per cent interest rate) of some $23 billion to the US Treasury. A significant proportion of US banknotes are held by non-residents, and if the euro begins encroaching on the dollar, the US share of seigniorage gains will decline. This may be one reason why euro banknotes will include 500-euro denominations, while the largest US banknote is $100 – a limit established partly to increase the cost of money laundering and tax evasion.

Shock resistance

Stress on the euro will develop when and if euro-zone governments relax fiscal policies and begin running larger public sector deficits, financial sanctions incorporated in the Growth and Stability Pact notwithstanding. In that event, mounting national borrowing costs would increase political pressure on the ECB to ease monetary policy in order to facilitate national deficit finance. It seems likely that the institutional safeguards built into the ECB's operations would provide adequate armour plating to neutralize such pressure, as long as it remained moderate. Just such concerns were reflected in the market's reaction to Italy overstepping its Maastricht fiscal deficit target in June 1999.

The major stress test for the system will come in the case of severe 'asymmetric shocks' – i.e. when the economy of one of perhaps several EMU countries suffers serious recessions which cannot be fought by monetary policy (since there is no longer a national central bank) or exchange rate policy (since there is no longer a national currency) or fiscal policy (since deficit spending is subject to Maastricht-type budget constraints). In such a case the countries concerned will presumably argue for expansionary ECB monetary policy, a call which will be fiercely resisted by countries that are not in recession because of such a policy's inflationary impact and weakening effect on the euro. Again, the US case is instructive: asymmetric shocks are encountered regularly, yet the board of governors of the Federal Reserve targets on nationwide indicators. Regional stabilization in the US occurs through a combination of labour and capital flows from the affected regions, tax and expenditure reallocation within the relatively centralized federal fiscal system (reduced tax collections and higher budgetary outlays for unemployment and other support payments), and moderate fiscal policy changes at the state and local level. It is here that the differences between the euro-zone and the US become acute, with the former seeing much more limited labour mobility and fiscal centralization than the US where federal borrowing has dwarfed state and local borrowing ever since a wave of state debt defaults in the thirties.

Examples include the British, Irish, Spanish, Portuguese, Italian and Swedish cases of the early nineties, where the need to maintain a fixed peg against the DM by means of high interest rates and having to endure severe recessionary pressure was politically unacceptable. Without the exchange rate escape valve, in 1992 each of these countries might have entered a vicious circle of high interest rates, recession, excessive budgetary deficits correctable only through higher taxation or reduced spending, continued recessionary pressure, etc. – from which there is no escape without massive financial transfers from the EU itself or a currency depreciation sufficient to pull the affected country out of trouble. There are no provisions now for either of these policy options in euro-zone arrangements. Such stress, particularly early in the life of the euro, could lead either to a further weakening of it, imposition of exchange controls by the EU as a whole, revision of the Maastricht Treaty to allow the EU to assume the debt of member governments, or possibly the withdrawal of one or more of the affected nations.

One major flaw in the governance structure of the euro is that the political overlay for fiscal policy is very different to that for monetary policy, unlike the US and other countries where it is one and the same. In the euro-zone fiscal policy remains in the hands of the national political systems, unlike monetary policy which is in the hands of the collective management of the ECB. Despite the issuance of periodic reports and staging of press conferences, as well as regular testimony by the ECB chairman to the European Parliament, it has no direct political overlay – it seems remote from the body politic and is likely to remain that way. This fundamental gap in the politics of economic policy, some observers contend, is a sure-fire recipe for trouble.

These concerns notwithstanding, the betting remains that the euro is here to stay, and in usual European fashion the necessary policy convergence and political legitimacy will ultimately be achieved one step at a time, with a lot of noise and occasional backsliding on the way. Meanwhile the markets have been able to go to work, and even by the end of 1999 it was clear that they were doing just that with a vengeance.

Capital market dynamics and competitive structure

Besides the macro-economic policy determinants of the basic drivers of the euro-zone financial markets through exchange rates, interest rates and inflation rates, there is the micro-economic question of the kind of market structure wholesale banks will be facing in the years ahead.

The global financial market architecture

The overall market for financial instruments within which investment banking firms operate can perhaps be summarized by Fig. 9.1. At the core of the market are foreign exchange and money market instruments. There is virtually complete transparency, high liquidity and large numbers of buyers and sellers – probably as close to the economists' definition of 'perfect competition' as one can get in financial markets. Moving out from the centre of the diagram, the next most perfect market is that of domestic sovereign debt instruments in their national markets; they carry no credit risk (only market risk) and are usually broadly and continuously traded. Sovereign debt instruments purchased by foreign investors also, of course, carry foreign exchange risk and the (arguably minor) risk of repudiation of sovereign obligations. And if sovereign debt instruments (or bank loans) are denominated in foreign currencies, they carry country risk (the risk of inability or unwillingness to service foreign currency debt); this method ranges from AAA-rated debt that may be traded in broad and deep markets, to non-investment grade, highly speculative sovereign bonds.

Next come corporate bonds and municipal (muni) bonds (issues of states and municipalities), which range across the quality spectrum from AAA-rated issuers that trade in liquid markets fractionally above sovereigns, all the way to high-yield non-investment grade and unrated bonds. Also included here are repackaged bank loans and asset-backed securities that are sold to various types of institutional investors, as well as wholesale syndicated bank loans, which may involve a substantial amount of leverage on the part of the borrower. Finally there are stocks, which may or may not be properly covered by research analysts, with disclosure and reporting requirements imposed by the securities regulators and the accounting profession, and traded on more or less efficient organized exchanges or in over-the-counter markets. Each stock is different, with values dependent on both market and firm-specific developments. And between corporate bonds and equities lie hybrid financial

Fig 9.1 The global securities market structure

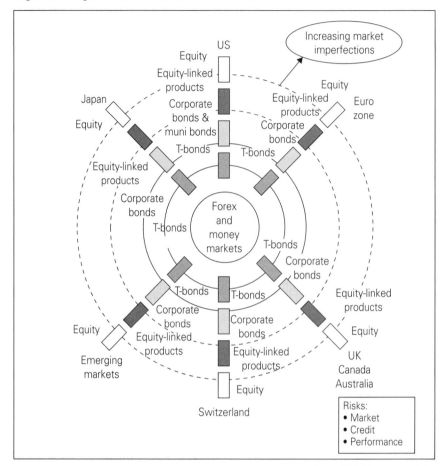

Source: Adapted from McKinsey & Co.

instruments such as convertible bonds and bonds with attached warrants to buy equities at a predetermined price at some time in the future, which in turn can be 'stripped' and sold in the market. Well out on the periphery of the diagram is venture capital and private equity, which tends to be highly speculative with little or no liquidity until an exit vehicle is found through sale to another company or an initial public offering.

As one moves from the centre of Fig. 9.1 to the periphery in any given financial market environment, information and transaction costs tend to rise, liquidity tends to fall, and risks (market risk, credit risk and/or performance risk) tend to rise. Along the way, there are a host of structured financial products and derivatives that blend various characteristics of the underlying securities in order to better fit into investors' portfolio requirements and/or issuer/borrower objectives. And finally, each geographic context is different in terms of size, liquidity, infrastructure, market participants and other characteristics. The substantial structural differences that have existed between the US and euro-zone debt and equity markets – and reasons why they may well converge in the future – have been outlined in previous chapters.

Financial intermediaries that tend to perform well for their shareholders seem to have strong comparative advantages in the *least* perfect corners of the global financial markets. They either specialize in those markets – often in the form of financial boutiques – or represent major firms that have strong businesses in those markets and are able to selectively leverage their operating platforms in the major wholesale markets to access them. They may also be able to cross-link on a selective basis both the major and peripheral markets opportunistically as interest rates, exchange rates, market conditions and borrower and investor preferences change – for example, financing the floating-rate debt needs of a US corporation by issuing fixed-rate Australian dollar bonds through currency and interest rate swaps. These cross-market links, creatively marrying users of finance to lenders and investors in ever-changing market conditions, is what separates the winners from the losers in this business – those firms which have created effective teamwork and information cross-flows in client coverage and transaction execution from those which have not.

The constant search for imperfections in global financial markets implies that global wholesale banks need to maintain highly cost-effective execution and trading platforms covering the markets at the centre of Fig. 9.1. They must be able to take sometimes massive securities positions off their clients' books on to their own, and then place them in the market quickly and profitably. Even in the absence of proprietary trading the importance of risk control, placing power, teamwork and operating efficiency is clear, as is the capital intensity of the business. None of the major firms in global wholesale finance can afford not to have such a platform, although none should expect to be able to extract very substantial risk-adjusted returns from it. Impressive profits are possible from time to time, but near-perfect markets make it unlikely that these are very durable.

It is from such a platform, however, that the firm can position itself to exploit the more imperfect markets towards the periphery of Fig. 9.1, as well as market anomalies that appear periodically, and to exploit market imperfections in the cross-links between them. Creation of the euro-zone is a major development in one of the spokes in that diagram. It is likely to grow disproportionately quick in terms of transaction volume and already did in its first year of life. It will provide new opportunities for arbitrages, both internally and between markets, and for firms that have operated successfully in the unified US market to introduce and adapt ideas that add value in the perception of clients. The point is that the euro-zone is an integral part of the global financial market, and a firm's competitive success in it is likely to reflect its competitive performance in the broader, global environment.

Competitive structure

A framework for considering the future competitive structure in the euro-zone wholesale banking sector can be discerned in Fig. 9.2. What in fact are the current standings of some of the principal wholesale banking businesses for which league table data are available? Figure 9.2 illustrates global client-based deal-flow concentration during 1999 achieved by the 25 leading global financial institutions most of which have a significant trading presence as well. Wholesale capital market origination is described in terms of four components:

- syndicated lending
- total underwriting of debt and equity issues
- global mergers and acquisitions advisory assignments
- management of medium-term note programmes.

The data reflect a 'full credit to book-running lead manager' basis. They do not purport to reflect profitability of the firms represented in the table, although a positive correlation seems to exist between high market share concentrations and profitability over the years.

For 1999 Goldman Sachs led the field with a market share of over 13 per cent. US firms comprised nine of the top ten in 1999, due partly to the large size of their home market (comprising perhaps half of global deal-flow) and their successful penetration of European markets. The sole European in the top ten Crédit Suisse First Boston (mainly US-based for investment banking purposes, although part of the Crédit Suisse group). Deutsche Bank and Warburg Dillon Read were just below the top ten in 1999. No Japanese firms were represented.

We would suggest that the euro-zone is unlikely to differ much from the global market structure depicted in Fig. 9.2 in the major lines of investment banking activity. This structure shows a highly uneven distribution of transaction volumes, with the top ten firms in 1999 handling almost 77 per cent of the combined global transaction volume and the top 25 firms responsible

Fig 9.2 Global wholesale banking rankings 1999
Full credit to book running manager only ($m)

Firm ranking 1999 (1998 in paren)	Syndicated bank loans	Securities U/W and private placements	M&A advisory	MTNs arranged	Total	Percentage of top 25
Goldman Sachs (1)	17,164	256,245	912,949	83,840	1,279,198	13.55
Merrill Lynch (2)	5,266	412,150	518,674	143,345	1,079,435	11.43
Morgan Stanley (3)		293,253	608,930	80,966	983,149	10.41
Citigroup*/SSSB (4)	94,964	323,206	291,841	117,550	827,561	8.77
Crédit Suisse Gp (5)	18,966	239,346	382,447	109,164	749,923	7.94
Chase Manhattan (7)	363,932	132,290	131,049	38,390	664,661	7.04
J.P. Morgan (6)	57,351	131,058	361,899	35,996	586,304	6.21
Lehman Bros (8)	10,378	202,679	182,056	106,869	501,982	5.32
DLJ (13)	9,830	72,739	326,061	27,330	435,960	4.62
Bank of America (11)	220,632	81,425	16,555	29,083	347,695	3.68
Deutsche Bank (9)	35,895	139,425	130,764	35,065	341,149	3.61
UBS/WDR (10)		80,604	155,616	26,455	262,675	2.78
Bear Stearns (12)		94,867	41,129	50,608	186,604	1.98
ABN Amro (14)	9,666	103,884	32,029	24,382	168,961	1.79
Lazards (16)			163,926		163,926	1.74
Dresdner KB (18)		51,005	99,529	13,225	163,759	1.73
Rothschild (19)			126,093		126,093	1.34
BNP Paribas (15)		53,073	31,609	13,961	98,643	1.04
Wasserstein Perella (–)			78,821		78,821	0.83
Paine Webber (24)		42,529		35,348	77,877	0.82
NatWest (25)	11,710	34,952		26,846	73,508	0.78
HSBC (25)		25,172	39,239	8,259	72,670	0.77
Fleet Boston Corp (22)	31,340	4,474	27,271		63,085	0.67
Barclays (17)		47,232		11,723	58,955	0.62
CIBC (–)	12,404	2,534	34,047		48,985	0.52
Top 10 firms	798,483	2,152,391	3,732,461	772,533	7,455,868	78.97
Top 25 firms	899,498	2,831,142	4,692,534	1,018,405	9,441,579	100.00
Industry total	1,089,931	3,278,721	2,311,834	1,141,059	7,830,545	
Top 10 as % of top 25	91.67	78.26	71.58	76.62	76.96	

Source: Thomson Financial Securities Data Company

* Citigroup included Schroders

for a combined market share of over 96 per cent. This suggests a high level of global market concentration and the emergence of a global 'bulge bracket' capable of forcing through monopolistic pricing and thereby appropriating substantial gains for their own shareholders. But a more careful examination shows otherwise, as suggested in Fig. 9.3.

A good way to measure market structure is to use the so-called Herfindahl-Hirshman index – the sum of the squares of market shares ($H=\Sigma s^2$), which lies somewhere between 0 (perfect competition) and 10,000 (one firm with monopoly control of the market). The value of H rises as the number of competitors declines and as market-share concentration increases among a given number of competitors. Many domestic markets for financial services have shown a tendency towards oligopoly, with very high levels of banking concentration in countries such as the Netherlands and Denmark and low levels in relatively fragmented financial systems such as the US. In wholesale financial markets, too, spreads and fees tend to be positively associated with higher concentration levels, as in the traditional US bulge bracket of securities underwriters and M&A advisers. But as market definition broadens from domestic to global, the H value invariably drops and market structure becomes increasingly competitive – more of the gains go to the clients and fewer go to the intermediaries.

Global wholesale banking shows very little evidence so far of systematically increasing market concentration. The Herfindahl-Hirshman index for the top ten firms rose gradually since 1990, as shown in Fig. 9.3 – based on the wholesale market-share data presented in the previous chapter – but was still only 664 in 1999. For the top 20 firms, the index rose from 393 in 1995 to 709 in 1999. But the number is still very low compared with many other industries, indicating a high level of market competition despite some evidence of an upward trend in concentration, especially among the top 20 players. This indicates a very competitive global wholesale market prevailing well into the future, one that is far tougher than the term 'global bulge bracket' suggests. Moreover, the structure of the leading firms has been in flux due to numerous mergers affecting the wholesale banking industry, as well as some failures and withdrawals, suggesting that there remains plenty of room for change.

The dominance of US firms evident in Figs 9.2 and 9.3 could of course shift in the years ahead, as the major European universal banks acquire or build significant market shares against their US rivals – especially if there is disproportionate growth in Europe's share of global transaction flow. Indeed, in the months following the launch of the euro, European banks such as Deutsche Bank and ABN Amro captured a disproportionate share of euro-zone debt and equity deals on the strength of their distribution capability and improving research, forcing the US houses to scramble to catch up.[5]

Wholesale banking thus remains a highly contestable business in the global financial system despite the fact that the amount of new securities issues, trading, corporate finance, risk management and investment advisory services has been rising much more rapidly than economic activity in general and is likely to continue to do so.

Fig 9.3 Global wholesale banking and investment banking: market concentration

	1990	1991	1992	1993	1994	1995	1996	1997	1998	1999
Top ten firms										
Percentage of market share	40.6	46.1	56.0	64.2	62.1	59.5	55.9	72.0	77.9	77.0
Herfindahl Index	171.6	230.6	327.8	459.4	434.1	403.0	464.6	572.1	715.9	664.0
Number of firms from:										
US	5	7	5	9	9	9	8	8	7	9
Europe	5	3	5	1	1	1	2	2	3	1
Japan	0	0	0	0	0	0	0	0	0	0
Top twenty firms										
Percentage of market share			80.5	75.6	78.1	76.0	81.2	93.3	97.1	96.3
Herfindahl Index			392.7	478.4	481.4	439.5	517.6	620.9	764.0	709.0
Number of firms from:										
US			8	15	15	14	14	13	11	12
Europe			11	4	5	5	6	7	8	8
Japan			1	1	0	1	0	0	1	0

Shareholder-value perspectives on wholesale banking

Given prospects for competitive structure in global wholesale banking, what are some of the factors that will determine the economic value of investment banks – or investment banking activities of broader universal banks and financial conglomerates – in the euro-zone and in the world capital markets of which it is an integral part?

One issue has to do with future competitive structure and the gradual erosion of margins in investment banking activities. In virtually every area of global wholesale banking, margin erosion has taken place. There has been some reversal from time to time, but the impact of stiffer competition is doing pretty much what economists would predict. Investment-grade debt under-writing margins have declined more or less consistently over the years, and may decline further as new (possibly Internet-based) distribution techniques take hold. More or less the same thing has happened to common stock under-writing margins, with the exception of initial public offerings which have been much lower in Europe than in the US and which may eventually come under further pressure as well. Even M&A margins are not immune. The result in the US has been the kind of progressive erosion of industry profitability shown in Fig. 9.4.

Fig 9.4 US securities industry profitability

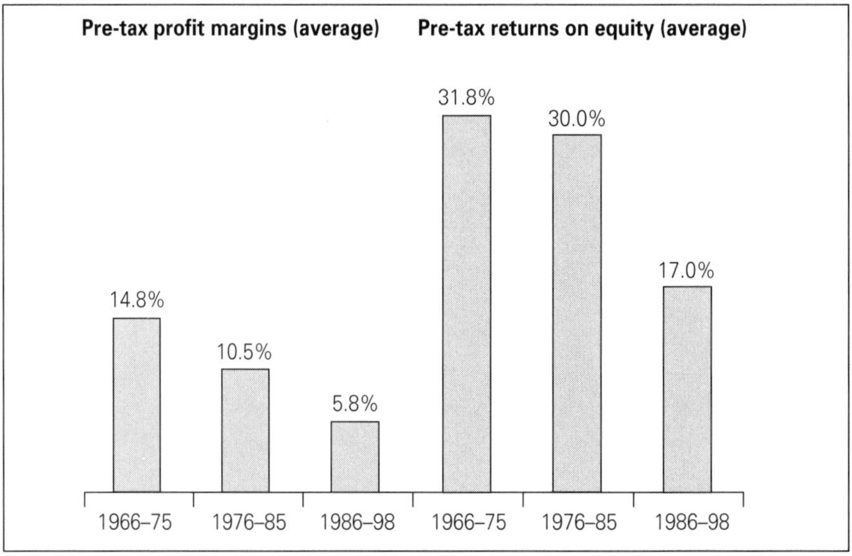

Source: Securities Industry Association

Meanwhile, brokerage commissions paid by institutional investors have been eroded even as Internet-based securities brokerage has basically caused retail commissions to collapse – first in the US and then in Europe – as investors find it increasingly easy to separate advice from trade execution. While most of the new distribution and trading vehicles have been introduced by non-traditional vendors like E*Trade, Charles Schwab and the electronic communication networks (ECNs), the major established firms have had to join in with a vengeance wherever innovative approaches showed signs of durability in order to protect their market shares. What this technical financial market infrastructure will look like in the future is by no means certain. What does seem certain is that the competitive structure will be affected in fundamental ways, so it is not at all surprising that virtually every firm active in wholesale banking is building, buying or seriously investigating technology-driven financial intermediation alternatives.

Technological innovation in wholesale financial intermediation has not so far had much effect on the market structure depicted in Fig. 9.2. A key question is whether it will do so in the future.

Technology tends to have a catalytic impact on market structure and competition in the financial services industry in general, and in wholesale banking in particular. There are three principal sources of competitive advantage in the financial services industry. One is an *information* advantage over clients or trading counterparties. A second involves *interpretation* advantages, and the third involves *transaction cost* advantages. Over time, information advantages have gradually declined as IT developments have progressed, and transaction cost advantages have also eroded in terms of differential cost structures among competing firms. But there remain very large differences between firms in terms of interpretation advantages, particularly as they relate to financial innovations, arbitrage and value-added in corporate finance. Interpretation advantages are imbedded in people, which is why returns to employees have outpaced returns to shareholders in the securities industry in recent years.

Another possible driving force of the competitive structure in wholesale banking is significant strategic rethinking on the part of the major established players, notably the US investment banks expanding their geographic scope into Europe and Asia and getting into new activities in an aggressive way. Another is US commercial banks pushing into the investment banking business. With the exception of J.P. Morgan they have had limited success, but Chase Manhattan has made some remarkable progress without major acquisitions and a few of the other emerging US megabanks are unlikely to eschew investment banking permanently. And there is Citigroup, which is already a force through its Salomon Smith Barney unit, and the big European universals like Crédit Suisse, UBS, ABN Amro, ING, Dresdner Bank and HSBC. Each has its own strategic targeting, and each has relatively deep pockets that can be used to cross-subsidize investment banking incursions from other business areas. Their impact on margins is pretty clear. They don't have to 'succeed' as major-bracket competitors in order to erode margins. The investment banking industry may in the future prove to be a remarkable study in efficiency, but not necessarily in sustained profit margins.

A third factor affecting shareholder value in wholesale banking has to do with earnings volatility – *see* Fig. 9.5 for an example of earnings volatility among US securities firms over 30 years. In essentially all full-service investment banking firms and securities units of universal banks, the role of trading and position-taking has become more prominent. The reason is that, in today's environment, price and execution is paramount. It drives the issuers and it drives the institutional investors. Both sets of clients are themselves highly performance-oriented, so they consistently want best price and best execution. Consequently, a world-class 'trading engine' is a prerequisite to success in this business, as is the ability to effectively manage the associated risks and allocate sufficient capital to carry them.

Fig 9.5 Pre-tax profits of US securities industry 1965–98

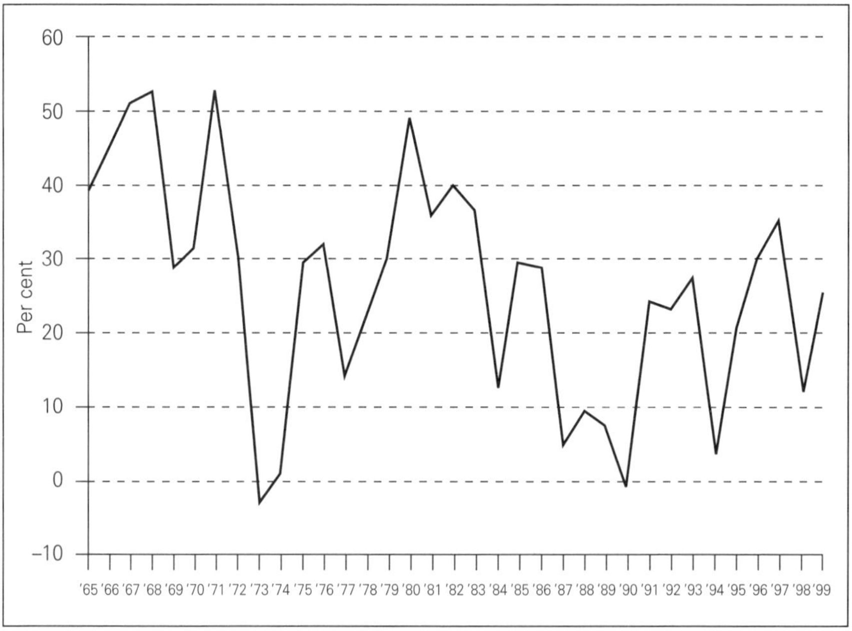

Source: Securities Industry Association (NYSE member firms dealing with the public), 1999

A fourth point that undoubtedly affects the value of wholesale banking from the perspective of shareholders is what some people call the BOB problem – 'bolts out of the blue'. Investment banking is perhaps an accident-prone industry, one that is capable of destroying shareholder value.[6] It may be that public perception of the professional standards in the industry has been eroded considerably in recent years. These standards, which incorporate the industry's reputation for integrity, service quality and expertise, may have been seriously tarnished by lapses in supervision, criminal indictments, regulatory complaints, customer litigation and all the attendant publicity. Top management tolerance (however distant) of low standards of conduct will almost certainly help to bring them about, sometimes at great cost to firms and their shareholders.

All things considered, the overriding question is what the industry's competitive structure will look like in the years ahead. Will there really emerge a global 'bulge bracket' capable of superior risk-adjusted returns on shareholder capital? Or will the competitive structure prove to be even more demanding than it has in the past?

Creating and maintaining a high-performance culture

Given the continued intense pressure of competition in the various parts of investment banking in the hotly contested euro-zone as well as globally, and its reflection in margins and shareholder value, what, besides finding (often temporarily) imperfect markets leveraged off a global wholesale banking platform, can be done to bolster the franchise value of investment banking firms? It is a business in which probably the principal distinguishing factor between successful and unsuccessful firms is the quality of its workers and leadership. Firms can raise financial capital and buy technology from many sources. It is much harder to establish a winning pool of human capital, especially in an industry where people are highly mobile. Firms that are well led, where people are carefully selected, trained and motivated, are likely to be the ultimate winners in the battle for market supremacy in the evolving euro-zone. Much depends on defining and maintaining a high-performance corporate culture.

Corporate culture has become one of the most actively debated issues distinguishing successful from lacklustre performers in the financial services sector. Culture is something every firm has, even if it is weak. It is central to the institutional environment in which people have to work. If a firm wants to get a lot out of people, the first thing management has to give them is a highly desirable and effective workplace, where they spend more of their time than anywhere else. Some key ingredients are:

● high-quality peers and role models to learn from, and compete with;

● a sufficiently non-hierarchical, loose organizational structure which permits ideas to be put forward, to be taken seriously, considered carefully on the basis of merit, and acted upon quickly – a structure that protects high-potential individuals from bureaucratic stifling;

● an *esprit de corps* that thrives on measurable competitive success – such as significantly increasing market share or profit margins – in a business where winners and losers are not difficult to distinguish and where valuable franchises are difficult to build but easy to lose;

● a performance-based compensation and advancement system that is generally respected as fair and right not less than about 80 per cent of the time. This must be an integral part of a benign form of ruthless Darwinism, one that includes a reasonably high level of involuntary turnover, in which only the best survive and progress.

In short, there has to be a climate in which bright people, if they are found to be suitable, will want to spend their careers. This climate requires a sense of continuity, admired and respected seniors, and a serious, consistent commitment to careful recruitment, management development and training. Especially in times of growing international activity globally and within the euro-zone, those who are not from the institution's home country cannot be deemed unworthy of high office.

Corporate culture in a highly competitive industry like investment banking has to be regarded by management and boards of directors as an important competitive weapon, centred on grasping and preserving the qualities of winning. This includes:

● sound strategic direction and leadership from the top – knowing the right thing to do, then getting it done promptly by providing sufficient resources;

● an overriding attention to teamwork, avoiding becoming dependent on so-called stars and stamping out arrogance – some apparently strong cultures are really not much more than examples of institutionalized arrogance;

● the selection of loyal and efficient 'platoon leaders', to carry out day-to-day activities at a high level of quality and professionalism. This must include a fine, ingrained sense of what is unacceptable conduct, including conduct that does not necessarily violate laws or regulations but never-theless could impair the reputation of the firm and compromise its responsibility to clients;

● a high level of adaptability by the whole organization in an industry subject to rapid change – *sic transit gloria*. Senior management must be keenly aware of the need for adaptability, and communicate it effectively by word and deed. A certain amount of corporate *angst* help keep people on their toes.

Being a market share winner today is no longer enough. To stay a winner, a firm must be able to adapt to wrenching industry change, intense margin competition and the management of vastly complicated technology and risk issues. Few of its people can do all this without becoming obsolete after a while. Then they need to be moved out of the way, with dignity and grace if possible, to make room for more up-to-date replacements. This implies that such a culture – not unlike professional athletics or an effective military – needs to have young blood on the front lines but with plenty of senior coaching backing it up. The young don't know everything, and a good institutional memory is an invaluable asset.

Leadership is important. The evidence suggests that the culture of a financial institution can be strongly influenced by one or two individuals at the top, either to push forward and improve upon a core culture that already exists or to dramatically change it. But most banks are run by committees on the basis of shared responsibility and power by people, however capable, who reached their positions largely through bureaucratic progression within the system. This may be less so in smaller institutions than in larger ones, and less so in investment banks than in commercial and universal banks. As products of the system, these people tend to promote the shared values and behaviour patterns characteristic of that system. Sometimes 'outsiders' with quite different perspectives are included on the top management team, often with great catalytic effect, but others may have only a limited impact on institutions.

The history of an organization is often a useful cultural anchor, particularly if that history includes a strongly positive social and political as well as economic impact. Employees quickly identify with a proud history and the cultural attributes associated with it, and leverage it in a productive way in client relationships. Business setbacks, strategic errors and even scandals may be more easily overcome if corporate culture is linked to a strong historical anchor. The problem with a history-linked cultural identity is that it either exists or it does not, and represents a factual basis that cannot be altered in the short-run. Most established banks have long and honourable histories, but few are so distinguished that they provide a powerful cultural asset.

Of much greater interest is a bank's overall franchise, the cumulative product of its business successes and failures in the relatively recent past. In the case of market successes or dominance, the positive lessons can permeate the entire firm. In the case of failures, the demoralization effect on corporate culture can far exceed the direct impact of the failure itself. Financial institutions that are repeatedly successful in financial innovation, for example, often acquire resonance in the market which can positively affect corporate culture over a relatively short time-span. People are generally proud to be considered innovative or to be associated with innovators, and this can pay cultural dividends. It is also well known that entrepreneurial and start-up ventures often have extremely positive cultures that place a premium on hard work well beyond formal responsibilities, self-motivation, attention to quality, and the like. The problem is that the excitement can dissipate fairly quickly, after which routine takes over and the cultural value is lost.

Then there is a sense of institutional vision. Mission statements are often helpful in the development of strong cultures as long as they are both realistic and 'alive' in the sense that management 'walks the talk', to use a popular phrase. Among the most useless and indeed damaging efforts can be mission statements intended to weld together a coherent corporate culture but which turn out to be opportunistic, unrealistic, frequently violated and pious. These mainly serve to create a sense of cynicism, dissent and disinterest. Many firms have a powerful corporate culture without a mission statement, only a strong sense of vision on the part of senior management.

Finally, a partnership or quasi-partnership form of organization may have significant positive cultural impact. In any collective mentality, people are the most important thing – they must be trained, led and given role models to emulate; they must be compensated well and fairly, but not excessively relative to what they contribute. The question is whether certain cultural attributes specific to partnerships can be synthetically introduced into corporate organizations in order to derive some of the benefits. Sometimes this can be achieved partly through well-designed and credible management information and profit attribution systems, which put earnings into 'pools' where they are properly allocated, whether directly or indirectly. This system must then be sold to employees as being both accurate and fair, so that it is trusted as much as possible by those doing the performing. Lateral flows of information across the organization and co-operative behaviour may thus be encouraged far more effectively than any amount of exhortation by management.

One question that constantly arises in banking is whether a single culture is appropriate for an organization that covers a very broad range of activities, from foreign exchange dealing to mass-market retail banking and to M&A transactions in investment banking. However, there may be some over-arching cultural attributes (a superculture) that can be an effective umbrella covering widely different business cultures and national cultures within an organization. If this is considered impossible to achieve, then it is likely that a holding company type of organization – where subcultures are closely aligned to the respective businesses – may be superior to more integrated structural links between banks. However, cultural fragmentation in such a structure is one potential drawback, including the fragmentation of market delivery and quality control – not to be taken lightly.

As the investment banking winners in the euro-zone emerge, whether European firms or firms based in the US or elsewhere, the chances are that they will have a highly developed, positive and performance-compatible culture coupled to and reinforced by strong and consistent leadership.

Where next?

Ultimately, the question is whether the enthusiasm we have projected about the euro-zone will prove to be well-founded – that the European marketplace will evolve into the world's most important centre for finance (or one of two such centres). In this chapter, we have identified first the hazard of the macro-economic policy environment of the euro-zone as well as the benefits – notably substantially lower interest rates for all of Europe which have been passed on quickly to market users and households, and have encouraged stock price rises, restructuring and market capitalism in general. We then took up the competitive structure of the industry, emphasizing that wholesale finance is necessarily global because of significant market integration, so the new euro-zone wholesale market structure is global as well and subject to the same competitive dynamics.

The most successful firms have been American, largely because of the massive US market underpinning their global activity, but also because of their organizational distinctions. Mainly these include an emphasis on special-ization, skill and delivering the best price and quality of service, as well as reliance on long-standing relationships. The euro-zone is in the process of absorbing US operating practices and adapting them for optimal performance in its own environment. US firms have been using this technique successfully, not least the employment and advancement of European nationals – some US firms have as many European employees and senior officials as they have Americans, with much of their capital allocated to Europe. They have also been able to easily operate across European borders.

Still, there is plenty of scope for change in the competitive running order in Europe. The competitive dynamics in the wholesale banking industry have forced all firms to emphasize performance above all else. As indicated, the highly competitive US model is likely to prevail, at least for the time being, but it has not yet finished evolving. As Europe increases in importance – perhaps along with a decline in the merger and capital market intensity of the US, where much of what needs to be done has now been done – this model will have to be adapted to reflect more intrinsic European characteristics.

Europe will be a very distinct marketplace. Its importance will grow as it reaches US levels of market utilization and continues with its privatization and restructuring efforts which may need several years to be completed. There is also the expansion of the marketplace into non-EMU Europe and Eastern Europe, as well as the special effects of Europe becoming the financial centre of the world. Turning back the clock is increasingly unlikely.

To be successful, wholesale banking firms in the future will have to develop the ability to be specialized and price-competitive (and well integrated into the global market environment), but they will also have to know how to create and preserve important relationships with clients. This requires:

● constant renewal of talent and capabilities

● superior risk-management controls, including control of human risks

● the ability to satisfy market investors who expect top operating performance, margins, market share and franchise preservation, and who will otherwise sell the stock and embark on a hostile takeover.

So a premium will be available for those firms with:

● good strategy and leadership

● good middle management at all operating levels, especially people and technology management

● success in creating a positive culture, so key employees want to be there to help their firm perform well.

NOTES

[1] For a detailed discussion, *see* Story, Jonathan and Walter, Ingo (1997) *Political Economy of European Financial Integration: the battle of the systems*, Manchester: Manchester University Press, and Cambridge: MIT Press.

[2] The ECB in 1998 had a staff of only 475, compared with some 60,000 employed by the central banks of euro-zone participants.

[3] 'Sailing Choppy Waters,' *The Economist*, 26 June 1999.

[4] Norbert Walter, chief economist of Deutsche Bank, as quoted in Gerard Baker's article 'The Emu has landed', *Financial Times*, 5 May 1998.

[5] Robinson, Danielle (1999) 'Ranking wars', Investment Dealers Digest,' 26 July.

[6] Smith, Roy C. and Walter, Ingo (1997) *Street Smarts: linking professional conduct and shareholder value in the securities industry*, Boston: Harvard Business School Press.

CHAPTER 10

The new frontiers:
strategies for success

The nineties were tumultuous for the worldwide banking and securities industry. The decade began with the US banks in deep trouble and in need of fundamental reorganization. European universal banks, meanwhile, were smugly accepting the admiration of figures such as the US Treasury Secretary Nicholas Brady, who praised their commitment to long-term client relationships and decision-making practices. The Japanese banks were generally held in awe, having risen to occupy nine of the top ten rankings on the list of the world's leading banks ranked by assets.

The decade ended with the US banks having been drastically restructured and rebuilt along both fiercely competitive and profitable lines, and the Japanese banks in financial disarray. Many of the mighty European universals had been through a period of disarray and confusion, and many believed they needed to 'restructure' or 'refocus' themselves – the industry's most popular buzzwords – but were unsure just how to do it.

The great US recovery

The US banks were flat on their backs in 1990 after years of painful restructuring. They had to rid themselves of too many bad loans, too many unprofitable products and services, and too many slow-footed managers who were unable to adapt to the new, far more demanding and competitive environment into which they had been plunged. Indeed, 1990 was the worst year for US banking since the Great Depression. Problem loans had reached a modern-day high, write-offs were soaring, and profits were sagging badly. The Federal Deposit Insurance Corporation was just about out of money, and its reserves would have to be replenished. Bad loans had been the plague of the decade, made by over-eager, under-supervised, aggressive bankers striving to boost their careers no matter what the hazards. They had nearly ruined a whole industry. It had taken most of the eighties to clean up the mess. But by the early nineties, the worst was over and a miraculous recovery had begun.

While the US banks were suffering and being downgraded across the board, the Japanese banks were at their peak. They had swollen in size by virtue of aggressive lending practices and mergers. Most were feared for their predatory, 'money-dumping' practices outside Japan when they made loans at rate levels thought to be below their cost of funds, just to get the business. But in the early nineties came the deadly market slump brought on by the end of Japan's 'bubble economy'. By the end of the decade, Japanese banks would appear denuded – all illusion with nothing much left to support their once-powerful reputations. Meanwhile, European banks were still sorting themselves out after a successive series of the shocks, beginning perhaps with the UK's Big Bang and the many little bangs that echoed throughout Europe in the late eighties, but paralleled by many changes in regulation, technology and competitive threats and opportunities.

Looking back, US banks would admit that they recovered from the eighties only by pushing through massive restructuring and refocusing their goals and objectives. Businesses were cut back to the bone, with everything not essential (including a great many overseas branches) being sold off. Staffing was reduced as sharply as enhanced computer operations and regulators would permit. It was back to basics and 'core competencies'. Those activities that did not fit, or could not be justified on profitability grounds, had to go. As a result, most of the banks chose to concentrate on their domestic opportunities in the consumer sector. This meant focusing on credit cards, marketing, information systems, repositioning branches, moving into adjacent markets for deposit collection and retail lending, and cutting opera-tional costs to the minimum. In-market mergers and acquisitions (combina-tions of banks in the same market area) speeded up the pace of cost reduction while increasing the size and scale economies of the bank. Out-of-market deals also were done to expand into new territory.

Mergers in the banking industry were principally responsible for the reduction in the number of banks in the US from about 15,000 in 1990 to less than 10,000 in 2000. Only a few – less than a dozen or so – made any signifi-cant effort to work their way more deeply into the fiercely competitive wholesale financial services sector dominated by the major investment banks.

Those few that did – Chase Manhattan, J.P. Morgan and Bankers Trust – managed to challenge the entrenched investment banks for a share of the wholesale market revenues, but not without a great deal of trouble and expense that sharply detracted from their success.

Nevertheless, by the end of the nineties they had recovered smartly. The average money-centre bank registered a return on assets of 1.46 per cent in 1998, up from a miserable 0.54 per cent in 1990, and a return on stockholders' equity of 18.5 per cent. Still, the banks were restoring their profitability in a bull market, in which interest rates were falling and stock prices rising, so that their cost of capital was falling. Capital cost is always important in a highly leveraged business such as banking. One study showed that as much as 33 per cent of the profit recovery in US banks since 1993 came from non-recurring factors such as lower deposit insurance costs, smaller loan loss provisions, and wider spreads between lending and deposit rates.[1]

The banks were also much larger at the end of the nineties as a result of the profusion of mergers, most of which were quite ordinary in- or out-of-market deals. One, however – the biggest of all – created the world's first, truly multi-business financial services conglomerate, Citigroup.

Figure 10.1 shows the top ten US banks ranked by assets in 1989. These rankings alone testify to a great deal of competitive change. Whereas five of the top ten remain the same, they were very different banks by the end of the decade. Nine of the top ten names of 1990 were combined with other banks. Only one, J.P. Morgan, eschewed acquisitions as a corporate strategy and remained independent, although it was frequently proposed as a possible takeover target.

Fig 10.1 US bank holding companies ranked by assets

Rank	31 December 1989	Assets (US$m)	31 December 1998	Assets (US$m)
1	Citicorp	230,643	Citigroup	668,600
2	Chase Manhattan	107,369	Chase Manhattan	356,500
3	Bank of America	98,764	J.P. Morgan	298,500
4	J.P. Morgan	88,964	BankAmerica	263,900
5	Security Pacific	83,943	First Union	234,600
6	Chemical Bank	71,513	Bankers Trust	156,300
7	NCNB	66,191	Bank One	120,200
8	Manufacturers Hanover	60,479	Fleet Financial	99,500
9	First Interstate	59,051	Wells Fargo	92,800
10	Bankers Trust	55,658	National City Corp.	83,100

People have been studying bank mergers for decades, and have in general come away with only a limited amount of agreed wisdom – consultants' pitches notwithstanding. Most would agree that there is no evidence that banks combining into entities with $10 billion or more of assets will experience any significant economies of scale. There are, of course, some one-time cost savings, in in-market mergers in particular, but only to the extent that work and functions overlap and can be rationalized. But operating a large enterprise has its own special costs that are found in growing bureaucracy, lost efficiency and agility, incompatible systems, and general organizational unwieldiness. Out-of-market mergers have their problems, as do cross-industry combinations. Economies of scope, to realize the benefits of cross-selling, are almost never more valuable than the cost expended to achieve them. Nor do cross-industry deals, such as combining commercial and investment banking or investment banking and insurance, have a very happy history, at least so far. Yet there seem to be plenty of managers who would try to be the first to make the combinations succeed.

European banking restructuring

During the nineties European banks were required to adjust to the Basle Agreement on consolidated supervision and minimum bank capital adequacy levels, to the EU's Second Banking Directive, to the modernization of capital markets, to increasingly complex demands of competitive technology, and to an unrelenting storm of competition, all at the same time. They also had to face changes in the rules governing insurance services, investment services and asset management, and had to cope with the transformation related to the creation of the euro. Nevertheless, they seemed to have survived these adjustments in pretty good shape. The Basle minimum capital requirements were not a problem for many European banks – they had plenty of capital and reserves. The movement towards the capital markets was not too difficult for the principal continental banks, which were after all structured as universal banks and had been in capital markets before. They would just have to get a little better at it. The hardest part – the part that caused the most difficulty for banks in all Europe's financial capitals – was dealing with an entirely new level of competition, a level that would (as intended) raise the quality of financial services in Europe and lower their clients' financing costs. But this new benefit could come only at the cost of terminally disrupting much of the European banking industry, the roots of which had held firm for hundreds of years.

New levels of competition

The Basle Agreement (scheduled to be overhauled in 2000) required that banks meet minimum standards of capital adequacy, so that many of the other practices designed to keep banks safe could be foregone. These included protectionist regulation, allowing for large banking spreads to be sure that the banks had enough capital and profitability to endure losses, and restrictions on new products and services that might involve assuming too much risk. Foregoing these practices would indeed open the door for more innovative financial services. The EU's Second Banking Directive affected banks too, by opening up competition in domestic markets to all European-based banks, and even the Americans and Japanese that were not European-based. The Directive encouraged competition by creating opportunities for some banks to move into other countries and causing others to consolidate their positions at home through mergers. And it emphasized the open nature of universal banking in declaring it to be the standard for the continent. Along with all this came the opportunity for competitors to cut across traditional sector boundaries, and for banks, securities firms, insurance companies and asset managers to compete openly for each other's business. Technological developments in the industry accelerated the pace of change – wholesale banking had become global, price-sensitive and rapidly changing even as retail banking adopted credit cards, ATMs, phone and mail solicitations, and life insurance was losing ground to mutual funds and annuities.

Marking strategies to market

The growing competitive pressures in European banking – pressures from regulators, from traditional national competitors and from an increasing array of foreigners offering a range of new services – began to be felt in the early nineties. Whereas the largest European multinationals were active users of capital market services, most European banks and other providers of financial services regarded the more numerous, less sophisticated, mid-sized companies to be their most important clients. According to a 1998 survey, about 75 per cent of all company finance in continental Europe is provided by banks, compared with 25 per cent in the US.[2]

The largest European corporations and government agencies had established easy access to eurobond and syndicated lending facilities, and the wholesale market had become highly competitive (based on price), global and transaction-oriented. Those companies that had access to the markets, of course, benefited handsomely by reducing their cost of capital. Their financing activities increased as the markets grew and became more efficient, drawing in even more transactions and increasing the disintermediation of the banks in customer business. Most banks, however, found this sophisticated wholesale business too difficult and de-emphasized or dropped it entirely.

These banks were at the same time facing a variety of changes in their traditional retail businesses. Automatic teller machines and other forms of electronic banking were being introduced, requiring all banks to substantially increase their investments in these areas in order to stay competitive. Money market funds were introduced, providing more competition for consumer savings. Banks were also offering investment services and various forms of insurance through their branch offices. All were competing hard for local customer business, and banking spreads began to narrow considerably in the late eighties. To offset the loss of interest income, the banks had to lower their operating costs and introduce more efficient procedures. Not all knew how to do this.

European banks also had to react to changes in business strategies enacted by their principal competitors. Some were merging to create larger domestic businesses. Others were specializing in pursuing particular pieces of the wholesale or retail businesses, threatening the banks' core businesses. The competitive position of banks was being reshaped by mergers and acquisitions, and by other restructuring actions. By the early nineties, each bank had to rethink its strategies to be sure they were still the most appropriate ones. In other words, their strategies had to be checked against the many changes in the competitive marketplace to ascertain whether they were still viable and suited to the banks' capabilities. The strategies had to be marked-to-market.

Institutional pressures

In addition, for the first time many banks came under the scrutiny of critical institutional investors and the equity analyst community that served them. Because of increased stock market activity, greater participation in European markets by US and UK institutional investors called attention to the low returns on investment generated by many European banks. In the past, banks (many of them state-owned or state-controlled) were not supposed to be optimal economic performers. They were meant to be safe havens for deposits and investments, even if they were excessively conservative, unimaginative and bureaucratic in the process. They were certainly not meant to be growth stocks. Still, the banks were subject to comparison with other banks inside their own country and the premier banks abroad. Many suffered under these comparisons, and gradually came under pressure from their boards of directors to do better. Many of those that succeeded in increasing returns were rewarded by strongly increased share prices; many of those that failed to do so were subjected to reorganization or merger.

Catching up

The European banks had not found the nineties to be an easy decade after all. The experiences of their principal competitors to the west and the east could not be avoided in the end. Deregulation and technology had stiffened competition. Market changes, especially unexpected interest rate increases and greater pressure for transparency, forced the European banks to admit asset-liability matching problems typical of the US savings and loan bank crisis. Then came a deluge of bad loans and overseas investment strategies that went wrong. Banks in the UK, France, Germany, Switzerland, Scandinavia and elsewhere – suddenly subject to market forces that had only recently been allowed to affect European banks – began to sink into difficulties. Stock prices plunged, business disappeared into the more comfortable arms of competitors or the capital markets, and credit ratings were chopped by the agencies. Many banks required government intervention to protect depositors.

After the Basle Accord and the Second Banking Directive, and the substantial reforms to capital markets all over the continent, the banks were in big trouble. They had to restructure, modernize, and become more competitive and more profitable. If they failed to do so, they faced a high probability of either being taken over by another bank or of falling into the arms of their government regulators. It was a rough decade. But as it came to a close, European banks were in much better shape strategically, most having moved in one of several viable directions. Bank mergers and acquisitions were as intense in Europe as they had been in the US, and by November 1998 the hierarchy of European market leaders was quite different from that of 1989, with seven of the top ten having been involved in major mergers (*see* Fig. 10.2). Since this figure was prepared, the merger of BNP and Paribas would move that bank into second place, in terms of assets, and the pending merger of NatWest and Royal Bank of Scotland would rank seventh by assets as of 31 December 1999.

European banks, like their US counterparts, have followed a 'bigger-is-better' acquisition strategy, with the average assets of the top ten banks settling in at $514 billion, 2.8 times the 1989 average assets of the top ten banks. The assets of the top ten US banks averaged $251 billion, also 2.8 times more than in 1989. The emphasis has been on in-market deals but, as in the US, there have been some significant out-of-market and cross-industry

Fig 10.2 European bank performance data, November 1998

Rank	Bank ($bn)	Total assets ($bn)	Market cap ($bn)	Market cap as % assets	Tier I equity	ROAE (post-tax)	Net int margin	Ln growth 8 years	P/E	P/B
1	UBS	749	69.2	9.24	7.5	21.6	1.0	Na	15.50	2.94
2	Deutsche Bank	693	33.4	4.82	5.1	15.0	1.3	11.9	11.70	1.76
3	ABN-Amro	501	31.8	6.35	7.2	18.3	1.7	28.1	16.00	2.12
4	Bayerishe Hypo Ver. Bank	492	31.3	6.36	5.0	17.7	1.3	Na		
5	HBSC	487	55.5	11.40	9.8	17.7	2.8	Na	12.00	2.02
6	Crédit Suisse	477	46.4	6.56	10.3	2.2	0.9	13.1	18.60	3.2
7	Dresdner	462	24.7	5.35	5.7	15.0	1.3	8.5	19.70	2.04
8	ING Group	456	55.2	12.11	7.0	13.5	2.3	17.0	15.60	1.47
9	Soc Générale	418	18.2	4.35	6.2	10.4	1.2	9.5	13.50	1.65
10	Barclays	406	35.6	8.77	7.3	22.9	3.4	-0.5	12.20	2.7
11	Banque Nationale de Paris	346	14.6	4.22	5.5	10.1	1.1	4.6	12.40	1.39
12	Commerzbank	343	13.8	4.02	6.0	10.4	1.3	14.6	13.90	1.37
13	National Westminster	311	30.2	9.71	8.1	18.6	3.3	1.2	12.80	2.37
14	San Paolo-IMI	200	12.0	6.00	11.0	5.2	1.8	11.8	20.80	2.25
15	Lloyds TSB	234	64.8	27.69	9.1	27.7	3.6	10.0	18.10	5.49
16	Santander	186	21.9	11.77	8.3	22.2	2.6	30.2	19.90	3.33
17	BBV	147	26.9	18.30	9.0	19.4	2.9	10.6	25.00	4.88
18	Bank Austria	126	6.9	5.48	5.9	8.5	1.5	Na	6.40	1.07
19	Banco di Roma	119	10.3	8.66	6.9	Na	2.4	Na	16.80	1.8
20	BCI	117	12.0	10.26	7.8	5.1	2.9	12.2	23.40	2.32
	Total	**7,270**	**614.7**	**8.46**						
	UK and continental average				7.4	14.6	1.7	10.9	14.5	2.06

Source: Goldman Sachs Investment Research

transactions. Among the top 20 banks in Europe, all but about four or five have chosen to concentrate on retail and middle-market banking and consumer financing services, largely in their home countries, just as all but four or five of the top banks in the US have done. Among the four or five banks in each area that have continued to specialize in wholesale market services are those which have had the most difficulty in integrating their commercial banking and investment banking activities.

The sum of the market capitalization of the top 20 European and US banks was about the same at the end of 1998 (approximately $620 billion), but US banks, averaging about half the assets of the Europeans, had twice the ratio of market capitalization to assets. This is probably best explained by the fact that European banks also lagged behind the US in terms of net interest margins – the top 20 European banks averaged 1.7 per cent against 3.6 per cent for the US. However, comparisons of other important banking ratios (including Tier 1 equity capital, return on equity, price-earnings and price to book-value ratios) were all about the same for the top European and US banks. After UBS, with the highest market capitalization among European banks at 31 December 1998, was Lloyds TSB, a UK retail banking and insurance firm. Lloyds was followed by HBSC (the former Hongkong Shanghai Banking Corp., which acquired Midland Bank in the UK and Marine Midland Bank and Republic National Bank in the US), and the ING and Crédit Suisse groups, both large mixtures of retail banking, insurance and securities. In the US, after Citigroup, the ranking in market capitalization at 31 December 1998 was led by BankAmerica (the recently merged NationsBank and Bank of America), First Union and Bank One (both regional bank groups), and Chase Manhattan.

Lagging in investment banking

Banking companies in both regions have adapted to the many changes affecting their respective competitive environments in much the same way, by increasing their market presence and striving to improve profitability. But most of their success has been the result of domestic restructuring and focus on traditional retail and middle-market business. By contrast, the wholesale market has moved to absorb the latest innovations and increased competition in the securities markets. Consisting of such transactions as syndicated bank loans, securities underwriting, medium-term note issuance and mergers advisory work, it has grown in size and importance, and has become consolidated into the hands of the leading ten firms, mostly US, as suggested by Figs 9.2 and 9.3.

This chapter focuses on the unfinished business of carrying these strategies forward into an environment that is still being shaped, not just by the market forces that dominated the nineties but by the competitive demands of the single currency.

Major components of European banking strategy

Strategies are the means by which organizations achieve their goals. In the past, banks in most countries were public utilities with goals limited to preserving the status quo. They wanted to remain as they were: large, respected, solid. Those with significant international activities wanted them preserved – for the sake of the prestige, the domestic clients they served, the contact with influential foreigners, and the opportunity to show the flag. Generally these activities contributed very little to banks' profits, but they were necessary. One bank stated that its long-term goal was simply to 'remain among Europe's ten most important banks'. After some chiding, it added the words 'and profitable', which changed the purported strategy quite a bit.

Setting goals

Today, most European banks would agree that their goals would be different, more sharply focused on profits and shareholder value. They now aspire to maintain return on investment in the 15–20 per cent area, a level that will require substantial improvement for many of them from their traditional ratios. Recognizing that competition is threatening their usual markets, the banks now sometimes also define their goals in terms of market share. They need to protect this share – to which much of their national recognition is tied – especially from foreign banks attempting to set themselves up locally under the liberal terms of the EU Second Banking Directive. Some other banks, though not all, would have a further strategic aim – to maintain their standing among Europe's (or the world's) leading banks.

These goals may conflict. To maintain high levels of profitability requires reducing low-yielding investments and cutting back on less profitable activities and on exposure to risk. Increasing market share can require substantial investments that do not pay off for a long time. But if a bank's reset goals require an improvement in its share of an increasingly competitive market, or an increase in profitability levels, there will need to be substantial changes in the way it operates. Banks often find it difficult to implement these changes, which may require replacing senior management, laying off large numbers of employees (something that is not done easily in most European countries) or abandoning long-term subsidized activities and sacred cows. Such draconian actions are rarely taken by any organization that is not in danger of failing or otherwise seen to be in serious trouble.

Implementation

The most difficult strategies to implement are the ones in which a bank wants to change direction entirely, to expand into a new area, solicit business from new clients or enter into different product lines. Along each axis, existing competition may be well entrenched and the route to success too often seems to involve throwing money at mispriced loans or bond issues, or in trading operations that get into trouble. Witness the difficulties of major banks in Britain (NatWest, Barclays), Germany (Deutsche Bank) and Switzerland (the old UBS) in breaking into or maintaining positions in the top ranks of the European securities business, an activity that has proven difficult and expensive for all that have tried it. In fact, the difficulties were perceived as being so great that some of the principal banks in the UK (Lloyds TSB, Midland) and Germany (Dresdner, Commerzbank) backed away, and major banks in France (Crédit Lyonnais, BNP), Italy and Scandinavia never tried.

The least difficult strategic moves are those that involve retrenchment from difficult areas into more comfortable ones in which the bank has local knowledge, expertise and an established brand name. The Lloyds TSB strategy of withdrawing from international and investment banking to concentrate on British 'high street' banking and insurance has paid off handsomely in higher returns and stock prices. Lloyds' success (28 per cent ROE in 1998, 3.6 per cent interest margin, market capitalization 5.5 times book value) has been hard to ignore by NatWest and Barclays, both of which to a large degree withdrew from the European securities markets after having made significant commitments to them.

Offence and defence

The new market configurations permitted by EU banking regulation (the 'single passport') removed longstanding barriers to competition from banks in neighbouring countries. It produced an environment in which a French bank could easily set up to do business in Holland, for example, under very competitive terms, offering high-tech products, fine pricing and a barrage of marketing expenditures to crack into a particularly lucrative segment of the Dutch market. The foreigners do not want to serve the whole market, as the Dutch banks do. They just want the most profitable, high-end part. The French, of course, might never actually do this, but the Dutch banks cannot be sure that they won't, or if not the French then maybe the Germans or the British, or even the Americans or the Japanese. The major international banks from these countries might be much more aggressive than the Dutch banks, leaving them bravely trying to defend their territory against an onslaught from more powerful competitors.

What should the Dutch banks do in a hypothetical case like this? Perhaps they are unable to think entirely as a shareholder-governed economic enterprise (which they are), rather than as a national utility (which they have been). They might prefer to set aside the questions of goals, returns and market share, and simply decide that individually, they are too small to mount a successful defence. So a merger between prominent national players might make the most sense. Without such a merger, few of them (that is, longstanding, traditional Dutch-owned institutions that the Dutch people recognize as their own) might survive. A large, fortress-like bank in Holland would confirm that 'bigger is better' or at least safer, and the combined market capitalization of the bank would perhaps make it immune to takeover and enable it to command all the resources needed to play an appropriately large role on the intra-European stage. Once a large national champion has emerged, the forward-looking strategic details can be polished up. Certainly the strategy would benefit from the ending of competition between the merging banks.

Partly driven by such thinking, Europe has seen a large number of in-market bank consolidations: SBC-UBS, HypoVereinsbank, Crédit Suisse-Volksbank, ABN-Amro, ING, Lloyds-TSB, Unidanmark, Credito Italiano-Unicredito, BNP-Paribas, NatWest-Royal Bank of Scotland and others (see Fig. 1.1). Unlike their US counterparts, however, they will not see an immediate substantial improvement in profitability because of their inability to reduce costs quickly. Still, these in-market deals are likely to continue, and indeed accelerate, as the impact of the euro begins to be felt.[3]

European cross-border and cross-industry initiatives

Other banks had an idea of Europeanization through cross-border initiatives – acquisitions or strategic alliances that would provide a platform for aggressive expansion aimed at achieving banking leadership across the single market. Crédit Lyonnais launched the only serious attempt of this type, and briefly achieved its objective of becoming the largest bank across the EU. But the price of such rapid movement was the acquisition of too many bad loans which, when they came undone, were nearly fatal to the bank.

Deutsche Bank acquired Banca d'America e de Italia in 1986 (from a distressed Bank of America), and in 1989 acquired Morgan Grenfell, a British merchant bank, and in 1999 Bankers Trust. It has backed away more recently from large European acquisitions as a means of achieving strategic cross-border objectives.

Almost all other intra-European banking acquisitions have involved relatively small deals (most in the securities business or in asset management) or small stakes in larger 'strategic alliance' partners (*see* Fig. 1.2). Small transactions do not make for major strategy changes, although they may seem to do so on paper, at least for a while.

Banks have also been active in making investments in other branches of financial services, especially between banking and securities, insurance and investment management, and these have frequently involved cross-border transactions. UBS owns an investment banking business, a derivatives business, and an institutional investment management firm, all but one of which were acquired in the US. Its remaining Swiss competitor, Crédit Suisse, has acquired an in-market retail banking business (Volksbank) and the Swiss insurance company Winterthur to go with its US-based investment banking business (CS First Boston). Zurich Insurance has acquired the US and UK insurance businesses of BAT plc. and US mutual fund managers Kemper and Scudder, Stevens & Clark, as well as Threadneedle Asset Management in London. Allianz, Europe's largest insurance group, acquired Assurances Générales de France in 1998. AXA, the French insurance giant, owns a controlling interest in the Equitable Group in the US that includes controlling interests in money manager Alliance Capital Corp. and the investment bank Donaldson, Lufkin & Jenrette. Generali Assicurazioni (Italy) has acquired Aachener & Muenchener Beteiligungs AG in Germany, and has fixed a mutual minority equity stakeholding – a strategic alliance – in Commerzbank. ING Groep, the Dutch multi-industry financial services company, owns ING Barings (UK), Banque Bruxelles Lambert and Furman Selz, a US securities firm.

Increasingly it appears practical for those groups with international ambitions to acquire companies that provide market share in promising areas, and have the talent and the skill bases to achieve their objectives though no one yet has forged the banking equivalent of the global Chrysler-Daimler merger of equals, though combinations such as that of Deutsche Bank and J.P. Morgan are periodically rumoured. Inevitably such a transaction will occur, perhaps leading to a run of matching, similarly global acquisitions.

Strategies for success

European banks will increasingly be compared with their US counterparts for market competitiveness and contributions to shareholder value. During the nineties they pulled even, by emphasizing modernization and profitability. Like the US, they have remained focused on their domestic consumer and middle-market businesses. Also like the major US banks, many have backed away from big commitments to the wholesale securities and syndicated loans businesses and from operating extensive branch systems outside Europe. Most of the larger European banks will stand on this strategy for several more years while assessing the impact of the euro and determining where they will best fit in. But as the European national markets become one and feel the increasing presence of US and other competitors, it will be more difficult to maintain the profitability and market shares they have so far been able to defend. Many banks will decide that their shareholders are better off accepting an offer to merge with a larger bank rather than continue alone. The growth in consolidation will throw up a smaller number of very large banks, which will be confident that, for them, being bigger is better.

The major decision facing most of these banks, however, will be whether or not to remain committed to a universal banking structure or to develop a more focused strategy supported by a specialized organization structure. Some may prefer to continue with a conglomerate-type universal banking approach because that is their legacy and tradition, and that is what the market seems to expect. But in highly competitive, increasingly disconnected businesses (e.g. wholesale versus retail) without much benefit accruing from the ability to pass capital in an emergency from one part to another (in part because the units are separately regulated), it is increasingly difficult to find the synergies from having all these activities under one roof. The lack of synergy could well leave these organizations with all the disadvantages of being large and cumbersome but none of the advantages.

A French fiasco

There have been several experiments with 'new' banking strategies and operating structures. The most spectacular of these was the rush to leadership of the entire European marketplace by Crédit Lyonnais, under the guidance of a former French Treasury officer, Jean-Yves Haberer. He believed that with the muscle of the French government behind him (which owned Crédit Lyonnais) he could gain the high ground before anyone else in Europe knew what was happening. Indeed, on 1 January 1993 (the first day of the EU single market) he was able to announce that Crédit Lyonnais had more assets, more branches and more employees across Europe than any other bank. This was the result of a ferocious effort to acquire assets (loans) in Germany, Britain, Italy and elsewhere, which unfortunately for the bank's owners left it with an ocean of bad loans that by 1997 required a $28 billion bail-out. The strategy was constantly criticized by competitors who claimed that the bank was being unfairly promoted in its strategic efforts by the French government, which agreed to finance its actions and to disregard its reckless accumulation of risky assets. In the end, market forces intervened, and the bank was unable to continue on its expansion track. The government, since changed, was able to see the folly of the policy of supporting Haberer and sacked him. In Crédit Lyonnais' case, bigger was certainly not better.

Sturm und Drang in Germany

Deutsche Bank, which began its Europeanization with acquisitions in 1986 in Italy (a retail bank) and in 1989 in Britain (Morgan Grenfell, an investment bank), was devoted until late 1998 to reconfiguring its banking businesses from within. For some time Deutsche had followed the objective of being Germany's most important bank, one of Europe's most important banking forces and an important force in global terms. To achieve these objectives, Deutsche correctly understood it needed to change much about the way it conducted business in Germany. It pushed capital markets and privatizations, built its own insurance business, advocated capital market reforms, promoted new banking laws and pushed for reorganization of the stock exchanges along lines that were similar to those in the US and the UK. It attempted to reduce its ownership in major industrial corporations. And it also recognized that it was unlikely to achieve leadership in European wholesale markets by remaining focused on Germany, so it shifted its capital markets teams to London and aggressively hired experienced market professionals in New York. It appointed British investment bankers to the bank's management board and gave them extensive authority to do what they thought necessary.

Retail banking is highly competitive in Germany, a country with many more branches than it needs, subsidized savings institutions on every corner, and customers whose loyalty is strong as long as the rates are reasonably attractive. Retail banking returns are low in Germany. Deutsche Bank struggling to raise its returns on equity did not want to increase its exposure to German retail banking, which in 1999 accounted for 18 per cent of its total income. So it needed a profitable non-German business to shore up its returns, and it made a mighty effort to create one. But the nineties was a tough decade for Deutsche Bank – several of its *Hausbank* clients needed to be rescued despite their close association with the bank. Morgan Grenfell involved the bank in a money management scandal that cost shareholders nearly $10 billion to make good on. Its investment banking efforts in the US, centred around a former Morgan Stanley managing director who attempted to build the business by hiring star performers at great expense, fell apart and had to be re-Germanized.

Frustrated by its lack of progress, in November 1998 Deutsche Bank announced it would acquire Bankers Trust for about $10 billion. This was a curious choice because of Bankers Trust's lack of success in forging a strategy for itself that would enable it to compete with the strongest US investment banks. In fact, in 1995 Bankers Trust had itself been rocked by scandals, lawsuits and penalties in its derivatives business, followed by a hasty management change and attempts to establish a new strategy based on serving middle-market companies for which it acquired the regional investment bank Alex. Brown in 1997 for $1.7 billion. It also bought the European equities business of National Westminster Bank (evidently to get it started in Europe) and the mergers boutique Wolfensohn & Co.

Market conditions in 1998 were difficult for Bankers Trust – it lost considerable amounts in Russia, in the junk bond and emerging market debt businesses, and in loans to hedge funds. Indeed, many observers in New York believed that Deutsche Bank's appearance on the scene was a blessing for the shareholders of Bankers Trust, whose stock price had plunged from $136 per share in April 1998 to a low for the year of $49 in October. Deutsche Bank agreed to pay $90 a share the following month. Scarcely anyone taking notice of this acquisition would have failed to observe that Deutsche Bank would have a major job ahead to fold Bankers Trust into its global wholesale banking activities, while at the same time meeting its objective of significantly improving shareholder returns.

Still, Deutsche Bank perseveres, maintaining a presence among the top ten European wholesale banks but one that is only rarely seen in non-German deals. It ranks well behind the major US and Swiss investment banks in global market share and even within the more narrow limits of investment banking in Europe. Deutsche's banking and financial services performance, after subtracting the market value of its portfolio of industrial holdings, has been mediocre throughout the nineties. At the end of 1999, the market valuation of the bank's financial services businesses was less than 13 times earnings, and only slightly greater than the bank's book value. The bank is well positioned, however, to benefit from changes in the German tax code that would permit it to sell off its part or all industrial holdings.

A Swiss colossus

In 1998, the Union Bank of Switzerland and the Swiss Bank Corporation merged to form Europe's largest bank, the new UBS (although former Swiss Bank Corp. officers turned out to be in charge). Swiss Bank Corporation had pursued an aggressive Anglo-American policy since acquiring a major interest in the talented and highly profitable Chicago derivatives house, O'Connor & Co. Later it brought in all the rest of the firm and sent its top managers around the world to head up different parts of SBC's securities business. The acquisition of Chicago-based Brinson Partners (pension fund managers) was next, and this in turn was followed by the acquisition of investment banks S.G. Warburg & Co. in London and Dillon Read & Co. in New York. The combined firms would be in three businesses:

● Swiss domestic (mainly retail and middle-market banking), which could benefit from closing branches and reducing headcount, although this would take about ten years to accomplish in Switzerland;

● non-Swiss wholesale businesses, which would be controlled from London;

● management of about $1 trillion of assets belonging mainly to non-Swiss private and institutional clients.

Historically, the asset management business accounted for significantly more than 100 per cent of the combined banks' profits as the Swiss domestic business was recovering from a five-year slump and the non-Swiss wholesale businesses had rarely been profitable.

Perhaps the sheer weight of the bank's combined placing power could now drive it to the upper ranks of European investment banking. If so, the bank would be less dependent on proprietary trading results. These had mixed benefits for UBS's predecessor banks, producing some sizeable losses during the decade – especially in 1994 (making Warburg available for acquisition) and again in 1998 (when an unfortunate investment in the failing hedge fund Long Term Capital Management by the old UBS caused the resignation of the bank's chairman, Mathis Cabiallavetta, and four senior officers).

The merger, largely the result of poor results and mismanagement on the part of Union Bank of Switzerland, which was hounded by a dissatisfied shareholder group, reduced Switzerland's major banks to two. The other was the reorganized Crédit Suisse Group. The Crédit Suisse Group, though similar in structure to UBS, was much more heavily into Swiss retail banking and insurance, and considerably lighter in asset management.

Both Swiss bank groups hope to manage themselves through actual or virtual holding company structures, with a small management group on top, and large operating businesses headed by powerful figures with considerable autonomy just underneath. The decentralization of control (to the extent that it actually occurs and is not undermined by the proximity of things in Switzerland, or by disappointments abroad) is intended to enable each entity to preserve focus and specialization. However, whether such large businesses can truly be run without constant and cumbersome reference to the bank's top people has yet to be shown.

Facing the future

European banking and other financial services businesses will be required to face many of the same problems in the next decade that they had to face in the last. These include:

● continuing high levels of competition for market share in an industry that is being rapidly reconfigured, leaving much excess capacity in its wake. This competition will be especially intense from US firms, especially in wholesale sectors of the market;

● pressure on the part of institutional investors and activist shareholders for increased profitability and share-price increases, with weaker institutions being forced by market pressures into mergers;

● continuing acquisitions of banks and other financial services companies leading to increasingly large, trans-European and global entities. As in the US, the number of banks is expected to decline further, perhaps by as much as half over the next ten years. Banks will soon be sorted into either buyers or sellers;

● the shareholders of those banks that are bought by others will generally do much better financially than the shareholders of the acquirers. Thus, some of the market pressure will be deflected on to the larger, consolidating banks to demonstrate that their strategic moves will in fact result in improved performance for shareholders. In particular, the banks will be expected to reduce costs and demonstrate superior management.

The largest of the banking superpowers will, no doubt, choose to continue as universal banks, but the services offered, clients served and the territories in which they operate are likely to vary a great deal. The biggest task for European banks in the new century is to re-address the old question: 'Who are we and what do we want to be?' There are several choices, even for large universal banks:

- Should the bank extend its retail banking (deposits, loans and mortgages offered through branches, ATMs and other channels) and other services (credit card, mutual funds, life and property insurance) into all of the other euro-zone countries? Should high priority be given to establishing its 'brand' in the consumer market across Europe?

- Should the bank attempt to challenge the US investment banks for a high market share in the wholesale financial services sector (syndicated loans, underwriting and distribution of securities, mergers)? Or should it develop its trading capabilities to cover the entire, globally integrated wholesale marketplace – from New York to Tokyo – in all instruments from stocks and bonds to derivatives and foreign exchange?

- Should it attempt to develop its asset management business with private clients (private banking and mutual funds) and institutions (pension funds) in competition with the Swiss, the British and the Americans?

- Should it continue, if the situation applies, to own significant positions in the shares of industrial companies and to influence their actions by board memberships and the ability to vote customer-owned shares held in trust? Will these *Hausbank* relationships (still prevalent in countries such as Germany, France, Italy, Sweden and Austria) play an important role in the bank's developing strategy or have the relationships become more of a hindrance than a help?

The answers to these questions will have to be based on whether there are profitable advantages to be gained from doing so, once the costs and risks of developing strategies along these lines have been taken into account. But even if a bank sees opportunities in developing these strategies, there remains the task of implementing them correctly. A bold strategy that cannot be implemented because of organization or management limitations is of no value. Many banking organizations have been stopped in their tracks because of an inability to manage the introduction of a strategy change well enough to emerge as a fully competitive player in the targeted sector.

Some questions for banks' boards of directors include:

- Do we have the leadership and the depth of talent that it takes to carry out the strategic initiatives we have identified? How many of these initiatives can we undertake at once?

- Is our organization too large and bureaucratic to manage such difficult changes? Can we accommodate the diversity necessary to operate effectively in 11 major markets as if they were one?

● Can we manage the disparities between investment banking, commercial banking, asset management and insurance businesses well enough to justify being in all of these businesses? Differences in marketing practices have halted most efforts to successfully introduce cross-selling. Large differences in compensation between performance-oriented investment bankers and seniority-oriented commercial bankers have been difficult to reconcile within the same organization. Will we be able to do so?

● Is a universal banking structure one that is likely to optimize shareholder value? Is greater value achieved by holding all the parts together as a conglomerate, or would shareholders be better off if we spun off the investment banking, or the fund management business? Are we sure that being bigger is better from a shareholder-value point of view?

● If we are not satisfied with the answers to some of these questions, should we not consider a different, more scaled-down strategy, one that emphasizes shareholder returns over amassing size and standing just for its own sake?

The last of these questions may be the most important for most financial services business planning to operate in the new Europe. Big may not be better to all players, certainly not if it cannot be managed effectively. It may be ironic that the European bank with the greatest market capitalization per dollar of assets held is Lloyds TSB, with almost the same market capitalization as UBS but less than a third of its assets. Lloyds is best known for backing away from the strategy it inherited in the early eighties of being a major international lending bank. After a number of losses and unhappy experiences with third world loans, Lloyds decided to withdraw from the wholesale business to concentrate on consumer banking, asset management and insurance inside the UK. At first this strategy was seen as timid and defeatist, but soon the profits came rolling in, and the bank has been the envy of the European banking world ever since. Lloyds is perhaps tempted to point out that the retail banking business in Britain has always been very profitable, but if these profits are squandered by losses in the international and wholesale markets, as has happened with Barclays and National Westminster, then the net result is much diminished.

Some untried approaches

With the exception of the largest British banks, whose approach has been mainly to withdraw from the increasing competitiveness of the global wholesale markets, the underlying objective of those relatively few European banks (primarily the big Dutch, German and Swiss universals) seeking a share of those markets has been to gain position by becoming bigger and more diversified. In the end, this approach may prevail. But for this to happen, the large US firms would have to be displaced or acquired, neither of which would appear feasible for any but a very small number of European financial institutions. However, there may be some other approaches that could yield a successful result, one in which European presence and profitable domestic business could be melded with an effective and not too risky global investment banking business.

The bank as a 'portfolio manager'

One can argue that a bank is less of a service provider than an asset accumulator and manager. If its assets are selected entirely for their potential profitability (and for no other, more traditional but possibly unprofitable reasons), the value of the bank should increase over what it otherwise might be. Under such a concept (not unlike the business of General Electric Capital Services, a major 'unseen' competitor in both retail and financial services businesses) the bank would convert its balance sheet into a massive 'investment portfolio' consisting of assets purchased and funded by liabilities sold.

Managers would carefully select the assets they want to hold, and fund them with the cheapest possible sources of finance, ranging from deposits taken to securities issued in capital markets. Management of the portfolio would have top priority in the bank. It would have the authority over all assets and liabilities retained by the bank and engage itself in whatever proprietary trading or hedging activities seem appropriate. The entire effort would be aimed at securing the highest risk-adjusted shareholder returns that are feasible and obtainable in the markets covered. These markets, of course, would not be limited to traditional territorial areas, but expanded opportunistically.

Surrounding the central portfolio, however, would be several asset-acquisition units – acquiring assets by selling financial products to consumers, middle-market and real estate corporate customers, and wholesale products in a variety of market arenas. The asset acquisition units would be required to offer the assets they attracted first to the core portfolio managers, and then to the market. A unit could act as market-maker in some areas but not in others, depending upon the choice of its managers. The purpose of these units would be to sweep investment opportunities into the centre, and to distribute any leftovers as best they could.

The portfolio managers too could create new asset products of their own to take advantage of market opportunities. The portfolio manager's funds might be augmented by setting up special investment opportunities for pension or mutual fund investors in such asset classes as emerging market securities, junk bonds, leveraged leases, private equity or other investments in amounts appropriate for the portfolio as a whole. Such types of portfolio investment structures are already in operation at some of the major investment banks.

Surely the next decade will offer some new thinking on ways to organize and streamline efforts to further participate in the European capital markets. If size is important, then equally important is finding ways to keep size from suffocating initiative, response time and profitability. If large size creates inflexibility and a lack of manoeuvrability, it can make a bank very vulnerable to competitive efforts from US investment banks, which have managed to lead the market by specialization, focus and flexibility – not size. The Americans, however, are themselves changing into enormous financial service conglomerates. In doing so, they may be shedding the very heart of their competitive competence, creating opportunities in Europe for the new Europeans. Time will tell.

NOTES

[1] 'The trials of mega-banks', *The Economist*, 31 October 1998, quoting a study by First Manhattan Corp., a bank consulting concern.

[2] 'Euro brief – Europe's US dream', *The Economist*, 21 November 1998.

[3] Goldman Sachs proceedings of a conference on European Bank Restructuring, 14 May 1998. *See also* 'Euro brief – unready for blast off,' *The Economist*, 7 November 1998.

References

Advisory Council on Social Security. *Report of the 1994–96 Advisory Council on Social Security: Findings and Recommendations*, Washington, D.C.: US Government Printing Office, 1997.

Akhavein, Jalal D., Berger, Allen N. and Humphrey, David B. (1996) 'The effects of mega-mergers on efficiency and prices: evidence from a bank profit function'. Paper presented at the *Conference on Mergers of Financial Institutions*, New York University Salomon Center, 11 October.

Bassi, Mario (1996) *Der Bankunabhängige Vermögensverwalter*, Zurich: Schulthess Polygraphischer Verlag.

Begg, David and Portes, Richard (1992) 'Enterprise debt and economic transformation', Centre for Economic Policy Research, Discussion Paper no. 695, June.

Berger, Allen N., Demsetz, Rebecca S. and Strahan, Philip E. (1988) *The Consolidation of the Financial Services Industry: Causes, Consequences, and Implications for the Future*, New York: Federal Reserve Bank of New York.

Berger, Allen N. and Mester, L. (1997) 'Inside the black box: what explains differences in the efficiencies of financial institutions?', *Journal of Banking and Finance*, 21.

Berger, Allen N., Hancock, Diana and Humphrey, David B. (1993) 'Bank efficiency derived from the profit function', *Journal of Banking and Finance*, April.

Berger, Allen N., Hunter, William C. and Timme, Stephen J. (1993) 'The efficiency of financial institutions: a review of research past, present and future', *Journal of Banking and Finance*, April.

Berger, Allen N. and Hannan, T.H. (1987) 'The price-concentration relationship in banking', *Review of Economics and Statistics*, 71.

Berger, Philip G. and Ofek, Eli (1995) 'Diversification's effects on firm value', *Journal of Financial Economics*, 37.

Bernstein Research (1996) *The Future of Money Management in America – 1977 edition*, New York: Sanford Bernstein.

Bishop, Graham (1997) *Post Emu: bank credit versus capital markets*, London: Salomon Brothers Inc.

Cable, J. (1985) 'Capital market information and industrial performance: the role of West German banks', *The Economic Journal*, pp. 118–32.

Cadette, Walter M. (1977) 'Social security: financing the baby-boom's retirement', The Jerome Levy Economics Institute, Working Paper no. 192, April.

Chordia, Tarun (1996) 'The structure of mutual fund charges', *Journal of Financial Economics*, June.

Corbett, Jenny and Mayer, Colin P. (1991) 'Financial reform in Eastern Europe: progress with the wrong model', Centre for Economic Policy Research, Discussion Paper no. 603, September.

Cummins, J.D. and Zi, H. (1998) 'Comparisons of frontier efficiency levels', *Journal of Productivity Analysis*, June.

Davis International Banking Consultants (1996) *Trends in European Asset Management*, New York: Smith Barney.

DeLong, Gayle, Smith, Roy C. and Walter, Ingo (1999) *M&A Database: financial services*, New York University Salomon Center.

Demsetz, Rebecca S., Saidenberg, Marc R. and Strahan, Philip E. (1996) 'Banks with something to lose: the disciplinary role of franchise value', *Federal Reserve Bank of New York Policy Review*, October.

Dermine, Jean (ed.) (1993) 'European banking after 1992', Revised edition, Oxford: Basil Blackwell.

— (ed.) (1990) 'European banking after 1992', Oxford: Basil Blackwell.

Edwards, James and Fischer, Klaus (1992) 'An overview of the German financial system', Centre for Economic Policy Research Working Paper, November.

Epstein, Neil and Brewington, Bruce R. (1997) 'The investment management industry in the United States', New York: Putnam, Lovell & Thornton.

First Consulting (1997) *European Pensions*, London: AMP Asset Management.

Giddy, Ian, Saunders, Anthony and Walter, Ingo (1996) 'Alternative models of clearance and settlement: the case of a single European capital market', *Journal of Money, Credit and Banking*, November.

Gnehm, A. and Thalmann, C. (1989) 'Conflicts of interest in financial operations: problems of regulation in the national and international context', Working Paper, Swiss Bank Corporation, Basel.

Goldberg, L.G., Hanweck, G.A., Keenan, M. and Young, A. (1991) 'Economies of scale and scope in the securities industry', *Journal of Banking and Finance*, 15.

Goldstein, Michael L. *et al.* (1997) 'The future of money management in America', New York: Bernstein Research.

Griffin, Mark (1997) 'The global pension time bomb and its capital market impact', New York: Goldman Sachs & Co.

Gruber, Martin J. (1996) 'Another puzzle: the growth of actively managed mutual funds', presidential address presented at the American Finance Association, San Francisco, January 1996, *Journal of Finance*, May.

Hale, David (1994) 'The economic consequences of America's mutual fund boom', *International Economy*, March–April.

Harrison, Debbie (1995) 'Pension fund investment in Europe', London: FT Financial Publishing.

Herring, Richard J. and Santomero, Anthony M. (1990) 'The corporate structure of financial conglomerates', paper presented at a Conference on International Competitiveness in Financial Services, American Enterprise Institute, 31 May–1 June (*mimeo*).

Herring, Richard J. and Santomero, A.M. (1990) 'The corporate structure of financial conglomerates', Journal of Financial Services Research, December, pp. 471–97.

Holzmann, Robert (1996) *Pension Reform, Financial Market Development and Economic Growth: preliminary evidence from Chile*, Washington, D.C.: IMF Working Paper 96/94, August.

Hoshi, T., Kayshap, A. and Sharfstein, D. (1991) 'The role of banks in reducing the costs of financial distress in Japan', *Journal of Financial Economics*.

— (1991) 'Corporate structure, liquidity and investment, evidence from Japanese industrial groups', *Quarterly Journal of Economics*, pp. 33–60.

Hurley, Mark P., Meers, Sharon I., Bornstein, Ben J. and Strumingher, Neil R. (1995) *The Coming Evolution of the Investment Management Industry: opportunities and strategies*, New York: Goldman Sachs & Co.

Investment Company Institute (1996) *Mutual Fund Fact Book*, Washington, Investment Company Institute.

Jensen, Michael and Ruback, Richard (1983) 'The market for corporate control: the scientific evidence', *Journal of Financial Economics* 11, April, 5–50.

John, Kose and Ofek, Eli (1995) 'Asset sales and increase in ficus', *Journal of Financial Economics*, 37.

Kaufman, George (ed.) (1992) *Banking in Major Countries*, New York: Oxford University Press.

Kim, S.B. (1990) 'Modus operandi of Lenders-cum-shareholder banks', Federal Reserve Bank of San Francisco, *mimeo*, September.

Krümmel, Hans-Jakob (1980) 'German universal banking scrutinized', *Journal of Banking and Finance*, March.

Kwast, M.L., Starr-McCluer, M. and Wolken, J. (1997) Market definition and the analysis of antitrust in banking', *Antitrust Bulletin*, 42, 973–95.

Lang, G. and Wetzel, P. (1998) 'Technology and cost efficiency in universal banking: a thick frontier approach', *Journal of Productivity Analysis*, 10.

Levich, Richard and Walter, Ingo (1990) 'Tax-driven regulatory drag: European financial centre in the 1990s', in Siebert, Horst (ed.) *Reforming Capital Income Taxation*, Tübingen: J.C.B. Mohr/Paul Siebeck.

Longin, François and Solnik, Bruno (1995) 'Is the correlation of international equity returns constant?', *Journal of International Money and Finance*, vol. 14, no. 1.

Mattione, Richard P. (1992) 'A capital cost disadvantage for Japan?', *Journal of International Securities Markets*, September.

Mayer, Colin P. (1992) 'Corporate control and transformation in Eastern Europe', paper presented at a SUERF conference on The New Europe: Evolving Economic and Financial Systems in East and West, Berlin, Germany, 8–10 October.

Neave, Edwin (1992) *The Economic Organization of a Financial System*, London: Routledge.

Pastré, Olivier (1981) 'International bank-industry relations: an empirical assessment', *Journal of Banking and Finance*, March.

Patel, Jayendu, Zeckhauser, Richard J. and Hendricks, Darryll (1994) 'Investment fund performance: evidence from mutual funds, cross-border investments and new issues', in Sato, Ryuzo, Levich, Richard and Ramachandran, Rama (eds) *Japan, Europe and International Financial Markets: analytical and empirical perspectives*, Cambridge: Cambridge University Press.

Pozdena, Randall J. (1989) 'Do banks need securities powers?', *Federal Reserve Bank of San Francisco Weekly Letter*, 29 December.

Prager, R.A. and Hannan, T.H. (1999) 'Do substantial horizontal mergers generate significant price effects?', *Journal of Industrial Economics*.

Prowse, S.D. (1990) 'Institutional investment patterns and corporate financial behavior in the US and Japan', Board of Governors of the Federal Reserve System, Working Paper, January.

Reid, Brian and Crumrine, Jean (1997) *Retirement Plan Holdings of Mutual Funds, 1996*, Washington, D.C.: Investment Company Institute.

Remolona, Eli M., Kleiman, Paul and Gruenstein, Debbie (1997) 'Market returns and mutual fund flows', *Federal Reserve Bank of New York Economic Policy Review*, July.

Röller, Wolfgang (1990) 'Die Macht der Banken', *Zeitschrift für das Gesamte Kreditwesen*, 1 January.

Rybczynski, T.N. (1989) 'Corporate restructuring', *National Westminster Bank Review*, August.

Saunders, Anthony (1996) *Financial Institutions Management*. 2nd edn. Burr Ridge, III: Irwin.

Saunders, Anthony (1990) 'The separation of banking and commerce', New York University Salomon Center Working Paper (*mimeo*), September.

Saunders, Anthony and Walter, Ingo (eds) (1995) *Universal Banking*, Burr Ridge, III.: Irwin Professional.

Saunders, Anthony and Walter, Ingo (1994) *Universal Banking in the United States*, New York: Oxford University Press.

Sheard, P. (1989) 'The main bank system and corporate monitoring and control in Japan', *Journal of Commercial Banking and Organization*.

Siems, Thomas F. (1996) 'Bank mergers and shareholder value: evidence from 1995's megamerger deals', *Federal Reserve Bank of Dallas Financial Industry Studies*, August.

Sittampalam, Arjuna (1993) *Coming Wars in Investment Management*, Dublin: Lafferty Publications.

Smith, George D. and Sylla, Richard (1992) 'Wall Street and the capital markets in the twentieth century: an historical essay', New York University Salomon Center Working Paper, September.

Smith, Roy C. and Walter, Ingo (1997) *Global Banking*, New York: Oxford University Press.

Smith, Roy C. and Walter, Ingo (1992) 'Bank-industry linkages: models for Eastern European restructuring', paper presented at a SUERF conference on The New Europe: Evolving Economic and Financial Systems in East and West, Berlin, Germany, 8–10 October.

Smith, Roy C. and Walter, Ingo (1977) *Street Smarts: Linking Professional Conduct and Shareholder Value in the Securities Industry*, Boston: Harvard Business School Press.

Steinherr, Alfred and Huveneers, Christian (1992) 'On the performance of differently regulated financial institutions: some empirical evidence', Université Catholique de Louvain, Working Paper (*mimeo*), February.

Story, Jonathan and Walter, Ingo (1997) *Political Economy of Financial Integration in Europe*, Manchester: Manchester University Press, and Cambridge: MIT Press.

Turner, John and Watanabe, Noriyasu (1995) *Private Pension Policies in Industrialized Countries*, Kalamazoo: W.E. Upjohn Institute for Employment Research.

Van den Brink, R.G.C. (1998) 'Universal banking: an answer to the challenges facing the financial sector', ABN AMRO (*mimeo*).

Walter, Ingo (1999) 'The asset management industry in Europe: competitive structure and performance under EMU', in Dermine, Jean and Hillion, Pierre (eds) *European Capital Markets With a Single Currency*, Oxford: Oxford University Press.

— (1993) *High-Performance Financial Systems*, Singapore: Institute for Southeast Asian Studies.

— (1993) *The Battle of the Systems, Control of Enterprises in the Global Economy*, Kiel: Kieler Studien Nr. 122, Institut für Weltwirtschaft.

— (1993) (ed.) *Reforming Japan's Securities Markets,* Homewood, III.: Business One/Irwin.

— (1988) *Global Competition in Financial Services*, Cambridge, Mass: Ballinger–Harper & Row.

— (1985) *Barriers to Trade in Banking and Financial Services*, London: Trade Policy Research Centre.

— (1985) (ed.) *Deregulating Wall Street*, New York: John Wiley & Sons.

Walter, Ingo and Smith, Roy C. (1990) *Investment Banking in Europe: restructuring for the 1990s*, Oxford: Basil Blackwell.

Warther, Vincent A. (1995) 'Aggregate mutual fund flows and security returns', *Journal of Financial Economics*, September.

Index

The location of figures is shown in *italics*